Contemporary
Thought
on Edmund Spenser

With a Bibliography of Criticism of The Faerie Queene,
1900–1970

Edited, with an Introduction by
Richard C. Frushell *and* Bernard J. Vondersmith

Southern Illinois University Press

CARBONDALE AND EDWARDSVILLE

Feffer & Simons, Inc.

LONDON AND AMSTERDAM

Library of Congress Cataloging in Publication Data

Frushell, Richard C   1935–
  Contemporary thought on Edmund Spenser.

  Includes bibliographical references and index.
    1.   Spenser, Edmund, 1522?–1599—Criticism and
interpretation.   2.   Spenser, Edmund, 1522?–1599. Faerie
queene.   3.   Spenser, Edmund, 1522?–1599.   Faerie queene
—Bibliography.   I.   Vondersmith, Bernard J., 1943–
joint author.   II.   Title.
PR2364.F7   821'.3   74–30159
ISBN 0–8093–0695–6

Contents

10789

Introduction

EDWIN A. GREENLAW did not live to enjoy a *Festschrift* from colleagues and students, and this book is not one, at least in the usual sense. The authors herein did not write their essays for Greenlaw or to his memory, although most of them recognize his achievements and importance. Rather, as asked, they wrote chapters for a book which represents contemporary thought on Edmund Spenser, thought, as it turns out, largely consonant with Greenlaw's vision of Spenser's capaciousness. And it is in this that Greenlaw is representative of twentieth-century Spenser scholarship and not in any single technique, approach, or subject matter that he used or encouraged. In fact, one would suspect that each author is in one or more of these regards quite unlike Greenlaw.

Greenlaw acceded to the Sir William Osler Professorship in English in The Johns Hopkins University upon the retirement of Professor James W. Bright in 1925. From then until his death in 1931, Greenlaw oversaw the building of a new department of English at Hopkins and experimented with the seminar system of teaching. "The Proceedings of Dr. Greenlaw's Seminary C" is the record of the seminar (hereafter used for Seminary, its equivalent) meetings, kept by his students from 1925 to 1931.[1] Included in "The Proceedings" are minutes, formal presentations by Greenlaw, guest lectures, and graduate papers in various areas of Spenser criticism. Greenlaw unquestionably influenced the style and format of graduate teaching at Johns Hopkins, but he acknowledged his debt to his predecessor, in the minutes of the November 29, 1926, meeting: " 'The Seminary at the present time should give a moment's pause in commemoration of Doctor Bright's work,' said Doctor Greenlaw, 'for, in addition to his scholarly work as a writer of articles and textbooks, and as editor of

Modern Language Notes, it was he [who] first applied the seminary system to work in English at the Johns Hopkins.' "

"The Proceedings" is significant to anyone seriously interested in Edmund Spenser and the evaluation of Spenser criticism. Of special importance is the relationship among Greenlaw's conduct of the seminar, the nature of some student papers, and the *Variorum Edition* of Spenser's works, of which Greenlaw was an influential part, though he did not live to see the publication of its first volume.[2] When he began the seminar in 1926, Greenlaw was already at work with colleagues, probably Charles Grosvenor Osgood and Frederick Morgan Padelford, on a variorum edition of Spenser's works. The *Variorum* became a central concern of the seminar, and the students researched sources, analogues, and historical allegory, gradually moving to complete annotations of cantos of *The Faerie Queene.* Greenlaw's students thereby received training in editing and literary criticism. The following advice, recorded in the minutes of the meeting of October 18, 1926, is representative:

Dr. Greenlaw then spoke of the nature of the notes desired for *The Faerie Queene,* and some of the problems involved, in the present study of the Seminary. The investigator, he said, should try to find notes that the editors have failed to include, but he should consider carefully whether the phrase or word which he intends to annotate is deserving of annotation; and he should be able to write the note. Since there will be a gloss, no note in the nature of a gloss will appear, unless the word or passage needs a completer analysis than the gloss gives; and since the edition under consideration is not a popular edition, but a variorum, the student must always consider carefully whether or not the note is elementary and obvious, or whether it has real interpretive value.

As another part of their editorial training, Greenlaw encouraged his students toward earlier editions of Spenser's works and offered his own commentary on their relative merits. The January 17, 1927, meeting was devoted to early editions of Spenser:

Dr. Greenlaw, who this summer had access to Warton's 1611–1613 folio of Spenser, introduced the general subject with a discussion of this folio. He had examined Warton's notes in this book as to their relation to the *Observations on "The Faerie Queene"* (1754), which is the first great book in Spenserian scholarship.

He spoke to the seminar about Warton's many annotations of Book I in the folio, which are "all the more curious when we consider how few romance conventions are in the first book and that Warton was primarily interested in this aspect of the study." Warton had no reverence for the folio because of "the many notes scribbled in, an unscholarly method." Greenlaw points out that many of Warton's notes are now classics and that Warton stayed close to his copy of the folio, since "this folio contains in addition many notes from Upton's edition of Spenser (1758)."

After a brief background to the eighteenth-century editions of Spenser, Greenlaw turned the seminar's attention to Upton's edition, which includes "a surprising amount of historical identification." He is the first to suggest that Amoret is Mary Queen of Scots and that Artegall is Lord Grey. Greenlaw adds that "Upton and the eighteenth-century critics had no idea of continued allegory" and concludes that the Warton-Upton-Todd school represents "the patient accumulation of facts; although they reach no conclusions and make no parallels, their method is sound." Greenlaw, then, expected his students to contribute annotations to the *Variorum* and demanded that they be informed annotators aware of the editors who had preceded them.

Annotations and editions were an important part of the seminar but not its life's blood. In casual as well as formal comments, Greenlaw defined his aesthetic and his critical attitude toward Edmund Spenser. At the beginning of the seminar in 1926, he asked for volunteers to summarize and evaluate essays which had appeared in that year's scholarly journals. Greenlaw's critique of H. S. V. Jones's *"The Faerie Queene* and the Medieval Aristotelian Tradition" [3] includes several of his own principles of literary criticism, which anticipate several critical movements: concern for structure, the place of Aristotle, and the meaning of numbers.

Concerning the general matter illustrated by the article, Professor Greenlaw laid down two principles of Spenser criticism: 1. It is very doubtful that attempts to find a book or books explaining the structure of *The Faerie Queene* will be fruitful. The poem is too long and too complex for us to say it is based on any one system or book. 2. Spenser probably did not want to give a systematic presentation. His systemizing is not that of a medieval writer, as, for example, that of Dante or Aquinas. Spenser's statement that he takes the 12 virtues "as Aristotle hath devised" does not mean that he is taking Aristotle's 12 virtues, but that he is going to treat philosophy in a story and that his attitude toward the virtues is what Aristotle's might have been. Spenser used 12 because that was a mystic number. (October 25, 1926)

Greenlaw then advised his students not to proceed without sufficient evidence, not to attempt to prove too much, and not to resort to special pleading.

In subsequent meetings, Greenlaw speculated on historical method: "We must seek to relive the past in the light of the present, and we do not understand the past until, by means of investigation, we can project ourselves into it. Dr. Greenlaw noted that too much of the present day criticism consists in what the present generation thinks about the past, impressionism" (November 1, 1926). In a later class meeting Greenlaw buttressed his own critical position by quoting from E. B. Andrews's translation of Johann Gustav Droysen's *Grundriss der Historik*:

"The essence of the historical method," says Droysen, "is understanding by means of investigation." There are three stages, namely, perception, investigation, and understanding. And if there is no understanding, the investigation is valueless. The way to get at this understanding or interpretation is by means of the utterances of the great spirits of an age. For every period is a complex of the spirit of the working potencies. The method for investigation depends upon the system belonging to the matter inherent in it and the systematic presentation of results. The essence of interpretation consists in seeing realities in past events. (January 17, 1927)

Greenlaw's paraphrase of Droysen reflects his own interest in the study of Spenser's sources: "One cannot possibly interpret out of his own intelligence, which is romantic. The true approach, then, is through the author's sources. In other words, we must try to see what he means by investigating his sources and noting how he uses them. And if there is only investigation with no understanding, the work is futile" (January 17, 1927).

Although source study was important to him, Greenlaw was no mere chaser after ghosts of authors past. On occasion, he would relate his European travels to the artistry of his poet's work. "His visit to an exhibition of Elizabethan pictures this summer in Europe more than ever impressed him with the belief that much description in Spenser was influenced by pictures" (October 18, 1926). He commented that one cannot appreciate the kitchen of Alma's physiological castle until one has visited some of the abbey kitchens. "The one at Glastonbury bears a rude resemblance to the stomach, which, of course, is just the point" (January 17, 1927).

Greenlaw coaxed and guided and defended his students. The four essays which Charles G. Smith collected under the title *Spenser's Theory of Friendship* (1935) may have grown from "The Place of Love in Spenser's World-Order," which Smith presented to the seminar in 1927 and for which Greenlaw suggested revisions. It is likewise probable that Jewel Wurtsbaugh's *Two Centuries of Spenser Criticism, 1609–1805* (1936) grew out of an essay which she presented to the seminar in 1930, "Upton's Edition of *The Faerie Queene*." When Ray Heffner took issue with Padelford and Winstanley over the association of Book I of *The Faerie Queene* with the reign of Henry

VIII [4] and offered the alternative of Elizabeth's reign, Greenlaw remarked:

Explaining an allegory completely is dangerous, for Elizabethan allegory is plain and when it is not plain, it has a tag to it. His conclusion was that it will not do to say that Bk. I of *The Faerie Queene* refers to Elizabeth's reign and that therefore Miss Winstanley's and Mr. Padelford's work must be thrown out; but that Mr. Heffner's work must also be considered in the interpretation. (January 21, 1929)

This treatment of Greenlaw and his seminar is highly selective and necessarily brief. In the five volumes of "The Proceedings," we have the minutes of the class meetings, but few of the parenthetical comments and little of the personal interplay among the members of the seminar, which met in the Tudor and Stuart Club Room in Gilman Hall, Johns Hopkins. In a nearby room, a large portrait of Greenlaw looks out on the tables of a modern seminar room.

Greenlaw knew his debt to earlier editors and critics, and he made his students aware of the past, present, and future of Spenser's works as they ranged in their studies from Spenser and the Bible, to Spenser and Elizabethan pageantry, to Spenser and Nathaniel Hawthorne. He led his students from annotation to criticism, demonstrating and teaching respect for both. Greenlaw was also sensitive to his students and colleagues, all of whom had his ear—but only his students had access to his office typewriter.

Since the time of Greenlaw and the completion of the *Variorum*, interest in the works of Spenser has grown. The contributors to this volume are part of that growth. They wrote with few restrictions on subject matter and no restrictions on scope. Our charge to them: what is your current thinking on Spenser, and what is or should be a feasible approach to Spenser and his art? The interest and encouragement of Professors Josephine Waters Bennett, Donald Cheney, Alastair D. S. Fowler, William Nelson, Louis B. Wright, and the late Don Cameron Allen are gratefully acknowledged, as is the counsel of Waldo F. McNeir. We also acknowledge Professor McNeir's essay on the *Shepheardes Calender*, which we regret could not be included since the chapters herein seemed to require a focus on *The Faerie Queene*.

A subtitle to *Contemporary Thought on Edmund Spenser* might be *The Realities of a Poet*, realities about him and in him. The first three chapters as well as the final chapter point to realities about Spenser: the twentieth-century criticism of *The Faerie Queene*, the text of this major poem, historical scholarship and the poet, and a bibliography of criticism of the poem, 1900–1970. Chapters four and five are concerned with the realities in Spenser. Chapter six views the poem and its poet from the Mount of Contemplation and in so doing implies an imperative for necessary readings, new readings, different realities.[5]

RICHARD C. FRUSHELL
BERNARD J. VONDERSMITH

Terre Haute, Indiana
28 May 1974

Notes on Contributors

RUDOLF B. GOTTFRIED, Professor of English at Indiana University, edited the variorum *Prose Works* of Edmund Spenser (1949) and received the Modern Language Association Distinguished Essay Award for his 1968 essay "Our New Poet: Archetypal Criticism of *The Faerie Queene*."

A. C. HAMILTON, Professor of English at Queen's University, Kingston, Ontario, wrote *The Structure of Allegory in "The Faerie Queene"* (1960) and edited Spenser's *Selected Poetry* (1966).

S. K. HENINGER, JR., Professor of English at the University of British Columbia, wrote *A Handbook of Renaissance Meteorology* (1960) and edited *Selections from the Poetry of Edmund Spenser* (1970).

A. KENT HIEATT, Professor of English at the University of Western Ontario, wrote *Short Time's Endless Monument* (1960), and with Constance Hieatt edited Spenser's *Selected Poetry* (1970).

CAROL V. KASKE, Assistant Professor of English at Cornell University, is the author of "The Dragon's Spark and Sting and the Structure of Red Cross's Dragon Fight: *The Faerie Queene*, I. xi–xii," *SP*, 66 (1969), 609–38 and "Mount Sinai and Dante's Mount Purgatory," *DS*, 89 (1971), 1–18.

FOSTER PROVOST, Professor of English at Duquesne University, is co-author of *An Annotated Bibliography of Edmund Spenser, 1937–1960* (1962).

BERNARD J. VONDERSMITH, Assistant Professor of English at Indiana State University, is a contributing editor to the *Annual Bibliography* of the Modern Humanities Research Association.

CONTEMPORARY THOUGHT ON EDMUND SPENSER

I

FOSTER PROVOST   *Treatments of Theme and*
Allegory in Twentieth-Century Criticism
of The Faerie Queene

"NO CRITIC, NO POET, no age has yet fully appreciated *The Faerie Queene*." Thus Herbert E. Cory, in 1917.[1] In the past twenty years, a rush of monographs and articles on the poem has demonstrated the continuing validity of Cory's statement, and has reduced the gap between current and full appreciation.

In these years no movement in the study of Spenser's poem has been more striking than the advance in the study of the allegory. It is the chief purpose of the present essay to review the major treatments in the twentieth century of the theory and techniques of allegory in *The Faerie Queene*. In pursuing this purpose, we shall begin with a general review of twentieth-century speculations on the theme of the poem, a preliminary dictated by the fact that allegory for Spenser is a poetical mode and technique which he employs to achieve certain ends, ends which are addressed in the thematic speculations. In this way we shall avoid discussing *how* Spenser's poem is made before we have at least a general view of what his poem is about.

I should acknowledge that this brief essay, aiming at the general picture, will bypass much of the detail, sometimes perhaps some very important contributions;[2] conversely, some of the influences which I trace will have been transmitted in ways which I do not account for, and in some instances what I call influences may not be influences at all. There is a *Zeitgeist* in critical thought; first an idea is nonexistent, and then it is everywhere, and no one can fully separate direct influence from indirect, or influence from independent occurrence. What I hope to demonstrate is the broad cooperative pushing-forward of knowledge and thought about the greatest of English allegories.

One line of speculation on the theme or themes of *The Faerie*

Queene leads out of the great essay by Edward Dowden, "Spenser, The Poet and Teacher" (1884),[3] which identifies the theme of the poem in accordance with Spenser's declared end "to fashion a gentleman or noble person in vertuous and gentle discipline." For Dowden, Spenser's poem is concerned to foster "a grand self-culture," "the formation of a complete character for the uses of earth, and afterwards, if need be, for the uses of heaven—this was subject sufficient for the twenty-four books designed to form the epic of the age of Elizabeth" (p. 125). In the poem as we have it, Dowden holds, this theme is articulated in three stages (pp. 123–24): man's relation to God (Book I), man's relation to himself (Book II), and man's relation to his fellows (Books III–VI). Dowden's exposition of the third stage especially emphasizes the treatment of love in Books III and IV, and this emphasis has been a dominant one in twentieth-century treatments of the theme of the poem as a whole.

We must note incidentally that Dowden's identification of the movement in the poem from personal to social concerns anticipates later conjectures that because Books IV through VI are progressively more concerned with public virtues than with the private virtues which are the declared subject of the first twelve books, Spenser has actually covered in six books what he proposes in the "Letter to Raleigh" to cover in twenty-four. The hypothesis that the poem is essentially complete as we have it, a conjecture moderately popular in the 1960's (see the treatment of Graham Hough below), derives ultimately from Dowden's observation that Books IV–VI concern man's relation with his fellows. The corollary inference is cogent, perhaps inevitable: justice and courtesy, the virtues of V and VI, are public as well as private virtues.

In 1925 we find W. L. Renwick[4] linking the theme of personal love with the public themes of social concord and justice by reference to the further and more comprehensive theme of mutability. In Spenser's concern with "love as the law of life . . . there is some hint of a solution to the problem which recurs through all his work, the problem of change" (p. 169). Renwick proceeds to cite the Mutabilitie Cantos, a passage in V.ii.40, and especially the Garden of Adonis as testifying to Spenser's belief that change itself is the articulation of the law of God's love: "Here the principle of continuance in change is the Venus of Lucretius, presiding over procreation, and representing 'nothing other than the power of God.' Thus Love is doubly sanctified, matter and spirit are reconciled, and the tragedy of mutability is resolved, not by blind submission or by abstention, but by comprehension" (p. 170).

But the love-theme is only part of the total matter. For Renwick

The Faerie Queene has one lesson throughout, the necessity of stability: "society must be held together by concord or Friendship, the individual must be controlled by Temperance, the state by Justice" (p. 171). This leads back to mutability and the vision of God's plan as working out its perfection through successive changes: every step and change is subject to this universal law. The achievement of stability is man's contribution to the process: "in every particle of existence, in man, in society, in the state, the temporary form is important as a phase of the permanent, and must therefore be brought to its best mode and noblest function" (p. 172). Thus Renwick articulates Dowden's "grand self-culture" into Spenser's instrument for battling the specter of mutability. This battle is for Renwick the fundamental theme of the poem.

Charles G. Osgood in his 1930 lecture "Spenser and the Enchanted Glass" [5] broadens the quest for theme by asserting that Spenser's moral allegory is predicated on the "issue between good and evil, between right and wrong, between life as it is and life as it ought to be" (p. 172). For Osgood this theme of moral struggle is worked out in terms of Spenser's own personal moral problems. The theme is developed in the poem in three sub-issues. The first and most prevalent is "the moral issue between carnal lust and pure affection or chastity" (p. 173). This issue is ubiquitous in the poem because "Spenser was more interested in the experience and spiritual potentialities of romantic love than in anything else" (p. 173). The second is the issue between worldly ambitions and the poet's sense of their unworthiness and his appreciation of higher values. "He longed for conspicuous position, while he knew its real worth in spiritual terms" (p. 175). This fact underlies both Spenser's continual concern in the poem with ambition and fame, and his parallel concern with the maneuvering and duplicity which are commonly employed as a means to conspicuous position and power. The third sub-issue sets "despondency and despair in a fluctuating world over against cheerful security in a sense of Absolute Goodness and Beauty" (p. 177).

Romantic love, ambition, mutability: Osgood's list adds one item, ambition, to the themes already discussed by Dowden and Renwick. The next step comes in Janet Spens's notable essay *Spenser's "Faerie Queene": An Interpretation* (1934).[6] Spens emphasizes the Neoplatonic aspect of the poem, especially in what she views as Spenser's kinship with Plotinus in their understanding of the relationship between the mutable phenomenal world and the ideal. Spens's orientation leads her to transfer the ambition theme, the theme of the quest for fame, from the worldly to the ideal arena. The most conspicuous ambition in the poem is Arthur's "prayse-desire," his quest for glory, personified in Gloriana, the Faerie Queene. But this is a quest for perfection, a "symbol of the soul's pursuit of the supreme good," equivalent to the total thrust and purpose of the poem; and since Arthur's quest is imaged in terms of romantic love, the themes of love and ambition here draw together as two aspects of the same drive toward the vision of perfection. The love-theme which is so dominant in the poem is simply an echo of Arthur's quest, and the primary usage of the word "love" in the poem is as a symbol of spiritual aspiration. Of course love is a broader term than this; it is also "Spenser's symbol for the unifying and dynamic forces in existence" (p. 99).

The unifying force is imaged in the marriage of the Thames and the Medway: "an example of the 'sustaining love' woven through the web of physical and inanimate being." The dynamic forces are imaged in the knights who pursue Florimell "inspired by an aesthetic passion for sensuous beauty" (p. 99); by the natural passion of virtuous figures like Amoret, which once freed of impure overtones is represented as entirely virtuous; and by the friendship of famous pairs like Hercules and Hylas, Jonathan and David, a relationship indistinguishable from that of successful married love.

Spens does not omit the mutability theme. Mutabilitie is a symbol of the shifting phenomenal world of existence; and opposed to legitimate ambition is the tendency to depression, the lethargy or accidie which the uncertainty of this world brings about (pp. 117–38). When the poem ends, she concludes, the poet was about to develop a further theme, viz., the reality of the eternal world which lies behind the mutable world of phenomena (p. 138). In Spens's book we observe, if not the actual influence of Osgood, a parallel to Osgood's thematic analysis, but weighted toward Arthur's quest, wherein romantic love images the search for the ideal.

In subsequent studies the influence of Osgood's lecture is very apparent; his pronouncement that "Spenser was more interested in the experience and spiritual potentialities of romantic love than anything else" appears to set the tone of a considerable proportion of subsequent writing on the theme of *The Faerie Queene*. Of course it is not certain that Osgood directly influenced every subsequent writer who strikes this tone. For instance, the issue between "lust and pure affection," as Osgood phrases the matter, is of deep concern in C. S. Lewis's celebrated study *The Allegory of Love* (1936),[7] although Lewis, while patently influenced by Janet Spens, whom he acknowledges, does not mention Osgood, and may not have read Osgood's lecture.

In 1937, Isabel E. Rathborne's book *The Meaning of Spenser's Fairyland*[8] (which I shall notice at greater length momentarily) stresses the contrast in the poem between "the love that immortalizes and the love that destroys" (p. 217), symbolized by Gloriana and Acrasia respectively. This phrasing suggests influence from both Osgood and Spens, for here Osgood's polarity between lust and pure affection has become a polarity between lust and the sublimated, Platonized *eros* which drives Arthur in his quest for perfection. Thus the love and ambition themes remain at least tacitly joined, as in Spens.

Almost two decades later John Arthos's book *On the Poetry of Spenser and the Form of Romances* (1956),[9] in developing the thesis that *The Faerie Queene* in its general scheme exemplifies the pattern of the knightly quest, finds behind this quest the drive to learn what it is that will "overcome the terror of mutability" (p. 41). The answer, "the single affirmation that is repeated again and again" is "the idea of the power and excellence of love" (p. 41).[10] Here once more the themes of love, ambition, and mutability are tacitly joined: the quest, ambition in the good sense, seeks the solution to mutability, and finds it in love. Arthos also points out Spenser's awareness that love "for all its promise of stability" (p. 41) is in some of its aspects destructive, as in Ariosto, where it leads in the end to madness; but Spenser's view of love "will show the way to justice, perhaps it will be known as the creator of justice" (p. 42).

William Nelson, in his distinguished study *The Poetry of Edmund Spenser* (1963),[11] holds that the general theme not only of *The Faerie Queene* but of all Spenser's poetry is expressed in the opposition between "love the creator" and "love the destroyer" (p. 52, et passim). Nelson's phrasing "love the creator" and "love the destroyer" suggests a synthesis in the critic's mind of Arthos's phrase "the creator of justice" and Rathborne's phrasing "the love that immortalizes" and "the love that destroys"; and even if the genesis of Nelson's key phrasing on the theme of *The Faerie Queene* is not so simple as this, it is clear that by the early sixties a critical tradition has developed which emphasizes the love-theme in terms that entail Arthur's ambitious quest for Gloriana and the mutability of earthly things.

A second line of speculation on theme concerns Spenser's idealization of Britain and the British destiny. This is the province of Edwin A. Greenlaw; his 1918 article, "Spenser's Fairy Mythology,"[12] gives form and direction to this whole body of scholarship and speculation. My treatment of these works will be somewhat more detailed than the treatment accorded to the works cited in connection with the previous line of thematic speculation, for a detailed treatment of this line of work is necessary as a preliminary to the review of developments in allegorical theory further along in the essay. Greenlaw's article outlines the relationship in Spenser's poem between the Tudor myth and its component elements of chronicle history and Celtic fairy lore. Three monographs bring into respective focus the principal items discussed in Greenlaw's article: Carrie A. Harper's *The Sources of British Chronicle History in Spenser's "Faerie Queene"* (1910),[13] which Greenlaw draws upon; Charles Bowie Millican's *Spenser and the Table Round* (1932),[14] which studies the rise and prevalence of the Tudor myth; and Isabel E. Rathborne's *The Meaning of Spenser's Fairyland* (1937), which links Spenser's "Elfin Chronicle" (*F.Q.* II.x) with Celtic fairy lore.

Perhaps Greenlaw's main achievement in the 1918 article is to establish that the principal affinity between *The Faerie Queene* and the Arthurian tradition is the element of Celtic myth. For him Spenser's poem involves a fusion of the literal realm of England with a magic fairyland inspired by the Celtic otherworld which figures prominently in Arthurian legend. Not only is Spenser's Fairyland in general inspired by the Celtic otherworld, but the most significant episodes, even when ostensibly from Ariosto, frequently turn on a faerie motif, e.g., Guyon's visits to the Cave of Mammon and Acrasia's isle, Artegall's capture by Radigund, and Calidore's experience at Mount Acidale. Most important of all is Arthur's vision of the Faerie Queene, a clear example of the tale of the faerie mistress.

This tale, Greenlaw asserts, establishes the basis on which Spenser's poem rests. The traditional Arthur, after his last great battle, was received into Faerie (i.e., fairyland) to be healed; the prophecy was that he would someday come again to rule Britain. This brings Greenlaw to his central proposition, that *"Spenser conceives the Tudor rule as a return of the old British line; he conceives Elizabeth Tudor as the particular sovereign, coming out of Faerie, whose return fulfills the old prophecy"* (p. 116). In the poem, Greenlaw continues, Britons and Faeries are always carefully distinguished, a fact which is emphasized when Arthur the Briton reads "Briton Moniments" and Guyon the faerie reads "Antiquitie of Faery Lond" at Alma's castle. The Britons are the ancient race, the rightful rulers of England; the Faeries are "the Welsh, or more accurately, the Tudors," (p. 121) whose dynasty brings back the ancient British line.

Finally, there is a close link and parallel between the Britomart-Artegall story and the story of Arthur and Gloriana. To the extent that they are distinguished, the former is concerned with Elizabethan foreign policy, the latter with the return of the native British race to power. The Fairyland to which Britomart comes is the Avalon to which Arthur went to be cured. It is ruled by a great fée who healed him, protected him, preserved him until "his return, in the Tudor house, to worldly empire." Spenser's only addition to the Arthurian myth is that "the great fée, in the person of Elizabeth, herself assumes the rule of Great Britain" (p. 121).

In stressing Spenser's tendency to mold his poem in accordance with the Tudors' policy of emphasizing their Welsh heritage, Greenlaw acknowledges (p. 118) that Carrie M. Harper had already perceived this tendency in Spenser's treatment of mythical British history. Miss Harper's painstaking monograph [15] deals specifically with the account of British kings in the "Briton Moniments" and in Merlin's prophecy to Britomart (III.iii). Harper shows that Spenser, drawing chiefly on Geoffrey of Monmouth but incidentally on Holinshed, Stow, Camden, and virtually every other available authority, manufactures a history which stresses the British point of view and the lineal continuity of British rule from Brut to Cadwallader, and does so by suppressing all mention of rival Saxon (and nonlineal British) kings and by excluding tangential incidents in Geoffrey which do not enhance the Britishness of the history.

The rise of the Tudor myth and its prevalence in the days of Elizabeth come into focus in the monograph *Spenser and the Table Round* (1932) by Charles Bowie Millican. The book documents Greenlaw's proposition that "*Spenser conceives the Tudor rule as a return of the old British line.*" [16] Millican traces the Tudor antiquarian movement from its institution in 1485 when Henry VII came to the throne to its dissipation in the days of the Stuarts. He additionally reviews (pp. 106–26) the context of Italian and French criticism in which the use of the Arthurian legend was an appropriate expression of the learning deemed appropriate to the epic poet.

Isabel E. Rathborne's *The Meaning of Spenser's Fairyland* (1937) also documents and extends Greenlaw's 1918 article and parallels both Harper's and Millican's studies. Rathborne's book identifies the sources and explains the rationale of the "Antiquitie of Faery Lond" or "Elfin Chronicle" read by Guyon at Alma's castle, and provides the historical and literary context for Spenser's treatment of the mystique of Fairyland. She proposes that the "Antiquitie" supplements the "Briton Moniments" by presenting the Tudor lineage from Adam via Noah's son Ham to Osiris (Spenser's Elfin) and Hercules (Spenser's Elfinan), founder of Troy, to Brut, and, passing over the British kings with a brief summary, celebrates the two Henries and Elizabeth. In Rathborne's view, the "Antiquitie" relates the history of Fairyland as the seat of an earthly fame which, purged of grosser elements, mirrors the fame of heaven; and the empire of justice "whose earthly seat passed from Egypt to Troy, and from Troy to Rome and London" (p. 104). "Spenser aspired to do for England what Vergil had done for Rome: to write an epic which should vindicate the excellency of the English tongue and celebrate the glorious destiny of the British Empire as heir of all the ages" (p. 128). We must note here Rathborne's emphasis upon the ideal aspects of Fairyland, a point which is crucial to Harry Berger, Jr.'s theory of Spenser's poetic.

In establishing the historical and literary context of Fairyland, Rathborne describes the features of fairy mythology current in Spenser's day which may, along with the Arthurian tradition, have influenced him "to symbolize the pursuit of glory through virtue in the story of Arthur's quest for the Faery Queene, and to present the history of the ideal just empire under the veil of an Elfin Chronicle" (p. 158).

At this point we may observe that at the end of the 1930's the two strands of thematic speculation are in one respect very close together, and in one respect widely separated. They are close together in their common focus on Arthur's quest for glory. In the first strand of speculation (Dowden, Renwick, Osgood, Spens) this is treated under the issues of love and ambition; in the second strand the emphasis is upon Arthur's part historical, part mythical status. The two strands have little in common, however, as regards the ideal just empire, which comes up only in the Greenlaw strand.

The next development in the Greenlaw strand suggests that both emphases, that on Arthur's quest and that on the chronicle history, are indispensable to an adequate comprehension of Spenser's overall theme and hence of his poetic. This next development appears in Harry Berger, Jr.'s 1957 study *The Allegorical Temper*.[17] It is the thesis of this book that the two chronicles—Arthur's "Briton Moniments" and Guyon's "Antiquitie"—constitute a deliberate juxtaposition of the two levels of being imaged in the poem, viz., England itself, the nonideal, evolving British kingdom ruled by the flesh-and-blood Elizabeth and the ideal, unchanging kingdom ruled by Gloriana. Arthur's quest is the trip from England to Fairyland, the thrust that moves humanity forward toward the ideal; and Fairyland, the realm of the poem, is at one and the same time an image of imperfect striving England and the perfected ideal represented by Cleopolis. Elizabeth I, the live monarch, is both herself and Gloriana: limited by her humanity, but animated toward perfection by the vision of the ideal—an ideal which is her perfected self and which has the living reality of all operative ideals. On this view, then, the theme is both personal and national: the personal quest for the ideal, Dowden's "grand self-culture," and the evolution of British destiny, a "grand national culture."

It will be evident that after Janet Spens's book there is a strong tendency to focus on the centrality of Arthur's quest in the poem; and in 1960 M. Pauline Parker, whose *The Allegory of the "Faerie Queene"* [18] is among the most eclectic of all studies, has no hesitation in identifying the "gentleman or noble person" whom, as Spenser tells Raleigh, he intends to "fashion" in "vertuous and gentle discipline" as "prince Arthur before he was king" (p. 7). Arthur, she continues, "moves through the poem seeking true glory," and that is what the poem is about. Parker deemphasizes the theme of British history, however; for her the poem is heavily and emphatically Christian in orientation.

Among critics of the 1950's and 1960's, it must be remarked, there is a split in the way the term "fashion" in Spenser's letter is read. For William Nelson especially, Spenser's emphasis in his intent to "fashion" a gentleman is on the total impression, the "image of a brave knight," rather than on the process of evolution; Nelson insists (pp. 121–23) that we must not expect to find in Spenser's knights a gradual process of moral development. Other critics, especially Berger and Parker, find a definite place for striving and education, for the process as well as the ideal of perfection. Both Berger and Parker emphasize the psychomachic tendency of the poem, and for Parker, Arthur appears to be (p. 169) the sum of the other heroes; on this view the whole poem would constitute a grand psychomachia of the general protagonist, Arthur, and each book a subordinate psychomachia of the individual protagonist, an arrangement which like the morality play lends itself to striving and achievement—and this extends to both levels, the subordinate heroes' and Arthur's as well.

Turning now to Graham Hough's A Preface to "The Faerie Queene" (1962),[19] we find in his final chapter, "The Whole in the Part" (pp. 223–36), a fairly complete synthesis of the Dowden-Renwick-Osgood strand and the Greenlaw strand of speculation on theme. Hough's general thesis is that the poem is an example of the romantic epic. He shares the general opinion that "the internal structure of the books is capricious"; it is "by its thematic content that each book is given its integrity" (p. 225). "It is characteristic of Spenser that the formal principle is given by his theme" (p. 226).

For Hough it is through thematic emphasis that Arthur assumes his true significance in the poem. Arthur's quest, Hough feels, is largely ineffective as a narrative device; and turning back from Spens's and Rathborne's emphasis on the story of Arthur and Gloriana, he asserts that "the loves of Artegall and Britomart provide a stronger narrative thread than those of Arthur and the Faerie Queene" (p. 226). Hough does not scuttle Arthur and Gloriana, however; the point is that their real significance lies in their function as "the main vehicles of that glorification of Britain that is the great thematic ground-swell beneath the diverse surface movements of the poem" (p. 227); in this, of course, Hough is adopting the Greenlaw approach.

Hough continues his synthesis of earlier thematic speculation by asserting that the glorification of Britain which carries the poem along is both a spiritual current (Parker's emphasis) and a historical current (Greenlaw's emphasis); it is "directed toward conforming the idea of Britain with the idea of a Christian kingdom" (p. 228). Arthur in this process "represents both a historic ancestor and a spiritual ideal" (Berger's emphasis, with overtones of Spens and Parker).

From this national program the old warfare against the infidel central to the Italian epics has disappeared, and its place is taken by the "warfare of good against evil in every relation of life" (p. 229); this draws in Osgood's general theme and almost his phrasing.

Turning now to the problem presented by the status of Fairyland in the poem, Hough follows Berger's articulation of the Greenlaw-Rathborne line: Queen Elizabeth is given two ancestries, one linking her with Arthur and the British kings, one linking her with Fairyland. "The one embodies the destiny of the historical Britain, culminating in the actual Tudor rule. The other embodies the destiny of an ideal Britain, the kingdom of love, of chivalry, of true devotion, culminating in that idealized version of queenliness that was so powerful a factor in the Elizabethan imagination" (p. 229). Hough finishes this section of the chapter by recasting Berger's thesis, "the Faerie Queene both is and is not Queen Elizabeth; Cleopolis both is and is not London. It is London and its court as they ought to be and are not. . . . It is also London and its court . . . as they really are in some ultimate depth of the imagination" (pp. 229–30).

Having established Fairyland as both an ideal locality and the locale of a typical, imperfect humanity, Hough implicitly criticizes Parker's approach (as well as, indirectly, Spens's) by insisting (like Dowden) on the nonanagogical orientation of the poem. *The Faerie Queene* is a religious poem in that "its earthly action is suffused with Christian thought and feeling, but not in the sense that it is occupied with a supernatural quest." Only in Book I, at the Mount of Contemplation, and in the final extant stanza of the poem, "in the aspiration towards the eternal Sabbath," does man's last end enter the theme directly. "Its field is the world and its theme the conquest of life in the sublunary sphere" (p. 230).

Now Hough turns to the love-theme and incorporates it. He acknowledges and accepts C. S. Lewis's argument that Spenser is striving to overcome the medieval split between "*amour courtois* and the severity of the Christian scheme of redemption," and that Spenser inaugurates the romance of marriage. Then, articulating Osgood's first issue in a way slightly different from Lewis, Hough adds that except for Britomart and Artegall it is love itself and not marriage which Spenser emphasizes. "A tender, chivalrous love is the highest human value in Spenser's world; and it is always an uncomplicated unwavering love that looks to its 'right true end,' to a human and earthly fruition" (p. 231). Hough bolsters his implicit attack on Spens's Neoplatonic conjectures by citing Robert Ellrodt's argument [20] that Spenser's poem is almost innocent of Neoplatonic orientation, and especially in its passages dealing with romantic human love (pp. 231–32). Hough then concludes this section on the love-theme by drawing in the mutability theme: the poignance of Spenser's lyrical celebration of human love is closely related to the fragility of it: "the Blatant Beast, the brigands and Mutability are always at large; and if Spenser is the great poet of natural happiness he also knows its limits and its lack" (p. 233).

The final section in Hough's chapter "The Whole in the Part" explains the title; here he argues that whatever the finished poem might have been like, the fragment we have gives an impression of completeness which may indicate that without exactly intending to do so in this way, Spenser actually did round off his work. Hough's argument here articulates Dowden's position that the poem as it stands deals progressively with man's relations with God, himself, and society. Like Dowden and his many successors through John Arthos, Hough gives most emphasis to the central area, Books III and IV, which deal with love; and like Spens he associates the essential fact of human love with unifying and sustaining forces woven through the universe (p. 235).

Hough's synthesis of thematic speculation is a terminus of sorts; since his book and William Nelson's, which appeared almost simultaneously, speculation on theme in a general sense has not been a major aspect of criticism of *The Faerie Queene*, except that Rosemond Tuve's *Allegorical Imagery* (1966) [21] strongly supports the thesis that the whole poem is religious (*quid credas, quo tendas*) as well as ethical in its orientation. Other critics have, by and large, turned to studies of individual books, whose themes are less in doubt, or to general commentaries proceeding on the same thematic assumptions as those we have already observed, or to speculations on sources, poetic, or style.

Of course, thematic concerns persist. Mutability, the third of Osgood's thematic issues, has been treated with special vigor and insight by Kathleen Williams in her 1952 article "Eterne in Mutabilitie" [22] and her 1966 book *Spenser's World of Glass*.[23] Harry Berger, Jr., has shown a continuing concern with what the poem has to say about the relation between the poet and his poem.[24] Another theme which this survey has not touched on but which has drawn repeated attention is the theme of Nature: Nature and Art, since the time of Lewis's *The Allegory of Love* (cf. pp. 326–28); Nature and Grace, since the time of A. S. P. Woodhouse's "Nature and Grace in *The Faerie Queene*" (1949); [25] Nature in its benign and forbidding aspects, in Donald Cheney's *Spenser's Image of Nature: Wild Man and Shepherd in "The Faerie Queene"* (1966).[26]

The recent trend, beginning with Berger's *The Allegorical Temper* (1957), to concentrate on single books has given special prominence to the thematic unity of the several books as opposed to the overall theme; love, justice, and courtesy as themes have had monograph-length prominence, respectively, in the works of Thomas P. Roche, Jr. (*The Kindly Flame: A Study of the Third and Fourth Books of Spenser's "Faerie Queene,"* 1964); [27] T. K. Dunseath (*Spenser's Allegory of Justice in Book Five of "The Faerie Queene,"* 1968); [28] Jane Aptekar (*Icons of Justice: Iconography and Thematic Imagery in Book V of "The Faerie Queene,"* 1969); [29] Arnold Williams (*Flower on a Lowly Stalk: The Sixth Book of the "Faerie Queene,"* 1967),[30] and Humphrey Tonkin (*Spenser's Courteous Pastoral: Book Six of the "Faerie Queene,"* 1972).[31]

A grand self- and national culture, forming the complete human being, the complete monarch, and the complete nation for the uses of earth and for the uses of heaven, spurred by the force of love, which moves Arthur and Britomart, and with them Tudor England, ambitiously toward an ideal of personal and civic perfection within the Christian world view, in defiance of mutability, vice, and Satan: this, in sum, is how the composite speculation of the twentieth century has articulated and expanded Dowden's statement of the theme of Spenser's *Faerie Queene*. It may be that, judiciously applied, this corporate understanding of the theme will enable Spenserians to lay bare the whole structure of the poem, helped as we are by Dowden's further perception (as I have noted earlier) that this "grand culture" unfolds in three stages, viz., man's relations with God (Book I), with himself (Book II), and with others (Books III–VI). Graham Hough's highly respectable conjecture about the general structure of the poem, we note, moves on these lines.

Early twentieth-century speculation on the structure of the poem, however, did not have the advantage of the hindsight available to Hough. What was most apparent at the beginning of the century was that the poem was a romantic epic, ostensibly dealing with Arthur's quest for the Faerie Queene, which not only did not devote much space to the hero's quest but shifted radically in narrative structure after Book II. That Arthur's part in the poem is disconcertingly small and that the poem is a romantic epic in the tradition of Boiardo, Ariosto, and Tasso had become common observations in the eighteenth century, and the fact that the poem shifts in structure after Book II had been emphasized by R. W. Church in his 1879 English Men of Letters Essay.[32] At the dawn of the twentieth century, speculation about the status and structure of the poem as romantic epic was dominated by R. E. Neil Dodge's observation in his 1897 article "Spenser's Imitations from Ariosto" [33] that in Books III and IV *The Faerie Queene* shifts away from the systematic and careful structure of abstractions which characterizes the first two books and assumes the structural type of the *Furioso*, a multiple action with frequent digressions, with a constantly changing scene and with fewer houses and abstractions (pp. 190–95).

This observation describes the phenomenon which has devastated all attempts to deal with the poem as a coherent *narrative* design. A romantic epic imitated from Ariosto which becomes Ariostan in design only after two books of very different construction: no one in the twentieth century attempting to describe the poem as a narrative structure has been able to do much better than John Hughes in 1715 when he suggested that the poem is Gothic rather than classical in its structure.[34] Individual narrative structures have indeed been perceived; for instance, the parallel arrangement of Books I and II, always obvious in a general way, has been articulated in detail by A. S. P. Woodhouse [35] and others, notably A. C. Hamilton; [36] also, the Britomart story as the narrative structure of Books III, IV, and V was elaborately described by H. Clement Notcutt in 1926.[37] Rosemond Tuve has written brilliantly on the interlacing of tales as a principle of design derived not only from Ariosto but from medieval romance in general.[38] And John W. Draper found a reason why Spenser did not imitate Ariosto more closely when he suggested in 1924 that Spenser was trying to follow not Ariosto but the canons of sixteenth-century Italian criticism.[39]

But by the 1930's it had become apparent that the theory of Spenser's poem as a unified narrative structure was not advancing, and a reaction against the quest for such a structure emerged in the work of Janet Spens (1934),[40] J. H. Walter (1941),[41] and Josephine Waters Bennett (1942).[42] These writers disparaged the whole idea that the poem as it stands has any consistent narrative structure. Bennett's book in particular was a bombshell among Spenserians, to judge by the desertlike sparseness of books on Spenser between 1942 and 1955; [43] but it provided a much-needed ground-clearing because scholars had for too long been occupied in the hopeless quest for overall narrative structure, whereas some much more stimulating conjectures about the unity and structure of the poem had arisen in the first forty years of the century as alternatives to an overall narrative design. For instance, the now-popular thesis that the poem's unity is to be found not in a continued narrative structure but in the tone of the individual books, determined as this tone is by Spenser's use of different types of romance in the several books, was abroad as early as 1920 in Greenlaw's review [44] of Herbert E. Cory's *Edmund Spenser: A Critical Study*; [45] this idea, expanded by B. E. C. Davis in his chapter on romance in his 1933 book *Edmund Spenser: A Critical Study*,[46] pp. 78–99, lies behind both William Nelson's and Graham Hough's opinions concerning the thematic unity of individual books. Also, C. S. Lewis's proposal in 1936 that each book is organized around an allegorical core [47] is an alternative to the quest for a conventional narrative structure.

The effect of Josephine Waters Bennett's book was, in my opinion, to drive Spenserians back to the study to try to perceive anew the bases of the unity which many readers felt but which was so hard to identify. By 1954 C. S. Lewis is acknowledging that in *The Allegory of Love* he did not emphasize strongly enough the unity of the poem, which he finds not in the plot but the milieu, the atmosphere. This approach, he holds, leads to the structure of the poem: it is Fairyland itself which provides unity, for each place or person in Fairyland is a state of mind, and the poem is about states of mind. This theory links together the continual implications in *The Allegory of Love* that the Bower of Bliss, the House of Malecasta, the House of Busirane, etc., symbolize states of mind.[48] But this is a theory of allegorical structure, not narrative structure, and it indicates the direction in which thought on *The Faerie Queene* was turning. Similarly turned toward allegorical theory are A. C. Hamilton's premise in 1961 that Books II–VI are an expansion of Book I [49] and Thomas P. Roche's almost incidental observation in 1964 that the poem forms a double triptych, with correspondences between Books I and VI, II and V, and III and IV.[50]

These are all stimulating ideas, even if they raise difficult questions; they indicate a new ferment of thought about the poem and suggest that the place to search for structural unity might be in the allegory. The forward movement in Spenserian criticism, though somewhat attenuated in the 1970's, is by no means spent; and if we are, as a result, still not ready to advance a final reading or analysis of the poem, it is nevertheless in this movement that we find many of the most suggestive and incisive ideas about *The Faerie Queene* in the criticism which has appeared since 1942.

Any attempt to deal with the allegorical significance of *The Faerie Queene* requires certain points of reference, especially in view of the expanding realization in the past twenty years that Spenser's allegory is much more complex than earlier critics suspected. The traditional definition of the literary allegory is roughly this: it is a composition whose author intends some further significance or significances besides the primary or most obvious one or whose audience construes it as having such further significance(s). As a simple working definition, this covers almost everything allegorical in *The Faerie Queene*; yet when we try to elaborate on the relationship between the primary or literal aspect of the poem and the one or more further aspects suggested by the literal we encounter severe difficulties, not for lack of articulate theorists to draw upon, but because it has become increasingly apparent that the significance of the poem derives in an impressive degree not only from a tenor carried by or within a vehicle but also by the juxtaposition of two parts of the primary term, the vehicle, itself. As becomes clear in Harry Berger, Jr.'s seminal work *The Allegorical Temper* (1957), the Elvish and the British histories respectively record, in the same manner and on the primary level of the poem, the serene, stable, ideal Faerie state and the turbulent, unstable, imperfect Britain which seeks to achieve this ideal.[51] Similarly, as Berger further suggests, ideals and strivers are both characters in the poem, and the energy, the tension which provides meaning, is gained as much by the confrontation of Elvish ideal and Briton as it is by a figurative construct wherein image suggests analogous idea.

If we speculate further on this matter we find that Berger has only opened the door. This juxtaposition on the primary level of Faerie and British entities whose state of being is radically disparate, this interpenetration in the story itself of the existential and the ideal worlds, suggests other relationships in the poem which do not operate in exactly the fashion usually signified by the figurative relationship between image and meaning, vehicle and tenor, but rather involve relationships between two parts of the primary level. For example, if the first episode in the poem, Redcrosse's battle with Error, is a "cosmic" image, if it contains implicitly the whole story of Redcrosse,[52] then the tenor implied by the vehicle is *itself* all vehicle: the quest to slay the dragon is of course symbolic, and a part-whole relationship is established between two symbolic tales (Battle with Error, quest to slay dragon) quite independently of the fact that each monster-slaying enterprise is itself symbolic of something outside the story. Turning to the common technique of psychomachia, we find another such whole-part juxtaposition on the primary level. Redcrosse and Orgoglio, for instance, are both symbolic figures; Redcrosse is Holiness and all that the struggle for Holiness implies, and Orgoglio is Pride of some sort. But if Orgoglio is *Redcrosse's* pride, then Orgoglio symbolizes or embodies something about Redcrosse, and a relationship appears between two symbolic figures in the story which is of a somewhat different order from the image-meaning relationship between Redcrosse and Holiness or between Orgoglio and Pride.

Further, the heroes of the various books are sometimes viewed as merely parts of Arthur,[53] psychomachic fragments of him, as Orgoglio is perhaps a fragment of Redcrosse. Thus, when Arthur saves Redcrosse by killing Orgoglio, we might have the juxtaposition on the primary level of the *whole* both with the *part* and with the *part of a part*, a very complex relationship to deal with in terms of the traditional primary-secondary assumptions.

This speculation can be extended, but not in a way which will further clarify my procedure here. The point is that the simple traditional definition of the literary allegory, while helpful, is not sufficient for dealing with all the criticism; and so I shall expand my points of reference to include a descriptive list of characteristics of the allegorical poems and the allegorical theory available to Spenser. The characteristics will serve both as points of reference and as an organizing principle for the review of the criticism.[54]

One or more of the examples of allegorical writing and allegorical theory available to Spenser exhibit explicitly or implicitly the following characteristics. First, whatever relationships may have been perceived recently between parts of the primary, literal, or narrative level of the work, the "further significance" beyond the primary signification is often in some respects nonliteral and may be multiple. Second, these nonprimary or nonliteral significations are subject to various classifications such as the famous "allegorical, tropical, anagogical" significances of medieval biblical exegesis. Even if we set aside the complexities initiated by Berger in addressing the literal or primary significance, it is doubtful whether a mutually exclusive categorization of nonprimary significations is possible; but it is helpful in studying Spenser to be cognizant of the distinction between the signification which relates especially to Christian doctrine (*quid credas*) and the signification which relates especially to problems of prudential behavior (*quid agas*). Some writers, following a late medieval trend, would limit the term "allegory" to the first (*quid credas*) and would insist on another term like "moral allegory" for the second (*quid agas*); but since medieval theorists were not consistent in labeling even these limited aspects of the nonprimary signification, it seems more important to recognize the distinction than to insist upon particular labels.[55]

Third, the nonliteral signification either does or does not depend upon the reader's knowledge of one or more relatively esoteric bodies of traditional knowledge. For example, when Dante uses Cato to suggest the four cardinal virtues he is calling upon the reader's (more or less) esoteric knowledge of classical antiquity and of the values assigned to classical figures in the medieval tradition. But when Dante dresses hypocrites in robes of gilded lead, he is simply invoking the common experience of mankind that lead is heavy and hidden guilt hard to bear.

Fourth, in invoking traditional and/or esoteric knowledge the allegorist may engage in a practice modeled upon typological readings of the scriptures. Medieval exegetes, following the example of St. Paul, placed allegorical interpretations upon Old Testament passages; notably, these exegetes regarded various figures in the Old Testament as "types" of Christ because their actions prefigure and foreshadow the later activities of Christ as related in the New Testament. Thus Moses in leading the Israelites out of Egypt to the Promised Land is a type of Christ leading humanity out of the bondage of sin and death into eternal life. When Spenser has Redcrosse conquer the dragon and release Una's parents, he doubtless intends Redcrosse to be, like St. George in the parent legend, an echo of Christ breaking Satan's grip on mankind. This usage may loosely be called "typology," although some critics would limit "typology" to a prophetic rather than an echoing parallel; thus, by the curious alchemy which Spenser applies to time in *The Faerie Queene*, Belphoebe may be referred to as a "type" of Elizabeth in the more limited sense.

Fifth, the allegorist may employ a particular locale—a house, a garden, a castle, a forest, a temple—as a symbol for a state of mind or soul.[56] Significant in this connection is the garden or landscape, which from classical times has been a symbol of a state of mind or soul.[57] Guillaume's garden in *The Romance of the Rose,* whether a deceptive and destructive locale of cupidinous desire as D. W. Robertson would have it, or the seat of ennoblement and ecstasy as older theorists of courtly love would have it, is clearly a symbol for, or figure of, a state of mind or soul; so are other garden settings large and small from the enormous French woods of the *Orlando Furioso* to the "grove most rich of shade" of Sidney's Eighth Song in *Astrophil and Stella.*

Sixth, the experience of the protagonist in the poem may be a dream vision, as in *The Romance of the Rose,* or may contain dream visions, as in Dante's *Comedy.* Seventh, the protagonist may be involved in a quest or pilgrimage. This tradition stems from the *Odyssey* via Virgil's Aeneas, whose quest-pilgrimage was, thanks to allegorizing commentators, among the most popular nonscriptural allegories of medieval times. In the tradition of Aeneas, the quest-pilgrimage is frequently intended as signifying the journey of a soul through life.

Eighth, again in the tradition of the *Aeneid* but also in the tradition of the Neoplatonic soul journey, one or more figures in the allegory may visit one or more extraterrestrial or subterrestrial regions, as in Martianus Capella's *De Nuptii Philologiae et Mercurii* and Dante's *Inferno* and *Paradiso.*

Ninth, the allegory may employ the device of fragmenting one or more characters into parts, each of which may appear as a separate character or nonhuman entity. In *The Romance of the Rose*, as C. S. Lewis observes, the lady is nowhere seen except in fragmented form: her pride, or something close to it, is Danger, her inviting looks Fair Welcome, etc. The nearest we have to the whole lady in this poem is the rose itself, and it might be construed as representing only her love (Lewis's view), or her favors or her beauty. The dreamer, however, is present in person and encounters various fragments of himself, some personified or deified, as with the Lady Reason and the God of Love respectively, others symbolized, as with the golden arrows, which represent various states of mind into which his infatuation brings him. This device of fragmentation frequently goes under the name of "psychomachia" from the poem by Prudentius which introduced it into the medieval tradition.

Tenth, the poem may employ the "cosmic image." This technique parallels the widely dispersed Neoplatonic doctrine which holds that each fragment of the phenomenal world contains, at least implicitly, the whole cosmos. The image of man as a microcosm containing within himself the universe in little is only the most prominent instance in medieval and Renaissance times of this ubiquitous idea. In allegories it appears to underlie the tendency to use individual images, incidents, or passages which contain in capsule form a larger portion of the work or even summarize the whole work. For example, in the first lines of Dante's *Comedy*, the protagonist emerges from a dark and terrifying wood to view a sunlit mountain difficult of access and ascent. Here the reader experiences a condensed version of the whole work, the dark wood being hell, the mountain purgatory, the sunlight itself an emanation from God in paradise. Such a cosmic image need not be the first incident, however, as exhibited by the Fradubio incident in Book I of *The Faerie Queene*, which contains by implication almost the whole of Redcrosse's experience.

Eleventh, the allegorist may avail himself of the mystical numerology and/or alphabetology, dating back at least to Pythagoras and the Psalms respectively, in which a convenient scheme of numbers or letters serves as an organizing or simply as a suggestive or symbolic device. Dante's *Comedy* is full of suggestive and symbolic threes, and the total of cantos is a perfect hundred; Psalm 119 is organized by the letters of the Hebrew alphabet; and the common acrostic by the letters of a word.

It may be well to add to this list the observation that in Spenser's day "allegory" was defined in the rhetorical manuals as a "continued metaphor." It is not clear that "allegory" was commonly applied to whole works, but Spenser presumably had the rhetorical phrase in mind when he called his poem a "continued Allegory" in the "Letter to Raleigh." Metaphor was not precisely defined in the manuals as a particular kind of analogy or comparison; it signified the use of a single word in a figurative sense, whereas allegory signified the extension of the figurative sense to a whole sentence, or occasionally a whole speech.[58] "Continued Allegory" suggests, but does not insure, that Spenser's entire poem is to be viewed as a single metaphor or figure of speech. It is clear, however, that Spenser's figurative intent is flexible, not to be encompassed by any single definition of metaphor.

Finally, a word about allegorical obscurity. Although the broad lines of Spenser's didactic intent are quite clear, the poet speaks in the "Letter to Raleigh" of the "colour" or cloak which his historical fiction provides for the didactic purpose, and mentions precepts "clowdily enwrapped in Allegoricall devises." His reference to "clowdiness" is borne out by the obscurity of a number of the images and incidents in the poem; and it is evident moreover that he places very heavy demands upon the reader's fund of knowledge. Anyone trying to assess the poet's rationale for proceeding in this way should be cognizant at least in a general way of the traditions respecting clarity and obscurity in allegory which Spenser inherited.

All allegories deliberately composed as allegories appear to fall into one (occasionally both) of two fundamental categories depending on whether the author made his work primarily elucidative or primarily enigmatic in character. Of course an author might intend to elucidate and actually produce a conundrum; but among authors of reasonable skill in medieval and Renaissance times the relative degree of elucidative and enigmatic elements appears to depend on the degree to which the author was dominated by the first or the second of two powerful artistic and cultural traditions, namely the didactic tradition, in which the author's aim is to instruct the audience, to communicate as effectively as possible the author's vision of things, and the obscurantist tradition which from ancient times held a powerful grip on intellectuals: the tradition of sacred, or at least of privileged, esoterica which are to be shielded from corruption by the common herd. The theory of allegory, generated largely by persons fascinated with enigma and conundrum and heavily indebted to Neoplatonist cultists, is from ancient times couched in terms which acknowledge the obscurantist tradition: chaff and fruit, rind and kernel, veil and truth, these are the common medieval labels for the relationship between the underlying meaning and the polished surface of the allegorical work.

The two traditions are not, of course, mutually exclusive; from very early the obscurity of enigmatic allegories was viewed as a sauce to the appetite of at least the qualified part of the audience, and St.

Augustine, with his happy talent for adapting what he needed from inimical or partly inimical sources, baptized the enigma as a teaching device by remarking that we value most those things which we have worked hardest to get. We can hardly doubt that Spenser was cognizant of these two standard arguments for obscurity: it is a sauce to the appetite, and it enhances the value of the meaning once obtained. It will be no surprise, then, if we find Spenser assuming that a certain degree of obscurity does not conflict with his clearly didactic purpose.

We may now proceed to an examination of the allegorical criticism. The working definition of "allegory" and the list of characteristics described above will, as I have said, serve as a guide in the examination of the criticism. To begin with the general area covered by the definition, what allegory is, one prominent strand of development concerns the status of the allegorical itself in Spenser's poem: what range of vehicles the poet uses to convey his theme and what part of these can legitimately be labeled "allegorical." This particular strand culminates in Graham Hough's schematic diagram (*Preface*, p. 107) which sets forth relationships between the presentation of concepts and straight verisimilitude in literature. The strand includes portions of the writings of W. L. Renwick, C. S. Lewis, W. B. C. Watkins, and Northrop Frye.

We see the line beginning in Renwick's *Edmund Spenser: An Essay on Renaissance Poetry* (1925). Renwick opens his treatment in the most orthodox fashion of his day by saying that *The Faerie Queene* is "moral allegory couched in a form reconciling epic and romance" (p. 133). For Renwick the allegorical aspect of the poem is an unhappy product of the didactic assumptions governing poetry: "The speaking picture had to have a meaning; that the duty should have been interpreted so literally as to result in allegory was perhaps a failure of the critical imagination" (p. 140).

Renwick proceeds to distinguish (pp. 140–42) topical, political significances from the artistically more important intellectual, moral, and spiritual values conveyed by the poem. These values Spenser conveys symbolically by a series of devices, the crudest of which is the emblem (p. 141). More sophisticated modes of symbolism range through a spectrum extending from personification to "true myth" (pp. 146–47). In between lie "the parable of the preacher, the fable, the interpretation of mythology, the exemplary episode, the simple but suggestive story, the illustration of a truth or of a theory, the dramatic personification as distinct from the symbolic" (p. 147). These devices of course are flexible and overlap; they are all used to convey the didactic meaning, which is fundamental.

This passage in Renwick is, I take it, an important anticipation of the schematic spectra of poetical devices which appear later in the works of Frye and Hough. Renwick does not attempt visual spectra, but he indicates a range of devices from easily translated emblems to pure myth which suggests at a distance the kind of diagramming which Hough later applies to his expansion of Frye's spectrum.

The devices named by Renwick vary widely in their technique and in the accessibility to the reader of the meanings they convey. In *The Faerie Queene*, Renwick points out, a proposition will often be expressed in symbols (the rose of love, the Christian armor, the parable) whose referents are sufficiently clear that the symbols are easily translatable back into the proposition. The true myth, however, conveys a philosophical intuition for which no terms exist; its appeal is purely imaginative, and it cannot be paraphrased. The illustration, finally, bypasses the intellect, appealing directly to the reader's humanity through the simple emotions (p. 149). Renwick's analysis appears to be entirely descriptive and empirical; he does not invoke medieval allegorical theory, not even the fourfold meanings; and we may say that the descriptive, empirical tendency persists through this whole line of thought on the nature of allegorical technique. Both Lewis and Watkins, among Renwick's successors, do of course draw heavily upon medieval scholarship in their treatments. We notice too that Renwick does not acknowledge the Coleridgean, romantic distinction between allegory and symbolism which bedevils Lewis's theory in *The Allegory of Love*. For Renwick, allegory is a symbolic way of writing, and all devices which convey meaning in any way besides the straightforward explicit statement of a proposition are equally symbols.

In *The Allegory of Love* (1936) C. S. Lewis is much more edgy about the status of symbolism. In his chapter "Allegory" (pp. 44–111) he limits the allegorical to the representation of immaterial facts by *visibilia*, and he emphasizes personification as the prime instance of this (p. 45). Symbolism, on the other hand, he defines as the "attempt to see the archetype in the copy," the attempt to see eternal and permanent realities as represented in sensible phenomena. This sacramental symbolism he excludes from his definition of the allegorical. Later, however, Lewis speaks (p. 140) of the necessity for the reader of *The Romance of the Rose* to keep "two stories—the psychological and the symbolical—distinct and parallel before his mind." We note also that at another point in his book Lewis advances a definition of "allegory" as a label for a whole composition as opposed to "allegory" as a label for the device of personified abstraction: a "radical allegory" is a story "which can be translated into a literal narration . . . without confusion, but not without loss" (p. 166). Further on Lewis acknowledges that clothing and jewelry in *The Faerie Queene* are "the symbol of a spiritual radiance" (p. 329); we may suppose, thus, that if he indeed is maintaining his distinction between the allegorical and the symbolic, he at least does intend to say that the kind of poem which Spenser is writing has room for both symbol and allegory.

The tendency to keep shifting the basis of what is meant by "allegory" and the "allegorical" unfortunately extends throughout this celebrated study. In the passage on p. 334 which most clearly places Lewis in the line of thought begun by Renwick, the "allegorical," the representation of immaterial facts by *visibilia*, has become only one device among many, presumably including symbols, though Lewis does not say so explicitly. Here he applies, like Renwick, a graded classification to the description of Spenser's narrative devices: "Not everything in the poem is equally allegorical. . . . We shall find that it is Spenser's method to have in each book an allegorical core, surrounded by a margin of what is called 'romance of types,' and relieved by episodes of pure fantasy" (p. 334).

Moving on to W. B. C. Watkins's *Shakespeare and Spenser* (1950),[59] we find his remarks on allegorical theory concentrated in the essay entitled "The Painted Dragon," pp. 111–45. For seven pages (pp. 114–21) he tilts with Lewis over the latter's unconvincing distinction between the allegorical and the symbolic. He begins this polemic by observing that "symbolism, one thing standing for another, includes not only allegory but all literature"; that "in its more restricted sense of a specific poetic technique, something concrete standing for something immaterial, it is a conscious emphasis on words and images used as symbols, their immaterial meaning paramount"; and that "allegory is never found without symbolism in both senses of the term" (p. 114). Watkins then rejects Lewis's absolute separation of the allegorical and the symbolic as invalid,[60] and in essence returns to the implicit position of Renwick, namely that the symbolic, the conveyance of immaterial meanings through words and images, is a ubiquitous technique in allegorical writings.

Having freed the word "symbol" from the connotation of being in opposition to allegory, Watkins follows Renwick and Lewis in devising his own graded array of techniques in *The Faerie Queene*: Spenser's method, he observes (pp. 123–44), moves between the poles of symbolic personification and rounded characterization, as with Una, whose symbolic features sometimes receive more emphasis—her whiteness, her donkey, her lamb, all emblematic—but whose womanly features are sometimes emphasized, as when she fears that Duessa will escape unscathed after having captured Redcrosse: "Ne let that wicked woman scape away." In no instance is Una either purely symbolic or purely a realistic characterization; but the mix varies greatly from incident to incident.

Watkins acknowledges (p. 126, n. 20) that this schema or spectrum was inspired by T. M. Greene's symposium volume *The Arts and the Art of Criticism* (1940).[61] The schema might be described as a way-station leading into Northrop Frye's schema in *The Anatomy of Criticism* (1957),[62] pp. 89–92, although Frye either ignores or does not know of Watkins's rejection of the fundamental opposition between the allegorical and the symbolic; in fact, taking "symbolism" to mean in this context "thematically significant imagery," he acknowledges and approves the opposition. We notice the echo of the romantic approach also used by Lewis: "The contrast is between a 'concrete' approach to symbols which begins with images of actual things and works outward to ideas and propositions, and an 'abstract' approach [the allegorical] which begins with the idea and then tries to find a concrete image to represent it" (p. 89). The only thing wrong with the distinction, Frye feels, is that in modern literature "allegory" is used to indicate such a large variety of literary phenomena that any reference to it may inspire confusion. He therefore begins by defining: "Allegorical interpretation" is "an attaching of ideas to the structure of poetic imagery" (p. 89). *All* commentary, thus, is allegorical interpretation; but we have "actual allegory" only when "a poet explicitly indicates the relationship of his images to examples and precepts, and so tries to indicate how a commentary on him should proceed" (p. 90). Frye then sets up his own spectrum, ranging from "naive allegory," which is a disguised form of discursive writing, so heavily and obviously interested in making its point that it is not literature at all, to the most indirect and obscure use of "symbolism not intended to be fully understood." In between are, in order, "continuous allegories" like *The Pilgrim's Progress* and *The Faerie Queene*; free-style allegories whose direct suggestions for commentary are intermittent, as in Ariosto, Goethe, Hawthorne; poems like Milton's epics, with large and insistent doctrinal content, whose internal fictions are *exempla*; in the exact center, works like Shakespeare's plays where the structure of imagery has only implicit relation to ideas and events; then metaphysical poetry with its paradoxes; and finally the poems of *symbolisme* which avoid naming the things which their symbols are supposed to evoke (pp. 91–92).

To evaluate briefly, what renders Frye's schema virtually useless for helping us get at a poem like *The Faerie Queene* is that it is unhistorical in its rejection from "allegory" of the "symbolic," of images whose doctrinal significance is not patent to all readers. The fact is that many images in medieval and Renaissance allegories depend upon esoteric information; and the paradoxical and obscure was a feature so prominent in the tradition of allegorical writing which Spenser inherited that three scholars describing and documenting this tradition in the past twenty years have entitled their works, respectively, *Pagan Mysteries in the Renaissance*,[63] *Paradoxia Epidemica*,[64] and *Mysteriously Meant*.[65] Once it is acknowledged that the most prominent of allegories have depended heavily on mere suggestion and have engaged in deliberate obscurity in the relation between image and meaning, then the whole point of Frye's distinction between the allegorical and the symbolic disappears, and the word "symbol" is freed of its antiallegorical meaning.

We now arrive at Graham Hough's schematic diagram (*Preface*, p. 107), which illustrates his contention that the poem is not primarily allegory as opposed to epic-romance in its genre: "as far as the structure of *The Faerie Queene* as a whole is concerned allegory is not so decisive a factor, theme not so dominant over image, as we have sometimes been led to expect" (p. 112). Hough, as we already see from this quotation, accepts Frye's definition of "real allegory" as that writing in which the author points the direction in which a commentary should proceed, in which the theme insistently dominates the image. Hough is uneasy with that part of Frye's schema which touches upon the obscure practices of *symbolisme*; unfortunately he does not reject the schematic approach entirely but rather constructs a schema of his own. He adopts Frye's polar distinction between theme-dominance and image-dominance; he attaches image-dominance to straight verisimilitude and converts Frye's spectrum into a clock-arrangement with "naive" (absolutely childish, explicit and lifeless) allegory at noon, realism at six o'clock, and symbolism, redefined as "image simple, theme complex" at nine o'clock. On the other side at three o'clock is the perfect wedding between simple theme and complex imagery achieved in Shakespeare's plays. This Hough labels "incarnation." Hough then places *The Faerie Queene* at about 1:00 to 1:30, ranging between a point where the image, though still the vehicle for an obvious theme, begins to take on an interesting life of its own, and a point where the "romance of types," still more lifelike, appears (p. 108). This places *The Faerie Queene* right next to Ariosto's even more lively epic-romance which stands, with its intermittent allegory, at two o'clock, not far away from Shakespeare's dramatic incarnation at three. We note here Lewis's phrasing ("romance of types") and also, presumably, the influence of Watkins's polarity between symbol and characterization; but we are still left in the anomalous position of being unable to talk about the symbolic in relation to allegorical meaning in *The Faerie Queene*, for symbolism is on the other side of the clock from Spenser's poem. We must infer then that the schematic approach, besides being involved almost from the beginning with an untenable distinction between the allegorical and the symbolic, as it develops gets us progressively further away from being able to deal with the flexibility of Spenser's poem.

This inference is borne out by the fact that Robert Kellogg and Oliver Steele, in the remarkable introduction to their edition of the first two books, *Books I and II of "The Faerie Queene,"* [66] first advance the diagrammatic approach (pp. 6–7) and then are forced to set it aside (pp. 7–8) in order to get at the symbolic dimension of the figures in the poem. Kellogg and Steele adopt that part of Hough's arrangement which extends from naive allegory at noon to straight realistic "history and reporting" at six o'clock, and place *The Faerie Queene,* as Hough does, between naive allegory and the midpoint (Hough's three o'clock) where "the representation of actuality and idea are in balance" (p. 7), as in Shakespeare's plays.

This schema does not, however, accommodate the function of the image as symbol which occurs when an image suggests to the reader, without explicit statement on the author's part, one or more traditional associations which it has accumulated. Hough labels this symbolic function "image simple theme complex" and places it at nine o'clock on his diagram, far away from *The Faerie Queene* at one-thirty; Kellogg and Steele rightly recognize that Spenser extensively employs images in this way and simply describe this function (p. 8) as an adjunct to their adaptation of Hough's schema.

The next strand of criticism of the allegorical dimension of *The Faerie Queene* concerns itself not only with what allegory is but with the nature and classification of the nonliteral or nonprimary meanings, the first and second items in my list of allegorical characteristics.

Generally speaking the medieval classifications evolved for exegetical study of the Bible—e.g., allegorical (*quid credas*), moral (*quid agas*), and anagogical (*quo tendas*)—were little attended to in criticism of *The Faerie Queene* until the 1960's. B. E. C. Davis does observe briefly in *Edmund Spenser: A Critical Study* (1933),[67] pp. 106–7, that the four modes can be applied at various points in the poem; but in 1936 C. S. Lewis sets the approach aside by casting doubt on the usefulness of the multiple senses of exegetical study for examining erotic allegory (*The Allegory of Love,* p. 48, n. 2). In 1950 W. B. C. Watkins, pursuing his argument against the arbitrary and untenable distinction between the allegorical and the symbolic, makes the important point (*Shakespeare and Spenser,* p. 119) that in modern usage Dante's moral and anagogical senses have been subsumed under the term "allegorical," which thus becomes a blanket term covering all sorts of secondary meanings, including Lewis's sacramental symbolism which, Watkins adds, Dante would probably have called "anagogical" (*quo tendas*).

Rosemond Tuve's revival of the distinction between the terms "allegorical" (*quid credas*) and "tropological" (*quid agas*) as a useful and necessary distinction in dealing with *The Faerie Queene* accompanies her insistence in *Allegorical Imagery* (1966) on a flexible, informed response to Spenser's romantic fiction with its large variety of secondary meanings. Her remarks along this line in *Allegorical Imagery* are anticipated by those of her student Thomas P. Roche, Jr., in *The Kindly Flame* (1964); the passage in Roche's book will serve to indicate the position of both scholars, although this should not be taken to mean that Roche is simply setting down what he heard from Tuve.

In "The Nature of Allegory," pp. 3–31, Roche suggests the response which Spenser expected of the reader by comparing the verbal universe of allegory to the quasi-Neoplatonic, Ptolemaic universe of medieval times. Phenomena in the sublunary world have their own individual identity, but they also suggest corresponding events in the celestial world of the planets and stars and in the supercelestial world of angels and Godhead. Fire burns; the sun, burning, nourishes life; angels burn with love for the creator. The three worlds are a progression from material to spiritual; and as our knowledge of seraphim is drawn from our knowledge of fire and the sun, so our knowledge of universal truths is drawn in part from our reading of the imitations of these truths which occur in the visible universe.

Correct allegorical reading, in Roche's view, parallels this. The poetical fiction adumbrates other meanings, sometimes several or many; this corresponds to the way in which fire suggests the sun or the angel burning with love. "When the structural patterns of the narrative coincide with any other events of nature or supernature, we as readers are entitled to view the conformity or analogy as an allegorical meaning" (p. 10). Translation is, in fact, often difficult to do precisely; but the added meanings are automatically summoned up by the associations stimulated by the fiction. The entire narrative of an allegorical poem, then, "is the vehicle of a continued metaphor and . . . the tenor may be any concept or object outside the poem that conforms to the pattern or patterns inherent in the narrative. . . . There is no single meaning, at least no single meaning to be stated apart from the experience of the poem" (p. 31).

In the first chapter of *Allegorical Imagery*, "Problems and Definitions," pp. 3–55, Tuve establishes the fact that in Spenser's day, as in earlier centuries, the secondary significance of an allegorical composition was normally viewed as double or multiple; the reader could be expected to look not only for the "moral" allegory (*quid agas*) but for the spiritual allegory (*quid credas*). Tuve is at pains to demonstrate that this would be true for the whole of *The Faerie Queene* and not just for Book I, so obviously directed toward spiritual matters. All allegorical composition in the time, she holds, is likely to be concerned with two human ideals, *Bon Chevalier* and *Bon Esprit*; and not only the quest of Redcrosse but also those of Guyon and Britomart must be read as both moral and spiritual quests.

This widening of the secondary meaning of the whole poem into the area of spiritual doctrine and spiritual development corresponds to the thematic widening into the spiritual area noted earlier in Tuve's book and that of M. Pauline Parker. Anyone who wishes to limit the thematic and spiritual scope of the poem after Book I must effectively refute Tuve's book; and we may take the argument of the book as a reply to A. S. P. Woodhouse's argument in "Nature and Grace in *The Faerie Queene*" (1949) that Book I moves on the level of grace and the other books on the level of nature, although Tuve mutes the argument by going out of her way to agree with Woodhouse wherever she can (e.g., pp. 131, 137n.).

The third item in my list of the characteristics of allegory asserts that a nonprimary significance either does or does not depend upon the reader's acquaintance with one or more bodies of (more or less) esoteric information. The "does not" part of this characteristic appears in the list largely as a housekeeping item, a means of acknowledging that Spenser incorporates into his allegory timeless aspects of human experience which all men share, and which the poet can suggest without having to appeal to the reader's learning. There are perhaps fewer instances of this kind of allegorical significance in Spenser than in Dante, but Spenser has them, too. For example, the image of being lost in the woods in *F.Q.* I.i, is patently an image of internal confusion and disorientation, drawing upon the discomfort which everyone feels when lost; and however much this passage may also draw upon traditional classical and medieval forest and garden imagery, any reader capable of more than the most childish response will see that it represents internal confusion. For this the reader has no need of scholarship. There is no point in going through the criticism and commentaries to point out instances where such nonesoteric significances have been recorded; there are plenty of instances, but obviously no developing critical tradition.

On the other hand, the symbolic allusion, the word or image which suggests one or more items of relatively esoteric knowledge, has been the focus of a huge proportion of Spenserian scholarship, including the majority of the commentary notes in the *Variorum* Spenser, a host of articles, and a few monographs like John E. Hankins's recent *Source and Meaning in Spenser's Allegory* (1971).[68] Most prominent in this area in recent years is the interest in iconographic explication. To the degree that the iconographic study of Spenser is merely a visual approach to the mythological allusion, interest in this area was already lively in the days of Jortin (1734), Warton (1752–62), Upton (1758), and Todd (1805), all of whom annotated or commented upon mythological passages, with remarks on probable sources.

The first attempt at a systematic treatment of this material appears in Alice Elizabeth Sawtelle's *The Sources of Spenser's Classical Mythology* (1896).[69] The defects in her book, largely matters of omission and failure to refer to Spenser's sources in the mythological handbooks of the day, were remedied in considerable part by Harry Gibbons Lotspeich in his *Classical Mythology in the Poetry of Edmund Spenser* (1932).[70] This dictionary provides longer and better essays than Sawtelle's, and adds many new entries. A most notable feature of Lotspeich's book is the introductory essay (pp. 3–28). Specific critical application of this kind of material can be seen already in C. S. Lewis's *The Allegory of Love* (1936), in the passages on the Bower of Bliss, the Garden of Adonis, and the houses of Malecasta and Busirane (pp. 324–44), and especially in the appended essay "Genius and Genius" (pp. 361–63). Lewis continues the approach in the essays in *Spenser's Images of Life* (1967).[71]

Beginning in the 1940's more strictly iconographical criticism, with reference to actual artifacts, begins to make itself felt. In spite of a great deal of cross-pollination, three broad lines of development appear in Spenserian iconographic study. One line derives from the nineteenth-century iconographic investigations of medieval art by A. N. Didron[72] and Émile Mâle.[73] The main Spenserians in this field are Rosemond Tuve and Samuel C. Chew; Tuve's "Spenser and Some Pictorial Conventions with Particular Reference to Illuminated Manuscripts" (1940)[74] indicates that she had already at that time developed the lifetime interest which resulted ultimately in the posthumous volume *Allegorical Imagery* (1966). Chew's *The Virtues Reconciled* (1947)[75] was followed in 1954 by "Spenser's Pageant of the Seven Deadly Sins"[76] and in 1962 by *The Pilgrimage of Life*.[77] All of these studies draw upon medieval visual art to illuminate Spenser's visual and symbolic techniques and references.

A second line begins with Erwin Panofsky's *Studies in Iconology* (1939)[78] and includes Jean Seznec's *The Survival of the Pagan Gods* (1940; 1st English ed. 1953)[79] and Edgar Wind's *Pagan Mysteries in the Renaissance* (1958). All three of these books, and most notably

Edgar Wind's, deal with the Neoplatonic interpretations of classic myth which served as programs for the compositions of the great visual artists of the Italian Renaissance. The continual references to Spenser in these volumes could not fail to suggest to Spenserians generally the similarity between the mythological images and programs in *The Faerie Queene* and those of Botticelli, Rafael, and Michelangelo.

Thirdly, interest in sixteenth-century printed sources of visual symbolic representation appears vigorously in Rosemary Freeman's *English Emblem Books* (1948) [80] and in the lifelong project of Don Cameron Allen, published in 1970 as *Mysteriously Meant: The Rediscovery of Pagan Symbolism and Allegorical Interpretation in the Renaissance.*

It is not until about 1964 that iconography emerges as a standard major tool in the reading of Spenser's poem. Alastair Fowler's immersement in the subject is evident already in his review of Berger's *The Allegorical Temper* in 1960; [81] and in 1964 Thomas P. Roche, Jr.'s *The Kindly Flame* and Fowler's *Spenser and the Numbers of Time* [82] include reproductions of contemporary visual art and in some degree depend upon these illustrations as a basis for their critical pronouncements. The remarkable application (1965) of Carpaccio's "St. George Slaying the Dragon" to a reading of Book I in Kellogg and Steele's edition (pp. 10–15) is certainly a landmark in Spenserian iconography, but only one of a number of highly useful contributions, including of course Tuve's *Allegorical Imagery* (1966), as well as T. K. Dunseath's *Spenser's Allegory of Justice in Book Five of "The Faerie Queene"* (1968) and Jane Aptekar's *Icons of Justice: Iconography and Thematic Imagery in Book V of "The Faerie Queene"* (1969), all of which include and employ reproductions of contemporary visual artifacts as a means of exploring Spenser's meaning.

The fourth item in the list of allegorical characteristics is typology, the name assigned by medieval exegetes to the prophetic parallels which they observed between Old Testament figures and the life of Christ: Moses, Samson, etc., are "types" of Christ. Spenser shows his awareness of the device when he calls Gloriana the "true glorious type" of Elizabeth (*F.Q.* I.Proem.iv.7); Gloriana, living at some indefinite time in the past, foreshadows the glory of Elizabeth I. Kellogg and Steele use "typology" in the loose sense, to mean simply an allusive parallel, in labeling St. George of the legend and Redcrosse as types of Christ (p. 13). The identification of such parallels is widespread in the criticism, as in the parallels between Guyon and Aeneas, Artegall and Hercules, Britomart and Camilla and Bradamante, and need not be dwelt on here.

Much more important for the examination of Spenser's poetic

world are the explorations of the most specifically typological relationship in the poem, the relationship between the mythological histories in Books II and III and the House of Tudor, a relationship
which is the special focus of the Greenlaw strand of scholarship on
theme, examined earlier in this essay. This scholarship has provided
the basis for some very important further speculation about the nature
of Spenser's poetic.

The crucial item here is Harry Berger, Jr.'s *The Allegorical Temper*, but we must notice briefly that Josephine Waters Bennett provides an important bridge between Isabel Rathborne's *The Meaning of
Spenser's Fairyland* and the speculations initiated by Berger, though
her article appeared too late to affect Berger's book. Bennett's article,
entitled "Britain Among the Fortunate Isles" (1956),[83] proposes that
Fairyland is simultaneously England itself, the Fortunate Isle of classical tradition, and the New Jerusalem, held together in an amalgam
made possible by the timeless character of the poem.

It would not be fair to Berger to attribute his inspiration to
Greenlaw, but the link is patent. We must begin, however, at some
little distance from Greenlaw. In chapter 8, "The Poem as Vision,"
Berger proposes that the poem is built on the interplay between the
ideal, imagined world of Faery and the existential world of the reader
and poet. This interplay can be recognized in various articulations:
the narrator's voice (in comments and interpretive passages) versus
the dramatic voice of Guyon and other characters in the poem; Gloriana the dream-ideal versus the Arthur who dreamed her and now
seeks to achieve his dream; Faery (land) versus Britain; Gloriana
versus Elizabeth. The visionary world of Faery is both stimulus and
warning to the denizen of the existential world, who grows toward
the perfections of the ideal and embodies or contains the ideal to
some degree, but who must be alert to the nonideal character of his
own existence and situation. Gloriana is the ideal toward which Arthur
strives, but he has dreamed her, and she represents a fundamental in-
gredient in his makeup which motivates him and which struggles for
realization. Guyon, stimulated by the Shamefastness (fear of doing a
disgraceful act) which is the heart of his inner being, strives toward
the ideal represented by Belphoebe.

More specifically related to the research of the Greenlaw school
is the relationship between Fairyland and Britain. The history of British Kings at Alma's castle, which records the doings of human monarchs, is an unrelieved tale of corruption and disaster; the History of
Fairyland, which records the doings of the Faery monarchs, is a
serene happy history. The reason, for Berger, is clear: Fairyland is
the ideal toward which turbulent imperfect Britain must strive. The

relationship between the two kingdoms, ideal and real, becomes specific in the relationship between Gloriana and Elizabeth. Gloriana is the ideal toward which the live existent Elizabeth strives; Gloriana is both stimulus and warning to Elizabeth, who grows toward the perfections of the ideal but must be alert to the nonideal character of her own existence and situation.

Berger's remarkable essay, in spite of its difficult style and its obvious alignment with the snook-cocking New Critics, crystallizes the poetic of Spenser's poem which is implicit in Greenlaw's and Rathborne's studies. This is a new poetic, not exactly typological, though akin to it; for in the relationship between Faeries and human beings, between the Elvish royal line and the British, we have something quite different from the relationship between primary and secondary term in metaphor, or between literal and tropological significances in allegory as traditionally conceived. Here both the Faeries and the human beings are participants in the poem on the literal level: here the ideal and the fallibly human interpenetrate, the world of the poem is simultaneously the locale of ideal polity and of struggling nascent Britain. The two aspects of Spenser's poetic world correspond to two aspects of the human being motivated by an ideal: such a person, imperfect and struggling, contains within himself the idea, the ideal, toward which he struggles.

I do not believe that Berger's poetic should be viewed as anticipating or duplicating the insistence that we focus upon the image, on the literal level of the poem, which characterizes A. C. Hamilton's *The Structure of Allegory in "The Faerie Queene."* Hamilton is concerned, like Northrop Frye, lest we forget that all the meanings of the poem are implicit in the word or the image and have no existence apart from these. He would not contend that the function of the images is neither symbolic nor metaphorical. But for Berger, there is in one aspect of the poem no symbol, no metaphor at all, for the two correlates whose juxtaposition reveals Spenser's meaning are both a part of the fictional narrative: human and Faery, the dynamic striver and the static goal.

With the next item in the strand of allegorical criticism now under consideration we draw in the fifth characteristic of allegory, the use of a locale as a symbol for a state of mind or soul. Janet Spens commented on this aspect of Fairyland in the early thirties, and we shall return to her shortly; but first, while Berger's speculations on the poetical implications of the Tudor myth in *The Faerie Queene* are fresh in mind, we should review further speculations in the same area. Chapter 8 of M. Pauline Parker's *The Allegory of "The Faerie Queene"* (1960), entitled "Spenser's Poetic World," in some measure parallels

Berger in working out the implications of Greenlaw's and Rathborne's concern with the Tudor myth and the Celtic otherworld. For Parker the word "fayerye" provides the link between the historical and the visionary aspects of Spenser's poem. The locale of the poem is simultaneously historical Britain and Fairyland. "Fayerye," she points out, is as much an adjective as a noun in the sixteenth century, and as an adjective it qualifies the name of a person or place in the state of fayerye, i.e., in the possession of or under the control of the elves or the fairies. The distinguishing mark of the fairies was their power of casting glamor, or making things appear as they wish in the eyes of others.

"There is no substantial, geographical, difference between the land of faerie and the land of humanity. It is the state which is different. The forest of Arden, or the wood near Athens, or Arlo-hill, are faerie land in the faerie presence. No imaginative violence is required to conceive of England as at once faerie land and the kingdom of Elizabeth, still less if the hero be Arthur" (pp. 276–77). In *The Faerie Queene*, Parker continues, Spenser synthesizes the faerie doctrine of glamor with the Platonist imaginative conception of the world as a transient insubstantial phenomenon, "little more than a fayerye vision." England, for Spenser, is the perfect locale for his epic of the human soul, simultaneously the great globe itself and the baseless fabric of a vision (p. 278).

The implication here is that the Arthurian element in the poem, the participation of Britomart and Artegall as forebears of Elizabeth (who is herself Arthur reborn), and the repeated suggestion in the poem that England is Fairyland, all provide a reciprocally convertible and permanently ambiguous matrix from which the poet derives the visionary land of the poem, simultaneously England under a historical aspect; the transitory, deceptive phenomenal world which we all experience; a symbolic landscape which represents the interior experiences of the human psyche in the struggle of existence; and a "golden world" peopled by denizens more perfected, nearer the ideal than can be found in our experience. Here we find drawn together the traditional primary-secondary aspects of allegorical signification, implicit in the symbolic landscape (a vehicle whose tenor is a state of mind or soul), and the newer concept of Spenser's poetic world, set forth by Berger, as a simultaneous presentation, in the narrative itself, of the phenomenal, the historical, the imperfect, the striving, the human, and the ideals toward which the imperfect striving human beings move. In *The Kindly Flame* (1964) Thomas P. Roche, Jr., similarly articulates the theory of Spenser's poetic world which has its roots in the Greenlaw school of historical scholarship. It is evident, I think, that Roche has benefited from the speculations both of Berger and Parker.

In his section on "The Nature of Faeryland," pp. 31–50, Roche quotes Coleridge's remark that the poem is "truly in land of Faery, that is, of mental space" (p. 33). Roche notes that there is no jarring shift from this land of mental space back and forth to the real world of history; on the contrary there is no break from one to the other. Yet the two worlds are carefully distinguished in the poem on the basis of the parallel histories of British kings and Elf monarchs read by Arthur and Guyon respectively. "Spenser's apparent confusion of Britain and Faeryland is in reality a careful poetic discrimination. The poem is a fulfillment of the ideal of civil life that is to occur historically during the reign of the Tudors. From the point of view of the narrative Elizabeth is only a descendant of Britomart, still far off in the future. From the point of view of the poet Elizabeth is the fulfillment of the prophecy in the chronicle of British kings. The action of the poem is the evolution of the civil ideal and is conceived as a reciprocal interchange between England and Faeryland" (p. 46).

We must observe, further, that the recent book by Angus Fletcher, *The Prophetic Moment* (1971) [84] is largely a speculation on the portrayal throughout the poem of the dichotomy which exists between the British and Elvish histories: the separate but reciprocal status of the striving imperfect world of historical reality, represented not only in the British history but also by the labyrinthine *selva oscura* which makes up most of Fairyland, and the static, perfect world of the fulfilled wish, represented not only in the Elvish history but also by the various "temples"—places of fulfillment, fruition and order—which provide allegorical centers in the various books: the Mount of Contemplation, the House of Alma, the Garden of Adonis, etc. Fletcher's approach is, in a sense, a completion of Berger's poetic, for it shows how the imperfect and the ideal are articulated into the geography of the whole poem outside the Castle of Alma.

The interest in the distinction between the two histories which reaches a certain poetic completion in Fletcher's book extends back all the way through the Greenlaw school to Greenlaw's own precursor, Carrie E. Harper; and if Harry Berger, Jr., may be said to have made the major step from speculating typologically about the fulfillment of the Tudor myth in Elizabeth to describing the relation between ideal and striver, still we find that this major line of speculation about the poetic of *The Faerie Queene* is clearly and firmly within "the province of literary history."

To continue with the fifth characteristic of allegory, the use of a locale as a symbol for a state of mind or soul, we notice that Fletcher, like Roche and Parker, is intensely interested in this aspect of Fairy-land. In this interest, these figures culminate another strand of criticism begun in this century by Janet Spens, who in turn borrows the idea from Coleridge. Coleridge and Spens, in viewing Fairyland as a symbolic locale, have a less localized conception than many of their successors. Spens expands Coleridge's proposal that Fairyland is the land of "mental space" by saying, in her chapter on symbolism, that "Faery Land is . . . the mind, the inner experience of each of us" (p. 52). In *The Allegory of Love* C. S. Lewis, chary of using the word "symbol" because of its antiallegorical overtones, favors other words in linking the gardens and houses to the states of mind they convey: the Bower of Bliss is the "home" of "vicious Pleasure," the "place" of "paralysis in appetite" (p. 339); the House of Busirane is a "picture" of adulterous romantic love with its "suffocating monotony," a "place" of death (p. 341). But it is clearly a matter of diction, for to him the gardens and houses convey states of mind. In his 1954 essay "Edmund Spenser 1552–1599" [85] he adopts the word "symbol" freely; the "moral" or "philosophical" allegory is couched in symbols, which are the "natural speech of the soul," a truth which "was accepted and acted upon by the ancient and medieval world" (p. 99). He then discusses (p. 101) the House of Busirane as a symbol, first for the wretched state of mind of a person trapped in an illicit love affair, and second for other psychic imprisonments unrelated to love.

From the time of Curtius, whose book precedes Lewis's 1954 essays on *The Faerie Queene*, the idea has been heavily buttressed by documentary evidence of its existence in medieval texts, and in the 1960's it is widespread in Spenser criticism, in Parker's and Roche's books, as noted above; and, significantly, in A. Bartlett Giamatti's *The Earthly Paradise and the Renaissance Epic* (1966), which contains a study of symbolism of this sort in ancient and medieval literature (pp. 11–93) and an essay on Spenser's Bower of Bliss (pp. 232–94).

Especially fascinating is the growing awareness among these and parallel critics that not only are specific locales states of minds but that the vast wooded landscape of the poem is itself a *selva oscura*, a symbol of the confusion which characterizes human existence generally — a fleshing out of the notion intuited by Coleridge and Spens. This idea, approximated by Fletcher in *The Prophetic Moment*, pp. 24–34, had been anticipated by Graham Hough in a passing comment in his *Preface*, pp. 98–99; he in turn may be extending from A. C. Hamilton's proposal that Spenser's Wood of Error and Dante's dark wood are parallel paradigms for the whole adventure of the respective travelers. Of Redcrosse, Hamilton says, "Error is all that which stands between the knight and his entering upon his salvation" (*Structure of Allegory*, p. 39).

In a parallel development in 1969, Judith H. Anderson proposed, in "Redcrosse and the Descent into Hell," [86] that the experience of Redcrosse from the time he goes to sleep in Archimago's cell takes place in an "inner landscape," an "inner world" which "will increasingly reflect and embody the knight's own passions." The passage into this inner world has been through the dreams stimulated by Morpheus, himself an aspect of Redcrosse (pp. 473–74): this links up with the dream vision, with the subterrestrial visit, and most strongly with the psychomachia, all of which are treated below; and we shall delay a consideration of Anderson's article until we come to the psychomachia.

There is, I believe, no study placing *The Faerie Queene* in the context of the medieval dream vision, unless we are to so label Bennett's *The Evolution of "The Faerie Queene,"* which proposes that Spenser's poem may have grown out of, or been suggested by, Chaucer's *Sir Thopas.* In spite of the ubiquitous assertion that *The Faerie Queene* is "dreamy" or "like a dream" and the widespread acknowledgment that Arthur's dream of Gloriana is somehow central to the poem, there appears to be no essay of any sort whose purpose is to explore the status of the work as a dream-poem until Hough's *Preface.* Hough makes no pretense of placing the poem in the tradition of the dream vision, but does treat of the dreamlike qualities of the work in two chapters, "Structure" and "Allegory." Under "Structure," Hough pursues briefly the assertion that "the organization of *The Faerie Queene* is like that of a dream" (p. 95). This is why the inconsequential developments of the poem do not disturb us; we are used to this in dreams. The situation calls up an appropriate setting, which evaporates when no longer needed. Personages appear and disappear. And it is the kinship with dreams which in large measure gives the poem more consequence than is registered in the limited number of explicit moral interpretations provided by the poet; Spenser himself was not equipped to go further in conceptual analysis, although the latent content is much greater, since the poem images the inner world: "a huge panorama of man's inner experience, political, military, social, erotic, moral, and religious" (p. 98). The relationship of this last point on the content of the poem to Spens's remarks on the inner experience of man (*Spenser's "Faerie Queene,"* pp. 117–18) should be noted.

Section 6, pp. 131–37, in Hough's chapter on allegory also deals with the dream aspect of the poem. Hough does here what few Spenserians have attempted: he applies Freudian and Jungian dream theory to the poem, and his application is cogent, at least to me. He points out first that, just as in Freudian dream theory a single item manifested in a dream may have latent within it several separate experiences or ideas, so a single element in an image of *The Faerie Queene* may refer to more than one element of the theme. This characteristic of Spenserian imagery, the double, triple, even quadruple reference (Redcrosse equals holiness achieved, English religion, *miles Christianus,* and the struggling, imperfect Christian) is one of the most widely observed phenomena in the poem, and it is enlightening to see this synthesizing faculty of Spenser's imagination allied with the synthesizing faculty which produces dreams.

Secondly, Hough points out that the opposite poetical effect, i.e., the representation of a single element or theme in various images, is also closely allied to a prominent dream mechanism described by Freud: a single idea or experience may be manifested in various ways in the dream. One of many examples of Spenser's use of more than one image for the same theme can be seen in Lucifera and Orgoglio; and though other explanations can be found (e.g., two different forms of pride), "the resemblance to the dream-mechanism can hardly be missed" (p. 134). Turning to Jung, Hough elaborates Berger's suggestion (*The Allegorical Temper,* p. 200) into a proposal that the various women in the poem, Amoret, Florimel, Belphoebe, who are not specifically virtues, are "a composite portrait of the anima," "each is a glimpse . . . of the total image of womanhood that dominated Spenser's imagination" (p. 135).

Finally, and this is extremely suggestive for reading the poem, Hough sees in the curiously alogical sequences in the poem an analogue to Freud's inferences about the expression of logical relations in dreams: since dreams have no way of expressing "if," "although," "because," etc., causal relations in dreams are expressed by mere succession. Thus soon after Redcrosse is separated from Una, Duessa appears; this sequence, mere succession in the story, is obviously cause and effect in the theme. So also is the appearance of Busirane on Amoret's wedding day before the bride is bedded: her desire and/or Scudamour's *causes* Busirane's appearance. Moreover, other logical relations are also simple sequences, as the procession from the seductive beauty of the Bower of Bliss to its destruction: *although* it is beautiful, still Guyon must destroy it.

All the studies which identify the poem as romance or Virgilian epic or epic romance touch upon the frequent use of the quest and/or pilgrimage; and the parallel tendency in thematic criticism to focus upon Arthur's quest for glory as a major theme makes this allegorical characteristic, the seventh in my list, too widespread a subject to deal with in detail here. We may note, however, that some emphasis has been placed upon the psychomachic quest in the tradition of the romances wherein the lady whom the knight protects or rescues symbolizes his own soul. This aspect of the quest will be noticed under the psychomachia.

The eighth characteristic, the soul-journey to extra- or subterrestrial regions might be expected to figure prominently in the scholarship which records the parallels between Dante and Spenser; but in fact almost nothing has been made of the relationship between Spenser's underworld and Dante's *Inferno*, between Spenser's Mount of Contemplation and New Jerusalem and *Purgatorio* or *Paradiso*, or between Mutabilitie's journey through the spheres and Dante's; it is not that the similarities have not been noted, simply that this has not been the focus of Spenser-Dante studies. Anyone interested in pursuing these studies will find his bibliographical spadework done in Matthew Tosello's "The Relationship Between Dante Alighieri and Edmund Spenser" (1970).[87]

Interest in the Mutabilitie Cantos has largely centered on aspects other than the otherworld journey itself; but there has been a good deal of attention to the underworld visits in Books I and II. Guyon's temptation in the Cave of Mammon has been the focus of vigorous critical consideration since well before the time of Harry Berger, Jr.'s *The Allegorical Temper* (1957). The episode well exhibits the aspect of deliberate enigma with which the poet spiced the poem for the delectation of the initiate, and also stands as perhaps the crucial episode marking the shift from dominantly thematic and narrative to dominantly allegorical and poetic focus in the study of the poem; for it is on Guyon's faint and its causes in the Mammon episode that Berger's pioneering book opens.

Nonetheless the controversy about Guyon's visit to the Cave of Mammon does not proceed along allegorical lines; rather, it is an argument over theme and narrative structure: does the visit to the cave portray heroic virtue, analogous to Christ's temptation in the wilderness, or does it reveal, as indicated by the faint, inadequate temperance on Guyon's part? Secondly, is the virtue displayed by Guyon up until the faint purely Aristotelian, and therefore inadequate for a Christian hero, or is it Christian all along? Thirdly, is this faint structurally a turning point in the book, marking the bankruptcy of Guyon's approach to virtue up to this point? Those wishing to survey the controversy will find a summary of previous scholarship in Chapter 1, pp. 3–38, of Berger's book, and can then proceed to the treatments of Frank Kermode, M. Pauline Parker, A. C. Hamilton, Maurice Evans, Priscilla Barnum, Lewis Miller, Kathleen Williams, and Paul J. Alpers.[88]

For the development of study in Spenser's allegory, however, the underground passages in Book I are much more important. And at this point we pass into the area of the psychomachia, fragmentation of one or more characters. Vigorous interest in the Morpheus and Sans Joy-Aesculapius passages developed only about the time of Rosemond

Tuve's observations on *entrelacement*, and is related to her proposal that the passages in the poem which intervene between episodes in a particular narrative have a way of moving the interrupted narrative forward, beyond where it had been when we left it (*Allegorical Imagery*, p. 363). Actually Donald Cheney was already at work on a similar assumption when Tuve's book appeared: the *Zeitgeist* was ready. Cheney proposes in his *Spenser's Image of Nature* (1966) that the image of Morpheus is closely related to Redcrosse's state at the cell of Archimago (pp. 29–31); and that the visit of Sans Joy to Hades, and his curing, details a stage in Redcrosse's tendency to joylessness and depression (pp. 49–54).[89]

The most extensive analysis of the Morpheus-Sans Joy-Aesculapius material appears in Judith H. Anderson's "Redcrosse and the Descent into Hell," which as noted above draws together several allegorical characteristics: the locale as symbol of state of mind (Morpheus's cave represents Redcrosse's own somnolence and depression; also, the remaining events in Redcrosse's story take place in an inner world); the dream vision (Redcrosse's erotic dream); the subterrestrial journey (the sprite goes to Morpheus's cave; Duessa takes Sans Joy to Hades); the psychomachia (the denizens of Redcrosse's inner world, from Archimago's cell on, are his own motives and passions). Anderson's analysis of Duessa's visit to Hell proceeds on the assumption that Duessa (*duo-esse*) signals the fragmentation of Redcrosse's psyche and that the descent into hell registers a sickness within Redcrosse of which he is not fully conscious until he meets the actual figure of Despair in canto ix (p. 482). She also conjectures that the visit to Hell is Redcrosse's dream while he lies abed after his battle with Sans Joy. The Hippolytus story is a "Psychomachy" (p. 488), with a fragment of Redcrosse in all the major roles: the wrathful Theseus, the lustful Phaedra, the too simple Hippolytus. Aesculapius facing Night is a prefiguration of Redcrosse facing Despair (pp. 490–91).

Anderson's subtle and resourceful reading of Book I as inner experience, dream vision, underworld journey, and psychomachia is not, of course, without roots in earlier criticism. There are previous suggestions that the underworld trip is related to, or images, Redcrosse's state of mind just before he flees the House of Pride: Donald Cheney[90] and Kathleen Williams,[91] for instance, make suggestions along this line. The psychomachic aspect of Anderson's article goes back at least to Harry Berger, Jr.'s *The Allegorical Temper*. C. S. Lewis had described the psychomachia of *The Romance of the Rose*, identifying the various characters as one or another aspect of the lover or the lady (*The Allegory of Love*, pp. 120–24); Berger makes the very important suggestion (pp. 177–207) that Belphoebe, and by inference other personifications in Book II, are fractions of Guyon. Berger later, in "At Home and Abroad with Spenser," makes the inference much more explicit, explaining the "dynamics of projection" in Book I thus: "an evil condition of psyche (permitted or induced by the hero) confronts him as an external enemy, while simultaneously, good forces (Una and Arthur) are at work within helping to sustain him." [92]

Donald Cheney's book, though primarily directed to Spenser's light and dark green worlds, makes highly stimulating remarks about Spenser's psychomachia, e.g., that the separation from Una signals Redcrosse's loss of integrity and that the second Redcrosse in Book I (Archimago in disguise) is an image of the hero's loss of integrity (*Spenser's Image of Nature*, pp. 34–48). And both Kellogg and Steele (p. 5) and Tuve (*Allegorical Imagery*, pp. 34–36) note the medieval stories wherein the lady whom the knight protects or rescues symbolizes his own soul. The psychomachic approach is now fairly standard, and we find it adopted into Maurice Evans's *Spenser's Anatomy of Heroism* (1970),[93] e.g., pp. 89–109, simply as one of a number of instruments drawn together eclectically (see pp. 47–68) for getting at the poem.

One of the most stimulating aspects of Angus Fletcher's *Allegory: The Theory of a Symbolic Mode* (1964) is his identification of the cosmic image (pp. 70–146), which contains implicitly a larger portion, or all, of the work in which it occurs. This phenomenon is at least hinted in C. S. Lewis's discussion of the "allegorical core" (*Allegory of Love*, p. 334). Here Lewis comments on Spenser's tendency to extend the implications of the core throughout the "allegories" and "romances" scattered through the book.

Before Fletcher's book appeared the phenomenon had been discussed extensively by A. C. Hamilton (*Structure of Allegory*, pp. 29–43). Hamilton compares the struggle with Error to the initial lines of Dante's *Comedy*, wherein the opening scene forecasts the whole configuration of the journey beyond: in the Error episode the whole movement of Book I is implicit. Hamilton notes a similar relationship between the Fradubio story and the course of Redcrosse's career; he calls Fradubio's story an "allegory" of Redcrosse, but "cosmic image" is a more precise term. Less cogent, but not less interesting, is Hamilton's assumption (pp. 128–29) that the remaining books after Book I work out at length the pattern of fall, redemption, regeneration, and restoration outlined in Book I. On this view, Book I is a cosmic image of the whole poem.

The fact that Hamilton has not demonstrated this part of his thesis to the universal satisfaction of his readers does not diminish the cogency of the cosmic relationship between the Error episode and Redcrosse's total career, or between the Fradubio story and the same career; and once this relationship is established, we see a new respect in which the traditional conception of primary and secondary terms does not apply in the usual sense: for the secondary term of a cosmic image is simply a larger part of the primary term.

A further complexity enters when we consider that dreams, underground journeys, and psychomachic figures in the poem frequently symbolize something about the protagonist, who in turn has a symbolic reference to human life outside the poem. And if we add the proposal that the various heroes are only fragments of Arthur, himself symbolic, we have four arrangements:

1. No secondary term: Britons (strivers); Elves (ideal).
2. Primary-secondary: Redcrosse, who symbolizes Holiness.
3. Primary-secondary-tertiary: Una, who symbolizes part of Redcrosse, who symbolizes Holiness.
4. Primary-secondary-tertiary-quarternary: Una, who symbolizes part of Redcrosse, who symbolizes part of Arthur, who symbolizes Magnificence.

All of these figures, with their varying tiers of symbolic relationships, are juxtaposed on the primary level, sometimes in cosmic images whose secondary terms are larger parts of the primary term. The inference is that in Spenser's literary allegory the traditional definition of primary level plus various secondary symbolic meanings can be applied only in the loosest way.

We come finally to the numerological aspect of the poem, a topic introduced into Spenser criticism by the remarkable demonstration of the numerological-astrological dimensions of "Epithalamion" in A. Kent Hieatt's *Short Time's Endless Monument* (1960).[94] This aspect of *The Faerie Queene* receives brilliant and learned, if ultimately disenchanting, treatment in Alastair Fowler's *Spenser and the Numbers of Time*, which argues that every complete book is permeated with reference to and suggestive application of its own number in the Pythagorean series: Book I is the Book of the Monad, II of the Diad, III of the Triad, etc., with associated references to the planets in the order of the planetary week.

I believe it is just to say that we do not yet know whether these numerological studies will blossom into a major tool for eliciting permanent significance in *The Faerie Queene*. Many lovers of the poem were impatient with the historical swamp-slogging of the Greenlaw school, but that school was entirely correct in pursuing the implications of the *theme* it was interested in, i.e., Arthur's quest and the related Tudor myth, and we see that no movement in Spenserian scholarship has carried us further into the poetic and the structure of the poem. We must also welcome any serious investigation in technique which can be intelligibly related to a validly described thematic concern of *The Faerie Queene*.

2

A. C. HAMILTON *On Annotating Spenser's* Faerie Queene: *A New Approach to the Poem*

OF THE MAJOR POEMS in our language, only Spenser's *Faerie Queene* has not been adequately annotated. I came to realize this fact only through considerable personal anguish. Several years ago when I was asked to produce an annotated edition of the poem, I refused because I knew that the text did not need to be edited and I assumed that any annotation required by a reader was enshrined in the fat volumes of the Johns Hopkins *Variorum.* Later upon being asked again, I accepted for two reasons. First, I saw more clearly that the poem ought to be easily available in a readable text: the two-volume Oxford edition is too expensive, the one-volume is notoriously unreadable, and the standard Cambridge Poets' edition with its double columns allows no space for a reader's marginal notes. The thirteen hundred pages of the edition proposed to me would provide at least a readable text even for a poem of some four thousand stanzas. Secondly, I was prepared to allow that the general reader needs a text with commentary at the bottom of the page. The only available edition with any annotation at all, the Cambridge, includes only spasmodic notes hidden at the end of the volume where they are awkward to consult and too brief to be of much use.

I was confident that the text itself would cause no trouble. By the grace of the gods, no manuscripts had been allowed to survive; the 1590 and 1596 editions apparently were guided through the press by the poet himself; and a thoroughly reliable modern text had been established by J. C. Smith for the Oxford edition and by a panel of distinguished editors for the *Variorum Edition.* I was unaware, however, that there was no tradition of annotating the poem. The poem has been subjected to much scholarship and interpretation but to very little commentary, glossing, and annotation. I discovered that the *Variorum Edition,* by what must have been deliberate editorial policy, excludes almost all annotation unless it concerns the study of sources. There are only late nineteenth-century or early twentieth-century annotated editions of Books I, II, and V, and modern editions of Books I and II. For Books III and IV, there is no edition at all, and for Book VI only an edition for schoolchildren. Instead of being borne upon the shoulders of my predecessors and sustained by their labors, as I had confidently expected, I found myself almost alone in my effort to annotate the poem for the modern reader. Almost, but not quite: there is Upton's superbly annotated edition of the poem in 1758, which has never been bettered, there is the pioneer edition of Books I and II by Kellogg and Steele, and, most important, there are a number of recent critical studies which involve the close reading required of the annotator. In between was, for my specific purposes, largely a wasteland.

This chapter has its genesis in my effort to annotate *The Faerie Queene* adequately. In that effort I have become more aware of the change in critical approaches to the poem: from the older criticism, which interpreted the poem through abstract ideas and general moral background, to the newer criticism, which interprets it either through a direct and immediate response to the words in the experience of reading or through a growing recognition of the larger structure or patterning of the episodes. One of the two essential ways to understand the poem, as we are beginning to realize, is through close analysis. This way is followed, for example, by Donald Cheney when he argues that we should read Spenser "under the intensive scrutiny which has been applied in recent decades to metaphysical lyrics," and by Paul Alpers who stresses the rhetorical nature of Spenser's poetry.[1] The other way, which is better known and generally allowed, is through the poem's sustaining archetypes, informing myths and unifying structures. This way was prepared by Northrop Frye's seminal essay on the structure of imagery in the poem,[2] and it has been extended in such diverse works as Angus Fletcher's study of Spenserian myth [3] and John Hankins's study of the archetypes in Spenser's allegorical landscape.[4] In the course of annotating the poem, it has become increasingly clear to me that the tangent at which these two ways touch provides the center at which the modern reader may understand and possess the poem. Ideally, the annotator occupies this center, and acting as mentor, guide, trickster, confidant and accomplice draws the reader to it so that he may understand the whole poem as a "continued Allegory, or darke conceit."

The role of the annotator in relation to the roles of the scholar and critic may be roughly defined by the response to the famous catalogue of trees in the poem's opening episode. Here Spenser employs a familiar epic formula to announce his relationship to Chaucer, Virgil and Ovid, and through Ovid to Orpheus who is the archetype of the poet's power to move trees and gather a forest around him as he plays upon his lyre. Thus the poet of Fairyland gathers a forest around his knight:

> Much can they prayse the trees so straight and hy,
> The sayling Pine, the Cedar proud and tall,
> The vine-prop Elme, the Poplar never dry,
> The builder Oake, sole king of forrests all,
> The Aspine good for staves, the Cypresse funerall.

> The Laurell, meed of mightie Conquerours
> And Poets sage, the Firre that weepth still,
> The Willow worne of forlorne Paramours,
> The Eugh obedient to the benders will,
> The Birch for shaftes, the Sallow for the mill,
> The Mirrhe sweete bleeding in the bitter wound,
> The warlike Beech, the Ash for nothing ill,
> The fruitfull Olive, and the Platane round,
> The carver Holme, the Maple seeldom inward sound.

These stanzas display the poet's craftsmanship and formally announce his role as the poet of Fairyland. His device of characterizing trees by their usefulness or stock associations suggests that the Wandering Wood, like Dante's *selva oscura*, is an emblem of man's life within society. A contemporary reader, John Dixon, notes succinctly in the margin of his copy of the poem: "worldly delighte." [5] In the same vein Upton writes: "Let us not forget the continued allegory of our poet, who plainly appears to me to allude to the wilderness and labyrinth of this world with its amusing vanities. Our knight is got into a wood, where he amuses himself till he loses his way: so it is in human life." [6] Since Upton's time, scholars have noted similar tree-lists in earlier writers and critics have interpreted the stanzas chiefly in biographical terms as a comment upon the knight's moral state.

In its summary of earlier scholarship and criticism, the *Variorum* omits Upton's penetrating observation; instead, it summarizes the earlier study of sources. It cites Jortin who catalogues tree-lists in Ovid, Seneca, Lucan, Statius and Claudian; then Warton who noted correctly that Chaucer was Spenser's immediate source and commented that the poet's minute and particular enumeration of various trees is "highly consistent, and indeed expedient" because the beauty of the grove draws the Knight and Una deeper into the center where Error hides. It cites Lane Cooper who found tree-lists in Virgil's *Culex* and Chester's *Love's Martyr*. It records Hallam's inane horticultural complaint that no forest ever contained such a medley of trees; Gilfillan's

reply, equally inane, that the poet was only dreaming anyway; and
Percival's pertinent reply that the allegorical point of the medley of
trees is that "the ways and means of error are manifold, confusing."
In this summary, the *Variorum* offers only one example of close analysis: Upton's prose rendering of line 6 of the second stanza to clarify
the syntax, and a specific source of one tree: Percival's reference to
myrrh in Scripture.

Excluded from this summary is close commentary upon words,
such as may concern any reader whose interest in the words is not in
their sources, or at first in what together they signify, but in what
each says. Why is it "*sayling* Pine"? Only the annotator is prepared to
suggest: "because the tree may be said to soar or sail in its height,"
or, "because ships or their masts were made out of pine." Why is the
"Poplar never dry"?—because the tree grows by water, or was anciently
associated with springs, or because the Heliades, weeping for their
brother Phaeton's death, were transformed into poplars and their tears
into its oozing amber, according to Ovid (*Met.* II.340–66). Or the annotator may note that the "vine-prop Elme" was a popular Renaissance
emblem of marriage, in order to point to the witty reversal: the feminine vine seems to support the masculine elm. Or he may reassure the
Canadian reader that the "Maple seeldom inward sound" is not his national emblem but that bastard Renaissance variety of which the
Trojan horse was made, and about which Lyly may rightly ask: "Is not
. . . dunge [taken] out of the Maple tree by the Scorpion?" [7] Commentary may extend from words themselves to their juxtaposition:
from the simplest kind, as the birch and the sallow, the one being stiff
and the other supple, or to more complex kinds, as the Olive and the
Platane, the one being associated with Christ and the other with
Socrates. Further, for the line, "The Mirrhe sweete bleeding in the
bitter wound," the reader may need more than Upton's two readings:
"first, the myrrhe that affords its odorous gums, which surgeons use
in dressing of wounds. The second, the myrrhe that distils a sweet gum
from its wounded bark." For in this line, the myrrh is noted as an
incense for its sweet smell (cf. Prov. 7:17), as an herb for its bitter
taste (Mark 15:23), and as the Arabian myrtle for its medicinal gum
(cf. "flowing myrrh, Exod. 30:23) which preserves the body. These
traditional associations are wittily collapsed in order to refer obliquely
to Adonis's painful birth from Myrrha's torn body (Ovid, *Met.*
X.503–13).

The different responses to Spenser's stanzas roughly distinguish
the different activities of the scholar, critic and annotator. The scholar
supplies general background, the critic interprets general meaning,
and the annotator explicates the specific meanings of the words. Meta-

phorically speaking, the scholar moves out and down to the literary context which sustains the stanzas while the critic hovers above to interpret the stanzas in the light of this context, and their context in the poem. Ideally, the one offers the deep root and the other the fine flower of our response. Certainly we are more informed readers when we relate the passage to its historical and literary contexts, and we read in vain if we do not understand what we read. The activity of the annotator is essential because we are no readers at all if we do not know what specifically the individual words and phrases mean. Metaphorically speaking again, the annotator occupies the foreground of the work itself. From this vantage point, his work must precede both historical scholarship and interpretative criticism and later he must judge the relevance of the contexts supplied by both to the plain reading of the poem. In practice, the work of the annotator is ignored or hurried over for the more professional and exciting work of the scholar and critic. That the maple is "seeldom inward sound" does not concern the scholar at all. The maple may be sound or not, seldom sound or always unsound, inwardly or outwardly sound or unsound, or even be absent altogether provided enough trees remain to be called a wood. Similarly, the critic may infer that since some trees are cited for their usefulness to society, together they signify worldiness, and so ignores the maple whose inward unsoundness makes it rather useless to society.[8] For the one, the poet may as well have substituted for the two stanzas a placard: "A List of Trees Follows," and for the other an added moral pointer: "Trees Generally Useful to Society." The one fails to see the trees for the wood; the other fails to see any trees at all but only abstract, generalized significance. Both fail to see the words for the woods; and for all that the words themselves matter, they could read the poem as well in a prose summary.

The failure to annotate *The Faerie Queene* derives in part from a failure to define the art of annotation. "Notes are often necessary, but they are necessary evils": Dr. Johnson's emphasis falls heavily upon the final word.[9] Annotation is generally considered a drab and demeaning activity that involves neither the scholar's learning nor the critic's sensitivity except at secondhand. The chief skill allowed it in the past has been philology. In the Proem to Book V, Spenser observes the reversal of virtue and vice since the Golden Age: "For that which all men then did vertue call, / Is now cald vice; and that which vice was hight, / Is now hight vertue." So far as I am aware, the scholar has ignored these lines, and for the very good reason that he is concerned with what men have called virtue and vice and not with Spenser's reversal of them. It is not clear to me why the critic should have ignored them unless they seem too Blakean for the sober and serious teacher, which is our current image of Spenser. However, the annotator, Gough, appends the note: "*was hight*: was called. The history of this phrase is somewhat complicated. The Old Eng. verb *hātan, heht* or *hēt, hāten,* to call, had an isolated present passive (*ic*) *hatte,* I am called (cf. Gothic *haitada,* Ger. *heisse*). In Mid. Eng. this became identical in form with the present active, *hāte,* and the passive sense was naturally extended to the pret. *hiȝt, hight* (the Old Eng. *heht*). Until about 1700 *hight* was still occasionally used in the sense 'was called.' But the un- familiarity of a preterite, active in form but passive in meaning, caused *hight* to be often corrupted into *was hight,* as here." [10] Gough's con- siderable skill as a philologist could be applied when the study of literature was part of a study of language. Presumably, the student of language and literature profited by his note. For the modern reader, however, the simple note "*was hight*: was called" suffices: concern with the origin of words is as remote from his reading Spenser as the knowledge of Anglo-Saxon is from his reading any modern literature. Yet to take away from the annotator his skill as a philologist reduces him to a snapper-up of unconsidered trifles, usually crumbs which he steals from under the tables of the scholar and critic. For the most part, annotation is badly done because those who practice the art have little awareness of what they should be doing.

Everyone knows what ought not to be done in annotation. Its sins flourish: the seven deadly ones come readily to my mind by way of confession and repentance. 1. The annotator's cardinal sin is to stand between the reader and the poem, allowing him to see only through his gloss darkly. This is the sin of Pride, for the overweening ambition here is to supplant the text. 2. The sin of Idleness is displayed when the annotator is content to gloss over the text rather than gloss it. While he may note the meaning of an obsolete word or refer to a source, he will ignore all challenges to understanding. The lack of energy in responding to the text makes this sin the beginning of all the sins. 3. Its counterpart, the sin of Wrath, is displayed in the re- morseless determination to clarify everything, not to permit any line to be read without his imprimatur. 4. This sin leads to the sin of Lechery: the desire to possess and dominate the text, to consume and destroy it. 5. The sin of Gluttony is shown when the annotator supplies information which is misplaced, superfluous or irrelevant, as it distracts the reader from responding to the poem itself. 6. The sin of Avarice is shown when the annotator allows the poem to exist only as it provides subject-headings for the encyclopedia that he is writing. 7. When the annotator's familiarity with the text breeds contempt, he becomes guilty of Envy in wanting to point out where Homer nods.

The reader of Spenser's poem has not been fully exposed to these sins because he lacks an annotated text. What annotation there has been provides abundant examples. For example, Idleness is shown when the annotator chooses to gloss "eftsoones" or note a source in Italian romance but does little more. The superfluous learning, which is a product of Gluttony, is shown in Kitchin's gloss to Spenser's comparison of the weeping Duessa to the crocodile whom the traveler meets "By the muddy shore of the broad seven-mouthed Nile" (I.v.18). "The crocodile [so Kitchin informs us] rarely descends below 27° N. lat., where the river banks are not 'muddy' (as they are in the Delta), but sandy." [11] Such information has its place only in a list of misconceptions in English poetry concerning the distribution of crocodiles along the Nile, and not in reading Spenser's line. Yet Kitchin's note is entirely representative of the annotator's usual practice, which is to align the poem's words to fact. The self-contained footnote, which is the product of the annotator's Avarice, uses the text to review a set subject. Let Spenser refer, however obliquely, to the chain of virtues which link his knights, and the annotator by his nature and training must insert an extended history of the concept, from the golden chain of Zeus in Homer, through the Middle Ages to Chaucer's chain of concord, to the linking of the elements in the Elizabethan World Picture, and so relentlessly on to the latest scholarly treatments of the subject.

It is more difficult to know what annotation ought to do because the art is rarely discussed. In *The Study of Literature* George Watson writes: "It is remarkable how little formal attention has been paid in any language to the writing of a commentary. There is no philosophy of the footnote, though any editor with experience in establishing a text and writing a commentary upon it will know that the second function is usually more demanding than the first." [12] Then he proceeds to supply a "philosophy of the footnote" by arguing that the annotator should gloss three species of obscurity: (1) linguistic difficulties, whether verbal or syntactical; (2) social, historical and especially classical allusions; and (3) complexities and errors in the text which are the result of authorial confusion. Since the business of the annotator is to remove difficulties, Mr. Watson argues that he must not comment where there is no difficulty: he would exclude, then, any personal response, whether aesthetic or critical, by the annotator as reader. Finally he claims that it is essential for the annotator to know for whom he glosses.

The nature of Spenser's poetry is such that almost any of the nearly 4,000 stanzas of the poem could be used to illustrate the first two kinds of obscurity, and I select I.ix.19 because it includes the third:

> Prince *Arthur* gave a boxe of Diamond sure,
>   Embowd with gold and gorgeous ornament,
>   Wherein were closd few drops of liquor pure,
>   Of wondrous worth, and vertue excellent,
>   That any wound could heale incontinent:
>   Which to requite, the *Redcrosse* knight him gave
>   A booke, wherein his Saveours testament
>   Was writ with golden letters rich and brave;
> A worke of wondrous grace, and able soules to save.

Upton initiated commentary upon this stanza by noting the custom of exchanging gifts in Homer, by glossing *of Diamond sure* "i.e., true and without flaw," and *Embowd with gold* "i.e., arched, or fashioned like an arch in gold. Ital. *Archegiato*," and by noting that the liquor is needed by the knight because he was wounded by Sans Joy and that it is later used by Arthur in Book IV. He notices that such liquor is found in romance writers and he identifies the book as the New Testament. The *Variorum* editor prints the second half of Upton's annotation and adds a parallel from *Orlando Furioso*—the gift of a book which is able to preserve from evil. Other commentators have added little: Kitchin asks whether *Embowd* means "embossed," and Percival notes that *sure* means "real," qualifying *Diamond*, or "secure," qualifying *boxe*. Kellogg and Steele suggest that the *liquor* may represent the Eucharist and that "the two gifts are the Blood and Book of the new Covenant." [13] Of linguistic difficulties, there is only one: *incontinent* means "straightway"; but as it modifies *wound*, it refers to the sin of concupiscence which the liquor heals. For this reason Arthur may use it to cure Amoret's wound at IV.viii.20. *Excellent* is not obscure to the modern reader because of its modern usage; yet there is an obscurity because the use here signifies "preeminent" or "supreme." Similarly *brave* will be misread: it signifies "splendid." Of the second obscurity, through allusions, there would seem to be none. That gifts are exchanged or offered in earlier literature does not concern any reader of the poem: there is no allusion to the custom: on the other hand, if the reader is aware of the parallel in Ariosto, he would recognize more fully perhaps the religious significance of the gifts in Spenser. Of obscurity through textual error, there is only one: the 1590 edition prints "this Saveours testament" but the error was noted in "Faults Escaped."

Apart from obscurities, there are difficulties in reading which arise because the poem is an allegory. These also are the business of the annotator to clarify. While *Diamond* may refer to the stone or to the rock, adamant, what matters is its emblematic significance which it gains in the poem through Arthur's diamond shield. The significance of the shield itself is gained through the use of the spiritual armor of the Christian knight in Book I. Similarly, *liquor pure* carries religious significance, suggesting the blood of Christ which "clenseth us from all sinne" (1 John 1:7).[14] More precisely, the two gifts are complementary: Arthur's gift heals wounds, the Redcrosse knight's gift saves souls. Hence the annotator needs to observe that the difference between the gifts is that between the water from the Well of Life and the balm from the Tree of Life in canto xi. Finally, the annotator may note that the example of textual obscurity in the 1590 edition is an interesting "fault": from Arthur's Christ-like function in Book I, it is fitting that the New Testament should be given to "this Saveour." Generally it may be said that the chief business of the annotator is to clarify the language of allegory. The sixteenth-century meanings of words, as defined by the *OED*, provide only a point of departure from which to explore the meanings defined by the poem itself. It is not enough for the annotator to gloss obscurities in words: he must show how Spenser defines the meanings of his words through repetition with variation, how he exploits etymological meanings and ambiguities in words, and how through his creative use of words he seeks to purify the English language.[15]

In Mr. Watson's classification of obscurities that the annotator should gloss, the simplest kind is allusions. Next to the citing of sources, the chief filler of annotation is the identifying of allusions. Spenser's use of classical mythology, in particular, needs to be glossed for the modern reader. Yet for a poem which so readily absorbs classical mythology into its larger structure of myths, the identifying of allusions may be too simple or too complex. An example of the first occurs in the debate with Mammon. Guyon describes the troublesome storms brought by wealth:

> Who swelling sayles in Caspian sea doth crosse,
> And in frayle wood on *Adrian* gulfe doth fleet,
> Doth not, I weene, so many evils meet.
>
> (II.vii.14)

Kitchin notes: "Horace's 'dux inquieti turbidus Hadriae' (*Od.* 3.3.5) will occur to every one." [16] Presumably the allusion occurred to the schoolchildren for whom Kitchin wrote; it need not occur even to an educated adult today, and may be missed as an allusion. If the annotator notes that the Caspian Sea and the Adriatic were cited by earlier writers for their violence, he suggests to the reader that there is an allusion to these waters, whether real or literary. Clearly it is not an allusion as it is when the shrewish wife of Shakespeare's Roman comedy is named Adriana; here not to recognize the allusion means that one does not understand the name. In Spenser's poem, there is no obscurity to clarify: the reader readily infers that these waters are violent; otherwise the reference would not support Guyon's claim about the evils of wealth. To suggest that there is an allusion, and then proceed to identify it, only distracts the reader from responding to the matter at hand, which is that Everyman by the proverbial force of common knowledge may answer Mammon's subtle rhetoric.

An example of an allusion too complex to be identified occurs in Scudamour's story of how Daunger threatened him when he seized Amoret from the Temple of Venus no less "Then *Cerberus*, when *Orpheus* did recoure / His Leman from the Stygian Princes boure" (IV.x.58). If the reader does not recognize the allusion, he needs to be told so that he may recognize the earlier allusion to the same myth when Scudamour first steps near to Amoret: "And by the lilly hand her labour'd up to reare" (53). Simply to identify the allusion, however, suggests misleadingly that it is simply an allusion, and ignores its complex use. For Orpheus did not recover Eurydice but lost her immediately, as Scudamour loses Amoret, and for the same reason: both are overcome by desire. A further connection, equally significant though not overt, is that Eurydice died on her wedding day as Amoret was stolen on her wedding day. Moreover, Eurydice died by the serpent wounding her heel, which signifies lustful love according to a common Renaissance interpretation. That interpretation is related, in turn, to God's curse upon man: the serpent shall bruise his heel. The classical reference to Scudamour as Orpheus is further complicated when he relates how he held Amoret's hand "Like warie Hynd within the weedie soyle." That is, she is the spoil whom he, as hunter, has ambushed; also, he is the ambushed deer whose refuge is Amoret. Clearly he is no Orpheus, as even his silence declares when he first seizes her. His arguments to claim her closely parallel Leander's sophistries to claim Hero, though there is no overt allusion for the annotator to identify. Clearly a simple note to IV.x.58: "Orpheus descended into the underworld to regain his lost Eurydice; see Ovid, *Met.* X.3 ff." to any reader who needs it would be an example of glossing over the text rather than glossing it.

Mr. Watson's claim that the annotator must know for whom he is glossing raises the problem that one may never know what obscurities prevent a reader's adequate response. Obviously all readers will find obsolete senses obscure and some readers will bring more knowledge to their reading than others. Yet the annotator's attention must be directed to the text rather than to the reader. The point may be illustrated by the lines that describe the tuft of hairs on the crest of Arthur's helmet:

Like to an Almond tree ymounted hye
On top of greene *Selinis* all alone,
With blossomes brave bedecked daintily;
Whose tender locks do tremble every one
At every little breath, that under heaven is blowne.

(I.vii.32)

If the annotator attends to the reader, it is sufficient to note, as does Kitchin, that "*Selinis*" is probably Selinus in Sicily. Upton adds a parallel in Homer, *Iliad* XVII.55–56, a passage in which Euphorbos before his death is compared to an olive tree "flourishing in beauty, and the blasts of winds from all directions shake it, and it swells with white blooming." While there are no further obscurities of allusions for the annotator to clarify for the reader, the true obscurity is found when one turns to the poem to ask why such an image is used. Why specifically the almond tree? Percival recognized that the tree is connected with the miraculous in both classical myth and Scripture. Phyllis, killed by grief at her lover's long absence, was changed into an almond tree; upon being embraced by him, the tree broke into fresh leaves and flowers. Aaron's rod which blossomed and bore ripe almonds was the sign that he had been chosen by God. A further important connection is suggested by folk etymology: the name yields "al monde," Lord of the World.[17]

Instead of trying to second-guess what may be obscure to a hypothetical reader, the annotator creates his reader in the course of responding himself to the text. Mr. Watson makes the shrewd comment that "commentary is not, and can never be, an aid to rapid reading."[18] Yet annotation which is restricted to clarifying obsolete words and obscure allusions is designed to hurry the reader through the text with minimum difficulty. Rapid reading is clearly at odds with the contemplation required to comprehend Spenser's allegory. Perhaps obscurities should be allowed to remain so that, being only dimly understood by the rational mind, they act as catalysts in our response to the lines as poetry. The kind of response that the lines cited above evokes is given by Kathleen Williams when she observes the effect inherent in the image: "the lightness and life and untroubled joy, the responsiveness to each breath of wind under heaven, each motion of the spirit: the sense of something high, remote, and untouchable which is at the same time sensitive and alive and delightedly aware."[19] To respond to the lines not as poetry but as fact leaves one in the position of wanting to observe, after the fashion of Kitchin, that the almond tree does not flourish on top of Mount Selinus but is found only on the lower slopes.

The problems of annotation through lack of a "philosophy of the footnote" have not prevented annotation of other major English poems. The exception of *The Faerie Queene* is not to be explained because of its length, although a reader may feel that it is enough to get through a poem of some thirty-five thousand lines without notes to interrupt, divert, and distract him. Generations of readers have not needed, or felt they needed, an annotated edition of the poem. In contrast, *Paradise Lost* was published with 321 folio pages of annotation less than thirty years after it first appeared; and recently there has appeared 1143 pages of annotation on Milton's minor poems alone.[20]

The obvious inference would seem to be that Spenser is not a difficult poet. If his language were less dated, only Chaucer would be easier to read without commentary. Neither poet has Shakespeare's complex allusiveness, Donne's crabbed complexity, or Milton's intellectual texture. Instead of the verbal economy that knots the syntax of a Donne poem, the sheer abundance of words in Spenser's poem makes any line in it clear in its context. Nor is he a learned poet, as is Milton: since he does not think in poetry, his poem is not as immediately and directly informed and sustained by ideas and doctrine. He remains a poet of images rather than of ideas. Although his images are images of virtues, vices, and passions with learned—and often abstrusely learned—traditions behind them, their surface is simple and clear. The characteristic quality of Spenser's verse was first noted by Sir Kenelm Digby:

Spenser in what he saith hath a way of expression peculiar to himself; he bringeth down the highest and deepest mysteries that are contained in human learning to an easy and gentle form of delivery—which showeth he is master of what he treateth of, he can wield it as he pleaseth. And he hath done this so cunningly that if one heed him not with great attention, rare and wonderful conceptions will unperceived slide by him that readeth his works, and he will think he hath met with nothing but familiar and easy discourses; but let one dwell awhile upon them and he shall feel a strange fullness and roundness in all he saith.[21]

Digby's extended interpretation of one stanza of the poem—II.ix.22—confirmed his judgment concerning Spenser's usual mode of writing: "although the beginning of his allegory or mystical sense may be obscure, yet in the process of it he doth himself declare his own conceptions, in such sort as they are obvious to any ordinary capacity." [22]

Although Digby's judgment stands, C. S. Lewis's judgment also stands: "*The Faerie Queene* is perhaps the most difficult poem in English." [23] It is difficult partly because it is a poem of acquired and accumulated meanings which emerge only through more careful reading of any passage in the continually extending contexts of the canto, book, and the poem as a whole. As Lewis notes: "Its characteristic thickness of texture is not a matter of local complexities (though there are plenty of those), so much as of resonances sounding at large throughout the poem."[24] These resonances may make any stanza of the poem truly obscure through its apparent simplicity without them, for alone it may seem to invite simply a psychological and mindless response. One of the simplest kinds of resonance is found in the opening stanza of II.viii:

> And is there care in heaven? and is there love
>   In heavenly spirits to these creatures bace,
>   That may compassion of their evils move?
>   There is: else much more wretched were the cace
>   Of men, then beasts. But O th' exceeding grace
>   Of highest God, that loves his creatures so,
>   And all his workes with mercy doth embrace,
>   That blessed Angels, he sends to and fro,
> To serve to wicked man, to serve his wicked foe.

There are few verbal obscurities to bother a reader, and although the stanza is based on Scripture, there are no allusions to be clarified before the stanza may be understood. Only in line 9 does the repetition of "serve" alert the reader to an allusion to the Latin and Greek root of "angel" as a messenger, as in Heb. 1:14: "Are they not all ministring spirits, sent forth to minister, for their sakes which shalbe heires of salvation?" As the repetition of "wicked" explicitly declares, Spenser extends the ministry of the angels to all men. But these are no more than the "local complexities" to which Lewis refers.

The "resonances" are established first with the abrupt beginning as it parallels the preceding line in the poem which ends the seventh canto: "And all his senses were with deadly fit opprest." By this beginning Spenser notes how God's grace follows directly upon man's defeat. A larger resonance is made from the comparable stanza at the beginning of I.viii, which also marks the entrance of Arthur as the instrument of heavenly grace to rescue the fallen hero. Such resonance is part of the significant paralleling between the first two books. The explicit reference to God's love for man, in contrast to Truth's love in the earlier stanza, marks the chief instance of God's direct intervention into the action of the poem, which the reader must measure against his indirect interventions at other parts of the poem in order to understand the complex relationship among the virtues, and the relationship of the virtues to grace, which the poem sets out to explore and define.

These resonances are realized chiefly through the poem's unity. For despite its length, vast scope, and universal significance, the poem is unified through a number of devices, such as the language of allegory in which it is written, by its extended, interlacing narratives, and above all, by its patterning of the virtues. As a consequence, the meaning of any one part of the poem is the rest of the poem. As an allegory, the poem continually expands, interprets, and defines its own meanings.

Recent scholarship and criticism recognize more clearly the nature of the poem's unity; as a consequence, the poem is understood more clearly as a "*continued* Allegory." As a further consequence, however, the allegory becomes unwieldy. Hence the more recent studies of the poem become more specialized and restricted in scope. In so doing, they fragment the poem and violate its unity, for they defy the simple principle that one who understands the whole understands the part but one who understands each part need not understand the whole. On the other hand, the significant modern studies that contribute to our understanding the poem are those that select certain themes or episodes or one book for analysis. General studies of the poem have become too general: they cannot hope to say much, for example, about the Mammon episode, for that one episode now has a book-length number of articles upon it, and yet fills only one canto of the seventy-four.

With all this heavy industry directed against the poem, the plight of the mere reader may seem desperate. He may allow (and rightly) that the poem contains all knowledge, since Spenser is the English Homer, and that it contains "infinite Allegories," [25] since he is the English Ariosto; yet a poem that means everything soon seems to mean nothing. As the reader proceeds through the poem seeking to grasp its unity in its manifold complexity, he may well feel that the surface he reads is both undermined by scholars who expose the slag they find below and made too dim for his sight by critics who cast their shadows down upon what he reads. In this plight, he needs the annotator who may serve as the moderator between the scholar and critic. Further, the annotator has a special role in relation to the text: while others may use the text for their own purposes, he seeks simply to preserve it. He seeks zealously to preserve each word and phrase against all assaults by scholar, critic, the reader himself, and especially by Time. His aim is to help the reader achieve "exactness." I take the term from Dr. Johnson's advice on reading Shakespeare, for it applies especially to Spenser: "Let him [the reader] read on through brightness and obscurity, through integrity and corruption; let him preserve his comprehension of the dialogue and his interest in the fable. And when the pleasures of novelty have ceased, let him attempt exactness, and read the commentators." [26] Annotation clarifies our understanding of the poem by forcing us to see more clearly. For we understand the poem by seeing clearly what is there. First we must see its images rather than learn what may lie behind them or meditate abstractly upon what they may signify. Once we see, scholarship and criticism may aid us to see with exactness.

I want to show how the annotator may help the reader "attempt exactness" by noting, though only very selectively, how certain kinds of commentary may be used for three episodes in the poem.

In the Redcrosse knight's meeting with Despair, exactness in reading may be gained by attending to emblematic description which is used throughout the poem. Here description may be broadly traditional: the owl that shrieks before Despair's cave is the bird of ill omen that inhabits desolation and wilderness (as in Isa. 34:11–15), or the omen of death (as in Chaucer's *Parl. Fowls*, 343), or more precisely, the conscious denial of spiritual values, as it has been taken to be in a Bosch drawing.[27] Description may be more narrowly literary, as in the account of the clothes worn by Despair: "His garment nought but many ragged clouts, / With thornes together pind and patched was." Such clothes declare his abandoned state, as the "olde rotten ragges and olde worne cloutes" which Jeremiah put on when he was taken from the dungeon (Jer. 38:11). The garment pinned with thorns seems to allude directly to the abandoned and despairing Achaemenides in Virgil, *Aen*. III.594, and declares Despair's cursed state without hope of redemption, according to God's curse in Gen. 3:18. Or description may belong to the language of allegory, as it does in the sudden appearance of Trevisan fleeing with his head unarmed and a hempen rope about his neck. In the religious iconography of Book I, the helmet signifies "the hope of salvation" (1 Thess. 5:8). The scriptural verse that follows presents the terms of the knight's argument with Despair: "For God hathe not appointed us unto wrath, but to obteine salvation." The loss of the helmet signifies, then, the loss of such hope; hence the knight's opening words, "For Gods deare love, Sir knight, do me not stay" as he flees from despair to God's love. The hempen rope comes from traditional iconography: it is the hangman's halter, which is associated with despair by the suicide of Judas.

Since the significant action of the Despair episode takes place within the knight's mind, description becomes internal: the thoughts of the despairing knight, as of the despairing Richard II, "do set the word itself / Against the word," When the angry knight accuses Despair of Terwin's death, for "What justice can but judge against thee right, / With thine owne bloud to price his bloud, here shed in sight?," he bases his argument on Gen. 9:6: "Whoso shedeth mans blood, by man shal his blood be shed." In so doing, however, he invokes the justice which condemns himself: "Therefore thou art inexcusable, O man, whosoever thou art that judgest: for in that that thou judgest another, thou condemnest thyself." As the argument unfolds in his growing despair, the knight remembers God's justice but forgets his mercy until by the end he may be named "O man of sin," as one who deserves only to die. Then Despair need only pose questions:

> Is not he just, that all this doth behold
> From highest heaven, and beares an equall eye?
> Shall he thy sins up in his knowledge fold,
> And guiltie be of thine impietie?
> Is not his law, let every sinner die:
> Die shall all flesh? what then must needs be donne,
> Is it not better to doe willinglie,
> Then linger, till the glasse be all out ronne?
> Death is the end of woes: die soone, O faeries sonne.

The questions that confirm the knight in despair also reveal the means to defeat despair. For the first two lines suggest the answering text: "The Lord is good to all, and his mercies are over all his workes" (Ps. 145:9). The rhetorical question in the next two lines suggests the answer: "Christ died for our sinnes according to the Scriptures" (1 Cor. 15:3). The fifth line suggests the answer to God's law: "For the wages of sinne is death; but the gifte of God is eternal life through Jesus Christ our Lord" (Rom. 6:23).

Spenser helps the reader understand the knight's inner conflict exactly by expressing it in outward action. The knight is overcome by despair when Una's presence is invoked by Despair's reference to "this Ladie milde" (46). Since her faith measures his sin, he is driven to despair. When Despair's speech "as a swords point through his hart did perse" (48), he must accept the dagger by which to stab himself. Since he cannot save himself, Una may save him; and she may save him only when she undergoes his despair: "Which when as *Una* saw, through every vaine / The crudled cold ran to her well of life" (52). Being true faith herself, she revives to save her knight by faith.

Such symbolic action, which is one of the most common devices used in the poem to contain meanings in an image, may be illustrated by the Maleger episode. A. S. P. Woodhouse first argued that Maleger may be identified with "original sin or human depravity, the result of the fall." [28] This identification is made manifest by Arthur's struggle with him. Against Maleger's fierce attack in full flight, which expresses his paradoxical state, first Arthur learns to "keepe his standing" (II.xi.27), which is the temperate stance of the Castle of Alma (15). At the next stage of the battle, he assumes Guyon's stance, which is that of the wrestler, for he fights on his behalf. Like him, he falls unconscious at the crucial moment of his testing. From this state he is able to arouse himself "As one awakt out of long slombring shade, / Reviving thought of glorie and of fame" (31); that is, he is awakened out of intemperance, which is the Cymoclean state of sleeping in the shade, by memory of himself, which is his "prayse-desire" (ix.39). When Maleger dismounts to attack him, he is caught, as Arthur was, and fills Arthur's place upon the ground.

The ensuing struggle reveals Maleger's nature:

> Flesh without bloud, a person without spright,
> Wounds without hurt, a bodie without might,
> That could doe harme, yet could not harmed bee,
> That could not die, yet seem'd a mortall wight,
> That was most strong in most infirmitee.
>
> (40)

These riddles, which defeat "reasons reach," suggest that Maleger is the Old Adam in us, against whom Paul laments: "O wretched man that I am! who shal deliver me from the bodie of this death?" (Rom. 7:24). Arthur's internal struggle is made clear by the unamended 1590 text: he "thought his labour lost and travell vaine, / Against his lifelesse shadow so to fight" (44). Since such a foe is "of the earth, earthlie" (1 Cor. 15:47), he is sustained by the earth. To defeat him, Arthur must go beyond what all other knights have done: he throws away his armor to wrestle with his foe. He subdues him by crushing his body, as Hercules overcomes Antaeus. (The classical parallel was first noted by Upton who cites Fulgentius's interpretation of the myth as reason's conquest over the lusts of the flesh.) Yet this action is not enough: while Hercules may prevent Antaeus from reviving by holding his crushed body off the ground, Arthur must also cast Maleger into a standing lake. As Woodhouse also suggests, this second action refers to baptism.[29] The significant parallel within the poem is the story of another son of the earth, Georgos, the Redcrosse knight, who also is sustained by the earth: when he is cast into the living water of the Well of Life, he rises renewed for the next day of battle. Maleger does not emerge from the lake on the next day; however, Arthur is left near death, needing to be sustained by his squire and nursed to life in the Castle of Alma. His "infirmity" (49) is Maleger's (40). While baptism may defeat the Old Adam in us, and allow lapsed powers to be renewed, the infection of original sin, expressed in concupiscence, remains in us according to Article 9 of the Thirty-nine Articles: "this Infection of Nature doth remain, yea in them that are regenerated, whereby the Lust of the Flesh . . . is not subject to the Law of God." On the third day, as II.xii.2 indicates, the final struggle against the lust of the flesh following baptism is shown in Guyon's triumph over Acrasia in her Bower of Bliss.

The characteristic syntax of Spenser's allegorical technique is ritual: characters undergo set sequences of action by which they (i.e., we) are initiated into more fully realized states of the virtues displayed through them. Exactness in reading may be gained by attending carefully to the key words which reveal the significant patterning of the action. A major example of ritual in the poem is Britomart's experience in the house of Busirane.

In the prelude to her progress through Busirane's house, Britomart discovers Scudamour by pursuing the embodiment of masculine vice. She shares his anguish because Amoret is imprisoned: "Both with great ruth and terrour she was smit, / Fearing least from her cage the wearie soule would flit" (III.xi.12). These companion emotions are specifically those that lead to love. For ruth or pity is the emotion that the lover traditionally seeks to awaken in his lady; once it is awakened, terror follows from the violation of the virgin state. Here the virgin encounters Cupid's man, to whose lord she is subject. She is prepared to aid Scudamour even though to free love seems hopeless: "Sith powre of hand, nor skill of learned brest, / Ne worldly price cannot redeeme my deare, / Out of her thraldome and continuall feare" (xi.16). Since neither force nor wisdom—the forces which defeat, respectively, the foes in Books I and II—is sufficient, Britomart prepares to submit herself as sacrifice to that power which imprisons love in "continuall feare." As the "Virgin" (8) she pities Scudamour's plight, and as the "bold Virgin" (13) she seeks to know its cause; now as the "warlike Damzell" (18) she seeks to free love.

The enchanted castle girded by fire is a traditional motif of Court of Love allegories and romance. Here, in keeping with the erotic allegory, the gate is open but guarded on the porch by unquenchable fire. For when Britomart first saw Artegall, love aroused such flames in her she despaired that nothing could "my flame relent" (ii.43). Now at last she prepares to act. That the maid should be "dismayd" (22) by the flames aroused by love prepares for the erotic initiation to which she boldly submits. Her sword must serve as her enchanted spear whose virtue manifests the magical power of chastity: with it she may pierce the flames and enter the Castle.

Within the castle she progresses through three rooms. An outside room displays tapestries of the gods transformed into beasts through love, and contains the statue of Cupid at its upper end. Behind the statue, a door leads to the second room which displays in bas-relief the monstrous forms of love and contains the spoils of love. In the first, Britomart gazes in wonder upon Cupid's statue; in the second, she gazes upon Cupid's mask of love. An iron door leads to the third and inmost room in which she sees Amoret tortured by Busirane. These rooms are carefully related and distinguished in each particular of decoration, furniture, the door with its motto, and the action for which they serve as setting. Time is carefully paced: Britomart sees the mask at the crucial testing time of midnight, which was the time of her testing in the House of Malecasta, and she enters the inmost room at the same hour, which begins the third day of victory.

The tapestries and the mask are related by significant numerological patterns, as Alastair Fowler has revealed.[30] The tapestries and bas-relief are related as both show love's effects: in the one, love's power is revealed in its pictures of the gods metamorphosed into beasts to satisfy desire; in the other, love's psychological power is revealed in the cruel and despairing love that leads to suicide.[31] In the first room, Britomart gazes in amazed wonder at the sight of the blinded Cupid triumphing over the blinded dragon-guardian of chastity. The corresponding vision in the second room is the mask which presents an anatomy of her love for Artegall. As it is a mask, and her mask, she is first an observer and then a participant: at the beginning the mask "forth issewd" (xii.3), but at the end she "issewed forth" (27) ready to put the antimask to rout. The symbolic thresholds over which she must pass in order to be confirmed in her chaste love for Artegall are identified by their mottos, "Be Bold," "Be not too bold." Their import encourages, and warns against, the importunities of the lover whose actions arouse fears of consummation. As phrased by C. S. Lewis: "In this false love, it seems, we are tempted to be bold in going a certain distance, and bold in leaving, i.e., exchanging the love for another; but we are not to be too bold in passing what Marvell called the iron gates of life and entering full intimacy."[32]

Britomart's final testing takes place in the inmost room where Amoret, bound by iron bands to a brazen pillar in parody of the married state, is tortured by Busirane who with her blood is "Figuring straunge characters of his art" (31) to gain her love. These "characters" signify those first woven in the tapestry, then outlined in the bas-relief, and finally paraded in the mask. Their power to hold love enchanted is broken when Britomart suffers the token wounding and endures the charms she forces Busirane to recite:

> horror gan the virgins hart to perse,
> And her faire locks up stared stiffe on end,
> Hearing him those same bloudy lines reherse;
> And all the while he red, she did extend
> Her sword high over him, if ought he did offend.
> (36)

Although her heart, too, is pierced, as Amoret's has been, and she experiences terror, as she had before she enters the Castle, now she triumphs by the power of her chastity. By her actions she frees love from all the fears that bind it to the virgin state—fears of the male, of herself, and of the bondage of constant love—so that it may freely enter the higher state of married chastity.

The Faerie Queene is an immensely stimulating poem: it appeals profoundly to a reader as it engages him wholly on many levels of awareness and response. In the future it will become more stimulating in its matter and form as scholarship and criticism reveal more fully the comprehensiveness of its scope and complexity of significance. Annotation provides the center for these activities, as it selects what is relevant to understanding the poem and presents it to be tested by the reader. Ideally, the annotator's role is a humble one: he serves as "the reader over the shoulder," an Anamnestes who reminds the reader what he should not have forgotten. His annotation is designed with built-in obsolescence: it supplies the reader with what he needs, but no more, to respond fully to the words before him. In what he selects as needing to be known, however, he creates the ideal reader for the poem. His role is not simply a humble one then for he shares the creative end of the poem itself. And even as he serves the reader, his true business is to serve the poem by showing how it unlocks the power of words. Annotation of *The Faerie Queene* is exacting but the rewards are great. It is a most humbling and, at the same time, a most exalting experience to stand at the center of this great poem around which the words whirl in their constellations, by their patterns illuminating man's nature, both as it is and as it should be, and sounding the harmonies that reveal his full and final harmony with Nature.

3

RUDOLPH B. GOTTFRIED   *Spenser Recovered:*
The Poet and Historical Scholarship

THE LONG ESSAY on Spenser which James Russell Lowell produced nearly a century ago occupies a somewhat ambiguous position today. That parts of it are frequently anthologized would seem to demonstrate its continued popularity. In fact, written as it is with a kind of jocular, metaphorical grace, it is still readable enough; and at least to begin with, in its late Victorian context, Lowell's view of Spenser as an idealistic dreamer with a genius for putting pictures into words rested on a conception of poetry which was widely held. But the essay has obviously declined in critical esteem since 1875; neither its manner nor its matter can entirely satisfy the more specialized reader of the 1970's. Lowell's graceful bonhomie descends at times to an unprofessional archness which, in spite of our flair for informality, surprises us in one who was soon to become president of the Modern Language Association; we are disconcerted to find him twisting Chaucer in order to characterize the English people during their Elizabethan springtime—"The yongë sonne / Had in *the Bull* half of his course yronne." [1] But far more damaging than an occasional lapse in taste is the fact that Lowell faces backward rather than forward in the history of Spenserian studies and that crucial elements in his evaluation of the poet are derived or even, as Alpers has pointed out, whittled down from the insights of earlier Romantic critics. [2] One is tempted to dismiss his essay as a period piece at second hand.

For all its defects, however, Lowell's essay raises questions which are not only provocative in themselves but also relevant to the course of literary scholarship today: What is the central weakness in his point of view? What in our experience as students of Spenser allows us to understand that limitation as Lowell's contemporaries did not? And to what use, in the vastly expanded flow of recent Spenserian studies, are we now putting the experience which differentiates us from the age of Lowell? The answer to this last, indeed, is my real subject.

An obvious, if not all-important weakness of Lowell's essay is revealed in a tendency to get the facts wrong. The undeveloped state of Elizabethan scholarship in his period, of course, partly accounts for this: when he speaks of Surrey's having brought blank verse back with him from Italy (p. 340), he is merely repeating a contemporary assumption; the date he gives for Spenser's death, January 16, 1599 (p. 357), was corrected to January 13 long after Lowell's time;[3] and his acceptance of the theory that the *Amoretti* were addressed to one Elizabeth Nagle (pp. 348, 389) antedates the publication of decisive evidence in favor of Elizabeth Boyle.[4] But Lowell himself is responsible for many of his undocumented or wrong assertions. We do not know that Spenser was domiciled for a time at Penshurst (pp. 348, 360) or that he was in the household of Leicester (p. 348); it is incorrect to say that the poet made only "flying visits to England" after 1580 (p. 348) or that he "did not stay long in London" on the trip which kept him in England from 1589 to 1591 (p. 350); he received the grant of Kilcolman shortly before, not after the grant of his pension (p. 352); the Mutabilitie Cantos were first published in 1609, not 1611 (p. 356); and—what is perhaps the outstanding example of Lowell's heedless approach to his material—in 1596 James of Scotland was clearly protesting the representation of his mother as Duessa on trial in a passage of *The Faerie Queene* which had just been published (V.ix), rather than the "nasty" divestment of Duessa in Book I, as we are told in the essay (pp. 371–72).

Each of these mistakes may easily be dismissed as immaterial in itself, but they add up to the profile of an attitude. Lowell is not much concerned with the given elements of Spenser's life and poetry; if he does not deliberately misrepresent them, he treats them, consciously or unconsciously, as matters of little importance. His nonchalance in handling literary fact has even, in one case, allowed him to alter Spenser's text: after quoting a stanza from *The Shepheardes Calender*, he admits, "In the first line I have put *here* instead of *hether*, which (like other words where *th* comes between two vowels) was then very often a monosyllable" (p. 362). The poet's words, in short, are subject to improvement by the critic.

In this instance Lowell's prevailing carelessness as a literary scholar is somewhat inconsistently joined with another element in his approach to Spenser: he revises the poet's words at the same time that he stresses the virtues and shortcomings of the poet's style, improving what he is simultaneously criticizing. Lowell's sensibility, in fact, is genuinely engaged in the stylistic judgments he makes throughout his essay; while they are often impressionistic or too concerned with metrical regularity, they are not apt to be delivered carelessly. When he finds Sternhold and Hopkins inspired in comparison with Gascoigne and Surrey and Wyatt (pp. 340–41), he may be wrongheaded, but he is scarcely halfhearted. He is attacking what he calls "pedantic" artificiality in the style of sixteenth-century love poetry, and for the same reason he gives the *Amoretti* short shrift (pp. 356, 385). Similarly the irregular pseudo-Chaucerian versification of "May" and other eclogues comes under fire (p. 362); yet *The Shepheardes Calender* as a whole is praised for the revived Chaucerian naturalness of its style (p. 359). "In general it is not so much the sentiments and images that are new as the modulation of the verses in which they float. The cold obstruction of two centuries thaws, and the stream of speech, once more let loose, seeks out its old windings, or overflows musically in unpractised channels" (p. 361). Thus, the essay puts a strong emphasis on poetic style divorced from content; and style, almost without examination of specific passages, is found good or bad as it is pronounced to be "natural" or "artificial."

Lowell's responsiveness to sheer stylistic effect accounts for the unexpected warmth of his tribute to *Muiopotmos*: "No other English poet has found the variety and compass which enlivened the octave stanza under his sensitive touch" (p. 365); and he goes on to quote more than eight of those stanzas, although he provides the reader with no help in analyzing the poet's sensitive touch. Later, when he praises the Spenserian stanza with even more fervor, he makes some attempt to explain its peculiar effectiveness. "This delicious abundance and overrunning luxury of Spenser appear in the very structure of his verse"; the poet deliberately draws out the ottava rima into a nine-line stanza, closing it with "an alexandrine, in which the melody of one stanza seems forever longing and feeling forward after that which is to follow" (p. 378).

But the question of poetic style is inevitably entwined with the content of *The Faerie Queene*, and in what is perhaps the most notorious passage of his essay, Lowell links Spenser's verse with the sensuous imagery of the poem:

The true use of him is as a gallery of pictures which we visit as the mood takes us, and where we spend an hour or two at a time, long enough to sweeten our perceptions, not so long as to cloy them. He makes one think always of Venice; for not only is his style Venetian, but as the gallery there is housed in the shell of an abandoned convent, so his in that of a deserted allegory. And again, as at Venice you swim in a gondola from Gian Bellini to Titian, and from Titian to Tintoret, so in him, where other cheer is wanting, the gentle sway of his measure, like the rhythmical impulse of the oar, floats you lullingly along from picture to picture. (P. 377)

Lowell's emphasis on the ear as the primary judge of poetic style leads him quite naturally to the eye as the primary source of poetic content in *The Faerie Queene*. Spenser is, "of all our poets, the most truly sensuous" (p. 370); "he is court-painter in ordinary to each of the senses in turn" (p. 371). Yet his poetry, we are told, can properly make only a purified appeal to the senses: the irregular versification of "May" fails to satisfy our aural expectations, and the picture of Duessa stript to her ugliness fails to "sweeten our perceptions" as it should. The poet's art has not only been reduced to its sensuous elements; it has been still further narrowed down to those sensuous elements which the critic is willing to find "beautiful."

But ideally, as a fastidious gondolier, the poet has much more to avoid than the choppy waters or malodorous channels of his Venetian world; and Lowell repeatedly tempers his enthusiasm for the sensuous appeal of *The Faerie Queene* with contempt for its moral allegory. This is not merely a hollow shell; it is a bore, forced on us against our will (p. 373). Spenser

loves to prolong emotion, and lingers in his honeyed sensations like a bee in the translucent cup of a lily. So entirely are beauty and delight in it the native element of Spenser, that, whenever in the "Faery Queen" you come suddenly on the moral, it gives you a shock of unpleasant surprise, a kind of grit, as when one's teeth close on a bit of gravel in a dish of strawberries and cream. (P. 382)

Recognizing the poet's need to convince British readers that his art was useful and serious, Lowell sees *The Faerie Queene* as an attempt to answer that need in the crudest terms, in the form of "a rhymed moral primer"; he explains, "Allegory, as then practised, was imagination adapted for beginners, in words of one syllable and illustrated with cuts, and would thus serve both his ethical and pictorial purpose" (pp. 375–76).

Spenser's unfortunate excursions into allegory are thus accounted for by his desire to satisfy the taste of an unsophisticated, moralistic audience; but genuine though his purpose is, the argument continues, the very nature of his mind disqualifies him for allegorical writing of this kind. Lowell denies that "the Don Quixote of poets" should be taken seriously as a discursive thinker: "whoever wishes to be rid of thought and to let the busy anvils of the brain be silent for a time, let him read in the 'Faery Queen'" (p. 394).[5] What the poem gives us is food for a process far more passive than thought: "The land of Spenser is the land of Dream, but it is also the land of Rest. To read him is like dreaming awake, without even the trouble of doing it yourself, but letting it be done for you by the finest dreamer that ever lived, who knows how to color his dreams like life and make them move before you in music" (p. 393). And Lowell is so pleased with his conception of the poet as a dream-maker that when he refurbishes the essay in 1890, he spins new phrases and metaphors around that delicate cocoon:

Spenser's is a magic glass in which we see few shadows cast back from actual life, but visionary shapes conjured up by the wizard's art from some confusedly remembered past or some impossible future; it is like one of those still pools of mediaeval legend which covers some sunken city of the antique world; a reservoir in which all our dreams seem to have been gathered.[6]

The failure of *The Faerie Queene* as an allegory and a poem of ideas is offset in large part by its effectiveness as the musical and pictorial expression of our dreams.

Under Lowell's explicit statement of this view, however, his criticism implies without completely acknowledging a more fundamental attitude to Spenser's poetry. When we are told that "the bent of his mind was toward a Platonic mysticism" or that he was "lifted away from the actual by . . . that ideal Beauty whereof his mind had conceived the lineaments in its solitary musings over Plato" (pp. 369, 389), Lowell is skirting the problem posed by the relation of art to reality. Himself the least Platonic of critics, he shows almost no interest in the *Fowre Hymnes* as such; but he cites Spenser's Neoplatonism in order to rationalize the insignificance of reality, as ordinarily understood, in the poet's work. Not only the stripping of Duessa but the homely description of the body as the House of Alma and the "Teniers-like realism" of Britomart's passion while she waits for Artegall are decried as uncharacteristic intrusions into the idealized world of *The Faerie Queene* (pp. 372, 375, 365). *The Shepheardes Calender* was intended to be "an escape from the realism of daily life" by artificial means; "but he was soon convinced of his error, and was not long in choosing between an unreality which pretended to be real and those everlasting realities of the mind which seem unreal only because they lie beyond the horizon of the every-day world and become visible only when the mirage of fantasy lifts them up and hangs them in an ideal atmosphere" (p. 347).

This passage betrays an ambiguity which lurks at the center of all that Lowell has to say about the poet's art. Since a *mirage* by definition represents what does not exist, how can it possibly make us see *realities*? Furthermore, what are "the everlasting realities of the mind" which "the mirage of fantasy" makes visible to us? He contrasts them with "the realism of daily life," which he disparages, and they might conceivably be identified with the moral allegory or the conscious development of thought in *The Faerie Queene*; yet for these, as we have already noted, he also feels contempt. His "everlasting realities of the mind" seem rather to be the all-important "dreams"—perhaps we should call them daydreams—which the poet's fantasy re-creates in stylistic and pictorial terms for his reader; and on them, if this is what Lowell means, he has apparently conferred a kind of real existence as pseudo-Platonic forms.

But ambiguous as this passage is, and speculative as any interpretation of it is bound to be, it serves to reveal the blind spot at the center of Lowell's essay: he fails to see that Spenser's success as a poet is more than an internal matter, that it largely depends on his response to what exists outside of himself. Lowell is keenly sensitive to the musical and pictorial effects he finds attractive in the poet's work, but he does not know, and does not care to know, much about the external realities which enter into its substance. Assuming that his own narrowly subjective emphasis includes all that is valuable in Spenser's work, he overlooks or condemns any discussion of the poet's contacts with the daily life, the historical views, the political affairs, the religious and philosophical problems, or even the literary criticism of his time; and thus he overlooks not only the variety of the poet's interests but the marvelous versatility with which the poet accommodates his art to the expression of what he has to say about all of these realities. Lowell has let most of Spenser slip through his graceful fingers.

Today, indeed, such a conclusion verges on truism, and it should prompt a twentieth-century Spenserian to ask: "What did you expect? Lowell's essay may have its serious precedents in Romantic criticism; but if all that you have just been telling us is true, he also represents a decadent, late Victorian tradition which reduces poetry to a belletristic exercise. In his gondola he is simply a tourist who travels through literature for his entertainment. After a century we have no reason to take his shallow view of Spenser seriously. If Lowell, from his grave, will pardon another man's metaphor: why beat a dead horse?"

To reply that the horse may not yet be quite dead is not to beg the question altogether, but it is a better answer that the horse, alive or dead, serves a much more useful end than beating. Lowell helps us to clarify the standards by which we find him wanting; he throws into relief the development of literary studies between his time and ours; and in particular, he underlines the role of historical scholarship in determining our view of Spenser as a poet who is seldom out of contact with the realities, material and intellectual, which surround him.

The sheer quantity of Spenserian scholarship which has been published in the twentieth century may be called impressive in itself, but the effect of that scholarship on the way we look at the poet has been revolutionary. The student has come to rely on such exact professional tools as the three bibliographies which cover the whole Spenserian field through 1960, on Charles Osgood's concordance, on Alexander Judson's biography, on the Oxford text of the poetry, and on the *Variorum Edition* with its even more nearly definitive text and textual variants as well as the accumulated commentary of the last three hundred years: all of them works which general readers may be tempted to dismiss as mere compendia of information, but which have set standards of completeness and accuracy for the host of specialists who have used them. What is more important, these implements of research have had their numerous counterparts in related fields, both literary and nonliterary, which reinforce not only standards of completeness and accuracy but a common agreement on the essential orientation of Spenser's poetry. Working with the materials provided by historical scholarship, the most distinguished Spenserians of the twentieth century—writers as varied as Edwin Greenlaw and A. S. P. Woodhouse and C. S. Lewis and Rosemond Tuve and Paul Alpers—have all assumed that the poet absorbed much of his art and his material from the world outside himself and that if he transmuted these impressions and ideas and techniques in his mind, he later restored them, in a form which was characteristically his own, to that portion of the outside world which read his poetry. Clearly, the creative process began and ended in external reality, and external reality has provided the basis for almost every credible conclusion we can draw about Spenser as an artist: even the most subjective elements in his poetry can only be descried, like the dark nebulae, against the shining points of our objective knowledge.

This approach to Spenser may seem so obvious today that it is difficult for us to recognize the fundamental change it represents. Indeed, historical scholarship had already, a century ago, become a significant element in literary studies, and Lowell's influential essay repeatedly alludes to its findings; but he does not accept the consequences of historical scholarship in his basic attitude to Spenser's work. On the one hand, he focuses his praise on the poet as a melodious dream-maker; on the other, he refuses to deal seriously with the poet's relation to the world around him. The break between nineteenth- and twentieth-century views of Spenser is nowhere more sharply revealed than in the naive assurance with which Lowell writes, "Allegory, as then practised, was imagination adapted for beginners, in words of one syllable and illustrated with cuts" (pp. 375–76): an assertion whose plausibility had vanished even before Rosemond Tuve began to investigate the nature of allegory on a broad comparative basis. But the meagerness of his information is less important than his terse dismissal of a subject which historical scholarship was later, by a dramatic reversal, to place once more at the center of Spenser's poetic experience.

The revolution which transformed Spenserian studies after the turn of the century can now be seen to have depended on various favorable circumstances. The personal influence of a few scholars like Edwin Greenlaw undoubtedly directed younger men into specific kinds of research; yet Greenlaw's influence was also supported by the general drift of almost all the literary research published during his period. Other men in other fields were making the same kinds of investigation, and their labors were accumulating information and insights which could be effectually applied to the understanding of Spenser's poetry. These factors, however, will not of themselves account for the sweeping character of the change in Spenserian studies: not only was historical scholarship extensively applied to the poet's work for the first time, but the poet's work turned out to be peculiarly fitted for interpretation by historical scholarship. Ideally, the approach which an informed criticism makes to any artist should, as far as possible, conform to the character of that artist's mind, not to his specific doctrines or subject matter, of course, but to what may be called the orientation of his consciousness. The whole body of Spenser's poetry faces outward in one sense or another—toward the circumstances and the people who made up his personal life, toward the immediate problems of the English Church and Elizabethan politics, toward history and myth and topography, toward traditional beliefs concerning morality and religion and philosophy and poetry itself, toward all the techniques of poetic communication, language and imagery and rhetoric. If Spenser stands high among English poets today, it is not because we think of him as Lowell's dreamer, but because we can understand the richness of his response to the world around him as well as the skill and versatility with which he sets forth his vision of reality. And to what do we owe this understanding if not to the historical scholarship of the twentieth century?

The question, nevertheless, is not entirely rhetorical today, nor the answer a self-evident yes from every quarter. If our reaction to Lowell's essay indicates that the birth of modern Spenserian studies occurred soon after 1900, there has been a recent tendency to date it fifty years later and to assign it a somewhat different parentage. Harry Berger, Jr., for example, has explained the anti-Spenserian bias of the New Critics in a curious way:

to be fair to his detractors, the Spenser they disliked was the Spenser presented to them through the somewhat fusty gentility of the Variorum Edition and not the Spenser we have more recently been enabled to recover through the agency of that very new criticism, in its aspect of close interpretation. Spenserians of the fifties and sixties have clearly benefited from this aspect, and have combined it with other benefits received from such sources as the long line of studies of Renaissance culture from Burckhardt through Cassirer to Wind.[7]

In a similar diagnosis, though limited to scholarship on *The Faerie Queene,* Jane Aptekar assures us that "the real nature of Spenser's poem is only beginning to be understood in this age which had assimilated Donne and Joyce and accepted the critical validity of William Empson's 'hierarchies of level' and Northrop Frye's 'structures of imagery.'"[8] And even Alpers has endorsed the view that "Settled and purposeful study of Spenser did not begin until after the Second World War," though he attributes this late fruition to the influence of both the nonacademic criticism of the twenties and thirties and the academic tradition which is chiefly represented by the *Variorum.*[9] All of these assessments agree that the serious study of Spenser has come into existence quite recently and that the New Criticism of the previous generation has played a significant part in the happy event; Berger also gives credit to the cultural historians, but only Alpers acknowledges a sizeable debt to the historical scholarship produced by earlier twentieth-century Spenserians.

The theory that serious study of the poet began not more than twenty years ago is based, I think, on an understandable mistake. By 1952, the four-hundredth anniversary of the poet's birth, Spenserian scholarship had reached an impasse which was to some extent the immediate consequence of its previous success. It had specialized in certain of the narrower areas of historical research—biography and the establishment of the text, for example—where a job well done eliminated most of the opportunity for further investigation; and the wider possibilities for research and its critical application to the poet's work were not yet recognized. Paradoxically, the completion of the *Variorum* coincided with a sharp decline in the publication of Spenserian material,[10] and this at a time when the bibliographies registered, year after year, the ever-increasing popularity of Donne and Shakespeare as subjects of research and criticism. In his quatro-centennial lecture W. L. Renwick asked, "Why has so little been heard of Spenser from our recent critics? Why has he lost the position which he held so long, of being one of the obvious, necessary points of reference and judgment in any discussion of English poetry?" and Renwick found the answer in the resistance of his poetry to the newer critical techniques and even more in his reputation as an "easy" poet.[11] Whatever the causes—his reputation, the nature of his poetry, the newer critical techniques, or a conservative lag in scholarship—by 1952 it looked as if an informed interest in Spenser had been seriously curtailed on both sides of the Atlantic.

This Spenserian lull, however, was to be only a temporary respite; within a few years it was followed by the torrent of academic publications with which we have become so familiar—articles by the hundred, books by the dozen, and some ten volumes of edited selections, intended to introduce the poet's work to a wide circle of newly initiated readers. The older lines of research have not entirely disappeared, and general handbooks are still on the market; but the prevailing tendency has been to investigate the more distant and esoteric corners of Spenser's intellectual background and to analyze the text of his poetry far more closely than before, in order to uncover new critical insights. As a result, he has even been readmitted to the company of Shakespeare and Milton. Thus the sudden increase in their number and the sharp change in their direction have made it natural to assume that recent Spenserian studies owe their success, if not their very existence, to a revolution which occurred during the last twenty years.

But this assumption disappears under wider scrutiny. The great majority of twentieth-century Spenserian studies, the most recent as well as the earlier, stem from the same revolution which occurred two generations ago; they employ the same objective skills and imply the same conception of their poet as one who perceives and transforms the realities around him. For the "historical" scholar of the last sixty years, no matter where he comes in them, Lowell's prehistorical criticism inevitably rings hollow at its subjective, undocumented core. To be sure, the temporary break in Spenserian studies which occurred after the Second World War seems to indicate that there was a radical discontinuity at that point; but the newer critical approaches that followed the break were themselves the natural outgrowth of the research which preceded it (a close analysis of texts depends on having well-established texts). Furthermore, the research of the last twenty years may have tackled strange and unexpected problems, but it is still, for better or worse, a natural outgrowth of earlier research: although the numerologists have sometimes based their findings on questionable logic or incorrect statistics, their methods and objectives are still firmly rooted in the tradition of historical scholarship. It is the continuity of the tradition, not its demise, which characterizes Spenserian studies during the last twenty years; and the perspective of their development during the last century, running the whole gamut, so to speak, from Lowell to Hieatt, serves to reinforce that conclusion.

To assert the continuity of historical scholarship is not, of course, to deny that there have been significant changes in its direction,

changes which we should recognize and evaluate in terms of the tradition to which they still belong. For these purposes we need to consider an example which is both striking in itself and characteristic of
other new departures. Such a case is found, I think, in a significant
reinterpretation which the last twenty years have placed on a major
episode of *The Faerie Queene.*

In 1936, C. S. Lewis published his controversial view that the
Bower of Bliss embodies Spenser's considered attack on a static, dis-
eased, sterile, unnatural form of sexuality which is chiefly represented
by Acrasia and the two girls bathing in the fountain;[12] he relates this
attack to the poet's thinking on sexuality and artifice in other episodes
of the poem and thus provides an implicit justification for the deliberate violence with which Guyon and the Palmer destroy the Bower at
the end of Book II. Agree or not as one may with Lewis's interpretation, it is an influential example of literary criticism which is broadly
based on historical scholarship.

When Harry Berger, Jr., comes to the Bower in 1957, he notes that
its spectacles are all artificial and refers their unnaturalness obliquely
back to Lewis;[13] at the same time he questions Lewis's conclusions
and subordinates his Stoic interpretation to a very different knot of
meanings. The similes with which Spenser describes the bathing
girls (II.xii.65) —

> As that faire Starre, the messenger of morne,
>   His deawy face out of the sea doth reare:
>   Or as the *Cyprian* goddesse, newly borne
>   Of th'Oceans fruitfull froth, did first appeare —

reveal, according to Berger, not only Guyon's naive response to their
charms, but a good deal more:

The Creation image [of the goddess] corresponds to the dawn of the hero's
sex awareness. The difference between the mystical, dynamic image of
Venus and the burlesque reality of the girls emphasizes Guyon's lack of
experience and adds a certain charm to his awakening. . . . But the star
and goddess images convey at once the unconscious daily fulfillment of
natural order (Venus as planet) and the supernatural love which invests
every dawn, every renewal of life and light with the mystery of fresh
creation. What happens to Guyon happens to Everyman—it is eternal
recurrence; but for the hero it is "newly borne." (Pp. 218–19)

In what follows, Guyon is transformed from the righteous knight who
destroys the Bower as an unmitigated evil, into a typical son of Adam
whom the Bower has taught that he himself is subject to Original Sin
(p. 236). At the end of Book II, he and the Palmer are left in a state
which parallels that of Adam and Eve at the end of *Paradise Lost*:

In the final moment they stand on the edge of the false paradise waiting for the fresh wind of Creation to take them home. In a sense they have found themselves; they have a feeling, at least, that they are not home. Perhaps there is even a faint echo of hopelessness. Perhaps their essential selves harbor a vague uneasiness too profound to be articulated or clearly felt: that they are ordained to wander "on the foam / Of perilous seas, in faery lands forlorn." This is a modest revelation. But it is the best temperance can do. The goodly frame is complete, and the world lies all before them. (P. 240)

This eloquent conclusion represents a striking departure from almost all that Lewis had to say about the Bower twenty-one years earlier; yet it is also founded on the tradition of historical scholarship. In his book Berger supports his case with specific evidence from the text of *The Faerie Queene*; he cites the commentary in the *Variorum* as well as some works contemporary with Spenser; he frequently makes use of twentieth-century theories on myth and symbolism; and at the same time that he directs attention to the poet's mind as evidenced in metaphorical meanings, he seems, in general, to recognize that Spenser faces outward and that his poetry must be apprehended largely through applying to it our knowledge of the world around him.

And yet Berger's interpretation of Guyon's role in the Bower of Bliss leaves us with a curious sense that if he really apprehends Spenser's meaning in the episode, he has replaced it with one of his own. The cool, ferocious destruction of the Bower, which can only be a climactic announcement of the poet's theme, is laid aside; and we are asked to concentrate on the four lines which compare the bathing girls to the star of dawn and the newborn Venus. The imagery becomes the message, and the message includes not only Guyon's but Everyman's loss of sexual innocence, the fulfillment of the natural and the supernatural orders of the universe, and the Fall of Adam and Eve for good measure.[14] If a little textual evidence has been cited, the several deductions which are made from it lead us so far afield that we become incredulous: is the reader being taken, perhaps, on another gondola ride? Actually, Berger does not assume, as Lowell does, that the poet is essentially a subjective dreamer and that therefore it is appropriate for an interpretation of his poem to be subjective too; but historical scholarship, committed though it be to the use of objective criteria, is not immune to subjective distortions which are no less serious than Lowell's because they are less openly acknowledged. Berger's conclusion, with its speculation on the "hopelessness" and the "vague uneasiness" that Guyon and the Palmer may perhaps feel at the end of Book II, is peculiarly vulnerable to the

evidence of the poem itself; and its subjective afflatus is only under-
lined by the phrases borrowed from Keats and Milton, depending as
it does on those not so very fresh winds to fill our slack Spenserian
sails and waft us out into the dawn.

The case of Berger brings our subject into sharpened focus. He
himself, as we have seen, believes that Spenserian studies have been
revolutionized in the last twenty years, benefiting in large part from
the "close interpretation" which the New Criticism had taught us,
however belatedly, to use; and presumably his own discussion of the
Bower represents the way in which he feels that historical scholarship
has been revitalized by close analysis of the text. At any rate, most
of the scholars who reviewed his book soon after it was published in
1957 were highly favorable to the kind of textual interpretation,
called "poetic" or "metaphorical allegory," which he applies to *The
Faerie Queene*; none of them detected any danger of subjective dis-
tortion in that method, and one of them specifically praised the results
it achieved in Berger's interpretation of the Bower.[15]

These reviews, of course, are not exceptional in any way. Since
1957 many other scholars than Berger have profited from the tendency
to view ourselves as living in a new golden age of Spenserian studies
which dates from the recent discovery of close interpretation or irony
or iconography or archetypal patterns; and if the older historical
scholarship is grudgingly admitted to a share of the glory, it is apt
to be treated as a kind of preliminary day-labor, leveling the ground
on which better minds are now engaged in erecting their splendid
aperçus. Without denying that the last twenty years have seen various solid achievements in the Spenserian field, one may reasonably
account for them as a significant outgrowth of earlier scholarship;
but the prevailing emphasis suggests that discontinuity with the immediate past is itself a primary virtue.

The weakness which such an emphasis unconsciously conceals
might easily be traced in a score of books and articles which have
appeared since 1957; none of them, however, tells us more about the
recent course of Spenserian studies than a long "essay" of Angus
Fletcher's entitled *The Prophetic Moment*. Published in 1971, it has
already received several reviews which are clearly favorable to most
of its insights and to its central thesis.[16] Even at a first reading, one
can see that in a sense it is a more carefully organized book than we
have come to expect of Spenserians in the last twenty years, and it
obviously belongs to the tradition of historical scholarship. Many of
its 304 pages are shod with oversized footnotes, not merely documenting the text but supplying additional ideas and their bibliographical support. The range of Fletcher's learned references is

considerably broader than Berger's, and he implicitly accepts the view that the more we can know about the poet's world, the better we can understand the poet.

Fletcher's partiality to historical learning, indeed, has its awkward consequences. His central thesis, of which more will be said in a moment, is carefully developed in the actual text of the book; but its firm organization is achieved, not by discarding a number of marginal and submarginal matters, but by segregating them in the footnotes. As a result, the upper and lower halves of the same page may deal with subjects which are clearly too remote from each other to be aligned in the text; and a single annotation may sprawl across two or three or even four pages. Footnotes, for example, provide us with unalphabetized lists of works on the Renaissance concept of history and on Milton's typology;[17] again, in two of the longest and least conclusive of his annotations Fletcher runs through threshold symbolism from Dante to Herbert (pp. 45–47) and the implications of an allusion to the Argonauts, in the *Amoretti* but not in the passage from *The Faerie Queene* to which the note is attached (pp. 112–15); or, to take a different kind of case, his discussion of "social banditry" in Book V of *The Faerie Queene* is underpropped with a long quotation on Carpathian, Sicilian, and Corsican bandits from the nineteenth century to the present (p. 229). Yet the irrelevance of these and many other footnotes is not so disturbing as the contrast they make with the much less fully documented thesis at the center of the book: historical scholarship, for the most part, supplies a kind of elaborate packaging rather than the real substance of the argument.[18]

The central argument of Fletcher's book is ingenious. He defines prophecy, in the sense in which he applies it to *The Faerie Queene*, as a tradition "which is only partially predictive, a tradition that balances anticipation of the future with a concern for the past and, even more important, for the present. . . . History is useful and necessary to the prophet because it presents him with a theoretical wholeness of past, present, and future. In prophetic hands, however, the three aspects of time condense into a single moment" (pp. 4–5). In literary works the prophetic moment is located at the juncture between two thematic elements:

Centering upon this moment, the prophetic mode of literature employs two great archetypes, the temple and the labyrinth. More specifically, in the romantic tradition of English poetry a dialectic of the temple and the labyrinth enables the poet to develop a mythological grammar, whereby he can combine myths with various matrices in a large, loose, yet harmonious syncretic union. (P. 6)

These two archetypes organize the overall shaping of *The Faerie Queene*, and while other archetypal images play a part throughout the poem, the temple and the labyrinth, as "poetic universals," are sufficiently large and powerful images to organize an immense variety of secondary imagery, leading thereby to an equally varied narrative. (Pp. 11–12)

The way in which these archetypes are related to the prophetic moment is elaborated in a later passage:

The structure of the prophetic moment is given by the dialectic of the temple and the labyrinth, between which there is a theoretical threshold, corresponding spatially to the temporal crossover defined as a moment. Thresholds are openings or doorways between two spaces or places. Moments are doorways between two spaces of time. These metaphors diagram the emergence of vision. At the theoretical meeting place between the temple and the labyrinth there bursts forth a higher order, which the great syncretist of ancient allegory, Philo Judaeus, would call "the Immanent Logos." (Pp. 45–46)

Fletcher's account of his central thesis suffers from certain obscurities: the meanings of such metaphorical phrases as "the dialectic of the temple and the labyrinth" and "a mythological grammar" are not self-evident, and the allusion to "the Immanent Logos" of Philo Judaeus hardly throws much light on the immediate subject. Nevertheless, a distinct concept has been outlined. The prophetic poet, it is clear, looks before and after, yet concentrates on the present and particularly on the specific moments of the present when the enclosed, ordered world of the temple makes electric contact with *the* World, the boundless, disordered labyrinth of existence. Stated in such general terms, the theory of the prophetic moment has an impressive completeness and simplicity. How well, then, does it account for the content and the structure of *The Faerie Queene*?

The numerological approach to the poem, however far it strays afield, does find a very concrete if narrow justification in the well-known arithmetical stanza describing the House of Alma (II.ix.22); and in the same limited way the prophetic approach might seem to be directly authorized by one or two oracular stanzas, for instance, by Merlin's gloomy prediction to Britomart:

> Then woe, and woe, and euerlasting woe,
> Be to the Briton babe, that shalbe borne,
> To liue in thraldome of his fathers foe.
>
> (III.iii.42)

But Fletcher, for whatever reason, makes nothing of so obvious an example. On the other hand, the evidence provided by Osgood's *Concordance*, which he apparently uses on occasion, hardly confirms the importance of his crucial archetypes: "temple" and its cognates occur only nineteen times, "labyrinth" only three times in the entire *Faerie Queene*. Twelve of the occurrences of "temple" are clustered where one might expect them, in the episodes of the Temple of Venus (IV.x) and the Temple of Isis (V.vii); in a single curious instance, "Labyrinthes" are found in the enclosed garden surrounding the Temple of Venus (IV.x.24), precisely where the prophetic hypothesis would lead one to expect them least. The text of the poem, in other words, gives no convincing verbal proof that Spenser's mind was deeply or continuously occupied with Fletcher's archetypal images.

Thus the theorist must necessarily rest his case for them on evidence which is not verbal, and he turns to the evidence provided by a system of equivalent forms:

The image of the temple is probably the dominant recurring archetype in *The Faerie Queene*. Major visions in each of the six books are presented as temples: the House of Holiness, the Castle of Alma, the Garden of Adonis, the Temple of Venus, the Temple of Isis, the sacred round-dance on the top of Mount Acidale. Even the Mutabilitie Cantos display this "symbolism of the center," as the trial convenes at the pastoral *templum* of Diana, Arlo Hill. (P. 12)

Here, except for the Temples of Venus and Isis, which Spenser has literally described as such, "the temple" becomes a concept so tenuous as to be almost meaningless: in most of these cases the term does not refer to a place of worship, in some of them it does not refer to an enclosed area, and in one of them it does not even refer to a place. What the seven episodes do have in common is their function as symbolic centers for the books of *The Faerie Queene* in which they occur, and it would be both more honest and more persuasive to call them "symbolic centers" or "allegorical cores," in Lewis's phrase, than to tie them together with the misleading image of "the temple."

Fletcher, of course, borrows that image, along with its archetypal opposite, from authorities on myth and esoteric thought;[19] but mere learning hardly accounts for his exuberant discovery of the temple and the labyrinth, singly or together, in every corner of Spenser's poem. The magic glass in which Britomart sees her future husband is a temple of alchemical foresight (p. 120); in its historical presentation of customary behavior, canto x of Book II assumes an idealized templar form (p. 179); Christ's statement "I am the vine and ye are the branches" confers templehood on the tree and branches of the Trojan race in Book III (p. 227); in Book V Spenser shows that law aspires to the timeless cyclical uniformity of a sacred temple (p. 183), and yet, while equity is templar in nature, the *lex talionis* resembles a labyrinth (p. 287). The whole poem, like England in the marriage of the Thames and Medway, becomes a temple of echoing verbal elements (p. 106); but "If *The Faerie Queene* is by its concentric form a templar vision, its flowing narrative is the image of error and experience. . . . The templar structure gives meaning to the labyrinthine ways of Faerieland" (p. 217). Even the versification is made to fit the same archetypal pattern: while the stanzas of the poem are "the ultimate templar monuments of which the whole templar vision is made," the enjambment of the lines is a metrical equivalent of labyrinthine error (pp. 130–31). And Fletcher cites other temples and labyrinths than these to prove that *The Faerie Queene* is dominated by a single pair of images; yet each assertion only stretches the plausibility of his case a little thinner. In the end they no longer bear any relation to what is actually in the poem itself: they are stamped on it, just as a Gothic church, springing out of an Elizabethan maze, is stamped on the cover of Fletcher's book.

Moreover, even if the temple and the labyrinth were acceptable as the dominant imagery of *The Faerie Queene*, they would not of themselves establish Fletcher's thesis; he subordinates them to a more important concept, the prophetic moment of which they are alleged to be the parents. The title and the early pages of his book raise the expectation that he will fully demonstrate the existence and significance of such a concept in Spenser's poem. The text that follows, indeed, asserts or implies that prophetic moments appear in several episodes: Redcrosse on the Hill of Contemplation (p. 50), the Garden of Adonis (p. 94), the dance of the Graces on Mount Acidale (p. 126), Britomart's praise of Troynovant (p. 135), the Temple of Isis (p. 262), the four pageants described in the course of *The Faerie Queene* (p. 52), and the annual feast of the Order of Maidenhead (p. 74). Since the last of these is not part of the actual poem and probably was never written, it can hardly provide evidence of any kind; yet the other episodes, which do exist, are available for analysis and a full discussion of the prophetic moments they are said to contain. In them we should be able to savor the proof of Fletcher's thesis. But the proof, which would necessarily consist of a detailed and logical examination of such passages, is curiously missing; and what we find instead is merely a reassertion, in each case, of the grandiose hypothesis which was assumed from the first. Under all its accumulated learning, *The Prophetic Moment* is hollow, like a polished geode, at the center of its argument.

It would be unjust, however, to linger over the deficiencies of Fletcher's book as if they were unique: not only Berger's interpretation of the Bower of Bliss but a number of more recent studies testify, with varying degrees of clarity, to the same weaknesses. Historical scholarship, supplemented by all the new approaches which have followed in its wake, has had few mature achievements to record as yet in the field of Spenserian criticism; writing under its aegis but against its spirit, scholars and critics have often in recent years distorted the poet's meaning almost beyond recognition. After a century, the subjectivism which colors the most striking passages of Lowell's essay is easily exposed in its untutored brashness; the subjectivism of our more knowledgeable time, partly because it is of our time and partly because the preceding revolution in historical studies disguises it, has often eluded us. We forget that, unlike Lowell, we are committed to a rational examination of Spenser on his own terms, as he saw himself and his world.

And yet, in spite of the pitfalls which beset our blindness and our self-indulgence, the case for Spenserian scholarship is never hopeless in the end. If we have often forgotten the poet's vision of reality, that great object in all its complex magnificence of rhetoric and image and belief is still as always there, to be recovered.

4

S. K. HENINGER, JR.   *The Aesthetic*
Experience of Reading Spenser

SPENSER suffered what must surely be the most demeaning of fates
for a poet. His high reputation survived intact, while the taste for
his poetry rapidly declined. As a consequence, he continued to be
read, but for the wrong reasons and in the wrong way, and therefore
with less and less understanding. His poetry has certain qualities that
please the aesthete and lead to a sobriquet such as "the poet's poet."
It was for these reasons that John Keats and Leigh Hunt read Spenser.
But in the seventeenth century, changing assumptions—about art,
about nature, about reality—made it increasingly unlikely that a reader
should understand Spenser's poetic method or his poetic statement.
The rapid change in ideas and attitudes during what has come to be
called the scientific revolution very quickly rendered Spenser obsolete.

Already by 1674 Thomas Rymer had formulated the censures
that became commonplace in later Spenserian criticism. In the preface
to his translation of Rapin's *Reflections on Aristotle's treatise of poesie*
Rymer is careful to praise Spenser, but is basically unsympathetic to
The Faerie Queene:

Spencer, I think, may be reckon'd the first of our *Heroick Poets*; he had a
large spirit, a sharp judgement, and a *Genius* for *Heroick Poesie*, perhaps
above any that ever writ since *Virgil*. But our misfortune is, he wanted a
true *Idea*, and lost himself, by following an unfaithful guide. Though besides *Homer* and *Virgil* he had read *Tasso*, yet he rather suffer'd himself
to be misled by *Ariosto*; with whom blindly rambling on *marvellous* Adventures, he makes no Conscience of *Probability*. All is fanciful and
chimerical, without any uniformity, without any foundation in truth; his
Poem is perfect *Fairy-land*.[1]

Rymer is willing to maintain Spenser's high reputation. He actively
supports the primacy of Spenser in English epic and readily com-

pares him to Virgil, matters of grave concern to the harbinger of neoclassicism in England. But what he does not find in Spenser is exactly that which Spenser had taken greatest pains to provide: "a true *Idea*." Rymer laments the absence of a plan, a structure, a unifying theme—"a true *Idea*" to lead the reader along some continuous path through the maze of episodes. And Rymer ascribes this deficiency to Spenser's emulation of Ariosto, who was notorious as a meanderer.

But Rymer makes against *The Faerie Queene* an even more serious charge than disorganization. It lacks veracity. Instead of being valid, "all is fanciful and chimerical . . . without any foundation in truth." This is the perennial charge against poetry. In the vocabulary of Elizabethans, poetry is "feigning" and "counterfeiting." It is a wholly mental construct contrived by the poet without reference to reality. Or at best, it is an inevitably inaccurate reconstruction of the objects and events in physical nature. As Rymer concludes here about *The Faerie Queene*, the "Poem is perfect *Fairy-land*"—a product of the poet's unrestrained imagination, not to be believed by the prudent reader because it does not accord with his sense perception of the universe. Spenser does not apply the criterion of probability to the actions in his fiction; and therefore, while he may be the airy-fairy poet's poet, he is certainly not your poet and mine. Rymer's assumptions are fundamentally detrimental to *The Faerie Queene*, and to poetry in general.

Rymer's censures against Spenser were heartily seconded by later critics in the century. In 1690 Sir William Temple similarly found *The Faerie Queene* an offence to his neoclassical tastes:

Spencer endeavoured . . . to make Instruction, instead of Story, the Subject of an *Epick* Poem. His Execution was Excellent, and his Flights of Fancy very Noble and High, but his Design was Poor, and his Moral lay so bare, that it lost the Effect.[2]

In 1693 John Dryden praised Spenser (along with Milton) for "genius" and "learning," but he complained that "there is no uniformity in the design of Spencer: he aims at the accomplishment of no one action."[3] In 1695 Sir Richard Blackmore confirmed the deleterious influence that Ariosto had exerted upon Spenser and railed against the unruliness of allegories:

Ariosto and Spencer, however *great Wits*, not observing this judicious Conduct of *Virgil*, nor attending to any sober Rules, are hurried on with a *boundless, impetuous* Fancy over Hill and Dale, till they are both lost in a Wood of Allegories. Allegories so *wild, unnatural,* and *extravagant,* as greatly displease the Reader. This way of writing mightily offends in this Age; and 'tis a wonder how it came to please in any.[4]

Of course, by this time a critic had expectations for literary art quite different from those which prevailed in Spenser's day. And it was not merely a matter of imitating Virgil or following the rules, as Blackmore would have us believe.

Evidently, by the end of the seventeenth century *The Faerie Queene* was being judged with the same expectations and by the same criteria as those soon to be applied to the novel. *The Faerie Queene* was being read not as a poem, but rather as a narrative. My distinction can be made clear most easily, perhaps, by considering those intellectual conditions which attended the rise of the novel as a major genre. The novel appeared on the literary scene at that time in our intellectual history when the data of this world became the constituents of ultimate reality. The novel reflects the new concepts of reality and time that developed during the seventeenth century.

Previous to that century, as part of its medieval heritage, renaissance Europe had adopted certain notions about ultimate reality, about the relationship of physical nature to that ultimate reality, and about the relationship of art to both. Many notions about these topics were current, of course, but the prevalent assumption placed ultimate reality at some level beyond perception by our senses. For the philosopher, ultimate reality lay in some Platonic world of archetypal ideas; for the theologian, it lay in some Christian heaven; for the historian, it lay in some time-tested legend. Whatever the context for ultimate reality, it could not be perceived directly. It could be imperfectly suggested by objects and events that are sense perceptible; it could be "mirrored" or "shadowed" for our perusal at secondhand. But the data of this world are transient and even illusory, and any readings from the book of nature must be interpreted with care. The truth of ultimate reality was elusive, and certainly not to be achieved through the senses.

For us in this post-Baconian era it is difficult to accommodate such an epistemology. But for contemporaries of Spenser the perception of truth was reserved for the human intellect (or the soul, in a religious context). To use Platonic terms, truth was intelligible, not sensible. And even so, despite its desirability, not everyone could activate his intellect (or soul) to acquire this absolute knowledge. Discernment of ultimate reality was no more than a possibility, and even this possibility was allowed to but a few: to the mystic through vision, to the scholar through study, to the poet through inspiration, and perhaps to the lover through service to his mistress. Greatly simplified, this was the Platonic-Christian heritage of the Renaissance as it came down from the Middle Ages.

Given the location of ultimate reality at some level beyond our senses, there were a limited number of relationships that could be postulated between art, nature, and truth. Again to use Platonic terms for convenience, we recall from the *Timaeus* that nature (Gr. *phusis*, "physics") is but a projection of the world of ideas into a time-space continuum. The insubstantial, though changeless, ideas are given physical extension into a dimensional continuum, thereby producing our sense-perceptible universe. The objects of nature are replicas, albeit imperfect, of the archetypal ideas, and nature as a whole is a replica, albeit imperfect, of that truth which is ultimate reality. In this scheme the relationship between nature and truth is distinct and fixed.

Art may relate to truth, however, in two different ways. First, art may imitate the objects of nature in some representational fashion, so that art is an imitation of an imperfect replica of ultimate reality — that is, art is twice removed from truth. It was upon the basis of this argument that Plato drove the poets from his ideal commonwealth. But also art may be the immediate transcript of truth. If the poet has direct perception of ultimate reality, he may reproduce in his poem the archetypal ideas without need of any intermediary such as nature. In this scheme, art does not depend from nature as an imperfect facsimile of it, but rather art is coordinate with nature, each stemming directly from ultimate reality. As Philip Sidney puts it, the poet produces a "second nature," an alternate man-made nature which bears the same relation to truth that God's nature bears.[5]

In this latter scheme, art is the straightforward exponent of truth, and the validity of art is equal to that of nature. In fact, the poet can control his materials, removing the deficiencies of matter and the accidents of time — as Sidney says, the poet produces a golden world, while nature's world is only brazen. Therefore the creation of the poet has greater validity than physical nature, because it more nearly approximates the perfection of ultimate reality. In substance, this argument is the basis of Sidney's apology for poetry.

By the end of the seventeenth century, however, as a result of the so-called scientific revolution, all of this had changed. Assumptions about the relationship between art, nature, and truth radically altered, because there was a fundamental change in the location of ultimate reality. No longer was ultimate reality believed to reside with Plato's timeless ideas, or with a benign deity, or with the heroes and heroines of old. Rather, according to prevalent assumption, the objects of physical nature became the constituents of ultimate reality. The ascendant ontology was materialistic and the ascendant epistemology was empirical. Phenomenalism was inaugurated as the dominant intellectual mode. As a result, art perforce must imitate physical objects, since nature and truth are conflated. There is no alternative for art to mirror. And if art does venture to forsake nature as its obvious model, it becomes "fanciful and chimerical," to repeat the damning epithets of Rymer, "without any foundation in truth." Furthermore, to say that "his Poem is perfect *Fairy-land*" is the grossest condemnation of a poet, relegating him to the fictitious and irrelevant. Under these strictures, a poem as Sidney and Spenser conceived it is impossible.

Another aspect of the change in the location of ultimate reality bears upon the development of the novel as a literary genre and perhaps explains why it became the dominant genre by the late eighteenth century. Plato's world of being, the Christian heaven, and the realm of legend are all timeless in a literal sense. In them there is no time. There is no past, present, and future. Periods are not distinguished, or perhaps they are all concurrent. But time is not a duration to be measured. Eternity is measureless, not only in the sense of being without limit, but also in the sense of not submitting to dissection. Eternity is all-inclusive but atemporal, and ultimate reality conceived as timeless is homogeneous. In consequence, a poem that reflects this ultimate reality must also display these qualities: all-inclusiveness and homogeneity. Or to state it another way, such a poem must demonstrate how to achieve unity out of multeity. Or to push it one step farther, such a poem must demonstrate a favorite maxim of the renaissance, "All contraries agree in unified nature." The poem must resolve the discords observable in time and space to produce a perfect concord.

When ultimate reality is placed among the objects of physical nature, however, a different concept of time necessarily results. Physical objects undergo continual alteration—a fact which became an obsession of the Renaissance under the rubric of "mutability." As a result of this observation, reality does become indubitably a durational process. And a literary genre to reflect this notion must perforce emphasize time and must arrange its parts to represent the passage of time. To meet this expectation, the novel as a genre came into existence; and as this expectation became more insistent, the novel gained importance, until it dominated the literary scene. The novel (at least until recently) is a sequence of episodes following one another in a chain of cause-and-effect. One episode grows out of its predecessor and prepares for the next, or else the plot is decried for lacking realism and seeming contrived. In sum, the novel is the representation of a finite portion of passing time. It begins at one point in time and proceeds more or less in a straight progression to its conclusion at a later point in time. It is not a circular progression, like *The Shepheardes Calender*. Recent writers have reacted against the expectation that a novel imitate sense-perceptible nature and follow a course in linear time, but they are responding to yet other and newer assumptions about ultimate reality. They are attempting to record the effects of subjectivism and irrationality.

To return to the comments of Rymer and his successors, we can see that their disappointment in *The Faerie Queene* stems largely from its dissimilarity with a novel. It is distinctly not a novel. And despite the conditioning we have received from our own age and our own literature, we must not read it as though it were.[6] It is not a sequence of episodes taking place in chronological order within a finite period of time. It is instead a poem in a special sense. *The Faerie Queene* is based upon a set of assumptions about art, nature, and truth quite different from those which prevail today. We can still appreciate Spenser's poem and can make it relevant to our own times, but the only safe starting-point for such an enterprise must lie with Spenser himself.

By 1579 Spenser had written a treatise on poetics, as we know from E. K.'s argument prefixed to "October" in *The Shepheardes Calender*. It was entitled *The English Poet*, and according to E. K. dealt at least in part with "[*enthousiasmos*] and celestiall inspiration." Apparently, it was never printed; in any case, it is no longer extant. At this point, I wholly subscribe to the sentiment of William Webbe, who in 1586 while writing his own *Discourse of English poetrie* gave this item priority in the Spenser canon: "Among all other his workes whatsoever, I would wysh to have the sight of hys *English Poet*."[7] It would indeed be helpful to have a manifesto from Spenser. Upon sober reflection, though, we may not be willing to forego *The Faerie Queene* for the author's youthful effusions upon the poetic craft. Besides, we do have a reasonable substitute, or at least some basis for making surmises.

During the years 1578 to 1580 Spenser was enjoying his closest comradeship with Philip Sidney. One was a resident of Leicester House and the other a frequent visitor. These were the days of the Areopagus. And no matter how facetious the remark of Gabriel Harvey or how tenuous this literary circle, there is no doubt that Spenser and Sidney were in conversation about poetry as well as politics. Their intimacy and interaction are indisputable, as the dedication of *The Shepheardes Calender* attests. Shortly after these years (did he begin during them?), Sidney wrote his celebrated *Defence of poesie*. Without stretching probability or prudence beyond the limits of reason, we can look to Sidney's *Defence* as a statement of poetic principles that Spenser very likely shared.

In that sophisticated apology for the human imagination there is much that bears upon the aesthetic experience of reading Spenser. I hope in another place to consider at full length the way in which Sidney and Spenser elucidate one another. For the purposes of this essay, however, I shall draw from the *Defence* a single quotation. Quite early in the treatise, when Sidney is defining the poet in Timaean terms as a "maker," he concludes with a statement which is surprisingly dogmatic: "The skill of ech Artificer standeth in that *Idea,* or fore conceit of the worke, and not in the worke it selfe." [8] This statement implies an entire poetics that constitutes the gist of Sidney's defence for poetry.

In this passage Sidney is thinking of the poet as an "artificer" in the literal sense of the term (which, incidentally, was the usual sense for Elizabethans). The artificer performs a skill, as the etymology of the word (L. *ars* plus *facere*) indicates. The *poet* is a "maker" from the Greek *poiein,* "to make or fashion," as Sidney had just explained, and *poiein* is cognate in meaning with Latin *fingere.* The past participle of *fingere* is *fictus,* and it is from this word that our term "fiction" comes. Literally and originally, "fiction" means "that which has been made by an artisan." "Fiction" and "poem," be it noted, are synonyms—the same word, in fact, though in different languages. Only later, after the seventeenth century, does "fiction" acquire the sense of being unreal or untrue, and "artificial" acquires the sense of being unnatural and therefore phony.[9] For Sidney and his contemporaries, however, the poet was an artificer who performed the skill of making fictions that were both real and true, and the product of this operation was a poem.[10]

And Sidney tells us more in this quotation. The artificer begins with an "*Idea,* or fore conceit." He begins with a mental concept which he then makes particular and concrete by means of counters which are sense perceptible—what T. S. Eliot has called "objective correlatives." If narrative is the vehicle of expression, the poet produces "an historical fiction," to use Spenser's term,[11] where "historical" of course has its latinate meaning preserved in our "story."

Quite clearly, the term "idea" suggests a Platonic reading here, and the context confirms the relevance of Plato and points to the account of creation reported in the *Timaeus.*[12] There the deity is called "the poet of the universe" (28C) and his creative act is described in detail. Starting with the archetypal ideas, he proceeds by giving them physical extension until our time-space continuum is perfected. The universe is his fiction, his poem. From the time of St. Augustine it was commonplace to see the poet as an analogous creator who gives extension to his foreconceit by means of characters and actions and settings—i.e., by means of fiction in the applied sense of narrative. The poem, then, continuing the analogy, is the poet's universe in a more than loosely figurative sense.[13]

Finally, the skill of the artificer lies in his "*Idea*, or fore conceit . . . and not in the worke it selfe." Our judgment of the poet's art, therefore, must bear upon the poet's original concept, rather than upon the narrative fiction whereby he expresses his foreconceit. Apparently, our judgment should concern itself more with the truthfulness of his idea than with the means whereby he makes this idea perceptible to us. The essence of a poem is its intellectual content, not its dynamics or its technique. The narrative fiction is but the external manifestation of the poem's meaning, a secondary effect to be perused and passed through as quickly as possible. It is not the *raison d'être* of the poem. As Sidney later in the *Defence* advises his audience, "They shall use the narration but as an imaginative ground-plat of a profitable invention." [14] Our aim in reading a poem should be to discern the poet's original idea, his "invention," to use the Ciceronian term employed by Sidney.

It seems likely that Rymer had in mind this principle from Sidney's *Defence* when he complained that in *The Faerie Queene* Spenser "wanted a true *Idea*." But how unjust an accusation. Spenser is unmistakably clear in enunciating his foreconceit. He calls his poem "The Faerie Queene," and certainly the court of Gloriana provides both the containment and the cohesion for the entire work.

To use the title of a poem to announce its foreconceit was a common practice for Renaissance poets. As an example near to Spenser, George Herbert in *The Temple* uses the title to announce his controlling idea; and for individual poems within the larger structure, such as "The Collar" or "The Pulley," he uses the title to designate an idea which he then makes understandable to us by elaborating it in durational terms. The poem is the extension of a foreconceit, which without this extension would remain ineffable. The poem explicates the foreconceit announced by the title. Conversely, without the title we would have difficulty understanding the poem. We need the title to provide a context for what follows. So title and poem are mutually dependent. In just such a way, *The Faerie Queene* in its narrative fiction unfolds its title, and likewise the title gives essential meaning to every part of the poem. The court of Gloriana is an omnipresent point of reference for every episode.

The fairy queen lies behind Spenser's poem and permeates it in much the same way the mistress initiates a sonnet sequence. The sonneteer begins with an idealized concept of his mistress as the repository of all celestial values, and then he composes a series of sonnets which praise particular qualities and record particular events. The individual sonnets make knowable the idea of feminine perfection that otherwise would remain inaccessible to mere mortals. The mistress is measured out in parcels of fourteen lines, and in this reduced form can be experienced. In the sequence as a whole, in fact, she is fully revealed. The sonneteer in his sequence of small poems reports his responses to her at various times and in various moods, until he exhausts her infinite variety. Thereby through a summation of his transient experience he glimpses eternal bliss. And we, the readers, share this experience vicariously until we too transcend the temporal confinement of this world and contemplate the absolute beauty of the mistress as an idea. In the course of reading the series, sonnet by sonnet, we come to know the mistress bit by bit, until we comprehend the totality of her being; and thence we can abstract the perfection of her absolute beauty.[15]

Just so, Spenser begins with an idealized concept of Queen Elizabeth, whom he implores in the Proem to Book I:

> raise my thoughts too humble and too vile,
> To thinke of that true glorious type of thine,
> The argument of mine afflicted stile.
>
> (I.Proem.4.6–8)

The "type" of Elizabeth is of course Gloriana, avowedly the argument of this humble "stile" (i.e., song). Spenser wishes us to gain gradual knowledge of Gloriana through her effect on Arthur and his fellow knights. Bit by bit, through the numerous episodes that we witness, we come to know her greatness. Eventually we perceive her all-pervasive beneficence in the realm, and consequently perceive in her the abstract quality of glory, heavenly as well as mundane. This is the mechanism of Spenser's compliment to the aging queen, and no doubt it would have been more manifest had he completed his poem.

In fine, the concept of glory embodied in a fairy queen is the "*Idea*, or fore conceit" which Spenser proceeds to give durational extension by means of his narrative fiction. This process is explicit, and when disclosed seems almost embarrassingly mechanical. One wonders how Rymer could have missed it. Spenser tells us just what he is doing in the explanatory letter to Raleigh which has been appended to most editions of *The Faerie Queene* since the first in 1590. Apparently, Raleigh had requested some aid in reading the poem, so Spenser complied by writing this letter "to discover unto you the general intention and meaning, which in the whole course thereof I have fashioned,[16] without expressing of any particular purposes or by-accidents therein occasioned." At the appropriate point in the discussion, Spenser confides:

In that Faery Queene I meane glory in my generall intention, but in my particular I conceive the most excellent and glorious person of our soveraine the Queene, and her kingdome in Faery land. And yet in some places els, I doe otherwise shadow her. For considering she beareth two persons, the one of a most royall Queene or Empresse, the other of a most vertuous and beautifull Lady, this latter part in some places I doe express in Belphoebe.[17]

Spenser's idea, his "generall intention," is glory, which he reduces to an objective correlative in the well-known personage of Queen Elizabeth.

Furthermore, Spenser recognizes that this deputy of Gloriana has "two bodies," to use a phrase from Kantorowicz's famous study: her public life as a monarch, and her private life as a woman.[18] Therefore through the agent of Elizabeth he deduces his concept of glory from the insubstantial realm of Plato's ideas down to the public level of human society, and thence he further deduces it to the most intimate of personal affairs. He elaborates its meaning by unfolding [19] Elizabeth, the queen, into an array of secondary entities, such as Belphoebe, who adumbrate her personal qualities. And we can identify other characters who unfold Elizabeth in a similar fashion, such as Una, Britomart, Mercilla, and perhaps even Radigund. Each of these characters projects some particular quality of Elizabeth, some portion of her total being. She is fragmented into knowable parts which are purveyed to the reader through the episodes of the poem. Consequently, in the reverse process of infolding these parts together, the reader arrives at some notion of the Queen based upon dependable experience. The sum of these characters taken together comprises the personality of the Queen, and the narrative fiction provides the reader with a means of knowing that whole at first hand. In addition, as a bonus, that whole is greater than the sum of its parts. Continuing the process of infolding, the reader abstracts and idealizes until he arrives at some notion of Gloriana. And thence it is an easy step to comprehend the idea of glory. In Sidney's words, the characters and their actions have provided the "groundplat" of that "profitable invention."

But Spenser does not stop with the salient structuring of that idea. He supports and confirms it by devising a suitable mate for the fairy queen, by presenting a male counterpart who reinforces and enhances and amplifies her qualities by means of a parallel process of unfolding. Prince Arthur has had a dream of Gloriana, and his quest to realize this vision—his search for this perfection, this absolute—provides the narrative framework for the welter of individual episodes. His engagement to Gloriana, proposed for an uncompleted twelfth book as Spenser intimates in the letter to Raleigh, was to be the culmination of *The Faerie Queene*.

This conclusion of the poem will engage our attention in a moment. At this point, however, let us again turn to Spenser's explanatory letter and see what he says about Arthur:

In the person of Prince Arthure I sette forth magnificence in particular, which vertue for that (according to Aristotle and the rest) it is the perfection of all the rest, and conteineth in it them all, therefore in the whole course I mention the deedes of Arthure applyable to that vertue, which I write of in that booke. But of the xii. other vertues, I make xii. other knights the patrones, for the more variety of the history.[20]

Once more Spenser is unequivocal about his foreconceit: "In the person of Prince Arthure I sette forth magnificence." And in this instance, he is more explicit about the structure for unfolding this idea. He notes that "according to Aristotle and the rest"—that is, according to accepted authority—the "vertue"[21] of magnificence "is the perfection of all the rest." Here we should read "perfection" with its literal definition from the Latin *perficere*, "to work through to an end." So "perfection" means a completed action which has gone through and thereby subsumed a multitude of phases. As Spenser himself immediately explains, magnificence is the perfection of all the other virtues because magnificence "conteineth in it them all." To use our terminology, magnificence "infolds" all the other virtues.

Arthur infolds each of the partial virtues to be bodied forth by the other knights. As the summation of virtue, he represents holiness, temperance, chastity, friendship, justice, courtesy, and so forth. In consequence, he could be Spenser's agent for performing any of the manly deeds which occur in the narrative fiction. But Spenser recognized the incipient monotony of such a plan, and therefore "for the more variety of the history" he unfolded Arthur into twelve subsidiary knights, each one of whom represents a partial virtue, a constituent of Arthur's magnificence. Nonetheless, Arthur will ride through each book, and Spenser comments that "in the whole course [of the poem] I mention the deedes of Arthure applyable to that vertue, which I write of in that booke."

So Arthur rides through *The Faerie Queene*, a poem "disposed into twelve bookes, fashioning XII. Morall vertues," as the titlepage announces. In each book he is unfolded into a subsidiary knight who demonstrates a particular virtue, a portion of the inclusive virtue of magnificence demonstrated by Arthur. Therefore Arthur is immanent in each episode involving one of his subsidiary knights, and he often makes an appearance in his own personage. Not even the neoclassical rage for order could obliterate a good poet's sensitivity to this intent, as Dryden grudgingly admits: "Magnanimity, which is the Character of Prince *Arthur*, shines throughout the whole Poem; and Succours the rest, when they are in Distress." [22] In actual fact, Arthur appears in the narrative fiction only when a lesser knight has proved inadequate to a degree which renders him impotent—for example, when Redcrosse is imprisoned in Orgoglio's dungeon and when Sir Guyon is despoiled by Pyrochles and Cymochles. Then Arthur rescues his beleaguered surrogate. Spenser's meaning clearly is that a partial virtue, no matter how intensely developed and assiduously exercised, cannot withstand the trials and tribulations of life; only an all-inclusive virtue can succeed.

And Arthur does succeed. As he rides through each book, succoring the hero of that particular book, he activates the partial virtue represented by that hero. Spenser set Arthur upon the super-quest of seeking the fairy queen; and as he journeys toward this transcendent goal, he vicariously participates in the particular quest of each knight, and through this experience he enhances his own virtue, building gradually toward the super-virtue of magnificence. By the end of the twelve books which Spenser planned for *The Faerie Queene*, Arthur would have gone through all the partial virtues until he achieved perfection. In the letter to Raleigh, Spenser is forthright about his intention: "I labour to pourtraict in Arthure, before he was king, the image of a brave knight, perfected in the twelve private morall vertues." [23] After completing this circuit, thereby incorporating the totality of all virtues, Arthur would be a fit consort for Gloriana.

Once we outline this superstructure for the poem, we can see that the quest of Arthur to find the fairy queen and his eventual union with her provides the prototype for the quest of each lesser knight. Spenser thought he had been clear on this point, as the conclusion of his letter to Raleigh indicates:

Thus much Sir, I have briefly overronne to direct your understanding to the wel-head of the History, that from thence gathering the whole intention of the conceit, ye may as in a handful gripe al the discourse, which otherwise may happily seeme tedious and confused. [24]

The "continued Allegory, or darke conceit" of *The Faerie Queene* is no more than this superstructure of Arthur's search for Gloriana. Arthur's quest contains the separate quests distributed in the twelve books, and is therefore a "continued Allegory"—"continued" not in terms of durational time as the narrative progresses, but in terms of the structure's provision for a continuum.

As a corollary, the twelve subsidiary knights unfold and amplify Arthur "for the more variety of the history," so the quest of each knight is a partial enactment of Arthur's quest. Indeed, not only does each knight participate in Arthur's quest, but he epitomizes it, seeking his own lady, his own vision of perfection. In addition, since it follows Arthur's pattern, the quest of each knight is correspondent to the quest of every other knight. That is why Sir Guyon has "like race to runne" after Redcrosse: [25] Guyon will follow the same pattern for his quest, but of course with variations to accommodate his context of temperance, which is different from the context of holiness. From the reader's point of view, we have a series of variations upon a single theme. But this theme gains its definition through our perception of the particular variations. From the flux of the variations arises the stasis of the theme. The quest of each knight makes an individual and distinct contribution to the meaning of Arthur's quest. We can comprehend the quest of Gloriana's knight, in fact, only by following the fortunes of the other twelve.

What we have for structure, to conclude, is the comprehensive virtue of magnificence arising from the partial virtues of holiness, temperance, chastity, and so forth. The unifying theme of Arthur's quest develops from the multifarious quests of the other twelve knights. *The Faerie Queene* by this structure convincingly demonstrates the motif of *e pluribus unum,* the paradox of unity out of multeity. It shows how an all-inclusive and self-consistent entity can exist simultaneously with its incomplete and autonomous parts. There is at once amalgamation and divisiveness, stasis and continual movement, cotemporaneity and discursiveness, essence and appearance.

An important element in the poetic statement of *The Faerie Queene* is the demonstration of this very paradox, which is achieved through the twelve-partite structure. Much of the meaning of the poem is conveyed by this structure. When it is discovered, we can see at once that in this narrative fiction the poet must perforce disregard any concept of time as a sequential progression of events. Any particular quest (e.g., Redcrosse's or Guyon's) will seem to take place in durational time; but considered within the context of Arthur's super-quest, it is co-temporaneous not only with Arthur's but also with every other quest. The passage of time is, in fact, illusory. Or perhaps, the illusion of passing time is necessary for the extension of an idea in order to make it palpable to our senses. Then we have some feeling for the flux of events, and the experience of the poem accords with our experience of daily life. But the ultimate reality of any particular quest lies in the idea of magnificence, at some level beyond our sense perception, where time does not apply.

Spenser was very much aware of the difference between his intention and that of a historian, who must report events sequentially as they transpire in our time-space continuum. Spenser did not feel bound to respect time as are those who record the data of physical nature. As he observes pointedly in his letter to Raleigh:

The Methode of a Poet historical is not such, as of an Historiographer. For an Historiographer discourseth of affayres orderly as they were donne, accounting as well the times as the actions, but a Poet thrusteth into the middest, even where it most concerneth him, and there recoursing to the thinges forepaste, and divining of thinges to come, maketh a pleasing Analysis of all.[26]

Again, we must read "historical" with its latinate meaning, so that "a Poet historical" is not a poet dealing with historical material, but rather a poetic maker of a "story," a "fiction." His method, says Spenser, will differ from that of the writer who "discourseth of affayres orderly as they were donne," who must report "the times" along with the circumstances of events. The poet as maker can disregard the sequential organization of time—indeed, to reveal ultimate reality, he must. The injunction for the epic poet to begin *in medias res* is not simply a convenience for getting the story under way. As Spenser saw it, this epic convention is an open defiance of time, a declaration of independence from time. The poet perforce alludes to things past and proclaims things to come, shuttling back and forth between past and future, indiscriminately reducing events to their essence without reference to time. Only in this way the poet "maketh a pleasing Analysis of all." [27]

So Spenser expects the poet to follow some method different from that of the historiographer. In order to reveal the essence of our universe, in order to discover to our view its ultimate reality, the poet disregards time, begins his poem at that point which he considers most important for his foreconceit, conflates past and future, reduces the welter of particular events to a unity which the reader's mind perceives as truth. Within that method lies the aesthetics of reading Spenser.

After this general discussion about "the Methode of a Poet historical" Spenser proceeds to explain his own method in presenting the episodes of *The Faerie Queene*. He admits to perversity: "The beginning therefore of my history, if it were to be told by an Historiographer, should be the twelfth booke, which is the last." In effect, Spenser is here disclaiming any allegiance to ordinary time. Instead, in keeping with his foreconceit of glory embodied in Gloriana, he proposes a sequence which derives from the court of the fairy queen:

I devise that the Faery Queene kept her Annuall feaste xii. dayes, uppon which xii. severall dayes, the occasions of the xii. severall adventures hapned, which being undertaken by xii. severall knights, are in these xii. books severally handled and discoursed.[28]

Spenser establishes a temporal relationship between the quests of the particular knights which is definitely not seriatim. Gloriana's feast lasts twelve days, and one quest begins on each of these days. According to this statement, the twelve quests run concurrently, with their beginnings spaced just one day apart. Yet in the poem itself it seems as though the quests do transpire sequentially. The books are laid end to end, so that the quest of Guyon follows tandem to the quest of Redcrosse. But the appearance of chronological sequence derives from the fiction, from the extension of the foreconceit in order to make it palpable, and therefore the chronological sequence is only illusory, like all sense impressions. Or less severe (and more likely), the action is both chronological and atemporal, both multifarious and unified. In any case, this playing with time explains our difficulty in having any clear notion of before and after in *The Faerie Queene*.[29] And it justifies Spenser's license in reporting episodes which do not grow organically out of precedent events. The casual way in which he introduces an episode is not the simple naïveté of the fairy-tale teller, but rather the sophistication of the fictioneer who defies chronology.

One final point: we should note that this feast of the fairy queen is an annual occurrence. It happens at the end of the year. And presumably, just as it is the point of origin for each quest, it will also be the *terminus ad quem*, when all the quests are completed. At this point Arthur will be perfected, and his union with Gloriana will be imminent.[30] This union of the comprehensive virtues of glory and magnificence will achieve a stasis at the suprasensible level of ultimate reality, like the self-sufficient stability of the alchemical hermaphrodite.

But of course, paradoxically, within the coordinates of our physical universe all things change as the heavens circle around, and therefore events will continue to occur in sequential time. The annual feast of the fairy queen is a node, but not a stopping place. It recognizes the completion of one finite pattern, the year; but it also postulates the continuation of the process into another similar pattern until its completion, and then another, and another, and another. This explains why Redcrosse does not settle down with Una at the end of

Book I, but instead returns to the service of the fairy queen. And when we read the actions of Redcrosse as a type of the actions of Arthur, we see that Arthur also will not be allowed to continue uninterruptedly in the bliss attendant upon the success of his quest. In the perfect world of ideas he may perhaps gain permanent union with Gloriana; but in the imperfect world which we inhabit with its deficiencies and limitations, even the transcendent values of magnificence and glory are ephemeral.

Lest pessimism prevail, however, Gloriana holds her feast each year. The presence of these values in ultimate reality is thereby reconfirmed, and their promulgation through surrogates in the phantasmagoric world of mutability is demonstrated. Perhaps Spenser is more successful than Milton in asserting eternal providence.

Gloriana's feast is "annual," moreover, not only in the sense that it occurs once a year, but also in the sense that it represents the passage of the year, the annual unit of time, the integer of eternity. Her feast is an ongoing process, extended through the cycle of the seasons and further articulated through the sequence of months. For this reason, there are twelve knights, twelve quests, twelve books, as Spenser insistently emphasizes. But though they are "xii. severall adventures" and "xii. severall knights" which are "severally handled"— that is, although each is a distinct entity—yet they all meet together once a year to celebrate the feast of the fairy queen. Again the motif of unity arising out of multeity.

Spenser had demonstrated this motif with even greater directness in his earliest poem, *The Shepheardes Calender*.[31] There his foreconceit quite evidently is a concept of time, as indicated by the title and by the disposition of the poem into "twelve Æglogues proportionable to the twelve monethes." Each eclogue is unique, yet each fits into the familiar pattern of a calendar. Each contributes to a whole, to a year, again the annual unit of time. And this whole, like Gloriana and Arthur, becomes greater than the sum of its parts. Although the year is a finite entity itself, being cyclical it can repeat an infinite number of revolutions without discontinuity, and thereby it can extrapolate to eternity. Considered as a totality, the calendar exhausts the possibilities of temporal change and is therefore self-complete, perfect, changeless. This structure, like that of *The Faerie Queene*, demonstrates the paradoxical interdependence of movement and stasis, of appearance and reality.

Furthermore, Spenser deduces this idea of time into the realm of human affairs by means of Colin Clout, who of course can be further deduced into the personage of Spenser himself. Or conversely, Spenser abstracts his own experience (for example, in "October") to that of Colin, who as shepherd is lover, poet, and clergyman combined. From thence he can abstract Colin to a figure representing everyman. In any case, Colin Clout embodies the foreconceit of man in the abstract. And the events of the poem, unique for each month, exhaustively display the experiences of man distributed along the individual's allotted time. The twelve eclogues in sum postulate a relationship between man and time, between man and the cosmos. *The Shepheardes Calender* is a model of the human condition.

As a shepherd, Colin Clout inhabits Arcadia, which is another literary construct to define man's relationship to time. Arcadia is a figment of the poet's imagination, a fiction to project the concept of perfection. For the limited period of the poet's fantasy and by an act of his will, however, it exists as a reality (at least for the euphoric poet). Arcadia is perfect in every way. It is perfect in every way, that is, except one: it suffers the limitation of time. The Renaissance with exquisite masochism delighted in quoting an anonymous speaker who averred his ubiquity by the well-known phrase, "Et in Arcadia ego"; and that speaker is Death. The ineluctable passage of time destroys even Arcadia, as Colin Clout so painfully knows. It is this knowledge, in fact, that sets him apart from the other inhabitants of his universe and makes him fit to be its protagonist. But despite the death (or disillusionment) of the individual poet, Arcadia survives undiminished as a concept, as a value in the changeless world of ideas. So Spenser chose the pastoral mode as the best means of unfolding his foreconceit because it, like the calendar, embodies a concept of time as both static and yet ever-changing. As Spenser expresses the paradoxical ambiguity of Nature in the Mutabilitie Cantos, time is "still mooving, yet unmoved from her sted" (VII.vii.13.3).

The Faerie Queene is more artful than *The Shepheardes Calender,* but it derives from the same poetics of making. It proceeds according to much the same poetic method and it makes much the same poetic statement. There is no chance of mistaking *The Shepheardes Calender*—nor *Teares of the Muses, Epithalamion,* or *Fowre Hymnes*—for a novel. And since *The Faerie Queene* is similarly constructed to project the motif of unity arising from multeity, it also should be distinguished from a novel. In *The Faerie Queene,* ultimate reality resides at the court of Gloriana, among the ideas of Plato's world of being, and the reader's task is to discover this foreconceit which lies beyond the fiction. In a novel, ultimate reality resides in physical nature, and the reader's task is to perceive this nature in a phenomenalistic way since the novel reproduces nature as faithfully as mimetic literature will allow.

Moreover, the assumptions about time in *The Faerie Queene*

differ from those in a novel. A novelist, like a "historiographer," re-counts the events of his tale in chronological sequence, "orderly as they were donne." The plot is a chain of causes and effects, and the reader experiences (vicariously) each event as a reality to be known by its phenomena. The result is a reconstruction of transient nature. In *The Faerie Queene*, however, the parts are not linked by cause and effect in a time sequence. An episode does not necessarily arise out of what went before and prepare for what follows any more than "May" in *The Shepheardes Calender* grows out of "April" and pre-determines "June." Each eclogue is autonomous; and it relates not with its neighbors, which are equally autonomous, but with the calendar as a whole. Just so an episode in *The Faerie Queene* must be related not with its contiguous episodes alone, but with the poem as a totality. The super-quest of Arthur in search of Gloriana pro-vides a prototypical pattern for the action in each book. Therefore any given episode must be referred to this encompassing structure. When each episode is related to the total structure rather than just to its immediate neighbors, we begin to see a large synthesis com-prising contrasts as well as reiterations. *The Faerie Queene* then be-comes an image of that unified nature wherein contraries are reduced to agreement. The poem, as poems must be if they successfully pro-pound an optimistic cosmology, is a model of *concordia discors*.

Without preempting the reader's right to interpret for himself, I should like to suggest by example how the comprehensive totality of *The Faerie Queene* conditions the meaning of its aliquot parts. In Book I, to sketch broadly, Gloriana is represented in the delimiting terms of holiness by Una, just as Arthur's inclusive virtue is deduced partially into Redcrosse. Continuing, Redcrosse's particular relation to Duessa in canto vii and his particular relation to Celia in canto x must be read in the context of his relation to Una, which has been stipulated at the court of the fairy queen. Una proves, in the long run, to be both his mistress and his salvation. But at the beginning of his quest, Redcrosse doesn't know this; in fact, this is the truth he seeks. During the course of the narrative fiction, therefore, Duessa by negative example defines Redcrosse's proper role as Una's lover, while Celia adumbrates the holy benefits of service to Una. Red-crosse's seduction by Duessa and his subsequent resurrection by Celia are then properly seen as complementary phases in the same large pattern: his search for a rapprochement with Una, his effort to per-ceive truth, his struggle to become a knight worthy of Gloriana's court. If Duessa had not corrupted Redcrosse, he would not have sought the restorative ministrations of Celia. In this Panglossian uni-verse, good derives from evil, and the fall of Redcrosse is fortunate.

But this significance for Redcrosse's dalliance with Duessa can be seen only when the particular episode is placed within the totality of Gloriana's court. Only then can we see its contribution to the overall scheme. Only then do we realize that although Duessa is evil when considered *sui generis*, in the best of all possible worlds she must perforce be good.

Furthermore, when we view *The Faerie Queene* as a whole, *sub specie totius*, we can see that in Book II Phaedria is correspondent to Duessa and Alma is correspondent to Celia, though of course in the context of temperance rather than holiness. We see that the pattern of Book I is repeated in the other books, and thereby confirmed. We see, in fact, that each book is an epitome, with distinctive modulations, of the poem as a whole. In fine, we are led toward comprehension of that cosmic wholeness which derives from the union of glory and magnificence, Spenser's foreconceit for the poem.

It is true that upon first reading *The Faerie Queene* we are apt to proceed discursively—that is, a new reader probably starts with the first line and intends to read through to the end. This is the procedure for reading a novel. And it is likewise true that we, modern readers, will perceive the poem phenomenalistically—that is, we will attempt to know the poem by its phenomena, by the events it describes; and we will assume that the poem has no other existence. Perhaps as heirs of the New Criticism, we will assume that the poem has no existence except the words of the text, which we should respond to as phenomena, and we may forget that there are other constituents in a poem's meaning besides our own affective response to these stimuli. To concede the worst, we might admit that a modern reader may experience *The Faerie Queene* like Joseph Spence's mother—that is, as "a collection of pictures." [32] He will read it discursively and phenomenalistically, reflecting the assumptions about time and ultimate reality which prevail in our own day. He will work inductively, piecing the poem together from fragmentary data like a scientist arriving at a hypothesis based on empirical observation.

That, however, is only half a reading of *The Faerie Queene*. Such a reading may well reproduce our awareness of transience, even the sense of bewilderment and fright that often overtakes us, like Dante, "midway the journey of this life." But such a reading, with its emphasis on mutable nature, leads to a pessimistic response. *The Faerie Queene*, in its determination to be real and true, painstakingly reproduces the motion of passing time and suggests the randomness of this world's cavalcade. But in its total effect the poem precludes any residue of pessimism. Rather, the mighty maze through which the knights wander does have a plan; all roads do lead to Gloriana's feast. And this sacramental event subsumes the trivialities that we have witnessed in the individual books and combines them into a single world view that Spenser valued—a world view which was threatened by the forces that changed the world in the seventeenth century, but which was therefore all the more to be cherished.

To understand *The Faerie Queene* as it was intended, we should strive to reorient our thinking to accord with assumptions that prevailed in Spenser's day.[33] We should read it in the context of an ontology which placed ultimate reality on some suprasensible level, and in the context of an epistemology which made truth dependent upon perception of that ultimate reality through exercise of the intellect rather than the human sensory apparatus. *The Faerie Queene* projects a world view different from our own, and a sympathetic approach is prerequisite to making any headway in it. We must take at face value Spenser's announcement of a foreconceit in the title, and we must accept literally the confidences about method he reveals in the letter to Raleigh. We must strive to reconstruct the foreconceits of glory and magnificence which he bodies forth in Gloriana and Arthur, and which he unfolds even further to our view in the multitude of knights and ladies (both good and bad) that inhabit the microcosm of Fairyland. We must learn to relate each episode not only to adjacent episodes in the durational narrative of its own book, but even more cogently to the encompassing pattern of Arthur's quest and to the enduring ideal inherent in Gloriana's court. Then we will perceive the endless variety of the world around us; and because the episodes of *The Faerie Queene* conform with our own experience, we will accept the events as true. Moreover, because in their totality they lead to a greater whole, to a vision of life not only in its completeness but also abstracted to essential beauty, we will have an aesthetic experience by reading Spenser, an experience wherein we will recognize the relationship between art and nature and reality that aspires to. . . . We have reached the limit of words, even the limit of poetry.

5

A. KENT HIEATT   *A Spenser to Structure Our*

Myths (Medina, Phaedria, Proserpina,

Acrasia, Venus, Isis)

DESPITE the fifteen years of heroic exploration that now lie behind us, two items in the standard literary-historical picture of Spenser remain in much the same shape that they received in the third decade of this century. For students of the general tradition of poetic narrative in the Christian West, the possibility does not usually even arise that incident and detail in *The Faerie Queene* are governed as rigorously by a luminously logical, overarching plan as is the case, for instance, in the *Commedia* or in *Paradise Lost.* For students of the general tradition of English poetry in the Elizabethan period and the seventeenth century, the inherited assumption is still a commonplace that the virtues of precision, specificity, economy, and control in the writing of English verse were only slowly developed in that tradition by a kind of trial-and-error method in which the errors were usually committed by Spenser. Both of these positions are in need of modification in a related way.

The Faerie Queene establishes a moral and narrative realm or "country" (in the sense in which one speaks today of the "Faulkner country" or, at another level, of "Tolkien country") made up of the most various topography and populations but organized with an elegant economy. What at the verbal level looks to some readers like imprecision is, very often, a stretching of verbal possibilities in order to accommodate Spenser's larger-scale controlling plan. Once one sees what Spenser is after in any particular instance, one must generally be prepared to applaud the particular verbal configuration which he has chosen. This is not always true, it must be admitted, of the middle-scale phenomena between these two magnitudes. Particularly in the matter of narrative unity and verisimilitude he occasionally seems to be distorting incidents, scanting them, or elaborating them overintricately in the service of his major aim to weave all his material thematically into his larger tapestry. At the smaller-scale, verbal level an instance of what must appear to many readers to be poetically facile impressionism and slack imprecision will shortly afford us a way of beginning to see the integral character of the plan of *The Faerie Queene* and, while perceiving it, of comprehending the very precise poetic notion, part of a larger system of such notions, which Spenser had in mind in the instance with which we shall start.

Spenser is, in fact, the earliest of all writers of first importance whom we as speakers of English can read with a modicum of formal linguistic training; and, reaching us in deliberate and ample accents over the distance of so many generations, he addresses us with a voice of much authority. Contrary to what many Romantics have said, he is a mythmaker—a mythopoeic author—who validates, by giving concrete form to, part of the traditional moral heritage of Western culture which we can and should entertain with ultimate seriousness to this day. This minimum life raft includes certain principles of serious commitment and mutual respect and freedom in those of our relationships which are based on love and attraction, and includes as well the principle of a sane temperance in our attitudes toward the social fulfillment of egoistic drives, toward failure, defeat, and deprivation, and toward the satisfactions of the senses.

It is a characteristic of a mythic world like Spenser's that one can enter it at any point and allow its complexities to unfold around one. The evidence of the correspondences between the parts of this world is so intricate and arises so casually that the pleasures of mythic discovery meet one freshly at each reading. As with music, however, clear prior recognition of what is happening and of what is about to happen only increases our pleasure. The physical locales of *The Faerie Queene* correspond naturally to the parts of a mental and moral country, sometimes in terms of chivalric and romantic adventure, and at other times in symbolically more concentrated allegorical landscapes or dwellings—*paysage moralisé*. Spenser's favored device in *The Faerie Queene* is the multilayered allegorical conceit or metaphor, in which he brings together thematically a group of symbolic meanings in what musically might be called a chord, without much concern for the onward movement of his narrative.

We may now enter this world with the discussion of the episode of Phaedria in *The Faerie Queene*, II.vi. One sees differing fruitful relationships here with larger unities in the poem, according to which of a number of ways one approaches this episode, which concerns Phaedria's employment of her charms on, first, the knight Cymochles and, subsequently, the knight Guyon. One of her devices in the first of these two cases is to sing a song, in the action of which two parts are played by a female lily and a male fleur-de-lis. The symbolic use here of these flowers relates directly to at least five other such primary symbolic uses of flowers and vegetation in other parts of the poem, not simply by some kind of unconscious or adventitious association but as part of a larger system of organized images and meanings, extending into other parts of Book II and into Books III, IV, and V. Another way of approaching this episode is through Phaedria's successfully deployed arguments to stop a combat between Cymochles and Guyon: these relate, with elaborate verbal parallels, but with a more important difference, to a similarly successful intervention on the part of Medina earlier in Book II. Yet a third approach depends upon the biblical context of Phaedria's obvious use, or rather misuse, of the parable of the lilies of the field, and brings us to yet a sixth primary instance of symbolic vegetation. Of these three kinds of relationship, the first is the most elaborate and extensive.

We first meet Cymochles lying upon a bed of what are in fact lilies (II.v.32.3), pouring out his "idle mind / In daintie delices, and lavish joyes," [1] in the island of Acrasia, far in the sea. This island is the Bower of Bliss. A Circe-figure, Acrasia unmans her lovers and turns them from reasonable beings to beasts through the voluptuousness which she offers. Cymochles is her servant. He has been reduced to near-somnolence by lustful pleasures and by the delights of gentle breezes and running water. He pretends to sleep, but in fact watches through barely opened eyes a wanton flock of damsels and boys. He lecherously connives in accepting whatever amorous stimulation he can get from the scene. Glances, words, kisses (softly embrewing "The sugared licuor through his melting lips") are directed at him. One girl bares herself to the hips before him; another, competitively aroused, strips off everything. His mistress's name means "want of power," "debility," "incontinence," "lack of self-control"; he lies by choice on this sea-surrounded isle, and his own name signifies in its first two syllables the waves of the sea, ceaselessly fluctuating, purposeless, fruitless, formless. Over him stretches an arbor of flowers framed in ivy, intertwined with "pricking" eglantine and roses. The arbor is a work of art, or artifice, not nature, for art strives here to compete with nature and to surpass it (v.29.1–2). His arms are cast aside. In one sense he is Mars who has been reduced to impotence by Venus.[2] In the great Renaissance commonplace, he has forsaken honor for pleasure.

Nevertheless, he is a man of great ability, tied to others by established social obligations which he can be brought to remember and acknowledge. A squire named Atin, who has been searching for him, now comes upon him and pricks him with a spear. Atin (meaning "challenge," "defiance")[3] is the attendant upon Cymochles's brother-knight Pyrochles, who suffers from a defect opposite to his sibling's. He is wrathful and vengeful, always seeking occasion for combat, for he conceives of no satisfaction beyond surpassing others and can endure no one's surpassing him. He lives for honor, but that honor is a false and invidious one, for it has nothing to do with socially useful achievement, everything to do with the irritable desire to dominate and never to be dominated. When decisively conquered he turns to the bitter luxury of self-destruction: he later tries to kill himself, but cannot, in the lazy waves in which his brother luxuriates, and still later he casts a final defiance in the teeth of Arthur, obliging that good man, an instrument of Grace itself, to behead him, removing the seat of the reason of which he had already deprived himself. His name has in its root the Greek for "fire," as his brother's is connected with water. Atin arouses Cymochles temporarily to what is apparently his duty: vengeance for an only brother, who is believed by his squire already to have been dispatched by Guyon, the hero of Book II.

When he is blocked in his ensuing wrathful progress by a body of water, Cymochles sees Phaedria on it in her small boat. Mounted on this vessel is a shelter of intertwined branches, which seems natural but is in fact woven together by the most skillful of technical means (i.e., by "art," vi.2) so as to conceal all artifice. Promising him transport, she separates him from the spirit of irascibility who has been guiding him. Atin must stay behind, much against his will. Phaedria ("bright," "gleaming," "beaming with joy," "joyous," "jocund," from Greek *phaidros*) conveys him swiftly across the waves, with which his name is connected, to her island—a floating one— where, easily deflected from his purpose by her wanton laughter, he is soon sunk in the same forgetfulness in which we found him. He had been wading "in still waves of deep delight," slumbering on lilies on Acrasia's island; he is now put to sleep by a lily-song on Phaedria's island among the sluggish waves of Idle Lake. This island appears to be "picked out" by Nature "from all the rest" (II.vi.12); but, as will appear, it is, in fact like Acrasia's island, "pickt out by" those "that natures work by art can imitate" (xii.42). We know that, much like her boat, even her own voice strives to surpass "native musicke by her skilfull art" (vi.25).

> The lilly, Ladie of the flowring field,
>> The Flowre-deluce, her lovely Paramoure,
>> Bid thee to them thy fruitlesse labours yield,

And soone leave off this toylesome wearie stoure;
Loe loe how brave she decks her bounteous boure,
With silken curtens and gold coverlets,
Therein to shrowd her sumptuous Belamoure,
Yet neither spinnes nor cardes, ne cares nor frets,
But to her mother Nature all her care she lets.

(II.vi.16)

This is the central stanza of Phaedria's lily-song. A modern, sophisticated reader of the Renaissance lyric is likely to pause over it in sad perplexity What can one make of a poet engaged in attempting a delicate lyrical feat who asks us to imagine a lily mating with a flower of a different species? Herrick, Marvell, Donne, Cowley, Milton, and Jonson (not to go beyond the mother tongue) have their flower-lyrics, but none of them is guilty of anything so arbitrary, or indeed so grotesque, as this. We may recognize that Spenser shows us Phaedria singing a song about a lily partly because a song about a rose is later to be sung in the presence of her mistress Acrasia, and we may go beyond this in perceiving that the rose-song is intended to establish an axis of polarity with the self-perpetuating flowers of the Garden of Adonis, which in turn relate to a larger system. Notwithstanding, outraged poetic sensibility stands stock-still at the verbal level to demand satisfaction from a poet who appears to have stooped to the facile quick profit of a lushly sensuous, but poetically unspecific and abstract, merely impressionistic, effect of color and tactility in asking us to imagine a lily's having a fleur-de-lis (whatever that is) for a paramour.

We cannot begin to save the case by showing that a "flower-de-luce" is just another lily, although its true identity leads us incidentally to an etymological discovery. Spenser would certainly have recognized the association of this word with the arms of the French monarchy, the grouped fleurs-de-lis, which were sometimes (but by no means always)[4] associated with lilies. His follower Drayton makes Henry V talk of lopping the French lilies in "The Ballad of Agincourt" (line 48). Our form "fleur-de-lis" itself, however, is not known in English until the nineteenth century. A "flower-de-luce" "flour-de-lys," etc., is properly an iris, and the first of these forms is sometimes so recognized in American English to this day.[5] The word was fancifully etymologized in English-speaking areas in the late Middle Ages and the sixteenth century, because English, unlike French, possesses for "lily" no native word which in resembling "luce" or "lys" would offer a ready-made explanation of how "flower-de-luce" or "flour-de-lys" arose. One of these etymologies (of which there are only two) appears in the usual Anglo-Latin name for this flower, *Flos* (*Flor-*) *deliciae* or *deliciarum,*[6] "flower of pleasure(s)" or "of delight(s)" (perhaps with an overtone of "sweetheart," "leman," for English readers of Catullus).[7] The other of these fanciful etymologies is given by the Anglo-Latin *Flos* (*Flor-*) *de luce,* "flower of light."[8] It seems likely that Spenser would have been aware of both these explanations of the name of the flower. We have happened upon the felicity, then, that a girl whose name is derived from a Greek word meaning "bright" and "joyous" sings a song in the action of which the paramour's name by an etymologically different path associates the same two concepts of light and pleasure. We may add to this that the "daintie delices, and lavish joyes" in which we first found Cymochles probably chime together by intention with two of the words which we have just listened to. Yet, while agreeable, this conclusion does not get us over the main difficulty of the apparently careless, imaginatively almost impossible, mating of two species of plants.

Medieval allegorical traditions, as over against those of the Renaissance lyric, may be called in but are not ultimately of much help in this case. It can indeed be said that the opposition which is only nominally possible between the two parties of the Chaucerian *Flower and the Leaf* remains pleasing even though flowers do not in their own persons feel a prejudice against leaves, or vice versa. Chaucer's flower-lady Alceste in the Prologue to *The Legend of Good Women* is charming, even though she can be associated with the daisy only for a nonce-purpose. More to the point, perhaps, there is no difficulty, in terms of the informing conceit of *Le Roman de la rose,* in accepting the flower-metaphor of that poem's concluding episode, in which the successful climax of a courtship is mimed with the items a man, a staff, and a rose. With greater decorum, Dunbar's "The Thrissil and the Rois" successfully represents a marriage combining the royal houses of Scotland and England, by describing the alliance of the heraldic flowers of the two houses, the thistle having a protective role in relation to the gentler flower.

In Spenser's song, however, no such monarchical symbolism validates the notion of one flower's being shrouded in the petals of another of different species, and, in a more general sense, the particular lyrical character of this stanza makes rather different demands in terms of imagery from those of these longer poems. A song awakens no expectations of elaborate figurative preparation, as do such poems, or as does the more closely woven intellectual texture of a sonnet. The image should have a traditional universality or an immediate concrete application, and the mating of a magnificent male iris with a richly furnished lily seems to meet neither of these requirements.

Nevertheless, the heraldic form of the fleur-de-lis, resembling the flag of an iris, in the French royal arms and in many others, is probably the key to an image of high specificity and concreteness which Spenser intended to set, in the sixth canto of Book II, against the now generally recognized sexual image of the Mount of Venus, or *mons Veneris*, of the Garden of Adonis in the sixth canto of Book III, which we shall come to in due course. What Phaedria has in mind when she speaks of love is plainly what St. Paul means by chambering and wantonness. In her song she gives silken curtains and gold coverlets to the lily to "shrowd her sumptuous Belamoure"; when she speaks later (vi.34) of the joys of love, she does so in Propertian accents of physicality, like those used by Campion in one passage of "My sweetest Lesbia," [9] referring to the act itself. When Mars spends the passing hours in amours, it is not conventional war and conventional weapons that she calls for:

> Another warre, and other weapons I
> Doe love, where love does give his sweet alarmes,
> Without bloudshed, and where the enemy
> Does yeeld unto his foe a pleasant victory.
>
> (vi.34.6–9)

It is in accord with Phaedria's quality that at the core of her imagination should be the human physical act of sex itself, executed in terms of the highly artificial and sophisticated conception of one sumptuous flower fitted within another lavish one. A simpler and entirely natural tradition comes close to what she means. An English flower of moist situations, resembling the American Jack-in-the-Pulpit, is called "Lords and Ladies." Within its white, lilylike, hollow cone, and running down to the flower's base, stands a single erect, dark pistil. The etymology is quite plain: the country folk who gave the flower this name had their own opinion of how lords and ladies occupied their entitled leisure. Phaedria's parallel, but artificial, notion depends on the heraldic image of the fleur-de-lis which has been fixed since the High Middle Ages as three petals or leaves, the central one erect, the other two curving right and left away from it, the whole joined at the base by a horizontal band. This indeed resembles the flag of the iris, but it can also be easily seen as a phallic image. What Phaedria sees in the nontoiling, nonspinning state of the lily's golden and silken shroud and of the latter's splendid paramour is simply an eternity of sexual pleasure, like the bliss of the Bower and the joy of Malecasta's Castle Joyeous (the latter to enter the discussion shortly); that is, what she objectifies in her image is sex laid on lavishly with maximum artifice.

To the question, then, of how we may accept poetically the

notion of a lily mating with a flower-de-luce, the answer is that we ought not to, but that through the agency of that image we are being presented with something else of a precision and specificity equal to what we first required: a shallow mind creating a highly unnatural and artfully obscene picture which disguises itself as natural and hides among the manifestations of Nature herself, thus profaned.

In the island of Acrasia, mistress of Phaedria and Cymochles, the most powerful technical means of a sense-deceiving art similarly strive to create an appearance of the natural. The best available practitioners have been retained: "A place pickt out by choice of best alive, / That natures work by art can imitate" (II.xii.42). When Guyon arrives here, in the last canto of Book II, the situation is analogous to that in the episode of Phaedria, but instead of a climax in a developed lily symbol, the development here culminates in the rose, for a reason which will soon be apparent. Acrasia and her new lover Verdant recline in the center of the seagirt island on a bed of roses, and a song about a rose is sung in their presence. As to Cymochles in his earlier visit, two girls have exposed their attractions to Guyon by turns, this time while they are bathing in the overflow from a central fountain. Upon this fountain itself is found ivy, like that previously found in the arbor over Cymochles's head, but the imitation of nature by a competitive and deceptive art is now made more explicit. The prurient tendrils of the plant are made of hard, mineral gold, colored expertly so as to suggest the most palpitantly living organic matter:

> And over all, of purest gold was spred,
> A trayle of yvie in his native hew:
> For the rich mettall was so coloured,
> That wight, who did not well avis'd it vew,
> Would surely deeme it to be yvie trew:
> Low his lascivious armes adown did creepe,
> That themselves dipping in the silver dew,
> Their fleecy flowres they tenderly did steepe,
> Which drops of Christall seemd for wantones to weepe.
>
> (xii.61)

So it is, as well, with some of the grapes on the vine from which the porter Excesse prepares a cup that she offers to all comers; and the weight of this gold is such as perilously to overburden the boughs provided by nature:

> And them amongst, some were of burnisht gold,
> So made by art, to beautifie the rest,
> Which did themselves emongst the leaves enfold,
> As lurking from the vew of covetous guest,

> That the weake bowes, with so rich load opprest,
> Did bow adowne, as over-burdened.
>
> (xii.55.1–6)

The principle on which the Bower is made attractive is that all stimuli should be intensified up to the breaking point, as though "With all the ornaments of *Floraes* pride, / Wherewith her mother Art, as halfe in scorne / Of niggard Nature, like a pompous bride / Did decke her, and too lavishly adorne" (an observation which applies just as strongly to Phaedria's gilding of the lily).

The great preoccupation of the artful supporters of this symbolic landscape is the evanescence of time, and the need to grasp sensual pleasure, as already defined by Phaedria, with an opportunism which in the event turns out to be murderously callous towards others. At the entry to the Bower of Bliss, as in so many other places in it, Spenser at first follows the description of Armida's garden in Tasso's *Gerusalemme liberata*, XVI. For the symbolic figures represented on the gate of the Bower, however, he discards Tasso's instances of man deserting honor for voluptuousness, and substitutes the enormities committed by the lover Medea in order to get and keep her sensual bliss. First, Medea drops the gobbets of the flesh of her dismembered younger brother from her ship to deflect her father's pursuit of her and her lover Jason; then, at a later point, she employs a stratagem to burn to death Jason's new love and affianced bride (xii.45). By a similar stratagem, as recorded in the first canto of Book II, Acrasia has caused the death of her former lover Mordant when his wife had temporarily recovered him, and sorrow for this bloody deed has provoked the suicide of this wife. The "death" which stands written in his name is replaced in the name of Acrasia's new lover by a signification of youthful growth and new hope—"Verdant." He, too, at the time of Guyon's arrival, is being blighted in this garden of only artfully simulated natural delight, as Cymochles, son of "Acrates" (II.iv.41.6; cf. "Acrasia"), had previously been shown to be wholly blighted (cf. v.28):

> His warlike armes, the idle instruments
>   Of sleeping praise, were hong upon a tree,
>   And his brave shield, full of old moniments,
>   Was fowly ra'st, that none the signes might see;
>   Ne for them, ne for honour cared hee,
>   Ne ought, that did to his advancement tend,
>   But in lewd loves, and wastfull luxuree,
>   His dayes, his goods, his bodie he did spend:
> O horrible enchantment, that him so did blend.
>
> (xii.80)

In Western culture the lyrical reminder of the mortal brevity of beauty has probably been more frequently expressed by the symbol of the rose than by any other, but what the rose is meant logically to support in Acrasia's garden is a culpable lie: so short is our time to love, says her sect, that by implication the fatal accompaniments of desire here, murder and the reduction of man's reason to beastliness, are justified if only we may prolong the one moment of bliss. As in the lily-song, we hear of the furnishing forth of a bedchamber, and of the physical act of sex itself with a paramour:

> So passeth, in the passing of a day,
> Of mortall life the leafe, the bud, the flowre,
> Ne more doth flourish after first decay,
> That earst was sought to decke both bed and bowre,
> Of many a Ladie, and many a Paramowre:
> Gather therefore the Rose, whilest yet is prime,
> For soone comes age, that will her pride deflowre:
> Gather the Rose of love, whilest yet is time,
> Whilest loving thou mayst loved be with equall crime.
>   (xii.75)

True Nature, as against the false artifices of a lying pornography, denies the premise. It is indeed true that each of us is bounded within his mortal prison and can live and love only briefly, yet the act of love itself is bound up with a circumstance that mitigates this hard fate and justifies (not only for dupes but also for the wise) a large-minded generosity towards others, not Acrasia's single-minded, murderous defense of her prey. In love we may beget copies of ourselves who engage our profound affection and in a sense continue us. They, too, will love and beget others, and each life bound by time may, for man's existence and throughout organic nature, become timeless. Of this timelessness the chief organic witness around us is the return of vegetation—of, for instance, the roses and the lilies—after their deaths, with the revolving year. The primeval tragedy of the descent of the Idea from the eternal and infinite into the bounded universe of temporal mutability and finite extension receives its classic mitigation in similar terms in the theory recorded in Plato's *Timaeus*. The Demiurge there arranges that the phenomenon of change in the universe should be circular and cyclical, so that all things, pitifully declining and perishable though they are, should by changing return upon themselves and continue the cycle afresh. Having lost the primeval true eternity of divine perfection, they yet are dowered with an eternity of recurrence, and the accomplishment of that eternity is through love.

It is in Mutabilitie, the incomplete seventh book of *The Faerie Queene*, that Spenser mounts his chief celebration of this circumstance

for the heavens above and the earth below; but for the life of our
species and its mirroring in the organic life of the animal and particularly of the vegetable kingdoms, the chief celebration in *The
Faerie Queene* takes place in the third of the moralized landscapes
to come under our view here: the Garden of Adonis in III.vi.

Here all is truly in accord with Nature, and a lying artifice has
no place. In "so faire a place as Nature can devize," "all the goodly
flowres, / Wherewith dame Nature doth her beautifie, / And decks
the girlonds of her paramoures / Are fetcht." "Franckly each paramour
his leman knowes," with emphasis on "franckly" and on the natural,
uninstitutionalized, physically sexual meanings of "leman" and
"knowes." As we have just pointed out, the arbor over Cymochles
had been of artfully arranged ivy with eglantine woven through it;
the same image of licentious ivy, artfully fabricated of gold, re-
appeared on the fountain of the Bower of Bliss, and the vines were
painfully bowed down by the weight of seeming grapes fashioned of
the heaviest metal. All of this now appears in a new guise:

> And in the thickest covert of that shade,
>> There was a pleasant arbour, not by art,
>> But of the trees owne inclination made,
>> Which knitting their rancke braunches part to part,
>> With wanton yvie twyne entrayld athwart,
>> And Eglantine, and Caprifole emong,
>> Fashioned above within their inmost part.
>
> (III.vi.44.1–7)

The generalization affirmed by Acrasia's song is here reaffirmed
up to a point, for Time cannot be denied:

> For formes are variable and decay,
> By course of kind, and by occasion;
> And that faire flowre of beautie fades away,
> As doth the lilly fresh before the sunny ray.
>
> (vi.38.6–9)

Yet Nature through her traditional helper and priest Genius [10] sees to
it that the supplies are constantly replenished, both of plants and of
human beings. Correspondingly, beneath that arbor just described, on
a hill in the center of the Garden (and of Book III) [11] lies a cave in
which Venus preserves her lover and can, unlike Acrasia, enjoy him
eternally. He is Adonis, the dying and reborn god, one of the chief
symbols of pagan antiquity for the rebirth of vegetation in the springtime. A Garden of Adonis is in the first instance a bowl of earth in
which grass-seed is ritually allowed to spring up as an earnest of the
return of the year after the desolation of winter. Adonis is described
as the "Father of all formes,"

> And sooth it seemes they say: for he may not
> For ever die, and ever buried bee
> In balefull night, where all things are forgot;
> All be he subject to mortalitie,
> Yet is eterne in mutabilitie,
> And by succession made perpetuall.
>
> (vi.47.1–6)

New shapes are continually imposed in the Garden upon the same enduring matter, of which the old shapes have had continually to pass away (vi.38). The myth here is the same as in the earlier part of this canto, where the annual encourager of plant life, the sun, is described as the "Great father" "of generation" to whom his sister the moon provides fit matter for the new living shapes (vi.9). In V.vii (Isis Church) there appears a similar image of sun and moon in cooperation, there equated with Osiris and Isis, who are both brother and sister and man and wife: Phoebus, correspondingly, is Phoebe's brother in III.vi, and Adonis is Venus's leman. The place where he knows her, in the central mount, is the hill of Venus, the *mons Veneris*, the central point of the female anatomy and the seat of pleasure. For Phaedria's tarted up bottle-and-stopper of the lily and the flower-de-luce is substituted a far graver symbol of unashamed physical pleasure in which account is taken of the moral and biological fact of the relation of this pleasure to the perpetuation of our race.

The next of the moralized landscapes to be considered here is a further rendition of the story of Venus and Adonis, this time in its picturesquely pretty Ovidian form. This appears on a tapestry (III.i.34–38) of Castle Joyeous, the abode of Malecasta. Suitably, it is a reversion to the egotistical and shallow formulae of Phaedria and Acrasia. The "joy" in the castle's name is a synonym for the "bliss" of Acrasia's Bower and the "joyfulness" to be found in the name "Phaedria" and the fanciful etymology *Flos deliciae*. "Malecasta" signifies "badly chaste," "unchaste." In the tapestry Venus woos Adonis to be "her Paramoure," "making girlonds of each flowre that grew," and leading him away from the sunlight and from "heavens vew" and his companions into secret and un-frank darkness. When he bathes, she, like Cymochles, craftily spies on "each dainty lim," and then throws "sweet Rosemaryes, / And fragrant violets, and Pances trim" into the water that holds him. Finally he is killed by the boar and transmuted "to a dainty flowre." She "Makes for him endlesse mone." *Finita la stòria*: there is no trace of the shackled boar and of the eternity in mutability of the classic rendition of Nature's truth in the Garden of Adonis. The flower here, like the other components of the story, and like the contents of the Bower, only appears to possess the lineaments of living nature, and is in truth a lying artifact, "Which in that cloth was wrought, as if it lively grew."

The great strength of the ingenuous, straightforward sex of the Garden of Adonis, as against all the other instances which we have discussed so far, is that it belongs to Nature; no sophistications of a feigning art pervert it. Yet it remains true that an acquired art of another kind in the management of personal relationships is universally acknowledged (although not universally practiced) as a necessary civilized complement to the stubbornly insistent libidinal urge with which we are naturally endowed. This art, in accordance with which natural affection is sublimated and amplified into a wise and friendly respect for the freedom and independence of those whom we love, is not a denial of nature but its perfecting. This desirable added dimension in our lives together is Spenser's concern in yet another allegorical locale, the Isle and Temple of Venus in canto x of Book IV, Of Friendship. In the other parts of this book, a number of the components of this moralized landscape are covertly supplied or reinforced in the course of chivalric adventure, which forms the other great category of narrative in *The Faerie Queene* in addition to *paysage moralisé*. Consequently, it is worthwhile in this instance to take a somewhat roundabout path via a brief selection of these adventures, in reaching the relevant flower-image in this landscape.

In the story in Book IV of the two friends Amyas and Placidas and their two loves Aemylia and Poeana, the libidinous prickings of natural desire are in the end complemented, through Arthur's agency, by mutual kindliness and friendship. The development is thus described in the case of Poeana:

> She whom Nature did so faire create,
> That she mote match the fairest of her daies,
> Yet with lewd loves and lust intemperate
> Had it defaste; thenceforth reformed her waies,
> That all men much admyrde her change, and spake her praise.
>
> (IV.ix.16.5–9)

Earlier in IV, "natural" [12] competitiveness for a love-object is similarly sublimated into friendly love in the story of the knights Cambell and Triamond and the damsels Canace and Cambina, when Cambina magically works a harmony between the contending knights while she bears a wand of two intertwined serpents crowned with a circular wreath. As a result, both natural love and acquired friendship bind the four together for life. Finally, and also in IV, the "Amazonian" lady-knight Britomart, the heroine of the whole central section of *The Faerie Queene*, adumbrates the self-sufficiency of a loving relationship where man and woman are bound by both nature and mental sympathy and accommodation. More than once, she enacts both a male and a female role in just such a group of four as the two groups which I have just described, but a single example of her bisexuality will suffice here. In a short, preliminary episode which sets the four-group pattern for Book IV, she first gains lodging for herself (as, apparently, a male knight) and for Amoret, the lady whom she is protecting, in a castle where it is the custom that no knight is accommodated unless he is accompanied by a lady whom he has in his charge. Britomart gains this shelter and entertainment by overcoming in fixed combat a young knight who had challenged her for Amoret in the hope of gaining board and room for himself at the end of the day. She and Amoret are thus assured of a place to stay, but Amoret's gratitude is tempered by her extreme fear that her protector (a male, as far as she knows) may molest her sexually: loving another knight, Amoret is in the socially uncomfortable position of having reason to feel both extreme gratitude for, and extreme fear of, the menacing strength of her companion. On the other hand the young knight is suffering extreme physical discomfort. After having been knocked violently from his horse he has nothing to look forward to but a supperless night in the open. Britomart, however, now proceeds to the friendly gesture which accords "all former strife." In the presence of her hosts she removes her helmet, allowing her blonde hair to flow down around her body to her heels, so as to create a miraculous effect, as though she were divine and as though a shower of falling stars had struck "common peoples sight" as "prodigious" (i.13.9). She then declares that she will be lady to the young knight as she has been knight to Amoret. He is fed and lodged, and consequently abounds in friendly gratitude; Amoret on her side is relieved and grateful to discover that the manly power of Britomart has a womanly base offering nothing but friendship to herself. One man, one woman, and an individual who seems to play the roles of both sexes are knit in concord.

Almost all of the motifs of these various incidents are united in the Isle and Temple of Venus in canto x. To enter the Isle, victory in fixed combat is required, but when this and certain other initial difficulties are past, the victor finds friendly concord within. A figure of the goddess Venus herself stands upon the central altar of the temple, partly hidden with a veil because she possesses both male and female organs (The hermaphrodite was a chief symbol in the Renaissance of harmonious wholeness and friendship, particularly in marriage).[13] A serpent, its tail in its mouth, encircles her legs, suggesting harmonious and loving concord in the same fashion as do the circular wreath and intertwined serpents of Cambina. Outside the temple, in the landscape of this island, the fulfillment of natural libidinal attraction in the ex-

quisite mental sympathy and willingly yielded mutual accommoda-
tions of an enduring intimate relationship is embodied in the complementary relation between nature and art. Even the natural force of
the current of the river bounding the island seems to serve the purpose of the artful constructor of the bridge reaching to it, as the
water murmurs softly in running past "The goodly workes" of the
artisans' bridge-piers; and the Isle itself is

> The onely pleasant and delightfull place,
> That ever troden was of footings trace.
> For all that nature by her mother wit
> Could frame in earth, and forme of substance base,
> Was there, and all that nature did omit,
> Art playing second natures part, supplyed it.
> (IV.x.21.4-9)

Above all, moreover, the landscape, with all its natural vegetation
and flowers (at which we now arrive) is cast in an artful pattern,
part formal garden, part "romantically" formulated landscape as
though mounted by Capability Brown:

> Fresh shadowes, fit to shroud from sunny ray;
> Faire lawnds, to take the sunne in season dew;
> Sweet springs, in which a thousand Nymphs did play;
> Soft rombling brookes, that gentle slomber drew;
> High reared mounts, the lands about to vew;
> Low looking dales, disloignd from common gaze;
> Delightfull bowres, to solace lovers trew;
> False Labyrinthes, fond runners eyes to daze;
> All which by nature made did nature selfe amaze.
>
> And all without were walkes and alleyes dight
> With divers trees, enrang'd in even rankes;
> And here and there were pleasant arbors pight,
> And shadie seates, and sundry flowring bankes,
> To sit and rest the walkers wearie shankes,
> And therein thousand payres of lovers walkt,
> Praysing their god, and yeelding him great thankes,
> Ne ever ought but of their true loves talkt,
> Ne ever for rebuke or blame of any balkt.
> (x.24,25)

The artificial vegetation of the island of the Bower of Bliss, and,
in turn, the exuberantly natural pullulating verdure of the Garden of
Adonis, give way here to a nature fulfilled in human, ethical terms by
cultivation. Much more intimately and variously than I have had time
to say, each of these "nuclear" landscapes at which we have looked
shares in the world of various characters' loves and adventures outside

its confines and in its particular Book. We shall not have time, either, to pursue here the further development of the motif of vegetation in the final moralized landscape of this series, the Temple of Isis, in V.vii, where the "fruitful vine" (vii.11) becomes turbulent, discordant, male force, moving Britomart's lover Artegall (under the form of a crocodile who is also Osiris and, temporarily, Bacchus-dominated) to attempt to dominate her [14] as Amoret's lover Scudamour had so unpropitiously mastered Amoret in the very Temple of Venus. Instead, we now turn back to another aspect of the episode of Phaedria with which we started, in order to see how it relates to yet another part of Spenser country.

Cymochles is no sooner drowned in sleep by Phaedria's lily-song than she descries a new subject for her attentions. Guyon, the hero of the Book of Temperance, arrives with his attendant, the palmer Reason, at the edge of the Idle Lake, and accepts her transport (II.vi.19). She separates him just as dexterously from his wise companion as she had separated Cymochles from the provoking and irascible force of Atin, but in the event Guyon's natural temperance saves him from his predecessor's fate. Although she sequesters him physically on her island, her most accomplished techniques fail to hold his attention or make him swerve from his purpose, and she resolves to disencumber herself of her embarrassing guest by ferrying him onward. At just that point, Cymochles awakes. Aroused temporarily by the jealous fury of the sensual man, he immediately assaults Guyon, who defends himself with equal energy but not equal loss of self-control.

Phaedria's fairly quick intervention in the combat seems to show her most attractive side. The description of this intervention begins a series of verbal and rhetorical parallels to corresponding passages in the apparently similar but in reality profoundly more charitable intervention of Medina, in canto ii of the same book, in the three-sided battle among Guyon, Huddibras, and Sans-Loy, where Guyon, again, fights unwillingly. It will be instructive to show the parallel passages side by side. Despite the similarity between the two interventions, Phaedria is only apparently a mediator. She does not intervene until Cymochles is about to be defeated (vi.29–32). She is in reality of his party, and her action, like everything else about her, achieves breathtaking natural affectiveness only because she mobilizes the astounding technical virtuosity of her art. Medina, on the other hand, is all natural sensibility, and she is a truly just mediator:

Still as he stood, faire
    Phaedria, that beheld
That deadly daunger, soone
    atweene them ran;
	Whilst thus they mingled were
	    in furious armes,
	The faire *Medina* with her
	    tresses torne,

And at their feet her selfe
   most humbly feld,
Crying with pitteous voice,
   and count'nance wan.
If ever love of Ladie did
   empierce
Your yron brestes, or pittie
   could find place,
Withhold your bloudie hands
   from battel fierce.
        (II.vi.32.1–4;33.1–3)

And naked brest, in pitty of
   their harmes,
Emongst them ran, and falling
   them beforne,
Besought them by the womb,
   which had them borne,
And by the loves, which were
   to them most deare,
And by their knighthood,
   which they sure had sworne,
Their deadly cruell discord
   to forbeare.
        (II.ii.27.1–8)

Phaedria, be it noted, appeals to man's love for woman, and to pity; Medina adds to this the source of life and also the knights' truly honorable vocation. Almost immediately after these initial appeals, both women employ the encomiastic epithet, rhetorical question, and paradox:

Ah well away, most noble
   Lords, how can
Your cruell eyes endure
   so pitteous sight,
To shed your lives on ground?
   wo worth the man,
That first did teach the
   cursed steele to bight
In his owne flesh, and make
   way to the living spright.
        (vi.32.5–9)

Ah puissant Lords, what
   cursed evill Spright,
Or fell *Erinnys*, in your
   noble harts
Her hellish brond hath
   kindled with despight,
And stird you up to worke
   your wilful smarts?
Is this the joy of armes?
   be these the parts
Of glorious knighthood, after
   blood to thrust?
        (ii.29.1–6)

The two argue almost in parallel against strife, with only the most delicately controlled distinction between their two different preferences:

Debatefull strife, and
   cruell enmitie
The famous name of knighthood fowly shend;
But lovely peace, and
   gentle amitie,
And in Amours the passing
   houres to spend,
The mightie martiall hands
   doe most commend:

Ne ought the prayse of prowesse
   more doth marre,
Then fowle revenging rage,
   and base contentious jarre.
But lovely concord, and most
   sacred peace

Doth nourish vertue, and fast
   friendship breeds;
Weake she makes strong, and

Of love they ever greater
  glory bore
Then of their armes.
              (vi.35.1–7)

strong thing does increace,
Till it the pitch of highest
  prayse exceeds.
              (ii.30.8–9;31.1–4)

As well, each introduces war as a paradoxical metaphor for the activity which each prefers, and names that activity's reward:

Another warre, and other
  weapons I
Doe love, where love does
  give his sweet alarmes,
Without bloudshed, and
  where the enemy
Does yeeld unto his foe a
  pleasant victory.
              (vi.34.6–9)

Brave be [Concord's] warres,
  and honorable deeds,
By which she triumphes over
  ire and pride,
And winnes an Olive girlond
  for her meeds.
              (ii.31.5–7)

Both women are similarly successful in their appeals:

Therewith she sweetly smyld.
  They though full bent
To prove extremities of
  bloudie fight,
Yet at her speach their
  rages gan relent,
And calme the sea of their
  tempestuous spight,
Such powre have pleasing
  words: such is the might
Of courteous clemencie in
  gentle hart.
              (vi.36.1–6)

Her gracious wordes their
  rancour did appall,
And suncke so deepe into
  their boyling breasts,
That downe they let their
  cruell weapons fall,
And lowly did abate their
  loftie crests,
To her faire presence,
  and discrete behests.
              (ii.32.1–5)

The difference between these mediators and their intercessions is of great structural significance, not solely because the artfulness of the one and the natural truth of the other reinforce a theme that we have already seen extensively used, but because this difference also reinforces no less than the central structural and moral idea of Book II. Phaedria is concerned with only two combatants, Medina with three, who represent the ultimately Platonic triad of the soul. Guyon is temperately reasonable; Huddibras is haughty, prideful, and melancholic, is the irascible, contentious, envious part of the soul, always concerned with the point of honor; Sans-Loy is boldly sensual and ungovernable. These three elements—the temperately reasonable, and, departing from it in two directions, the two forms of excess—reappear again and again in this book; in, for instance, the impatience at pain which leads to Amavia's suicide, and the impotence through pleasure that has doomed her husband Mordant, in canto i; in the Impatience and Impotence who are the two lieutenants of Maleger against the Castle of Alma in canto xi; in Pyrochles and Cymochles themselves; and even in the two forms of ridiculous attack with which Braggadocchio seeks to pervert Belphoebe in iii.38–42. Phaedria, defeating the forces of rancor in Cymochles and, to a less degree, in Guyon, is only one form of excess conquering another, with the inherent advantage that pleasure always possesses over pain (vi.1). She is right, as far as she goes, although she employs her preachments disingenuously for purposes of aiding someone who is only temporarily irascible and belongs in reality to her pleasure-sodden side.

Of the two forms of intemperance, the impotence and forgetfulness of honor and of our obligation to help our neighbors (which items of misbehavior follow from the elevation of the pleasures of the senses to a cult and a drug) reach their most intense form in Acrasia's Bower of Bliss, at the end of Book II, where they are overcome by Guyon. Guyon's overcoming of the most intense form of the opposite kind of excess—prideful, contentious striving for outward honor and high place for their own sakes—brings us to our last instance of the symbols of vegetation. The main form of this vegetation is at the precise center of Book II, in the three stanzas describing the central tree of the Garden of Proserpina. In the first of these stanzas occurs a phrase, "And in the midst thereof," similar to the phrase "Right in the middest" which introduces the central stanza of Book III in the 1590 edition, a stanza describing the central *mons Veneris* of the Garden of Adonis, which we have already discussed. The two gardens are of central importance, one for evil, the other for good. It is by a number of stages that Guyon reaches the Garden of Proserpina. First, on the earth's surface, he meets the tempter who is to bring him there—Mammon.

Surely it is a significant fact that of the two passages in the New Testament through which the figure of Mammon is known, one is in close proximity to the instance of the biblical lilies of the field which Phaedria uses for her own perverted purposes and with which we started. Spenser has so adapted these figures that Phaedria and her lilies stand for one of the two forms of intemperance which we have just mentioned, and Mammon stands for the other. The passage in Matthew 6.24–34,[15] embodying both these references, makes up the Gospel for the day for the fifteenth Sunday after Trinity in the Anglican Book of Common Prayer as Spenser would have heard and seen it (I quote from *The Second Prayer-Book of Edward VI*):

No manne can serve two Masters, for either he shal hate the one, and love the other, or els leane to the one, and despise the other: Ye canne not serve God and Mammon. Therfore I saye unto you; be not carefull for your lyfe, what ye shall eate or what ye shal dryncke: nor yet for your body, what raymente ye shall put on. Is not the life more worthe than meate? and the body more of value than rayment? Beholde the fowles of the ayre, for they sowe not, neither do they reape, nor cary into the barnes; and your heavenly father fedeth them. Are ye not muche better than they? Whiche of you (by takyng carefull thought) coulde adde one cubite unto his stature? And why care ye for rayment: Consider the Lylies of the fielde how they growe. They laboure not; neither do they spynne. And yet I saye unto you, that even Salamon in al his royaltie, was not clothed like one of these. Wherfore, if God so clothe the grasse of the fielde (whiche though it stand to-day, is to-morow caste into the fornace;) shall he not muche more do the same for you, O ye of litle fayth? Therfore, take no thought, saying; What shall we eate, or what shal we drinke, or wherwith shall we be clothed? After all these thynges do the Gentyles seke. For youre heavenlye father knoweth that ye have nede of all these thynges. But rather seeke ye first the kyngdome of heaven, and the righteousnes thereof, and all these thynges shalbe ministred unto you. Care not then for the morow, for the morow shal care for itselfe: Sufficient unto the daye is the travayl thereof.

Mammon almost immediately offers Guyon all the gold that would be necessary to gain honor in the world (II.vii.8–11), to which Guyon replies that true honor follows from honorable deeds, not from graft. He then accompanies Mammon beneath the earth to the latter's "House," annexed to hell, where, in the substance of exactly forty stanzas, he undergoes a course of temptation analogous to Christ's experience of temptation by Satan in the forty days in the desert.[16] Gold is first shown to him there as a means to invidious honor. When this does not make him fall, Mammon takes him to the chamber of his daughter Philotime ("love of honor"), where all the inmates strive to clamber above each other, to and upon a golden chain that reaches upward. Even though Mammon offers him this daughter in marriage (not, certainly, for sensual delight but as a means of getting ahead), Guyon humbly rejects union with a goddess. It is at this point that Mammon screws his offer up to the -nth degree by bringing Guyon into the Garden of Proserpina.

The plants of this anti-*locus amoenus*—our last instance here of this family of images—are all black and poisonous:

> There mournfull *Cypresse* grew in greatest store,
>   And trees of bitter *Gall* and *Heben* sad,
>   Dead sleeping *Poppy*, and blacke *Hellebore*,
>   Mortal *Samnitis*, and *Cicuta* bad,

> With which th'unjust *Atheniens* made to dy
> Wise *Socrates*, who therof quaffing glad
> Pourd out his life, and last Philosophy
> To the faire *Critias* his dearest Belamy.
>
> (vii.52)

The central tree itself bears golden apples, modulating from the temptation to gain honor through money into temptation to an honor of a more exalted kind. Fundamentally, since Guyon here imitates Christ, the second Adam, in refusing the proffered reward, the tree is Edenic; that is, it is the one whose apples Eve and Adam first ate, and, eating, fell. The biblical temptation which Satan offered Eve was that by eating she should become godlike. What, correspondingly, is being put finally before Guyon, who has rejected all temptation to high rank solely for the sake of surpassing other human beings (and not simply for the sake of worthy deeds), is that he should aspire above the human, either by becoming divine or at the least by enviously destroying divinity or aspiring to commerce with it.[17] In the Bower of Bliss, on the contrary, men are invited to descend below the human level, so as to be transformed into beasts. Tantalus (vii.58), up to his chin in the water around the Garden of Proserpina, and reaching unsuccessfully for the useless golden apples, had dared to test the gods' omniscience and to seek acceptance among them by offering them at a banquet a dish composed of his own dismembered son; he now rages at the ingratitude to him of heaven. Pilate, beside him, seeks unsuccessfully to wash his hands in the water and regrets his part in the murder of God, the son of man, killed at the instance of the Jews. Socrates, sometimes regarded in the Renaissance as the precursor of Christ and a godlike man, has been similarly condemned to death by the Athenians. Proserpina had succumbed, like Eve, to the temptation to eat the fruit (not the *malum*, the apple, but the *malum punicum*, or pomegranate) and had thus been forced to live in hell for half of every year; she is included here as a classical counterpart of Eve, and in fact takes the center of the stage. She is seconded by Atalanta (vii.54), interpreted in the *Golden Legend* as the soul of man falling prey to the devil, who, as her suitor, throws three golden apples successively before her in his race with her; and by the beloved of Acontius, of whom a parallel story is told of her downfall through the use of a golden apple by her lover. Paris (vii.55), like Tantalus, had presumptuously mixed in divine affairs, daring to award the prize of a golden apple in a contention among goddesses: he and his city were both destroyed. The fruit of the tree of contention and envy, on its island, is as mortal as the disguisedly golden vegetation and fruit of the island of the Bower of sensual Bliss.

So much, then, for the relation of the episode of Phaedria to that Bower, and to the Garden of Adonis, to Castle Joyeous, to the Isle of Venus, to Isis Temple, and to the Houses of Medina and Mammon. The directions are legion in which relationships, besides those considered here, ray out from this episode. The pleasures and profits of reading Spenser may be compared to those of examining, and for a time living with, the iconographical program of one or another of the greatest medieval cathedrals. With both exuberance and elegance they, and he, affirm the verities of a moral life which is still our own, by embodying these, not so much in individual, perfected corporealizations, as in the network of relations among them; and these mythic embodiments, once implanted in our imaginations, are among the richest and most satisfying heritages of our culture.

In speaking of Spenser's mythic structures it has not been directly to the chief user of this term, the anthropologist Claude Lévi-Strauss (as some readers may have expected), that we have looked for clarification. The application of his categories to Spenser's work does not seem to be immediately illuminating. The only point in *The Faerie Queene* where the distinction, for instance, between the Raw and the Cooked perhaps becomes important is in the Salvage Nation's expectation of eating Serena, and would probably not be of primary interest to that savant. These men are caught up, in VI.viii.37,38, in a discussion in which an incidental consideration seems to be (see 39.9) whether one or the other of these two states would yield them greater relish. Yet from whatever source we may borrow the term, the thing itself—mythic structure, a clothing for still operative moral imperatives—is one of the greatest gifts that Spenser gives us.

6

CAROL V. KASKE   *Spenser's Pluralistic Universe:*
The View from the Mount of Contemplation
(F.Q. I.x)

MOST MODERN READERS distrust a writer, such as Aquinas or Dante, with a unified system that furnishes an answer for everything. While Spenser does give answers, so that C. S. Lewis could maintain that "no poet was ever less like an Existentialist," he often gives contradictory ones and thus is more akin to our present world view than he is to that of Aquinas, Dante, or even Milton. It has been generally recognized that Spenser was interested in various combinations of what Arnold Williams has called "the two matters" of Renaissance art and thought—Christianity and classical culture. Because of this, Spenser is usually characterized as a syncretist, and if this is all syncretism means, he certainly is. But in what ways does he combine the two matters—in a reasoned Aquinian synthesis, in a loose, Ficinesque synthesis, in simple juxtaposition merely evoking a feeling of paradox, or in deliberate opposition taking one side or the other? (Explanations in terms of confusion or failure must of course be tabled as last resorts.) I suggest that while he uses all of these combinations at one time or another, his most basic position, as expressed by three crucial passages, is something else—opposition and yet affirmation of both sides. This qualified relativism of Spenser's should, I believe, be characterized as pluralism. Among literary works, some other specimens which I take to be pluralistic regarding their particular topics are Spenser's own *Fowre Hymnes*, Blake's *Songs of Innocence and Experience*, and, as extreme examples, *The Ring and the Book* and Akutagawa's "In a Grove," basis of the film *Rashomon*.

The most obvious though perhaps not the most conclusive evidence of pluralism in *The Faerie Queene* is its multiple structure. As Spenser's *Letter to Ralegh* will tell anyone who does not know it already, *The Faerie Queene* is an epic involving not one but many heroes, each in a discrete plot for the most part confined to one book, except that Britomart's and Artegall's plots are entwined with each other by a love-intrigue. This structure has taxed critics from the very beginning to find an aesthetic unity.[1] Of course, some doubts about unity are unresolvable due to the unfinished state of the work; but the additive structure allows nearly every one of the plots—for example Redcrosse's—to be for all practical purposes completed before the next one starts, so that the solvable problem of structure largely cancels out the insoluble one of incompleteness. Since, at least by the end of his book or plot, each hero is normative with respect to one virtue though segregated from the others, a corresponding hetero-geneity of thought is implied. Furthermore, a hero may be from either the Briton or the Faery race—a dichotomy which will take up most of our attention in this essay. I propose that Spenser chose this struc-ture not merely "for the more variety of the history," but because he felt that not all virtues are compatible. In particular, Spenser seems to have felt it impossible to embody all virtues in a single person as Virgil almost did in his Aeneas. True, precisely this was to have been the function of Prince Arthur according to the *Letter to Ralegh*—to comprehend all virtue in that overarching virtue which seeks the glory due one's merits. But in actual practice, Arthur comes across as more a link than a synthesis: he appears in each book as the perfec-tion of its titular virtue; and in the Book of Chastity he lacks even that, as the contrast between his distractibility and Britomart's stead-fastness shows (III.i.19.1–2). Spenser seems either to have failed in his announced plan for Arthur or more likely to have changed his plan, as he clearly did regarding the beginnings of Books II and III.

Book also differs from book. It is generally recognized that the philosophical point of view in *The Faerie Queene* somehow shifts from the exclusively Christian in Book I to the broadly humanistic in the later books. Then from Book II on, there is a progression from in-ward to outward virtues. The virtues of the later books may roughly be categorized as: II, Temperance, Aristotelian; III–IV, Good Love and Friendship, a combination of courtly and Neoplatonic like that found in the *Roman de la Rose*; V, Justice, Aristotelian; VI, the Courtesy of the courtesy-books. It is possible that Spenser conceived these differences between books in terms of successive genres. Certain books clearly fit into one genre and are labelled as such by allusions to specific models: Book VI is recognized to be pastoral, and its character Meliboe is from Virgil's *Eclogues* (I; III.1; V.87; VII); Books III–IV have close affinities with romance and romance-epic, and the odd word *belaccoyle* (IV.vi.25.4) is the name of a character in the *Roman de la Rose*; II is in many ways modeled on epic, and

Guyon's voyage to the Bower of Bliss reenacts the *Odyssey,* etc. Many medieval and Renaissance poets seem to have been willing in a larger way to pare down their personal Christianity to the requirements of the genre they were writing in, since obviously not all poems by Christians inculcate, though few deny, the distinctively Christian ideals. Spenser, however, goes further by performing the shifts within the same poem; and I will show that he portrays not only differences but contradictions between his world views, sometimes within a single passage.

There are three apparently pluralistic passages in *The Faerie Queene,* all involving the Christian perspective and some competitor to it. Two of them contrast British and Faery attitudes toward fame and toward the human condition—the debate between and within Redcrosse and the Hermit Contemplation as to whether Cleopolis is compatible with the New Jerusalem (I.x), and the contrasting chronicles of Britain and Fairyland (II.x). Third, Nature and the Christian poet-speaker provide differing answers to the problem of Mutabilitie in the conclusion of the poem as we have it. Besides these three passages, Spenser calls attention to the differences between books by capsule contrasts—treatments of the same topic that differ, or even verbally contradict each other, according to the viewpoints of their respective books. I will take up these evidences in reverse order, giving my last and closest attention to the debate over Cleopolis. I will demonstrate that at these points the poem is indeed explicitly pluralistic. It has often been discovered that for Spenser placement determines meaning. My approach, therefore, will stress the chronological development more than the simultaneous pattern; besides putting together the parallel passages, it will let each book speak to us in its own terms.

Let us begin with the more distinct of the capsule contrasts between books in order to establish that *The Faerie Queene* is somehow about contradictions, before we take up the passages that embody two points of view within themselves. The topics will be bloodshed, free will, and Cupid as god of physical lovemaking. The Hermit bids Redcrosse after his earthly victories to

> Thenceforth the suit of earthly conquest shonne,
> And wash thy hands from guilt of bloudy field:
> For bloud can nought but sin, and wars but sorrowes yield.
>
> (I.x.60)

In Book VI, however, the hero Calidore, who happens to sound here like a holdover from the Book of Justice, says, "Bloud is no blemish; for it is no blame / To punish those, that doe deserve the same"

(VI.i.26.4–5). Again, the following quotations reveal a gradual but distinct and orderly reinstatement of the human will. Just before the debate over Cleopolis, the poet-speaker says, echoing St. Paul:

> Ne let the man ascribe it to his skill,
> That thorough grace hath gained victory.
> If any strength we have, it is to ill,
> But all the good is Gods, both power and eke will.
>
> (I.x.1)

In Book II, however, the perfected Redcrosse says: "His be the praise, that this atchiev'ment wrought, / Who made my hand the organ of his might; / More then goodwill to me attribute nought" (II.i.33.2–4). In Book VI, another good hermit goes even further: "For in your selfe your onely helpe doth lie / To heale yourselves, and must proceed alone / From your owne will, to cure your maladie" (VI.vi.7). The first ascribes all to God, the last all to man, while the middle credits the power to God and the will to man; these represent in terms that would be recognizable, for example, to Calvin,[2] the three camps in the battle that was currently raging over free will. Whatever reconciliations their contexts might provide, these *sententiae* were constructed to sound contradictory, which is all I am trying to prove at the moment. Canto x of Book I is beginning to emerge as the hinge of the entire poem, since it not only contradicts itself in one of our pluralistic passages but is contradicted by these later books.

A threefold pluralism is likewise found in the three attitudes expressed toward Cupid as god of sexual love: that he is altogether bad in contrast to charity; that he is an analogue to God's charity; that he is good so long as he is unarmed. In the House of Holinesse, Charissa appears with her many infants: "Full of great love, but *Cupids* wanton snare / As hell she hated, chast in worke and will" (I.x.30).

Further descriptive details—Charissa's unabashed though purely allegorical sexuality (her "lovely fere," bare breasts, and pet turtle-doves, birds of Venus), her fecundity, her delight in the playfulness of her children but willingness to "thrust them forth" (x.4.30–31) — provide parallels to the two later passages. In Book II, Guyon's guardian angel, characterized as an embodiment of God's love to man (II.viii.1) appears

> Like as *Cupido* on *Idaean* hill,
> When having laid his cruell bow away,
> And mortal arrowes, wherewith he doth fill
> The world with murdrous spoiles and bloudie pray,
> With his faire mother he him dights to play,

> And with his goodly sisters, *Graces* three;
> The Goddesse pleased with his wanton play. . . .
>
> (II.viii.6)

The parallel of Venus to Charissa only intensifies the contrast by framing it. There is a great shift of emphasis between a book that takes pains to exclude Cupid from the picture and a book that devotes a stanza-long epic simile to bringing him into it. We are only halfway to the Cupid of Book III, however, for the virgin Alma in the allegorical house of Book II which corresponds to Charissa's house in Book I "had not yet felt *Cupides* wanton rage," though the implication is that she will (II.ix.18). This and the similar virginalness, or even downright puritanism, of the hero Guyon show that with regard to sex, Book II, while mediating, is not a synthesis. In Book III, on the other hand, in the Garden of Adonis, Cupid has lost any relation to God's love, but he is a good personage in his own right inasmuch as he has laid "his sad darts aside" (III.vi.49.8–9). He is again pictured as playing with kindred immortals; he is associated with the fecundity of the garden which bears "thousand thousand naked babes" and sends them "forth to live in mortall state" (32); he himself has fathered one infant and fosters another. The side of Cupid which is bad by Book III standards is portrayed five cantos later in Busirane's grotesque and horrible torture chamber; in this virtual temple of Cupid, his weapons are prominent (III.xi.29–30; 36; 44–48). But Cupid could not gain entry to the House of Holiness as he does to the Garden of Adonis simply by checking his weapons at the door; Charissa's wider objection is to his "wanton snare." That earthly love has actually replaced divine love in Book III is indicated by Spenser's ability to joke about Britomart's thinking only of her lover during the church service (III.ii.48). This contradiction is similar to that between the first and the last pairs of Spenser's pluralistic *Fowre Hymnes*.

Because of these contradictions, I suggest that *The Faerie Queene* is at least made to look pluralistic. They show that Book I keeps its Christianity pure, even Calvinistic at times, and that Book II alone is truly syncretic, providing a *via media* of Christian humanism, as Hoopes long ago suggested, between the exclusively Christian viewpoint of Book I and the exclusively humanistic viewpoint of Books III to VI.[3] While I cannot for all this proceed with him to hail Book II as the hinge and complete synthesis of the other two viewpoints, because of its incompleteness on the subject of sex, it clearly has its own distinct viewpoint, bringing the total to three and completing the correspondence to the three viewpoints recognized by Calvin. But such skipping around in the poem as we have done can never prove pluralism, for context might provide a synthesis, smoothing down contradictions into qualifications, as indeed it does smooth down the paired instances of bad and good beads, hermits, and cups within Book I into an Anglican *via media* between the denominational extremes of Catholicism and Protestantism. We must therefore examine those individual passages which explicitly contrast two sets of ideals and refuse to decide between them.

A brief pluralistic passage is the two successive answers to the problem of Mutabilitie which close the poem as we have it (VII.vii.58– viii.2). Nature, the first speaker, says in effect that although Change is in everything, she is not the ruler, i.e., she is not chaotic or destructive, but cyclical (as in the planets and in the replenishing of the species or "stock" mentioned in the parallel Garden of Adonis in III.vi), and constructive (working perfection, dilating Being). The poet-speaker retorts (VII.viii) that change does reign at least beneath the moon and that, as Mutabilitie said, "all that moveth, doth in *Change* delight" [4]—a condition that makes him "loath this state of life so tickle" and look forward not to accommodation of Change but to its opposite:

> steadfast rest of all things firmely stayd
> Upon the pillours of Eternity,
> That is contrayr to *Mutabilitie*:
>
> . . . .
> With Him that is the God of Sabbaoth hight.
> (VII.viii.2.3–5,8)

The view which he opposes to Nature's is an exclusive Christianity. Obviously, as the poet-speaker, he must pull more weight, especially since he has the last word. Yet Nature's attitude is supported by the evidence and is more reasoned, comprehensive, and viable than the poet's *contemptus mundi* for someone who cannot "streight way on that last long voyage fare" (I.x.63). Loathing of life is a frequent topos in *The Faerie Queene*, and it is always characterized as an unjustified or temporary mood. Therefore the poem as we have it ends in pluralism. As early as 1949, Woodhouse noted that the poet's answer was "the truth of another order" which he called "the order of grace" as opposed to "the order of nature"; and Judah L. Stampfer later elaborated the distinction.[5] This traditional dualism which Woodhouse traced throughout the poem is obviously the foundation for my thesis; but I have narrowed and rechristened his order of grace as the exclusively Christian viewpoint and his order of nature as the exclusively humanistic viewpoint; I have adopted Hoopes's addition that Book II is a *tertium quid* between them; and I have found a specific pattern in the ways the three viewpoints are related, thus arriving at pluralism.

The exclusively Christian and the exclusively humanistic views of man are embodied, separately but equally, in Spenser's paired nations, Britain and Fairyland, whose paired chronicles (II.x) delineate their racial characteristics by their histories. The differences are sharp. Most important, to my mind, the Faery is unfallen from his first estate (71) but at the same time created with some built-in vice or imperfection (stolen fire and parts of beasts) for which not he but his creator Prometheus is blamed (70). That we are to contrast this account of Faery origins with the biblical account is indicated by the widespread Renaissance custom (Ralegh's, for example) of beginning a history with the Creation, Fall, and Expulsion. The *Briton Monuments* itself, while it fortunately does not begin as far back as Adam and Eve, does mention Adam along with Christ in a rhetorically heightened aside. It recounts the two main events of any Christian history—the Fall and the Redemption:

> Next him *Tenantius* raignd, then *Kimbeline*,
>   What time th'eternall Lord in fleshly slime
>   Enwombed was, from wretched *Adams* line
>   To purge away the guilt of sinfull crime:
>   O joyous memorie of happy time,
>   That heavenly grace so plenteously displayd;
>   (O too high ditty for my simple rime.)
>   (II.x.50)

It is therefore in explicit contrast with the Britons that the Faery progenitors do not fall. Erasmus in his popular *Enchiridion Militis Christiani* elects to explain man's inner conflict by way of the biblical fall rather than by way of the Promethean creation from beasts:

But neither did that mythical Prometheus, if you will, implant this discord—a particle from every animal being mixed in with our mind—nor did the primal creation impart it, but sin evilly depraved what had been well-founded, between well-accorded things planting the poison of dissension.[6]

The Faery progenetrix, whom the Faery Adam "deemd in mind / To be no earthly wight, but either Spright, / Or Angell," is certainly a contrast to Eve and in fact suggests Calvin's statement that man as classical ethics views him is a "little angel," free of original sin.[7] As mankind here is contrasted with an angelic race, so mankind was contrasted with angels in the second chapter of the Epistle to the Hebrews: Christ "in no sort tooke on him the Angels nature," but that of man (2:16, Geneva version). Association with a sprite further dechristianizes Spenser's putative angel. Its contribution to Faery nature is to cap the parts of beasts and the stolen fire with the third and highest part of the classical hierarchy of the faculties, the quasi-divine intellect. In the same vein, the Garden of Adonis is the Faery Eden; but we hear only of an entry into it for breeding purposes, never of any Expulsion (II.x.71). Furthermore, as the reader learns when it is described in III.vi, the Garden of Adonis can be damaged not by sin but only by Time with its resulting decay, which its perpetual engendering replenishes. An unfallen man and world with some moral and metaphysical evil built into them by virtue of their corruptible matter—this is the world as classical ethics views it. So the heretic Pelagius viewed man, and he was accused of making Christianity too much like classical ethics. We can be sure, then, that in this respect Spenser's Fairyland contrasts with his Britain.

Nothing is done to allay this and other contrasts. Each of the two readers is a citizen of the country whose chronicle he reads, and he does not communicate its contents to his companion. The two readers are themselves contrasting but equally normative heroes. The main Faery-Briton contrast is borne out by the surrounding action, wherein Maleger, frequently identified as original sin (or better, in strict theological terms, as concupiscence), shows himself a threat not to the Elf Guyon (ix) but only to the Briton Arthur (xi).

Yet Spenser refuses to take sides as to which is the truer picture of man. The reality of Fairyland is first called in question and then reaffirmed by the Faery chronicle. Let us begin by observing that the same thing is done more obviously in the longer description of the Garden of Adonis in III.vi. Although, as Donald Cheney observes, the Gardens of Adonis seem "accessible only to the Fairy race," although "as a terrestrial paradise . . . they can be no more than a nostalgic daydream for the fallen Christian," [8] the poet-speaker pluralistically maintains he has been there (III.vi.29). There are more things in Spenser's universe than are contained in Christianity. The chronicle, to return to our subject, is made unrealistic and fanciful in mode by the introduction of fairy-tale motifs like a magic bridge and "two brethren gyants . . . / The one of which had two heads, th'other three" (II.x.73), whereas the Briton chronicle is in a quasi-factual mode. Although the Faery chronicle has violence, it is directed at non-Faeries, whereas the British history has also betrayal, interregna, and premature death. The only example of this sort of thing in Fairyland —the premature death of Elferon (75)—is inconsequential and necessitated by the historical allegory, to be glossed below. Instead, the Faeries' history is marked by the beautification of their capital, Cleopolis, with monuments reminiscent of ancient Rome—a sign of their higher culture. No doubt such internal troubles in the British as opposed to the Faery body politic symbolize the rebellion of the "flesh" in the little world of Christian man. My present point is merely literal—that these too locate Britain in relation to Fairyland as actual man to superman, as "life" to "literature." Moreover, the British history, besides being realistic rather than fairy tale in mode, has a content which most of Spenser's audience would still regard as factual an spite of contemporary scholarly refutation, partly because it established the antiquity of the Tudors' claim to the throne and their descent from King Arthur. Even its mention of Christ, while it brightens the pessimism, would no doubt seem to Spenser's Christian audience to make the Briton chronicle more factual rather than less so.

So far, then, Spenser's Faeries, while equally real in the world of the poem, are only a beautiful fiction, a "wouldn't-it-be-nice-if." They serve to make conspicuous, by their freedom from it, the human condition—its self-chosen Fall, original sin, possible childlessness, premature death, and internecine strife, but also its redemption by Christ. This function is like that of Homer's Olympian gods or Tolkien's Elves.

Actuality rears its head in the Faery history, however, with its climax in Tanaquil or Gloriana, whom we know from the Proem to parallel Queen Elizabeth. Fairyland itself, Spenser there announces, represents Elizabeth's "owne realmes," the real Britain outside the poem, which for the sake of clarity we will henceforth designate as England. Looking back from Gloriana to Elficleos, we recognize the entire Tudor dynasty—we see, for example, that Elferon corresponds to Prince Arthur Tudor (note the Tudors' eagerness to trace their lineage to King Arthur), who dying prematurely was "doubly" replaced by Henry VIII, here represented by Oberon, "in spousall and dominion." While Britain is the England of Arthur's time, Fairyland is also England—the England of Queen Elizabeth. Interestingly enough, along with using what we now call "the Tudor myth" as historical fact, Spenser by inserting this *roman à clef* in the Faery history has offered the Tudors a myth laudatory almost to the point of heresy. "The Tudor line," Spenser seems to be saying, "is like my super-human Faery race, of more innate dignity, less torn by rebellious passions. When I look at the history of England, I conclude that man is fallen; but when I look at our present glorious sovereign, Queen Elizabeth, I conclude that some individuals, at least, are not." In degree of actuality too, then, Spenser's Fairyland turns out to be equal to his Britain; though the world views are contradictory, both have real specimens to validate them.

These paired chronicles, then, set up Britain and Fairyland as one kind of thesis and antithesis in the poem. They must have seemed important to Spenser, for they are placed within the climactic allegorical house of Book II (Alma's Castle, ix–xi) and comprise the tenth canto of their book, the canto which he usually devotes to an allegorical scene summing up each book's particular virtue. We can draw another inference from their placement: since Spenser delayed this full-scale contrast of Britain and Fairyland as long as he did, whatever reconciliation the previous, shorter treatments may have achieved must be only partial. More fully than the two answers to Mutabilitie, these paired chronicles substantiate the presence of Woodhouse's dualism of nature and grace. Yet Woodhouse did not cite them; major critics as recent as Alpers still dismiss them; and they continue to be the first excision of the anthologist. Only Berger, Roche, and Frye appreciate their importance; my interpretation has drawn on all three, in that order of preference.[9] The *Briton Monuments* is too long? Granted; abridge it. It must also be admitted that some of the implications these and other critics have seen are contradictory or unconvincing or in need of evidence—such as the position of the Briton versus the Faery woman, the mixedness or singleness of Faery as opposed to Briton nature, and the suggestion of Roche that Fairyland is the exclusive realm of art and of all that we call civilization. It may even be true that the interest in later books shifts to other, unrelated contrasts. But the paired chronicles are at least equal in value with the *Letter to Ralegh* as an introduction to the entire poem.

We have seen not only from the separateness of the poem's heroes but also from the verbal contradictions among I, II, and the later books that *The Faerie Queene* is to some extent really about two or three contradictory pictures of man and his world. In the passages that explicitly contrast two ideals, the exclusively Christian and the exclusively humanistic views of man (II.x) and their characteristic answers to the problem of mutability (VII.vii–viii) have been seen as irreconcilable but for all that paradoxically true. Armed with this information, let us proceed to the third contrast of ideals, the much contradicted tenth canto of the Book of Holiness, to see whether it is indeed pluralistic about these ideals and whether any continuity or reconciliation is supplied. The opening stanza of the canto comprises that Calvinistic statement of "the bankruptcy of the natural man," as Woodhouse puts it, which is later verbally contradicted by Book II.

> What man is he, that boasts of fleshly might,
>> And vaine assurance of mortality,
>> Which all so soone, as it doth come to fight,
>> Against spirituall foes, yeelds by and by,
>> Or from the field most cowardly doth fly?
>> Ne let the man ascribe it to his skill,
>> That thorough grace hath gained victory.
>> If any strength we have, it is to ill,
> But all the good is Gods, both power and eke will.

Of course, this opening stanza may be primarily intended, like that of the ninth canto, as a moralized synopsis of the preceding episode; and as such it describes Redcrosse's close call with Despair accurately enough. In fact, it sums up Redcrosse's entire career ever since he left Una, in that what victories he won were not against spiritual foes but over external examples of vice such as Sansfoy (Sans Joy seems to be also within his spirit, but then he does not fully vanquish him either). That these merely physical victories are at best morally neutral is shown by the dubious prizes they have earned—Duessa and the shield of Sansfoy. The spiritual foes are Orgoglio or presumption on one's own strength, to whom he yields, and Despair whom he barely vanquishes through the grace of which Una reminds him.

Far from marking a change in the poet's viewpoint, then, as Alpers believes (pp. 118, 362), the Augustinian humility of this stanza has truly been learned by Redcrosse, as is confirmed by the first person he now meets, the porter Humiltá, and by the low doorway that now conducts him into the House of Holinesse. In the House, Redcrosse first learns "repentaunce" under Fidelia and Speranza, as well as unspecified doctrines "of God, of grace, of justice, of free will" (I.x.19), among which the term *free will* both evokes the controversy mentioned above and foreshadows a synthesis, especially in that it is linked with "grace" as the corresponding member of its pair in the series. More Catholic, though nonetheless Christian, is the idea that charity, not faith, merits heaven. At length he enters the tutelage of Charissa, the third theological virtue, and only now is there talk of "the way to hevenly blesse" (33.9; 34.9; 41.5–9). Mercy, a deputy of Charissa, teaches him to win God's mercy in order to save his soul at death by doing in the world the Seven Corporal Works of Mercy, including release of prisoners. Mercy then passes him on to a deputy of Fidelia, the Hermit Contemplation. His initial cold reception of them (49), by the way, shows that one virtue which is not compatible with contemplation is courtesy, the future subject of Book VI. The Hermit Contemplation forms part of the way to heaven too; in fact, he has the keys of it (50), meaning not that he has replaced St. Peter but that he can obtain foretastes of heaven for those still in this life, as he now proceeds to do for Redcrosse.

Let us pause again in our commentary to observe the importance for our theme of the first three lines of stanza 52. Heaven and the way to it "never yet was seene of Faeries sonne"—a distinction of Briton from Faery which has long been recognized. To this rule, Redcrosse is no exception, for we learn eight stanzas later that even he is "sprong out from English race / How ever now accompted Elfins sonne" (60). True, Redcrosse is not precisely a Briton but a Saxon; it matters little, for the two "nations different afore" are destined to unite, as the British chronicle foreshadows and as Merlin later prophesies (III.iii.49), in the Britain of the future. It has not always been understood that the same contrast is served by Redcrosse's being called "thou man of earth" (52.2). Adam was formed "of the dust of the grounde" (Gen. 2:7); whereas Faeries are not men of earth, being formed of parts of beasts and stolen fire (II.x.70). In these two phrases, therefore, the Hermit implies already both the lowliness and the privilege of the Briton race: Britons may start out worse, but they end up better than their pagan counterparts. In this treatment of Britons and Faeries, it will no longer be a question of which is the more accurate image of man, but of which one it is better to be. This questioning contrast of existing races seems to resemble that of the once-born and the twice-born types in William James's *Varieties of Religious Experience*—the Faeries resembling the once-born and the Britons the twice-born—and in a vaguer way that of paired nationalities or classes in the fiction of Henry James or of E. M. Forster.

The Hermit then leads his charge to a mountain likened in an interesting simile to Sinai, Olivet, and Parnassus or Helicon (53–54), which in turn symbolize, as I will show, Law, Grace, and Nature, the three different dispensations or ways to heaven. From there, Redcrosse sees a path to heaven and then heaven itself, pictured as a city, the New Jerusalem, peopled with saints and friendly angels (55–57). The knight exclaims that this city surpasses even Cleopolis, city of the Faerie Queene (58); and surrounding contrasts at least set up the competition between them. The New Jerusalem is described along the lines of the biblical heaven (Rev. 21:10–22:5; Heb. 12:22–24, 28) with the original addition of the "Angels towre" (58.9). Cleopolis means "fame-city," and its inhabitants—like classical man as characterized by Aristotle, the epics, and St. Augustine—live for fame (59). The New Jerusalem, on the other hand, is egalitarian (56.5; 57.8) and irradiated by love of the good-Shepherdly sort (57.9), in comparison to which the atmosphere of Cleopolis is that of a prize-day. The towers of the New Jerusalem are "strong," made "of perle and precious stone" (55.4–5), and onto one of them the friendly angels commute "from highest heaven," the abode of God (56); but Panthea, the tower of the Faery city, perhaps alluding to the Pantheon of Rome, is only of crystal glass, a substance often beautiful but transitory in Spenser (cf. III.ii.18.8–20.9; IV.x.39.9). The New Jerusalem, unlike Cleopolis, but like the Incarnation in the *Briton Monuments* (50), forms "too high ditty for my simple rime"—an *occupatio* which is Spenser's signal of literal reference to a Christian mystery. Both "that fairest *Faerie Queene*" (58) and "the great king" of heaven (55) bestow glory on Redcrosse; but the first kind is that of a famous knight (60.5–6), while the second is that of a patron saint (61.7–9). In her "booke of fame" (59.5–6) the Faerie Queene bestows a merely metaphorical immortality; but God gives the personal immortality of "eternall peace and happiness" (I.x.55.9). The God of Book II, we will learn, also keeps a social register; but our present passage stresses not merit but equality and God's grace. Whereas the Faerie Queene grants rewards ("guerdon") for specific achievements, Redcrosse's sainthood is not "won" by any special deed (as will be said of it in the syncretic Book II) but simply "ordaind" (61.5), or predestined. Because of these contrasts, Redcrosse sees Cleopolis to be an alternative value-system which will compete with the New Jerusalem—just as the chronicles of Britain and Fairyland implied that never the twain shall meet.

The New Jerusalem is clearly better *sub specie aeternitatis*; therefore we as readers also expect Cleopolis to be rejected. This expectation is reinforced by the tradition of the mountain-top or hermitage experience. In other works, such previews of heaven teach renunciation of earthly values: they either inaugurate exclusively Christian journeys to heaven, as in *The Pilgrimage of the Life of Man* or *Pilgrim's Progress*, or at least terminate earthly careers as in the case of Guy of Warwick, Lancelot, and even Larry in *The Razor's Edge*.

In spite of all this, the Hermit tells Redcrosse to go back to Cleopolis and to continue serving the Faerie Queene. One of his reasons is that he has an obligation to Una, "that royall maides bequeathed care," not as his beloved but as a needy human being (60.4; 63.6–9). This motive creates no problem, for it has already been enjoined by the Seven Corporal Works of Mercy. Redcrosse's subsequent Dragon-fight counts in Christianity as well as in Cleopolis, for it is a return to one of the recommended Works, release of prisoners, insofar as it is the release of Una's imprisoned parents. Even the imagery of the Dragon-fight looks back to the fourth Work, likened as it is to Christ's Harrowing of Hell (I.x.40); for Redcrosse's Dragon-fight, as several critics have noted, resembles the Harrowing of Hell in many ways, such as the echoes of the Passion story, the liberation of the "King of Eden," i.e., Adam (xii.26), the opening of the brazen gates, and the transfer of the liberated captives to Eden.[10] Spenser need not have mentioned Cleopolis, then, in order to justify the continuation of such a quest. But Cleopolis and the service of the Faerie Queene embrace much more.

It is also worth noting in this connection that the Hermit is quite as world-denying as one would expect him to be about the other motive for chivalric attainment, love. I do not see any reference in this passage to Una's symbolic role as religious truth, which might have given her a Dantesque importance here as it later does in Canto xii.[11] On the contrary, he says Una will ultimately be renounced. "Ladies love" is "vaine" not even because it is sinful, but because it "will vanish into nought" (62). In heaven they neither marry nor are given in marriage (Luke 21:34–35), just as there is no need of war in heaven (62.7); each is just another earthly circumstance—at most, raw material upon which to exercise the virtues of faithfulness and charity, which are indeed relevant for salvation. Spenser here passes over the synthesis afforded by Una's special symbolism, takes a hard Christian line on sexual love, and thus creates a further contradiction of Book III. I believe he does so because he intends the Hermit's pronouncement to cover the entire realm of sex—not only Redcrosse but also the later, less platonic lovers at the ends of their lives—just as with the realm of war. A drab view of love it is, but then, under the perspective of eternity, all "earthly things" are "darke . . . compard to things divine" (67.9). To this extent, then, the view from the Mount of Contemplation remains narrowly Christian and at least self-consistent. We were warned long ago, however, that such Christianity is not the last word: the Hermit's rejection of war and love rejects the entire poem he appears in, for "fierce warres and faithfull loves shall moralize my song" (I Proem i.9).

When the Hermit while conceding the inferiority of Cleopolis says that it well befits all knights to "haunt" it, in order "in th'immortall booke of fame / To be eternized"—advice which Redcrosse follows at the end of the book—Spenser breaks with his Christianity in a way for which neither the poem nor its traditions has prepared us. Critics such as Rathborne, MacNamee, and Quinones find this high ranking of fame among Christian values to be unparalleled in Renaissance literature—except possibly by Drayton and the Italians. Quinones expresses further surprise at its other-worldly context and spokesman, Contemplation. The only comparable praises of fame, says Rathborne, are all by Italians such as Poliziano and are from an exclusively pagan viewpoint. Spenser's fellow northerners, on the other hand, either "fail," like Gavin Douglas and Jean Lemaire de Belges, "to make explicit the difference between the pagan immortality conferred through fame and the Christian immortality secured by heavenly grace," or reject earthly fame altogether as did Chaucer and Milton.[12] Even the Italian Petrarch and the relatively humanistic Englishman Stephen Hawes specifically deny that earthly fame can make one eternal.[13] The Hermit Contemplation is not only other-worldly but, as the representative of the completest vision, comes closest of any speaker in the poem to being a spokesman for the author himself. He parallels the poet-speaker whose Christian and other-worldly solution to Mutabilitie gets the last word in the poem as we have it. Spenser here contradicts not only Christian tradition but himself; for, as Alpers puts it, "there is a contradiction of the sort that generated some of the profoundest theological controversies of the sixteenth century between the first stanza of Canto Ten and the praise of Cleopolis at the end" (p. 362).

One can think of a number of reconciliations between Cleopolis and the New Jerusalem which Spenser could have used. In terms of imagery, the New Jerusalem is clearly modelled on Augustine's *City of God*, and Cleopolis is Augustine's Earthly City, whose highest embodiment was pagan Rome, pursuing fame, when at its best, by means of virtue. Spenser has made Augustine's Earthly City good, as Rathborne long ago perceived (pp. 6 ff., esp. 12–14) and has relegated pursuit of undeserved fame to Lucifera's "sad house of pride" (p. 59). Lucifera's dungeon holds many of Rome's noblest (I.x.45 ff.), showing that her realm is a Rome *in malo*; but more important, it holds the "King of *Babylon*," and Babylon was Augustine's name for his (bad) Earthly City. In terms of ethics, however, it is still not clear how Spenser felt able to so reverse Augustine's judgment of the virtuous pagan Romans as to say that a Christian should join them.[14]

Let us see if any other reconciliations are embodied in Canto x. Whatever syntheses Book II may embody on the topic of fame should probably not be read back into it, since we have seen Book II contradicting it on two other heads. Though my undertaking here may seem to be an attack on a series of straw men, almost every solution I will mention has actually been propounded by one critic or another; and the world has seen how overeagerness to "read in" solutions to the problems of the characters has distorted criticism of, for example, *The Book of Job, Oedipus the King, The Romance of the Rose*, and *King Lear*, all of which deliberately leave certain problems unresolved. The absence of solutions here is not the sort of omission which cries out to be filled, as for example in the speech of an ignorant character; it must be acknowledged not only to refute error but to uncover a positive pattern—that of pluralism.

One solution is that good works inspired by charity get one into heaven. Spenser does indeed say this when he makes Charissa and her deputy Mercy, rather than Fidelia, the experts on how to get to heaven (33.9; 34.9; 51.3–4). In this respect, Spenser's stand is with the Catholics in the current faith-versus-works controversy. Moreover, as I have mentioned, the particular work to which Redcrosse immediately returns (the Dragon-fight) is characterized as meritorious by fulfilling one of Charissa's Corporal Works of Mercy. But if this were all he was saying, Spenser need not have mentioned Cleopolis, only Una. True, as long as Redcrosse is on the Mount of Contemplation, Cleopolis includes Una as a ladylove, a motive for worldly action, especially since her cause happens to have been assigned to the knight by Gloriana and will yield him fame whether he wants it or not. But when Redcrosse leaves Una to serve the Faerie Queene at the end of Book I (xii.41), they become as distinct in reality as they are here in theory. Once Redcrosse's charitable obligation to Una has been fulfilled, there is nothing in Christianity to make him go back to Cleopolis—in fact Una and her father wish he would not. He has a contract with the Faerie Queene, but this must itself symbolize that problematic hold which Cleopolis has on him; at any rate it is not particularly associated with charity, only with fame (e.g., I.i.3).

Another relation between Cleopolis and the New Jerusalem, which has been invoked earlier in canto x but which is not sufficient, is that of the Active to the Contemplative Life. Insofar as the keys of the New Jerusalem belong to Contemplation, Cleopolis must represent the opposite of contemplation or the Active Life. Contemplation is of course associated with heaven, not only as the faculty which apprehends it but as the chief occupation of its inhabitants. The paradox was traditional that the Active Life, while lower, is a necessary step; throughout the Middle Ages, it was thought to be symbolized in the Old Testament by Isaac's having to marry Leah before he could marry Rachel. Already in our canto, however, Redcrosse has had to learn Works of Mercy before being passed on to Contemplation; he has thus already reenacted the traditional sequence. When Contemplation subsequently orders Redcrosse back into the Active Life, he is adding something to the traditional sequence—something, I would argue, that is wholly new. It is true that a return from the Contemplative to the Active Life is recommended for one who is called to be a bishop.[15] In support of this, the soteriological imagery of the Dragon-fight definitely implies that Redcrosse is now so far an ecclesiastic as to be on the moral level engaged in "saving souls." But there is a difference between Cleopolis and any Christian activity; and that difference lies not at all in the matter of heightened spiritual responsibilities.

What differentiates Cleopolis from the Christian Active Life is its classical and this-worldly values—nobility, external achievement, and above all fame. These values are not endorsed in any Christian commendations of the Active Life; they are excluded, for example, from Luther's. Stephen Hawes's *Passetyme of Pleasure*, in many ways akin to if not a source for *The Faerie Queene*, identifies Fame, plus other classical values, with the Active Life, but then proceeds to downgrade the Active Life as irreconcilable with and inferior to the Contemplative Life which alone "eternizes." Conversely, the Italian writers Piccolomini and Sperone Speroni extolled the Active Life in preference to the Contemplative Life; in so doing, however, they not only preserved their mutual exclusiveness but spiritualized the Active Life, praising it as the means not to fame but to heaven. But in even this degree of closeness to Spenser these Italians are not typical, for Charles Trinkaus finds that in general, theoreticians of the Renaissance—humanists as well as reformers—were denying man's "rational capacity to lead a moral life in the ordinary secular pursuits of this world" and especially to do so, as Redcrosse is supposed to do, "while attaining salvation." [16] By canto xii, then, both of the main Christian motives for action in this world—charity for the sake of heaven and action for the sake of contemplation—have been satisfied, but something still remains for Redcrosse to seek: Cleopolis or fame.

While the sequence of Active to Contemplative to Active Lives fails to account for Cleopolis, it does, by a later recurrence, explain away an apparent contradiction which obscures the real one in the minds of critics such as Alpers (p. 119). The Hermit's predictions do not rule out another foretaste of the final contemplation similar to the one Redcrosse is now enjoying. Although Una's symbolism is ignored in Redcrosse's debate with the Hermit, so that she is there identified with action, it is finally invoked when Redcrosse is rewarded for his victory by betrothal to her. That this is a more-than-earthly reward for his action, that it is in fact another moment of contemplation as Harrison long ago perceived,[17] is indicated by Una's unveiling of her dazzlingly bright face (cf. Beatrice's unveiling to Dante) and the voices of angels singing to God in heaven that seem to sound through the earthly music of the betrothal ceremony (xii.21-23; 28-29). The first text shows that she symbolizes truth; the second identifies union with her as a relation like that of the angels to God, namely one of contemplation. "Truth" is of course a standard philosophical word for the object of contemplation. Redcrosse's betrothal to Una therefore symbolizes that penultimate stage of contemplation called "spiritual betrothal" by mystics such as Spenser's contemporary St. John of the Cross.[18] It was earned by his activity of the Dragon-fight, just as his first moment of contemplation was earned by his studying the Seven Corporal Works of Mercy. Spenser seems to think of action and contemplation as a lifelong alternation.

Another implication of these lines which will become relevant later is that here in canto xii—in an earthly mistress symbolizing divine truth, in the music of heaven resounding through an earthly "song of love"—we find that syncretism we sought for in vain in canto x; in fact, the translucence of divine and angelic love in and through sexual love is similar to Spenser's syncretic comparison, examined above, of Guyon's guardian angel to Cupid (II.viii.6). In the light of all this, the coming shift from Paulinism, with its black-and-white contrasts between natural and supernatural, to syncretism with its subtle fusion of the two is heralded here by another of Una's changes of costume—from the stark black stole over white to a single garment composed of "silke and silver woven neare / But neither silke nor silver therein did appeare" (I.xii.22 cf. i.4).

Redcrosse's anticlimactic abandonment of Una to return to the Faerie Queene for six years (xii.17–20; 41) now emerges as just another swing of the pendulum from contemplation to action. Likewise, Redcrosse's ultimate return in the seventh year to Una to consummate the marriage will of course be still another return from action back to contemplation. The significance of the number six is that it is almost, but not quite, the mystic number seven. "That Sabaoth," the seventh world-age, is the consummation of world history in the last line of the poem; and Jacob had to serve seven extra years to win Rachel, symbol of contemplation (Gen. 29:17–30). The Faerie Queene would seem to play Leah to Una's Rachel, especially since they are paired in Redcrosse's "love" (I.ix.17.1–3). Spenser has significantly reversed the traditional sequence, as noted above, so that he wins contemplation first and then has to work for action before he can fully enjoy contemplation.[19] (Spenser has borrowed from the numbers of years of service per lady only the basic idea of seven as the number of consummation, by giving the preliminary lady, or life, not another seven as in the Bible but the obviously incomplete number six.) Clearly, the necessity as Spenser saw it for continually inserting intervals of action into one's contemplation explains why he did not allow Redcrosse to marry Una at once. This is borne out by the separation of "spiritual betrothal" from "spiritual marriage" in treatises on mysticism like that of St. John of the Cross.

Redcrosse's terminal pilgrimage via the Mount of Contemplation to the New Jerusalem will be another and final period of contemplation. The absence of any predicted action in between the marriage and it, leads us to suppose that they symbolize the same thing. The marriage is described as "everlasting rest" (17.9); and the mystics' "spiritual marriage" similarly extends up to and into heaven—if, indeed, it is not deferred entirely to heaven, as is normally the case. Redcrosse's vow to come back to Una and his vow to come back to

Contemplation are therefore not really in conflict, and the more genuine conflict between these vows and his vow to serve the Faerie Queene, between contemplation and some sort of action, is reconciled in experience by alternating them.

The real conflict, however, arises not from the praise of action but from the praise of fame, which the two main Christian motives for action do nothing to justify. A Christian could justify pursuit of fame if it were for the state as a whole, as in the *Aeneid*, parts of Hawes's *Passetyme of Pleasure*, and in Spenser's own *Mother Hubberd's Tale*; but the glory of stanza 59 is the knight's, not the nation's, and Redcrosse in particular is not a citizen but an alien in Fairyland, as we soon learn. Redcrosse's one political role, as patron saint of his own nation, is not connected with Cleopolis, fame, or achievement; it is simply "ordaind" and comes only after he leaves Cleopolis for the New Jerusalem.

Again, the reasoned pursuit of fame could have been made a virtue in itself, as conducive to heaven as any other. But the Hermit does not say that the service of Gloriana will bring Redcrosse any nearer heaven; Cleopolis is not even on the "path" to the New Jerusalem, which leads directly from the Mount of Contemplation; it is a detour. Besides, even Aquinas—the Christian thinker who first counted Aristotelian magnanimity as a virtue meriting heaven, thus furnishing the solution MacNamee sees here (p. 155)—restricted the pursuit of glory to two kinds: glory for God as the ultimate source of the talent employed, and glory for the welfare of one's neighbor, as for example to inspire him to emulation (*ST* II–IIae, Q. 132, a.1). Although in Book II, Redcrosse will transfer some of his glory to God and will inspire his successor to emulation (i.32–33.4), neither of these purposes is mentioned here. The most that the Hermit can say to justify the pursuit of earthly glory is that it is the chief of earthly goods— "for earthly frame, / The fairest peece that eye beholden can"—and that for some unexplained reason, as Rathborne says, it is "to be renounced only after it has been won" (p. 59).

Another reconciliation between fame and heaven—one followed by the Christian humanists Dante, Petrarch, and Milton, and sometimes even by Augustine—is that true fame will be bestowed "lastly on each deed" in heaven. The notion that Gloriana bestows heavenly glory is entirely unfounded. Moreover, she cannot be a kind of earthly foretaste or analogue of it, for the Hermit's picture of heaven plays down any special distinctions and is utterly alien to the whole notion of "guerdon." It is egalitarian: "Now are they Saints all in that Citie sam." As I noted before, Redcrosse's special glory there of being the patron saint of England is simply "ordaind," and there is no connection between it and his "famous victory" beyond a temporal "when." Redcrosse does indeed seek for such a connection between deeds and heavenly glory when he asks, "Unworthy wretch . . . / How dare I thinke such glory to attaine" (62). The Hermit replies that all the saints were equally unworthy, in other words, that there is no such thing as worthiness—that sainthood is, as Redcrosse said, a grace. That Redcrosse had expected the answer to be "by deeds" is shown by his rejoinder, "But deeds of armes must I at last be faine?" Spenser does indeed use this justification in Book II—a "glorious name" and "everlasting fame" have been "wonne" in God's "heavenly Registers" by Redcrosse's "atchiev'ment (II.i.32)—but here where Redcrosse asks for it, the Hermit denies it: "What need of warres?"

I believe Spenser forgoes the appeal to heavenly fame as a reward for service in Cleopolis because he knows that while Redcrosse's quest merits both kinds of fame, some of the other quests do not. Besides being the spiritual high point of the poem (except perhaps for the concluding stanza), this passage is the second and longest reference to Cleopolis. It is therefore of as wide an application as the Faery chronicle, which forms the third out of four. Spenser is trying to characterize Cleopolis *per se* and the entire realm of Fairyland, then, not merely Redcrosse's part in it. In accord with this design, his only statement is a bare, pluralistic affirmation and an announcement that it has a place in a temporal sequence.

The justification for fame brought to bear on this passage by Quinones is that by prolonging one's "life" on earth it sustains and carries on God's work of creation (pp. 243, 246). I see no reference to this ideal in this or any of Spenser's treatments of fame, though it is used to justify procreation (III.vi.34.4–6).

One reconciliation between Cleopolis and the New Jerusalem which emerges later on is by way of the virtues demanded by each. Since the three Theological Virtues, faith, hope, and charity, as collectively represented in the House of Holiness, lead to the New Jerusalem, one would expect Cleopolis to represent the accompanying four Cardinal Virtues. Temperance and justice are already represented in the poem as we have it (II and V), and a knight of wisdom, Sophy, is mentioned in II.ix.6.9. The other virtues in the poem Spenser may, on the example of Aquinas, have associated with them. Magnanimity, for example, is a part of fortitude in Aquinas, and if Spenser followed him here, Arthur is the fourth cardinal virtue, whom Guyon prophesies will be equal in honor with Artegall (justice), Sophy, and, by implication, himself. This program does not in itself tell us very much, however, since the relation between the Cardinal and the Theological Virtues is loose and variable; and in any case, the characterization of Cleopolis as a court of virtues, while mentioned in the *Letter to Ralegh*, emerges in the poem only later on (e.g., VI. Proem).

Although magnanimity or pursuit of deserved fame is not portrayed as a virtue meriting heaven in this canto, it might be so in the character of Arthur. This study is not the place for a full-scale treatment of Arthur—a thornier subject than Cleopolis; but I think I can at least prove that Arthur reflects rather than reconciles the dichotomy between Britons and Faeries and their cities in I.x and II.x, i.e., that as stated at the beginning, he comes across as more a link than a synthesis. It is clear that Arthur in isolation represents magnanimity. He is given a conspicuously introductory characterization in the cantos just before ours: in ix, his "loves and lineage" which characterize him as magnanimity, and in vii, the opening description of his armor, whose richness characterizes him as magnificence.[20] The remark that after his death the arms, like Arthur himself in the legends, will be taken to Fairyland and preserved in a kind of temporal immortality by the Faerie Queene (I.vii.26.8–9) shows that the arms are not in themselves representative of Christian values, as the *Variorum* critics would have it, but of Faery values. Conversely, we simply never hear about Arthur's own eternal destiny, as we should expect to do if his magnanimity were Christian. I grant that since he is a Briton, his hoped-for marriage to the Faerie Queene, the only case of such intermarriage in the poem, will resolve Britain into Fairyland. This marriage, however, is felt as a goal remoter and less imaginable than Redcrosse's with Truth; and it recedes as the poem goes on.

According to the *Letter to Ralegh*, Arthur was supposed to comprehend all virtue by embodying that overarching virtue of magnanimity which pursues deserved glory by great achievements in each of the various virtues—presumably even holiness, the pursuit of heaven. I grant that if realized, this Arthur would be some sort of fusion of heaven with fame; but since even here the virtues are means to fame, it would still be holiness for the sake of fame rather than fame for the sake of heaven as in Aquinas's Christianized magnanimity. Let us see if this Arthur is realized. His "deeds applyable to" the virtue of holiness consist of his Christ-like rescue of Redcrosse from Orgoglio's dungeon—a deed which characterizes him, according to the opening stanza of the canto, as "heavenly grace" (viii.1). This distinctively Christian role, which seems also to recur in his rescue of Guyon in the corresponding canto of Book II, M. Y. Hughes has rightly seen as coordinate with his role as magnanimity.[21] The way in which Arthur's single character combines a Christian and a classical value is certainly another evidence of Spenser's yoking of "the two matters" of Renaissance thought. But the values remain almost antithetical, since insofar as one's virtue is from grace, one would ordinarily not receive glory for it—for which reason Redcrosse in Book II syncretically transfers part of the glory for his achievement to God. The only overlap Hughes finds between the two roles is a like stress on doing favors for people and a comprehensive place in their respective value systems. Particularly in cantos viii and ix, where his Christ-like identification with heavenly grace jars oddly with his secular and almost immoral love-story, Arthur seems to be divided, like the Hermit, into two alternating aspects: a Cleopolis aspect and a New-Jerusalem aspect. A similar though slighter incongruity is felt in II when Arthur's secular love and quest are again recounted right after his Christ-like rescue of Guyon, his other recognized appearance as grace (II.viii.18–ix.8). Though less schizophrenic than the Hermit because he is practicing the virtues and not theorizing about them, this Protean Arthur clearly does not represent a synthesis between Cleopolis and the New Jerusalem.

Finally, we come to the last lines of the episode proper. Going down the mountain, Redcrosse's eyes dazzle because "So darke are earthly things compard to things divine" (67.9). The word "earthly" has been used before: "Yet is Cleopolis, for earthly frame, / The fairest peece that eye beholden can; / And well beseemes all knights . . . that same to haunt" (59.2 ff.); and these constitute the only explicit statements in this canto of the relationship between Cleopolis and the New Jerusalem. The synthesizers make much of the earlier, positive passage; they rightly see it as the voice of Neoplatonic scalarism pronouncing everything good within its hierarchical place; but they do not put it together with the concluding negative usage. Such a scalarism—in which some earthly things are "fair" but *sub specie aeternitatis* all earthly things "dark"—virtually contradicts itself. "Darkness and fairness are relative" is a pluralistic statement. Here as in the *Fowre Hymnes* and the Mutabilitie Cantos, the Neoplatonic ladder is broken by contradiction and one has to leap from the bottom half to the top half; there is no intermediate stage in which, to shift the metaphor, earthly things are gray. An example of an unbroken Neoplatonic ladder would be the speech of Milton's Raphael on the "scale of nature" (*PL* V, 469–512); body working up to spirit is, after all, very different from the Redcrosse's unconnected oscillations. On the one hand he strives, be it physically or morally, for an immortality of earthly glory, and on the other he is "chosen" for an "ordaind" rank in an egalitarian heaven. The first is more pagan, the second more Christian than Milton's smooth ascent.

If Spenser's scale of nature is discontinuous, some continuity can be found by viewing the New Jerusalem and Cleopolis as stages of a single life in time. This is clearly how the Hermit views them, and he seems untroubled by the contradictions, serenely above his pupil's spluttering tergiversations. All the Hermit is really saying is that certain things—action, ladies' love, fame—are good for one time of life but not for another; and this commonsense insight, when dignified by philosophical attention as in this canto, is pluralism. One of the really paradoxical debates in *The Shepheardes Calender* is that between youth and age (Feb.). Shakespeare seems to be saying this about Prince Hal's first sowing his wild oats and then rejecting his drinking-buddy when he accedes to the crown. In the romances, the many knights who turn monks, insofar as their past lives are not actually sinful, also express pluralism. Critics have often suggested that the successive titular virtues of *The Faerie Queene* are cumulative, giving them either a logical or a temporal sequence. What distinguishes Spenser as a philosophical pluralist from these authors and these views of himself as author is his dwelling on the contradictions as much as he does, and, more important, his shifting back and forth several times between the more and the less worldly values, thereby attributing an equal value to each. Redcrosse after each of his three or four periods of action must return to his exclusively Christian starting point. Redcrosse likewise unites by alternation in time the polarities grace and free will which formed the subject of our second capsule contrast (I.x.1; II.i.33; VI.vi.7). In his Dragon-fight, Redcrosse alternates between utter passivity to divine grace during the nights—lying unconscious in the Well and under the balm-dripping Tree—and the most strenuous effort during the days.

After the resulting victory, Una's "his" is therefore deliberately ambiguous when "God she praysd and thankt her faithfull knight, / That had atcheiv'd so great a conquest by his might" (I.xi.55.8–9). Ambiguity is still not reconciliation, however; Redcrosse's apportionment of the praise for this achievement in Book II will be much more precise—to God for the "might," to himself, for the "goodwill"; there and only there will they be seen as reconciled in simultaneous, hand-in-glove cooperation (II.i.33). Book I also conveys the effect of ambiguity by the alternative causes, divine or human, and the alternative motivations, Christian or secular, assigned to so many of its events and actions (e.g., I.ix.7; I.x.9; I.xi.45). Alpers is right in his chapter "Heroism and Human Strength in Book I" that this habit of Spenser's conveys a feeling of ambiguity and paradox; but I would add that it merely sets the stage for the Hermit's explicit philosophical statement of pluralism.

This alternation as stages of a life is also a way of putting together Briton and Faery values at large. We have seen that it is not (except for the Seven Works) the orthodox Christian Active Life that Redcrosse alternates with his contemplation, but a Faery version of it paganized by the centrality of fame. There was in fact an alternation of Britain and Fairyland at the very beginning of Redcrosse's life: at the climax of the interview, Redcrosse learns he was born a Briton, or at least a Saxon, but was kidnapped and reared by Faeries. Though he lost social status by this change, the Hermit twice stresses that as an "impe sprung out from English race" he was and will be wise to come "to Faerie court to seeke for fame, / And prove [his] puissant armes" (64–66, cf. 60), just as it "well beseemes all knights" (59.4) to do so. While the contemplative stage was recommended for, among other times, the end of one's life, Fairyland seems particularly recommended for one's youth.

This inference is reinforced in typical Spenserian fashion by the similar alternation in Arthur's life as recounted in the preceding canto (I.ix). Arthur has on occasion been interpreted as less a personification of a virtue and more a *doppelganger* of the current hero.[22] Arthur, like Artegall (III.iii.26) and Redcrosse up to now, is ignorant of his parentage, though we know and he unlike them presumes that he is a Briton. While he was growing up in Britain, he was tutored by a Faery knight, evidently an *émigré*, for he had a geographically specific seat in the land (ix.3.8–9). Fairyland seems, then, to be associated with education. In support of this, before Arthur actually came to Fairyland, he had had a certain kind of pride, independence from love, which was cut down to a proper humility—proper as opposed to the love-despair which undoes Terwin and Trevisan in this same canto—by his falling in love with the Faerie Queene. Gloriana was his second Faery tutor. I therefore propose that Fairyland is praised as a realm of education, both by the Hermit Contemplation and in a large implicit way by Spenser's setting his epic there. This could explain why the people encountered in Fairyland are mostly personifications—a notoriously didactic mode of allegory. After all, the announced purpose of the entire *Faerie Queene* is "to fashion a gentleman or noble person in vertuous and gentle discipline."

Fairyland is for the education of youthful Britons. The vision afforded on the Mount of Contemplation, hard by the House of Holiness, is forbidden to "Faeries sonne." Yet despite their exclusive Christianity, these are places within Fairyland; for a definite boundary between Fairyland and Eden is mentioned in the immediate context, and it lies beyond the House of Holiness, cf. ix.20 with xi.2. Some parts of Fairyland seem, therefore, to be designed only for visiting

Britons. A character in Book II, Maleger, is so designed. Widely considered to be a personification of original sin, he is a threat not to the elf Guyon, who brushes him aside (ix.13–16), but only to the Briton Arthur (xi), putting up against him a fight big enough to compete in importance with the expected climax of the book, Guyon's struggle with Acrasia. That these signs "for Britons only" mean "for their education" is shown by Fidelia's "schoolhouse" (I.x.18.4). Conversing with Redcrosse and Una after a shared adventure in Fairyland, Arthur explicitly parallels his educational subjection to love with Redcrosse's recent fall resulting from his spiritual pride, and bids Redcrosse and Una learn from both (viii.44–45.2; ix.12.1–2).

If Fairyland exists to educate the Christian Britons, why the predominance of unchristian inhabitants and themes? Even for Christians, education is or at least was then a classical enterprise both in its subject matter and in its assumption that people can be improved by effort. As Fairyland adds just a leaven of Christianity to its predominantly classical instruction, so the famous Winchester School was ordered at the Reformation to add the Bible to its curriculum of "profane authors" and to refute their doctrinal errors therefrom, but not to drop or censor any of them.[23] This principle is the same as that which Spenser claims in his dedication to have followed, to an even more pluralistic degree, in publishing his profane pair of *Hymnes* but adding the Christian pair to correct them. Instruction can do little about the distinctively Christian entities original sin and grace beyond pointing out their existence. It can, however, inculcate the "discipline" and the "zeal for virtue" necessary to appreciate them, as Melanchthon says in defending the study of Aristotle.[24] The visiting Britons are then the models for Spenser's English readers, who are to go to his Fairyland of predominantly classical personifications in order to acquire "virtuous and gentle discipline."

What time of life, then, is *not* the time for classical ethics and their realm of Fairyland? That the typical Christian should not settle down in Fairyland is indicated by the predicted home-goings of Redcrosse as well as of Britomart and of Artegall, another changeling like Redcrosse (III.iii.26–27). In addition, the necessity of having some grace and some awareness of original sin before one is able to improve by human effort, is also indicated by Redcrosse's cautionary example up through I.x.1; and it will be made clearer in Book II, as I hope to show in a forthcoming study of Spenser's syncretism ("Reason and Grace in *The Faerie Queene*, Book II") designed as something of a companion-piece to this one. Redcrosse, indeed, had some grace to begin with, but did not appreciate it for lack of Fairyland experience and so lost it in his fall to Archimago. This partial reconciliation of contraries by alternation in time expounded in the last cantos of Book I is rather like the "things" in Nature's justification of Change, "turning to themselves at length again" in order to "work their own perfection"—provided the perfection is seen, at least in the case of Redcrosse in Book I, as one not of a spiral but of a circle, ending where it began. In Spenser here, I think we see a foreshadowing of that modern preference for experience over speculative reason exemplified in Goethe's *Faust*, wherein experience of contraries including action and contemplation somehow resolves the hero's philosophically unresolvable problems.

In conclusion, my case will perhaps be more credible if I suggest how Spenser might have come to devise his dichotomy of Britons and Faeries. Besides the strong general appeal of classical ethics to Renaissance man, there are certain values which seem from their repetitions in all Spenser's works to be built into his very nature. Among these a priori values are at least three—above all the intrinsic value and lastingness of earthly fame, but also the innate superiority of the aristocracy and the value of human sexual love—which do not fit very well with Christianity. Spenser is an author who, in Woodhouse's words, "recognizes the consequences of his position." Now at the same time the possibility—which had been mentioned as early as Augustine and which still fascinates readers of science fiction today—of totally different humanoid races, perhaps unrelated either to Adam or to Christ, had acquired new urgency from the races discovered in the New World. Spenser compares Fairyland to the New World in the Proem to Book II. He therefore, as I conjecture, constructed an alternative position in which these values could rank high and embodied it in his alternative humanoid race, the Faeries.

In order to complete my case, it will now be necessary to set the boundaries of Spenser's pluralism—to mention the instances in which he actually resolves the contraries he has set up, and is therefore rather a syncretist. An author cannot afford to have too many pluralistic passages, or else the poem's intellectual structure will collapse, as Alpers in fact believes it does. Looking at the beginning of Book I for the evidence that Redcrosse began with some grace, we are now surprised to find that it is not Calvinistic total grace, but that limited syncretic kind which is reconcilable with free will. For example, Una's cry, "Add faith unto your force" (I.i.19.3) and the resulting picture of Redcrosse "with God to frend" (28.7) recall that "partnership between God and man" classified by Calvin as a *via media* and exemplified in Redcrosse's disclaimer in Book II, "His be the praise, that this atchiev'ment wrought / . . . More then good will to me attribute nought" (II.i.33). Moreover, "Add faith unto your force" verbally contradicts "If any *strength* we have, it is to ill / But all the good is

Gods, both *power* and eke will" (I.x.1, italics mine). From this I conclude that Spenser is a Christian humanist not merely in Book II but whenever his hero is in a state of grace—that, like Erasmus and Hooker, he allowed man a limited free will *under* grace. The Pauline, black-and-white Christianity of "If any strength we have, . . .", while characteristic of Book I, seems not to be the only viewpoint represented; it refers in its immediate context to Redcrosse as he has become after his separation from Una—a hero without grace. This initial syncretism thus foretells and suggests a doctrinal explanation for the major shift to syncretism forthcoming in Book II.

In assessing the extent of Spenser's syncretism, it is important to distinguish between syncretism of thought, the kind I have been talking about, and syncretism of imagery. I admit that, as James E. Phillips has shown, syncretic imagery pervades *The Faerie Queene*, and nowhere more than in Book I, most of whose thought is obviously not syncretic but monolithically Christian. Important among Phillips's examples is the threefold comparison of the Mount of Contemplation to Sinai, Olivet, and Parnassus which precedes the vision of the New Jerusalem (53–54). Imagery, however, does not always determine theme. Because this epic simile, like so many others, juxtaposes classical and Christian elements, Phillips draws the inference that to Spenser all religions are parts of one truth, making him syncretic in thought and aligning him with those Platonic liberal Christians who traced all religions to a common source by way of a supposed *prisca theologia*.[25] If imagery were all we had to go on, this inference might be correct; but this canto happens to contain explicit philosophical statements which must by their very nature receive greater weight; and they (with the possible exception of 59.2–3 discussed above) are not at all syncretic. Besides, this simile is not as syncretic as the angel-Cupid simile (II.viii.6), for the differences between the mountains are more apparent than the similarities—one mountain flashing with fire, for example, while another is crowned with flowers. The three mountains are noncommittally juxtaposed and so could point a contrast as do Homer's similes; I would say that they represent the traditional three dispensations: Nature, Law, and Grace (see, for example, Erasmus, *Diatribe . . . on Free Will*, LB IX, 1222). It may even be that they define the three viewpoints of Books I, II, and III–VI as those of Grace, Law, and Nature (with her daughter Art). Like the alternations and the double causation, this schematic juxtaposition but not fusion of Christian with pagan contributes to that effect of iridescence rather than steady translucence of the divine in the human which distinguishes even the Christian-humanist parts of Book I from Book II.

To summarize the pattern in which the three separate viewpoints appear, then, Book I begins in syncretism, as if to forecast that for Redcrosse, at least, Christian humanism will prove at least partially viable. From his first fall to Archimago, whose tricks are proved Calvinistically impenetrable by his deception even of Una (I.iii.26 ff.), to his final fall to Orgoglio, representing presumption on one's own strength, Redcrosse's career illustrates in Calvinistic terms the bankruptcy of natural man. Despair's indictment is right so far as it goes, and only grace (expounded in and represented by Una's reminder) saves him. Building works onto grace in the exclusively Christian House of Holiness, he is suddenly told by the Hermit to become a pagan again for awhile—the first indication that this is not an entirely Christian poem. In saying this, the Hermit oscillates between Spenser's extreme positions—the exclusively Christian and the exclusively humanistic—because he is talking about "all knights" and about the New Jerusalem and Cleopolis in general. After this, Redcrosse on his way to syncretism alternates between grace and free will, between the Contemplative Life and a paganized Active Life, up through the end of Book I. Anticipatory syncretic notes occur in the betrothal ceremony (xii.21–23; 29).

In Book II, as our capsule contrast on the subject of free will and grace indicated, and as I shall prove in my related article, the eventual reconciliation of Redcrosse with Guyon and his Palmer nudges this particular Briton and Faery toward each other until they overlap in the late stage of Christian life known as sanctification. The necessity of grace as a foundation is shown by the tragedy of Mordant, Amavia, and Ruddymane which follows. Then in canto viii the relation of grace and free will is shown not as alternation but as a complex interdigitation and simultaneous cooperation of the angel and Arthur with various faculties of Guyon, like the "concurrence . . . the matching or marrowing together of God's grace and of the goodness that remaineth in man" in Calvin's *via media*. The interpenetration of earthly and divine love is seen in the truly syncretic comparison of the angel to Cupid (II.viii.6). The tenth canto of Book II, however, returns to the topic of Britons and Faeries in general and reiterates even more strongly and clearly the pluralism of its counterpart in Book I. The hard time Arthur has in canto xi subduing Maleger or original sin dramatizes the main difference between a Briton and an Elf such as Guyon, who kept Maleger away by his very presence, and who struggles instead with the Aristotelian counterpart of him, *acrasia*.

In Book III, another clash occurs between Guyon, the knight of the preceding book, and Britomart, his successor. Such clashes, I propose, herald the advent of a new viewpoint, in this case, the exclusively humanistic. In contrast, in Book VI, Artegall and Calidore have only the warmest feelings for each other when they meet in the first canto, because, I suggest, they both represent the same viewpoint. That the viewpoint of Book III is exclusively humanistic, despite routine references to church, God, and saints, is indicated by the qualified endorsement of Cupid, as we have seen, and perhaps most strikingly by Spenser's being able to joke about the fact that Britomart and Glauce were thinking about her love affair instead of paying attention to the church service (III.ii.48). The Garden of Adonis is pretty clearly sub-Christian in that despite the reference to the text "Increase and multiply" it deals with an area of life common to both classical and Christian—common, in fact, to man and beast, as is indicated by their frequent parallelism. I think it will be agreed that the remaining books are of a piece with Book III, with isolated brief references to Christianity in the syncretic similes and in pairs of classical-Christian contrasts—for example, Cambina in Book IV creating concord by means of her sacramental cup as opposed to Concord achieving it by main force, and Mercilla in Book V embodying God's mercy as opposed to Isis or classical equity.[26] Finally, like Redcrosse at the end of his life, Spenser, ending his poem prematurely in the shadow of death, returns to a vision of heaven perhaps more sublime, because more philosophical, than that of the New Jerusalem; but again it is paired with a vision through Nature's eyes of the cyclical perfection of earthly things, so that the poem as we have it ends in pluralism. This pluralism broadens the appeal of the first two books by mitigating somewhat the often-criticized sternness of their respective virtues. It assures us that Spenser did not "really believe" in them any more—or any less—than he believed in the free-and-easy Garden of Adonis. Our notions of the formal unity of The Faerie Queene must now be more complicated. If, as I suggested at the beginning, the structure is like a tree trunk, the center and its first growth-ring, Book I and Book II, must each be terraced upward, along with the outermost few stanzas of the poem, as representing more or less spiritual planes absent from the other books. Although the world of The Faerie Queene is not unified, it still has an intellectual structure; it has three worlds.[27] In this many-faceted poem, at least these three facets are clear-cut.

7

BERNARD J. VONDERSMITH   *A Bibliography of*
Criticism of The Faerie Queene,
1900–1970

THE FOLLOWING BIBLIOGRAPHY brings together for the first time the majority of the criticism of Edmund Spenser's *The Faerie Queene* published from 1900 to 1970. I am heavily indebted to the fuller bibliographies which precede mine: Frederic Ives Carpenter's *A Reference Guide to Edmund Spenser* (1923), Dorothy F. Atkinson's *Edmund Spenser: A Bibliographical Supplement* (1937), and Waldo F. McNeir and Foster Provost's *Annotated Bibliography of Edmund Spenser, 1937–1960* (1962). I am also indebted to Carolyn Burgholzer for the use of her unpublished bibliography of *Faerie Queene* criticism from 1948 to 1968.

Adams, Marjorie. "The Literary Relations of Spenser and Ronsard." Diss. University of Texas, 1952.
Aguzzi, Danilo. "Allegory in the Heroic Poetry of the Renaissance." Diss. Columbia University, 1959.
Ainsworth, Edward G., Jr. "The *Orlando Furioso* in English Literature before 1640." Diss. Cornell University, 1929.
Akrigg, G. P. V. "The Renaissance Reconsidered." *QQ*, 52 (1945), 311–19.
Albright, Evelyn M. "*The Faerie Queene* in Masque at the Gray's Inn Revels." *PMLA*, 41 (1926), 497–516.
———. "On the Dating of Spenser's *Mutability Cantos*." *SP*, 26 (1929), 482–98.
———. "Spenser's Connection with the Letters in Gabriel Harvey's *Letter-Book*," *MP*, 29 (1932), 411–36.
———. "Spenser's Cosmic Philosophy and His Religion. *PMLA*, 44 (1929), 715–59.
———. "Spenser's Reasons for Rejecting the *Cantos of Mutability*." *SP*, 25 (1928), 93–127.

Allen, Don Cameron. "Arthur's Diamond Shield in *The Faerie Queene*." *JEGP*, 36 (1937), 234–43.

———. "The Degeneration of Man and Renaissance Pessimism." *SP*, 35 (1938), 202–27.

———. *The Legend of Noah*: *Renaissance Rationalism in Art, Science, and Letters*. Urbana: University of Illinois Press, 1949; rpt. 1963.

———. *Mysteriously Meant*: *The Rediscovery of Pagan Symbolism and Allegorical Interpretation in the Renaissance*. Baltimore: The Johns Hopkins Press, 1970.

———. "A Note on Spenser's Orology." *MLN*, 61 (1946), 555–56.

———. "On the Closing Lines of *The Faerie Queene*." *MLN*, 64 (1949), 93–94.

———. "Spenser's Radigund." *MLN*, 67 (1952), 120–22.

———. "Spenser's Sthenoboea." *MLN*, 53 (1938), 118–19.

———. *The Star-Crossed Renaissance*: *The Quarrel about Astrology and Its Influence in England*. Durham, N. C.: Duke University Press, 1941; rpt. New York: Octagon Books, 1966.

———. "Symbolic Color in the Literature of the English Renaissance." *PQ*, 15 (1936), 81–92.

Allen, Percy. *Anne Cecil, Elizabeth, and Oxford*. London: D. Archer, 1934.

Alpers, Paul J., ed. *Edmund Spenser*: *A Critical Anthology*. Harmondsworth: Penguin Books, 1969.

———, ed. *Elizabethan Poetry*: *Modern Essays in Criticism*. New York: Oxford University Press, 1967.

———. "Narrative and Rhetoric in *The Faerie Queene*." Diss. Harvard University, 1958.

———. "Narrative and Rhetoric in *The Faerie Queene*." *SEL*, 2 (1962), 27–46.

———. *The Poetry of "The Faerie Queene."* Princeton, N. J.: Princeton University Press, 1967.

Alworth, E. Paul. "Spenser's Concept of Nature." In *His Firm Estate*: *Essays in Honor of Franklin James Elkenberry by Former Students*. Ed. Donald E. Hayden. Tulsa, Oklahoma: University of Tulsa Press, 1967.

Anderson, Judith H. "Aspects of Allegory in *Piers Plowman* and *The Faerie Queene*." Diss. Yale University, 1965.

———. "The July Eclogue and the House of Holiness: Perspective in Spenser." *SEL*, 10 (1970), 17–32.

———. "The Knight and the Palmer in *The Faerie Queene*, Book II." *MLQ*, 31 (1970), 160–78.

———. " 'Nor Man It Is': The Knight of Justice in Book V of Spenser's *Faerie Queene*." *PMLA*, 85 (1970), 65–77.

———. "Redcrosse and the Descent into Hell." *ELH*, 36 (1969), 470–92.

Aptekar, Jane H. *Icons of Justice*: *Iconography and Thematic Imagery in Book V of "The Faerie Queene."* Diss. Columbia University, 1967. New York: Columbia University Press, 1969.

Archer, Susan Mary. "Hawthorne's Use of Spenser." Diss. University of Pennsylvania, 1967.

Arestad, Sverre. "Spenser's *Faery* and *Fairy*." *MLQ*, 8 (1947), 37–42.

Ariail, J. M. "Some Immediate English Influences, *Faerie Queene*, Books I–III." Diss. University of North Carolina, 1925.

"Ariosto." *TLS*, 32 (1933), 385–86.

Arnold, Paul. "Occultisme Elizabethain." *Cahiers du Sud*, 34 (1951), 88–101.

Arthos, John. *On the Poetry of Spenser and the Form of the Romances*. London: Allen and Unwin, 1956; rpt. New York: Books for Libraries Press, 1970.

Ashley, Leonard R. N. "Spenser and the Ideal of the Gentleman." *BHR*, 27 (1965), 108–32.

Ashton, John W. "Folklore in the Literature of Elizabethan England." *JAF*, 70 (1957), 10–15.

Atabay, Ercüment. "Büyuk Ingiliz Destanlari" [Great English Epics]. *Yenitürk*, 10 (1942), 6–9.

Atkins, J. W. H. *English Literary Criticism: The Renascence*. London: Methuen, 1947.

Atkinson, Dorothy F. "Busirane's Castle and Artidon's Cave." *MLQ*, 1 (1940), 185–92.

———. *Edmund Spenser: A Bibliographical Supplement*. Baltimore: The Johns Hopkins Press, 1937; rpt. New York: Haskell House, 1967.

———. "A Note on Spenser and Painting." *MLN*, 58 (1943), 57–58.

———. "A Study of the Punctuation of Spenser's *Faerie Queene*." Diss. University of Washington, 1931.

———. "*The Wandering Knight*, the Red Cross Knight, and 'Miles Dei.'" *HLQ*, 7 (1944), 109–34.

Atteberry, James Lem, Jr. "Bartholomew the Englishman and Edmund Spenser: Medieval Platonists." Diss. University of Texas, 1961.

Auld, Ina Bell. "Woman in the Renaissance: A Study of the Attitude of Shakespeare and his Contemporaries." Diss. University of Iowa, 1938.

Awad, Louis. "Spenser and the Pleiade." In *Studies in Literature*. Cairo, Egypt: Anglo-Egyptian Bookshop, 1954, pp. 51–76.

Ayres, H. M. "*The Faerie Queene* and *Amis and Amiloun*." *MLN*, 23 (1908), 177–80.

Aziz, Paul D. "The Poet's Poetry: Edmund Spenser's Uses of the Pastoral." Diss. Brown University, 1969.

Babb, Lawrence. *The Elizabethan Malady: A Study of Melancholia in English Literature from 1580 to 1642*. East Lansing, Mich.: Michigan State College Press, 1951; rpt. Michigan State University Press, 1965.

Bache, William B. "Spenser and Deloney." *N&Q*, 199 (1954), 232–33.

Bahr, Howard W. "The Misery of Florimell: the Ladder of Temptation." *SoQ*, 4 (1965), 116–22.

Bailey, John. *Poets and Poetry, Being Articles Reprinted from the Literary Supplement to "The Times."* Oxford: Clarendon Press, 1911.

Baker, Carlos. "The Influence of Spenser on Shelley's Major Poetry." Diss. Princeton University, 1940.

———. "The Literary Sources of Shelley's *The Witch of Atlas*. I. Spenser and *The Witch of Atlas*." *PMLA*, 56 (1941), 472–79.

———. "Spenser, the Eighteenth Century, and *Queen Mab*." *MLQ*, 2 (1941), 91–98.

Baker, Donald. "The Accuracy of Spenser's 'Letter to Raleigh.'" *MLN*, 76 (1961), 103–4.

Baker, Herschel. *The Dignity of Man: A Study of the Idea of Human Dignity in Classical Antiquity, the Middle Ages, and the Renaissance.* Cambridge, Mass.: Harvard University Press, 1947; rpt. as *The Image of Man*, New York: Harper, 1961; Gloucester, Mass.: Peter Smith, 1967.

Baker, William Price. "*The Faerie Queene*, Book III: An Elizabethan Synthesis of Ethical Theory." Diss. Harvard University, 1949.

Baldwin, Charles S. *Renaissance Literary Theory and Practice: Classicism in the Rhetoric and Poetic of Italy, France, and England, 1400–1600.* New York: Columbia University Press, 1939; rpt. Gloucester, Mass.: Peter Smith, 1959.

Baldwin, T. W. "The Genesis of Some Passages Which Spenser Borrowed from Marlowe." *ELH*, 9 (1942), 157–87.

———. "The Genesis of Some Passages Which Spenser Borrowed from Marlowe." *ELH*, 12 (1945), 165.

Bale, John Christian. "The Place of Chaucer in Sixteenth-Century English Literature." Diss. University of Illinois, 1953.

Ball, Lewis F. "The Background of the Minor English Renaissance Epics." *ELH*, 1 (1934), 63–89.

———. "The Morality Theme in Book II of *The Faerie Queene*." *MLN*, 46 (1931), 371–79.

Baretti, J. M. "The Story of Fradubio and Fraelissa in *The Faerie Queene*: Notes on Witchcraft." *CLS*, 5 (1942), 25–27.

Barker, Sir Ernest. *Traditions of Civility.* Cambridge: Cambridge University Press, 1948.

Barnum, Priscilla H. "Elizabethan 'Psychology' and Books I and II of Spenser's *Faerie Queene*." *Thoth*, 3 (1962), 55–68.

Baroway, Israel. "The Imagery of Spenser and the *Song of Songs*." *JEGP*, 33 (1934), 23–45.

———. *Studies in the Bible as Poetry in the English Renaissance.* Baltimore: The Johns Hopkins Press, 1935.

Barrow, Sarah. "Studies in the Language of Spenser." Diss. University of Chicago, 1902.

Baskervill, C. R. "The Genesis of Spenser's Queene of Faerie." *MP*, 18 (1920), 49–54.

Bayback, Michael, Paul Delany, and A. Kent Hieatt. "Placement 'In the Middest' in *The Faerie Queene*." *PLL*, 5 (1969), 227–34. Rpt. in *Silent Poetry*. Ed. Alastair Fowler. London: Routledge and Kegan Paul, 1970, pp. 141–52.

Bayley, P. C. "Order, Grace, and Courtesy in Spenser's World." In *Patterns of Love and Courtesy: Essays in Memory of C. S. Lewis*. Ed. John Lawlor. Evanston, Ill.: Northwestern University Press, 1968.

Bayne, Thomas. "'Well of English Undefyled.'" *N&Q*, 117 (1908), 267–68.

Beale, Dorothea. "Britomart, or Spenser's Ideal of Woman." In *Literary Studies of Poems, New and Old*. London: G. Bell, 1902, pp. 25–51.

Beer, N. *A History of British Socialism*. 2 vols. London: G. Bell, 1919.

Beers, Henry Augustus. *A History of English Romanticism in the Nineteenth Century*. New York: Henry Holt and Company, 1901.

Belden, H. M. "Alanus de Insulis, Giles Fletcher, and the *Mutabilitie Cantos*." *SP*, 26 (1929), 131–44.

———. "Two Spenser Notes." *MLN*, 44 (1929), 526–31.

Bell, Bernard W. "The Comic Realism of Una's Dwarf." *MSE*, 1 (1968), 111–18.

Belson, Joel Jay. "Escaped Faults in the Spenser *Concordance*." *AN&Q*, 8 (1970), 69–72.

———. "The Names in *The Faerie Queene*." Diss. Columbia University, 1967.

Bender, J. B. "Pictorial Techniques in the Poetry of Edmund Spenser." Diss. Cornell University, 1967.

Bengtsson, Frans G. "Spenser, Edmund." *Svensk Uppslagsbok* [Swedish Reference Book], 26, cols. 1251–52. Malmö: Förlagshuset Norden, 1953.

Benjamin, Edwin B. "A Borrowing from *The Faerie Queene* in *Old Mortality*." *N&Q*, 202 (1957), 515.

———. "Fame, Poetry, and the Order of History in the Literature of the English Renaissance." *SRen*, 6 (1959), 64–84.

Bennett, Josephine Waters. "The Allegory of Sir Arthegall in *The Faerie Queene*, V, xi–xii." *SP*, 37 (1940), 177–200.

———. "Britain among the Fortunate Isles." *SP*, 53 (1956), 114–40.

———. *The Evolution of "The Faerie Queene."* Chicago: University of Chicago Press, 1942; rpt. New York: Burt Franklin, 1960.

———. "Genre, Milieu, and the 'Epic Romance.'" In *English Institute Essays 1951*. Ed. Alan S. Downer. New York: Columbia University Press, 1952, pp. 95–125.

———. *The Parlement of Foules: An Interpretation*. Oxford: Oxford University Press, 1957.

———. *The Rediscovery of Sir John Mandeville*. New York: Modern Language Association, 1954.

———. "Renaissance Neo-Platonism in the Poetry of Edmund Spenser." Diss. Ohio State University, 1936.

———. "Reply: On Methods of Literary Interpretation." *JEGP*, 41 (1942), 486–89.

———. "Spenser and Gabriel Harvey's *Letter-Book*." *MP*, 29 (1931), 163–86.

———. "Spenser's Garden of Adonis." *PMLA*, 47 (1932), 46–80.

——. "Spenser's Garden of Adonis Revisited." *JEGP*, 41 (1942), 53–78.

——. "Spenser's Hesiod." *American Journal of Philology*, 52 (1931), 176–81.

——. "Spenser's Muse." *JEGP*, 31 (1932), 200–219.

——. "Spenser's *The Faerie Queene*." *Expl.*, 1 (1943), Item 62.

——. "Spenser's Venus and the Goddess of Nature of the *Cantos of Mutabilitie*." *SP*, 30 (1933), 160–92.

Bensly, Edward. "The Name 'Hudibras.'" *N&Q*, 168 (1935), 160.

Berdan, John M. *Early Tudor Poetry*. New York: Macmillan, 1920.

——. "The Family of *The Faerie Queene*." *Johns Hopkins Alumni Magazine*, 12 (1924), 267–87.

Berger, Harry, Jr. *The Allegorical Temper: Vision and Reality in Book II of Spenser's "Faerie Queene."* New Haven, Conn.: Yale University Press, 1957; rpt. Hamden, Conn.: Archon Books, 1967.

——. "Archaism, Immortality, and the Muse in Spenser's Poetry." *YR*, 58 (1968), 214–31.

——. "At Home and Abroad with Spenser." *MLQ*, 25 (1964), 102–9.

——. "The Discarding of Malbecco: Conspicuous Allusion and Critical Exhaustion in *The Faerie Queene*, III, ix–xi." *SP*, 66 (1969), 135–54.

——. "*Faerie Queene*, Book III: A General Description." *Criticism*, 11 (1969), 234–61.

——. "The Prospect of Imagination: Spenser and the Limits of Poetry." *SEL*, 1 (1961), 93–120.

——. "A Secret Discipline: *The Faerie Queene*, Book VI," In *Form and Convention in the Poetry of Edmund Spenser*. Ed. William Nelson. New York: Columbia University Press, 1961, pp. 35–75.

——, ed. *Spenser: A Collection of Critical Essays*. Englewood Cliffs, N. J.: Prentice Hall, 1968.

——. "The Spenserian Dynamics." *SEL*, 8 (1968), 1–18.

——. "Spenser's Garden of Adonis: Force and Form in the Renaissance Imagination." *UTQ*, 30 (1961), 128–49.

——. "Spenser's Goodly Frame of Temperance." Diss. Yale University, 1954.

——. "The Structure of Merlin's Chronicle in *The Faerie Queene*, III (iii)." *SEL*, 9 (1969), 39–51.

——. "Two Spenserian Retrospects: The Antique Temple of Venus and the Primitive Marriage of Rivers." *TSLL*, 10 (1968), 5–25.

Bernheimer, Richard. *Wild Men in the Middle Ages: A Study in Art, Sentiment, and Demonology*. Cambridge, Mass.: Harvard University Press, 1952.

Bethell, S. L. *Essays on Literary Criticism and the English Tradition*. London: Dobson, 1948.

Beum, Robert. "Some Observations on Spenser's Verse Forms." *NM*, 64 (1963), 180–96.

Beutner, Sister Mary Louise. "Spenser and the Emblem Writers." Diss. St. Louis University, 1941.

Bezanker, Abraham. "An Introduction to the Problem of Allegory in Literary Criticism." Diss. University of Michigan, 1955.

Bhattacherje, Mohinimohan. *Platonic Ideas in Spenser*. London: Longmans Green, 1935; rpt. Wesport, Conn.: Greenwood Press, 1970.

————. *Studies in Spenser*. Calcutta: University of Calcutta Press, 1929.

Bieman, Elizabeth. "Britomart in Book V of *The Faerie Queene*." *UTQ*, 37 (1968), 156–74.

Black, J. B. *The Reign of Elizabeth, 1558–1603*. Oxford: Clarendon Press, 1936, 2nd ed. 1959.

Blair, Lawrence C. "The Plot of *The Faerie Queene*." *PMLA*, 47 (1932), 81–88.

————. "The Plot of *The Faerie Queene*: Reply to Mr. Perkinson." *PMLA*, 48 (1933), 297–99.

Blair, Seabury M. "The Succession of Lives in Spenser's Three Sons of Agape." *MLQ*, 2 (1941), 109–14.

Blanchard, H. H. "Imitations from Tasso in *The Faerie Queene*." *SP*, 22 (1925), 198–221.

————. "Italian Influence on *The Faerie Queene*." Diss. Harvard University, 1921.

————. "Spenser and Boiardo." *PMLA*, 40 (1925), 828–51.

Bland, D. S. "Shakespeare and the 'Ordinary' Word." *ShS*, 4 (1951), 49–55.

Blayney, Glenn H. "Nathan Field and *The Faerie Queene*." *N&Q*, 200 (1955), 59–60.

Blayney, Margaret S. and Glenn H. Blayney. "*The Faerie Queene* and an English Version of Chartier's *Traite de l'Esperance*." *SP*, 55 (1958), 154–63.

Blissett, William. "Florimell and Marinell." *SEL*, 5 (1965), 87–104.

————. "The Historical Imagination in the English Renaissance, Studied in Spenser and Milton." Diss. University of Toronto, 1950.

————. "Spenser's Mutabilitie." In *Essays in English Literature from the Renaissance to the Victorian Age Presented to A. S. P. Woodhouse*. Ed. Millar MacLure and F. W. Watt. Toronto: University of Toronto Press, 1964.

Blitch, Alice. "Etymon and Image in *The Faerie Queene*." Diss. Michigan State University, 1965.

————. "The Mutability Cantos 'In Meet Order Ranged.'" *ELN*, 7 (1970), 179–86.

Block, Edward A. "*King Lear*: A Study in Balanced and Shifting Sympathies." *SQ*, 10 (1959), 499–512.

Bloom, Edward A. "The Allegorical Principle." *ELH*, 18 (1951), 163–90.

Bloomfield, Morton W. *The Seven Deadly Sins*. East Lansing, Michigan: Michigan State College Press, 1952; rpt. Michigan State University Press, 1967.

Blum, Irving D. "The Paradox of Money Imagery in English Renaissance Poetry." *SRen*, 8 (1961), 144–54.

Boase, T. S. R. "The Decoration of the New Palace of Westminster, 1841–1863." *JWCI*, 17 (1954), 319–58.

Boatwright, Evelyn. "A Note on Spenser's Use of Biblical Material." *MLN*, 44 (1929), 159.

Boegholm, N. "On the Spenserian Style." *Études Linguistiques 1944, Travaux du Cercle linguistique de Copenhague*, 1 (1945), 5–21.

Böhme, Traugott. *Spensers literarischen Nachleben bis zu Shelley*. Berlin: Palaestra, 1911.

Bolwell, Robert. "The Pastoral Element in Spenser's Poetry." *Western Reserve Bulletin*, 19 (1961), 17–27.

Bond, R. M. "Ariosto." *QR*, 208 (1908), 125–54.

Both, Willy Hans. "Aristotelisches Gedankengut in Spensers *Faerie Queene*." Diss. University of Hamburg, 1940.

Botting, Ronald B. "Spenser's Errour." *PQ*, 16 (1937), 73–78.

Boughner, Daniel C. "The Psychology of Memory in Spenser's *Faerie Queene*." *PMLA*, 47 (1932), 89–96.

Bowe, Elaine C. "Doctrines and Images of Despair in Christopher Marlowe's *Doctor Faustus* and Edmund Spenser's *The Faerie Queene*." Diss. University of Oregon, 1969.

Bowers, Fredson T. "Evidences of Revision in *The Faerie Queene*, III, i. 2." *MLN*, 60 (1945), 114–16.

———. "*The Faerie Queene*, Book II: Mordant, Ruddymane, and the Nymph's Well." In *English Studies in Honor of James Southall Wilson*. Charlottesville, University of Virginia Press, 1951, pp. 243–51.

Bradbrook, Muriel. "No Room at the Top: Spenser's Pursuit of Fame." In *Elizabethan Poetry*. London: Edward Arnold, 1960, pp. 91–109.

———. *Shakespeare and Elizabethan Poetry: A Study of His Earlier Works in Relation to the Poetry of the Time*. New York: Oxford University Press, 1952.

Bradford, Gamaliel. *Elizabethan Women*. Ed. H. O. White. Boston: Houghton Mifflin, 1936.

Bradner, Leicester. "The Authorship of *Spenser Redivivus*." *RES*, 14 (1938), 323–26.

———. *Edmund Spenser and "The Faerie Queene*." Chicago: University of Chicago Press, 1948; rpt. 1959.

———. "Forerunners of the Spenserian Stanza." *RES*, 4 (1928), 207–8.

———. "Spenser's Connection with Hampshire." *MLN*, 60 (1945), 180–84.

Brady, Emily K. "The Probable Source for Spenser's Tobacco Reference." *MLN*, 71 (1956), 402–4.

Breslar, M. L. R. "Spenser and Dante." *N&Q*, 124 (1911), 447.

Brie, Friedrich. "The Design of the Poets." In *Sidney's Arcadia: Eine Studie zur Englischen Renaissance, in Quellen und Forschungen zur Sprach- und Culturgeschichte der Germanischen Völker*. Strassburg: Karl J. Trubner, 1918, pp. 23–65.

Brie, Friedrich. *Imperialistiche strömungen in der englischen literatur*. Halle: M. Niemeyer, 1928.

————. "Shakespeare und die Impresa-Kunst seiner Zeit." *SJ*, 50 (1914), 9–30.

Briggs, H. E. "Keats's 'Gather the Rose.'" *MLN*, 58 (1943), 620–22.

————. "Keats's Golden Tongued Romance." *MLN*, 58 (1943), 125–28.

Briggs, K. M. *The Anatomy of Puck: An Examination of Fairy Beliefs among Shakespeare's Contemporaries and Successors.* London: Routledge and Kegan Paul, 1959.

Briggs, W. D. "Spenser's *Faerie Queene*, III, ii, and Boccaccio's *Fiammetta.*" *Stanford University Publications* (Matzke Memorial Volume). Stanford, Calif., 1911, pp. 57–61.

Bright, James W. "Brief Mention [On Some Characteristics of Spenser and on Winstanley's editions of *The Faerie Queene*, I and II]." *MLN*, 31 (1916), 189–91.

Brinkley, Roberta F. *Arthurian Legend in the Seventeenth Century.* Baltimore: The Johns Hopkins Press, 1932; rpt. London: Cass, 1967; New York: Octagon Books, 1967.

Brittain, Kilbee Cormack. "The Sin of Despair in English Renaissance Literature." Diss. University of California, Los Angeles, 1963.

Broadbent, J. B. *Poetic Love.* London: Chatto and Windus, 1965.

Broadus, E. K. "The Red Cross Knight and Lybeaus Desconus." *MLN*, 18 (1903), 202–4.

Bronson, Bertrand H. "Personification Reconsidered." *ELH*, 14 (1947), 163–77.

Brooke, N. S. "C. S. Lewis and Spenser: Nature, Art and the Bower of Bliss." *CamJ*, 2 (1949), 420–34.

Brooke, Tucker. *Essays on Shakespeare and Other Elizabethans.* Ed. Leicester Bradner. New Haven, Conn.: Yale University Press, 1948.

————. "Stanza Connection in *The Faerie Queene*." *MLN*, 37 (1922), 223–27.

Brooks, Eric St. John. *Sir Christopher Hatton, Queen Elizabeth's Favourite.* London: Jonathan Cape, 1946.

Brown, J. R. "Some Notes on the Native Elements in the Diction of *Paradise Lost,*" *N&Q*, 196 (1951), 424–28.

Brown, P. F. "The Influence of Edmund Spenser on the British Romantic Poets, 1800–1840." Diss. University of Chicago, 1905.

Bruce, J. D. "Spenser's *Faerie Queene*, Book III, canto vi, st. 11 ff. and Moschus's Idyl, *Love the Runaway.*" *MLN*, 27 (1912), 183–85.

Bruser, Fredelle. "*Comus* and the Rose Song." *SP*, 44 (1947), 625–44.

————. "Concepts of Chastity in Literature, Chiefly Non-Dramatic, of the English Renaissance." Diss. Radcliffe College, 1948.

Bryan, Robert A. "Apostasy and the Fourth Bead-Man in *The Faerie Queene.*" *ELN*, 5 (1967), 87–91.

————. "Spenser and the Death of Arius." *MLN*, 76 (1961), 104–6.

Bryce, J. C. "Spenser's 'XII Morall Vertues.'" *TLS*, 32 (1933), 537.

Buchan, A. M. "The Political Allegory of Book IV of *The Faerie Queene.*" *ELH*, 11 (1944), 237–48.

Buck, Katherine M. "The Elfin Chronicle." *TLS*, 47 (1948), 345.

Buck, Philo. "On the Political Allegory in *The Faerie Queene*." *Nebraska University Studies*, 11 (1911), 159–92.

———. "Spenser's Lost Poems." *PMLA*, 23 (1908), 80–99.

Bullock, Walter L. "A Comment on Criticism in the Cinquecento." *PMLA*, 42 (1927), 1057–60.

Bullough, Geoffrey, ed. *Narrative and Dramatic Sources of Shakespeare*. Vol. 2, *The Comedies, 1597–1603*. New York: Columbia University Press, 1958.

———. *The Philosophical Poems of Henry More*. Manchester: University of Manchester Press, 1931.

Burgholzer, Carolyn. "Edmund Spenser's *The Faerie Queene*: 1948–1968." Diss. Duquesne University, 1970.

Burke, Charles B. "Humor in Spenser." *N&Q*, 166 (1934), 113–15.

———. "Keats and Spenser Again." *PQ*, 19 (1940), 149–150.

———. "The 'Sage and Serious' Spenser." *N&Q*, 175 (1938), 457–58.

Burke, Joseph. "Archbishop Abbot's Tomb at Guildford." *JWCI*, 12 (1949), 179–88.

Burt, M. K. "Verse Ancient and Modern." *Rev. de l'Enseign. des Lang. Viv. 50è an.*, 1 (1933), 420–22.

Bush, Douglas. *Classical Influences in Renaissance Literature*. Cambridge, Mass.: Harvard University Press, 1952.

———. "The Date of Spenser's *Cantos of Mutability*." *PMLA*, 45 (1930), 954–57.

———. *English Poetry: The Main Currents from Chaucer to the Present*. New York: Oxford University Press, 1952; rpt. 1963; 2nd ed., London: Methuen, 1965; London: Oxford University Press, 1967.

———. "Marlowe and Spenser." *TLS*, 37 (1938), 12.

———. *Mythology and the Renaissance Tradition in English Poetry*. Minneapolis: University of Minnesota Press, 1932; rpt. New York: Pageant Book Co., 1957; rev. ed. New York: Norton, 1963.

———. *Mythology and the Romantic Tradition in English Poetry*. Cambridge, Mass: Harvard University Press, 1937; rpt. New York: Pageant Book Co., 1957; New York: Cooper Square, 1963; New York: Norton, 1963; Cambridge, Mass.: Harvard University Press, 1959.

———. *The Renaissance and English Humanism*. Toronto: University of Toronto Press, 1939; rpt. 1956, 1968.

———. *Science and English Poetry: A Historical Sketch, 1590–1950*. New York: Oxford University Press, 1950; rpt. 1961, 1967.

———. "Some Allusions to Spenser." *MLN*, 42 (1927), 314–16.

———. *Themes and Variations in English Poetry of the Renaissance*. Claremont, Calif.: Claremont Graduate School, 1957; rpt. Folcroft, Pa.: Folcroft Press, 1969.

Butler, P. R. "Rivers of Milton and Spenser." *QR*, 29 (1953), 373–84.

Butterworth, Walter. "Symbol and Allegory in Spenser." *Manchester Quarterly*, 21 (1902), 229–43.

Buxton, John. *Sir Philip Sidney and the English Renaissance*. London: Macmillan, 1954; 2nd. ed. New York: St. Martin's Press, 1964; London: Macmillan, 1965.

Buyssens, E. "Aristotelianism and Anti-Puritanism in Spenser's Alllegory of the Three Sisters." *Englische Studien*, 18 (1936), 68–73.

———. "Calvinism in *The Faerie Queene* of Spenser." *Rev. belge de Phil. et d'Hist.*, 5 (1926), 37–69, 381–400.

———. "Spenser's Allegories." *TLS*, 33 (1934), 28.

———. "The Symbolism of *The Faerie Queene*, Book I." *PQ*, 9 (1930), 403–6.

Cain, H. Edward. "Spenser's 'shield of faith.'" *SAB*, 10 (1935), 163–66.

Camden, Carroll. "The Architecture of Spenser's 'House of Alma.'" *MLN*, 58 (1943), 262–65.

Camp, Charles W. *The Artisan in Elizabethan Literature*. New York: Columbia University Press, 1923.

Campbell, Lily B. *Shakespeare's "Histories": Mirrors of Elizabethan Policy*. San Marino, Calif.: Huntington Library, 1947; rpt. 1958; 3rd ed. London: Methuen, 1964.

Cantelupe, Eugene Benjamin. "Representations of Venus in Italian Renaissance Painting and English Renaissance Poetry." Diss. Washington University, 1959.

Carpenter, Frederick Ives. *A Reference Guide to Edmund Spenser*. Chicago: University of Chicago Press, 1923; rpt. New York: Kraus Reprint Co., 1969.

Carpenter, S. C. *The Church in England, 597–1688*. London: John Murray, 1954.

Carpenter, W. Boyd. *The Religious Spirit in the Poets*. New York: T. Y. Crowell and Son, 1901.

Carré, Meyrick H. *Phases of Thought in England*. Oxford: Clarendon Press, 1949.

Carscallen, James. "The Goodly Frame of Temperance: The Metaphor of Cosmos in *The Faerie Queene*, Book II." *UTQ*, 37 (1968), 136–55.

Carter, William Hoyt, Jr. "*Ut Pictura Poesis*: A Study of the Parallel between Painting and Poetry from Classical Times through the Seventeenth Century." Diss. Harvard University, 1951.

Cartigny, Jean. *The Wandering Knight: Reprinted from the Copy of the First English Edition in the Henry E. Huntington Library*. Seattle: University of Washington Press, 1951.

Caspari, Fritz. *Humanism and the Social Order in Tudor England*. Chicago: University of Chicago Press, 1954; rpt. New York: Teacher's College Press, 1968.

Cassirer, Ernst. *The Platonic Renaissance in England*. Trans. James P. Pettegrove. Austin, Texas: University of Texas Press, 1953; rpt. New York: Gordian Press, 1970.

Castelli, Alberto. *La "Gerusalemme Liberata" nella Inghilterra di Spenser*. Milan: Societá Editrice "Vita e Pensiero," 1936.

Cawley, Robert R. "A Chaucerian Echo in Spenser." *MLN*, 41 (1926), 313–14.

———. *Unpathed Waters: Studies in the Influence of the Voyagers on Elizabethan Literature*. Princeton, N. J.: Princeton University Press, 1940; rpt. New York: Octagon Books, 1967.

Cellini, Benvenuto. "Fantasie e Realtà nell' Opera de Edmund Spenser." In *Annuario dell' Instituto Universitario di Venezia* (1952–53 and 1956–57), pp. 12–23.

Chace, JoAn Elizabeth. "Spenser's Celebration of Love: Its Background in English Protestant Thought." Diss. University of California, Berkeley, 1968.

Chambers, E. K. *Sir Thomas Wyatt and Some Collected Studies*. London, 1933; rpt. New York: Russell and Russell, 1965.

Chang, H. C. *Allegory and Courtesy in Spenser: A Chinese View*. Edinburgh: Edinburgh University Press, 1955; New York: Humanities Press, 1957.

Chapman, Raymond. "Fortune and Mutability in Elizabethan Literature." *CamJ*, 5 (1952), 374–80.

Charles, Amy Marie. "The Poetry of Ralph Knevet (1601–c.1671)." Diss. University of Pennsylvania, 1951.

Chauvire, Roger. "L'Homme Élisabéthain." *BAGB*, 3 (1957), 53–80.

Cheney, Donald S., Jr. *Spenser's Image of Nature: Wild Man and Shepherd in "The Faerie Queene."* New Haven, Conn.: Yale University Press, 1966.

———. "Wild Man and Shepherd in the Spenserian Ethic: Studies in *The Faerie Queene* and Renaissance Pastoral Motifs." Diss. Yale University, 1961.

Chew, Samuel C. *The Pilgrimage of Life*. New Haven, Conn.: Yale University Press, 1962.

———. "Spenser's Pageant of the Seven Deadly Sins." In *Studies in Art and Literature for Belle da Costa Greene*. Ed. D. E. Miner. Princeton, N. J.: Princeton University Press, 1954.

———. "Time and Fortune." *ELH*, 6 (1939), 83–113.

———. *The Virtues Reconciled: An Iconographic Study*. Toronto: University of Toronto Press, 1947.

Cirillo, Albert R. "The Fair Hermaphrodite: Love-Union in the Poetry of Donne and Spenser." *SEL*, 9 (1969), 81–95.

———. "Spenser's 'Faire Hermaphrodite.'" *PQ*, 47 (1968), 136–37.

Clark, Earl John. "Spenser's Theory of the English Poet." Diss. Loyola University of Chicago, 1956.

Clark, Judith P. "His Earnest unto Game: Spenser's Humor in *The Faerie Queene*." *ESRS*, 15, iv (1967), 13–24, 26–27.

Clements, Robert J. "Pen and Sword in Renaissance Literature." *MLQ*, 5 (1944), 131–41.

Coe, Ada H. "Spenser and Ovid." *CW*, 22 (1929), 91–92.

Colbrunn, Ethel B. "The Simile as a Stylistic Device in Elizabethan Narrative Poetry: An Analytical and Comparative Study." Diss. University of Florida, 1954.

Colie, Rosalie L. *Paradoxia Epidemica: The Renaissance Tradition of Paradox*. Princeton, N. J.: Princeton University Press, 1966.

Collins, John Churton. *Ephemera Critica*. London: Archibald Constable, 1901.

Collins, Joseph B. *Christian Mysticism in the Elizabethan Age*. Baltimore: The Johns Hopkins Press, 1940.

Coogan, Mary Jane. "The Concept of Honor in *The Faerie Queene*, Books I and II." Diss. Loyola University of Chicago, 1964.

Cook, A. S. "Spenser's *Faerie Queene*, I, i, 6." *MLN*, 22 (1907), 208–9.

Cooper, Lane. "Spenser and Ovid." *CW*, 22 (1929), 166.

Corder, Jim. "Colin against Art, Again." *N&Q*, 206 (1961), 301–2.

———. "Spencer [*sic*] and the Eighteenth-Century Informal Garden." *N&Q*, 204 (1959), 19–21.

Cory, Herbert Ellsworth. *The Critics of Edmund Spenser*. Berkeley: University of California Press, 1917; rpt. New York: Haskell House, 1964.

———. *Edmund Spenser: A Critical Study*. Berkeley: University of California Press, 1917; rpt. New York: Russell and Russell, 1965.

———. "The Influence of Spenser on English Poetry." Diss. Harvard University, 1910.

———. *Spenser, the School of the Fletchers, and Milton*. Berkeley: University of California Press, 1912.

———. "Spenser, Thomson, and Romanticism." *PMLA*, 26 (1911), 51–91.

Cosman, Madeleine P. "Spenser's Ark of Animals: Animal Imagery in the 'Faery Queene.'" *SEL*, 3 (1963), 85–107.

Covington, F. F., Jr. "A Note on *The Faerie Queene*, IV, iii, 27." *MLN*, 40, (1925), 253.

———. "Spenser and Alexander Neckham." *SP*, 22 (1925), 222–25.

Craig, Hardin. *The Enchanted Glass: The Elizabethan Mind in Literature*. New York: Oxford University Press, 1936; rpt. Oxford: Basil Blackwell, 1960.

———. *New Lamps for Old: A Sequel to "The Enchanted Glass."* Oxford: Basil Blackwell, 1960.

Craig, Martha Alden. "Language and Concept in *The Faerie Queene*." Diss. Yale University, 1958.

———. "The Secret Wit of Spenser's Language." In *Elizabethan Poetry: Modern Essays in Criticism*. Ed. Paul J. Alpers. New York: Oxford University Press, 1967, pp. 447–72.

Crampton, Georgia Ronan. "The Protagonist as Sufferer: A Critical Inquiry into Topos in Chaucer and Spenser." Diss. University of Oregon, 1967.

Crane, Clara W. "A Source for Spenser's Story of Timias and Belphoebe." *PMLA*, 43 (1928), 635–44.

Crane, Ronald S. "Imitation of Spenser and Milton in the Early Eighteenth Century." *SP*, 15 (1918), 195–206.

———. "The Vogue of Guy of Warwick from the Close of the Middle Ages to the Romantic Revival." *PMLA*, 30 (1915), 125–94.

Crothers, Samuel M. *Among Friends*. Boston: Houghton Mifflin, 1910.

Culp, Dorothy Woodward. "The Bands of Civility: A Study of Spenser's Theory of Courtesy." Diss. Columbia University, 1967.

Cumming, W. P. "Ovid as a Source for Spenser's Monster-Spawning Mud Passages." *MLN*, 45 (1930), 166–68.

Cummings, R. M. "A Note on the Arithomological Stanza: *The Faerie Queene*, II, ix, 22." *JWCI*, 30 (1967), 410–14.

Curtius, Ernst R. *European Literature and the Latin Middle Ages*. Trans. Willard R. Trask. New York: Pantheon Books, 1953; rpt. New York: Harper and Row, 1963.

Cutts, John P. "Spenser's Mermaids." *ELN*, 5 (1968), 250–56.

Daiches, David. *A Critical History of English Literature*. 2 vols. New York: Ronald Press, 1960; 2nd ed. 1970.

———. *Literature and Society*. London: Victor Gollancz, 1938; rpt. New York: Haskell House, 1970.

Dallett, Joseph B. "*The Faerie Queene*, IV, i–v: A Synopsis of Discord." *MLN*, 75 (1960), 639–43.

———. "Ideas of Sight in *The Faerie Queene*." *ELH*, 27 (1960), 87–121.

Daly, John P., S. J. "'Talus' in Spenser's *Faerie Queene*." *N&Q*, 205 (1960), 49.

Danby, John F. "The Poets on Fortune's Hill: Literature and Society, 1580–1610." *CamJ*, 2 (1949), 195–211.

———. *Poets on Fortune's Hill: Studies in Sidney, Shakespeare, Beaumont and Fletcher*. London: Faber and Faber, 1952; rpt. Port Washington, N. Y.: Kennikat Press, 1966.

———. *Shakespeare's Doctrine of Nature: A Study of "King Lear."* London: Faber, 1949; rpt. 1958.

Daniells, Roy. "The Baroque Form in English Literature." *UTQ*, 14 (1945), 393–408.

Davidson, Clifford. "The Idol of Isis Church." *SP*, 66 (1969), 70–86.

Davie, Donald. *Purity of Diction in English Verse*. London: Chatto and Windus, 1952; rpt. New York: Schocken Books, 1967.

Davis, B. E. C. *Edmund Spenser: A Critical Study*. Cambridge: Cambridge University Press, 1933; rpt. New York: Russell and Russell, 1962.

Davis, W. H. "Castiglione and Spenser." Diss. Columbia University, 1908.

Davison, Francis. *A Poetical Rhapsody, 1602–1621*. Ed. Hyder E. Rollins. Cambridge, Mass.: Harvard University Press, 1931–32.

Dedeyan, Charles. *Dante en Angleterre: Moyen-Age Renaissance*. Paris: Didier, 1961.

Dees, Jerome S. "The Narrator's Voice in *The Faerie Queene, Christs Victorie and Triumphs*, and *The Locusts, or Apollyonists*." Diss. University of Illinois, 1968.

DeLacy, Hugh. "Astrology in the Poetry of Edmund Spenser." *JEGP*, 33 (1934), 540–43.

DeLattre, Floris. *English Fairy Poetry from the Origins to the Seventeenth Century*. London: H. Froude, 1912.

DeLattre, Floris and Camille Chemin. *Les Chansons Élizabéthaines*. Paris: Didier, 1948.

DeMontmorency, J. E. G. "The Red Cross Knight." *CR*, 101 (1915), 659–63.

DeMorgues, O. M. "A Comparative Study of the French and English Poets of the Late Sixteenth and Earlier Seventeenth Centuries." Diss. Cambridge University, 1950.

DeMoss, William Fenn. *The Influence of Aristotle's "Politics" and "Ethics" on Spenser*. Chicago: University of Chicago Press, 1918.

———. "Spenser's Twelve Moral Virtues 'according to Aristotle.'" *MP*, 16 (1918), 23–38, 245–70.

DeSelincourt, Ernest. *Oxford Lectures on Poetry*. Oxford: Oxford University Press, 1934; rpt. Freeport, N. Y.: Books for Libraries Press, 1967.

DeVere, Aubrey. *Great Thoughts*. 4th Series, 8 (1901), 219.

Dhesi, Nirmal S. "The Paynims and Saracens of Spenser's *The Faerie Queene*." Diss. Michigan State University, 1969.

Dickson, Sarah A. "Panacea or Precious Bane: Tobacco in Sixteenth-Century Literature," *BNYPL*, 57 (1953), 367–81, 419–32, 471–96, 544–66, 580–97; 58 (1954), 42–47, 55–73; 110–25, 174–85, 230–41, 274–304, 315–36.

Dimter, Margarete. "Der Adjectivgebrauch bei Spenser." Diss. University of Vienna, 1946.

Dixon, W. M. *English Epic and Heroic Poetry*. New York: E. P. Dutton, 1912; rpt. New York: Haskell House, 1964.

Dodge, R. E. Neil. "A Sermon on Source Hunting." *MP*, 9 (1911), 214–16.

———. "Spenser's Imitations from Ariosto." *PMLA*, 12 (1897), 151–204.

———. "Spenser's Imitations from Ariosto: Addenda." *PMLA*, 35 (1920), 91–92.

———. "The Well of Life and the Tree of Life." *MP*, 6 (1909), 191–96.

Doggett, Frank A. "Donne's Platonism." *SR*, 42 (1934), 274–92.

Doran, Madeleine. "On Elizabethan 'Credulity,' with Some Questions concerning the Use of the Marvelous in Literature." *JHI*, 1 (1940), 151–76.

Dorn, Alfred. "The Mutability Theme in the Poetry of Edmund Spenser and John Donne." Diss. New York University, 1970.

Douady, Jules. "Spenser et la Reine des Fees." In *La Mer et les Poetes Anglais*. Paris: Hachette and Co., 1912, pp. 66–84.

Dowden, Ernest. "Elizabethan Psychology." *Atlantic Monthly*, 100 (1907), 388–99.

Draper, J. W. "Classical Coinage in *The Faerie Queene*." *PMLA*, 47 (1932), 97–108.

———. "More Light on Spenser's Linguistics," *MLN*, 41 (1926), 127–28.

————. "The Narrative Technique of *The Faerie Queene.*" *PMLA*, 39 (1924), 310–24.

————. "Spenser's Talus Again." *PQ*, 15 (1936), 215–17.

————. "Spenser's Use of the Perfective Prefix." *MLN*, 48 (1933), 226–28.

Dressler, Graham McFarland. "A Study of Aphorisms in the Poetry of Edmund Spenser." Diss. University of Washington, 1937.

Dreyfus, Norman J. "Eighteenth-Century Criticism of Spenser." Diss. The Johns Hopkins University, 1938.

Duckett, Eleanor S. "Catullus in English Poetry." *Smith College Classical Studies*, no. 6. Northampton, Mass., 1925, pp. 8–199.

Duffield, Kenneth T. "The Elfin Chronicle." *TLS*, 47 (1948), 359.

Dunbar, Helen F. *Symbolism in Medieval Thought and Its Consummation in the "Divine Comedy."* New Haven, Conn.: Yale University Press, 1929.

Dundas, Judith. "Allegory as a Form of Wit." *SRen*, 11 (1964), 223–33.

————. "Elizabethan Architecture and *The Faerie Queene*: Some Structural Analogies." *DR*, 45 (1966), 470–78.

————. "The Imagery of Spenser's *Faerie Queene.*" Diss. University of Wisconsin, 1957.

————. "The Rhetorical Basis of Spenser's Imagery." *SEL*, 8 (1968), 59–75.

Dunlap, Rhodes. "Allegorical Interpretation of Renaissance Literature." *PMLA*, 82 (1967), 39–43.

Dunn, Esther Cloudman. *The Literature of Shakespeare's England.* New York: Scribners, 1936; rpt. New York: Cooper Square Publishers, 1969.

Dunn, Millard C. "Rhythm and Allegory: The Development of Narrative Structure in *The Faerie Queene.*" Diss. Indiana University, 1966.

Dunseath, Thomas K. *Spenser's Allegory of Justice in Book Five of "The Faerie Queene."* Princeton, N. J.: Princeton University Press, 1968.

Durling, Robert M. "The Bower of Bliss and Armida's Palace." *CL*, 6 (1954), 335–47.

————. *The Figure of the Poet in the Renaissance Epic.* Cambridge, Mass.: Harvard University Press, 1965.

Eagle, R. L. "The Arcadia (1593)—Spenser (1611) Title Page." *Baconiana*, 29, No. 116 (1945), 97–100.

Edwards, Calvin Roger. "Spenser and the Ovidian Tradition." Diss. Yale University, 1957.

Edwards, Jean M. "Spenser and His Philosophy," *CamJ*, 4 (1951), 622–28.

Elliott, G. R. *Humanism and Imagination.* Chapel Hill, N. C.: University of North Carolina Press, 1938; rpt. Port Washington, N. Y.: Kennikat Press, 1964.

Elliott, John R., ed. *The Prince of Poets.* New York: New York University Press, 1968.

Ellrodt, Robert. *Neoplatonism in the Poetry of Spenser.* Geneva: E. Droz, 1960.

Elmem, Paul. "Shakespeare's Gentle Hours." *SQ*, 4 (1953), 301–9.

Elton, Oliver. *Modern Studies*. London: E. Arnold, 1907; rpt. Freeport, N. Y.: Books for Libraries Press, 1967.

Emerson, Francis W. "The Bible in Spenser's Chaucer." *N&Q*, 203 (1958), 422–23.

———. "The Spenser-Followers in Leigh Hunt's Chaucer." *N&Q*, 203 (1958), 284–286.

Empson, William. *Seven Types of Ambiguity*. 3rd ed. London: Chatto and Windus, 1953; rpt. New York: Meridian Books, 1957; Harmondsworth: Penguin Books, 1961; London: Chatto and Windus, 1963; Cleveland: World Publishing Co., 1964.

Emry, Hazel T. "Two Houses of Pride: Spenser's and Hawthorne's." *PQ*, 33 (1954), 91–94.

English, H. M., Jr. "Spenser's Accommodation of Allegory to History in the Story of Timias and Belphoebe." *JEGP*, 59 (1960), 417–29.

Ericson, Eston E. " 'Reaving the Dead' in the Age of Chivalry," *MLN*, 52 (1937), 353–55.

Erskine, John. "Life, The Great Adventure: The Story of *The Faerie Queene*." *Delineator*, 110 (1927), 29, 66, 69.

———. "The Virtue of Friendship in *The Faerie Queene*." *PMLA*, 30 (1915), 831–50.

Evans, B. Ifor. *Tradition and Romanticism: Studies in English Poetry from Chaucer to W. B. Yeats*. New York: Longmans, 1940; rpt. Hamden, Conn.: Archon Books, 1964.

Evans, Frank B. "On the 1596 Printing of *The Faerie Queene*." In *RenP 1957*, pp. 4–8. Southeastern Renaissance Conference, 1957.

———. "The Printing of Spenser's *Faerie Queene* in 1596." *SB*, 18 (1965), 49–67.

Evans, Maurice. "Courtesy and the Fall of Man," *ES*, 46 (1965), 209–20.

———. *English Poetry in the Sixteenth Century*. London: Hutchinson, 1955; 2nd rev. ed. New York: Norton, 1967.

———. "The Fall of Guyon." *ELH*, 28 (1961), 215–24.

———. "Guyon and the Bower of Sloth." *SP*, 61 (1964), 140–49.

———. "Metaphor and Symbol in the Sixteenth Century." *EIC*, 3 (1953), 267–84.

———. "Platonic Allegory in *The Faerie Queene*." *RES*, 12 (1961), 132–43.

———. *Spenser's Anatomy of Heroism: A Commentary on "The Faerie Queene."* Cambridge: Cambridge University Press, 1970.

Evans, Robert O. "Spenserian Humor: *Faerie Queene* III and IV." *NM*, 60 (1959), 288–99.

Fairchild, Hoxie N. "Edmund Spenser." *Literary Digest International Book Review*, 2 (1924), 542–43.

———. *The Noble Savage: A Study in Romantic Naturalism*. New York: Columbia University Press, 1928; rpt. New York: Russell and Russell, 1961.

Falkiner, C. L. *Essays Related to Ireland*. London: Longmans Green, 1909.

Falls, Mother Mary Robert. "Spenser's Kirkrapine and the Elizabethans." *SP*, 50 (1953), 457–75.

——. *Spenser's Legend of Redcrosse in Relation to the Elizabethan Religious Milieu*. Washington, D. C.: Catholic University of America Press, 1951.

Faust, George P. "A Spenser Parallel." *MLN*, 49 (1934), 393.

Feinstein, Blossom Grayer. "Creation and Theories of Creativity in English Poetry of the Renaissance." Diss. City University of New York, 1967.

——. "*The Faerie Queene* and Cosmogonies of the Near East." *JHI*, 29 (1968), 531–50.

Ferguson, Arthur B. *The Indian Summer of English Chivalry*. Durham, N. C.: Duke University Press, 1960.

Ferguson, Wallace K. *The Renaissance*. New York: Holt, 1940; rpt. New York: Holt, Rinehart and Winston, 1960.

Finn, Sister Dorothy Mercedes. "Love and Marriage in Renaissance Literature." Diss. Columbia University, 1955.

Finney, Claude Lee. *The Evolution of Keats's Poetry*. 2 vols. Cambridge, Mass.: Harvard University Press, 1936.

Finster, Georg. *Homer in der Neuzeit von Dante bis Goethe. Italien. Frankreich. England. Deutschland*. Leipsig and Berlin: B. G. Teubner, 1912.

Fish, Stanley. "Nature as Concept and Character in the *Mutabilitie Cantos*." *CLAJ*, 6 (1963), 210–15.

Fitz, Irmgard Maximilians. "Theuerdank—Spensers Feekönigin." Diss. University of Vienna, 1950.

Fleischmann, Wolfgang B. "A Note on Spenser and Pope." *N&Q*, 199 (1954), 16–17.

Fleming, Charles F. "Spenser's *Faerie Queene*: Sans Loy, Sans Foy, and Sans Joy." *NQ*, 136 (1918), 71.

Fletcher, Angus. *Allegory: The Theory of a Symbolic Mode*. Ithaca, N. Y.: Cornell University Press, 1964.

Fletcher, James M. J. "Edmund Spenser and the Dorset Stour." *NQ for Somerset and Dorset*, 21 (1934), 180–82.

Fletcher, Jefferson B. "Edmund Spenser," *Encyclopedia Americana*. New York: Americana Corp., 1927. pp. 395–401.

——. "*Huon of Burdeux* and *The Faerie Queene*." *JEGP*, 2 (1898), 203–12.

——. "The Legend of Cambel and Triamond." *SP*, 35 (1938), 195–201.

——. *Literature of the Italian Renaissance*. New York: Macmillan, 1934; rpt. Port Washington, N. Y.: Kennikat Press, 1964.

——. "The Painter of the Poets," *SP*, 14 (1917), 153–66.

——. "The Puritan Argument in Spenser." *PMLA*, 58 (1943), 634–48.

Fletcher, Jefferson V. "Some Observations on the Changing Style of *The Faerie Queene*." *SP*, 31 (1934), 152–59.

Flint, M. K. and E. J. Dobson. "Weak Masters." *RES*, 10 (1959), 58–60.

Flower, Desmond and A. N. L. Munby, eds. *English Poetical Autographs*. London: Cassell, 1938.

Fluchère, Henri. *Shakespeare and the Elizabethans*. Trans. Guy Hamilton. New York: Hill and Wang, 1960.

Foltinek, Herbert. "Die Wilden Männer in Edmund Spensers *Faerie Queene*." *NS* (1961), 493–512.

Fowler, A. D. S. "Emblems of Temperance in *The Faerie Queene*, Book II." *RES*, 11 (1960), 143–49.

————. "The Image of Mortality: *The Faerie Queene*, II, i–ii." *HLQ*, 24 (1961), 91–110.

————. "A New Critic on Spenser." *EIC*, 10 (1960), 334–41.

————. "Numerical Composition in *The Faerie Queene*." *JWCI*, 25 (1962), 199–239.

————. "The Owl and the Turtle-Dove." *EC*, 12 (1962), 227–29.

————. "Oxford and London Marginalia to *The Faerie Queene*." *N&Q*, 206 (1961), 416–19.

————. "The River Guyon." *MLN*, 75 (1960), 289–92.

————, ed. *Silent Poetry*. London: Routledge and Kegan Paul, 1970.

————. "Six Knights at Castle Joyous." *SP*, 56 (1959), 583–89.

————. *Spenser and the Numbers of Time*. New York: Barnes and Noble, 1964.

————. *Triumphal Forms: Structural Patterns in Elizabethan Poetry*. Cambridge: Cambridge University Press, 1970.

Fowler, Earle B. *Spenser and the Courts of Love*. Menasha, Wisc.: George Banta, 1921.

————. *Spenser and the System of Courtly Love*. Louisville, Ky.: Standard Printing Co., 1934; rpt. Folcroft, Pa.: Folcroft Press, 1969.

Fox, Robert C. "Milton's *Lycidas*, 192–93." *Expl.*, 9 (1951), Item 54.

————. "Temperance and the Seven Deadly Sins in *The Faerie Queene*, Book II." *RES*, 12 (1961), 1–6.

"Frank Hogan's Library." *TLS*, 45 (1946), 288.

Freeman, Rosemary. *Edmund Spenser*. London: Longmans Green, 1957; rev. ed. 1962.

————. *English Emblem Books*. London: Chatto and Windus, 1948; rpt. New York: Octagon Books, 1966.

————. "*The Faerie Queene*": *A Companion for Readers*. Berkeley: University of California Press, 1970.

French, P. W. *A Commentary and Questionnaire on "The Faerie Queene."* London: Pitman, 1927.

Friden, Georg. *Studies on the Tenses of the English Verb from Chaucer to Shakespeare*. Upsala: English Institute in the University of Upsala, 1948.

Friederich, Werner P. *Outlines of Comparative Literature: Dante Alighieri to Eugene O'Neill*. Chapel Hill, N. C.: University of North Carolina Press, 1954.

Friedland, Louis S. "Spenser as a Fabulist." *SAB*, 12 (1937), 133–54, 197–207.

————. "Spenser's Sabaoth's Rest." *MLQ*, 17 (1956), 199–203.

Friedmann, Anthony Edward. "The Description of Landscape in Spenser's *Faerie Queene*: A Study of Rhetorical Tradition." Diss. Columbia University, 1965.

Fromm, Harold. "Spenserian Jazz and the Aphrodisiac of Virtue." *EM*, 17 (1966), 49–68.

Frye, Northrop. *Anatomy of Criticism: Four Essays*. Princeton, N. J.: Princeton University Press, 1957; rpt. New York: Atheneum, 1966.

————. "Levels of Meaning in Literature." *KR*, 12 (1950), 246–62.

————. "The Structure of Imagery in *The Faerie Queene*." *UTQ*, 30 (1961), 109–27; rpt. in *Fables of Identity*. New York: Harcourt, Brace and World, 1963, pp. 69–87.

Fucilla, Joseph G. "A Rhetorical Pattern in Renaissance and Baroque Poetry." *SRen*, 3 (1956), 23–48.

Fujii, Haruhiko. "Spenser no Graces." *EigoS*, 114 (1968), 442–43.

————. "Spenser no Shinko," *EigoS*, 115 (1969), 697–99.

Fuller, Ronald. *Literary Craftsmanship and Appreciation*. London: Allen and Unwin, 1934.

Fulton, Edward. "Spenser and Romanticism." *Nation*, 92 (1911), 445.

Funke, Otto. *Epochen der Neueren Englischen Literatur: Eine Überschau von der Renaissance bis zum Beginn des 20 Jahrhundert*. 2 vols. Bern: A. Francke, 1945.

Galimberti, Alice. *Dante nel Pensiero Inglese*. Florence: F. LeMonnier, 1921.

————. *Edmondo Spenser: "L'Ariosto Inglese."* Turin: Giuseppe Gambino, 1938.

Gang, Theodor M. "Nature and Grace in *The Faerie Queene*: The Problem Reviewed." *ELH*, 26 (1959), 1–22.

————. "Spenser and the Death of Socrates." *TLS*, 55 (1956), 643.

Garvin, Katharine, ed. *The Great Tudors*. 2nd ed. London: Eyre and Spottiswood, 1956.

Gayley, C. M. and B. P. Kurtz. *Methods and Materials of Literary Criticism*. 2 vols. Boston: Ginn and Co., 1920.

Geller, Lila G. "The Three Graces in Spenser's *Faerie Queene*: Image and Structure in Books III and IV." Diss. University of California, Los Angeles, 1970.

Giamatti, A. Bartlett. *The Earthly Paradise and the Renaissance Epic*. Princeton, N. J.: Princeton University Press, 1966.

Gibbon, John M. *Melody and the Lyric from Chaucer to the Cavaliers*. New York: E. P. Dutton, 1930.

Gilbert, Allan H. "Belphoebe's Misdeeming of Timias." *PMLA*, 62 (1947), 622–43.

————. "The Ladder of Lechery, *The Faerie Queene*, III, i, 45." *MLN*, 56 (1941), 594–97.

————. "A Poem Wrongly Attributed to Sidney." *MLN*, 57 (1942), 364.

Gilbert, Allan H. "The Qualities of the Renaissance Epic." *SAQ*, 53 (1954), 372–78.

——. "Spenserian Armor." *PMLA*, 57 (1942), 981–87.

——. "Spenserian Comedy." *TSL*, 2 (1957), 95–104.

——. "Spenser's Cymochles." *MLN*, 48 (1933), 230.

——. "Spenser's Imitations from Ariosto: Supplementary." *PMLA*, 34 (1919), 225–32.

——. "Those Two Brethren Giants (*Faerie Queene*, II.ii.15)." *MLN*, 70 (1955), 93–94.

"Giordano Bruno in England." *QR*, 196 (1902), 483–508.

Glasenapp, G. "Zur Vorgeschichte der Allegorie in Edmund Spensers *Faerie Queene*." Diss. Berlin, 1904.

Glazier, Lyle. "The Nature of Spenser's Imagery." *MLQ*, 16 (1955), 300–10.

——. "Spenser's Imagery: Imagery of Good and Evil in *The Faerie Queene*." Diss. Harvard University, 1950.

——. "The Struggle between Good and Evil in the First Book of *The Faerie Queene*." *CE*, 11 (1950), 382–87.

Glover, Terrot R. *The Ancient World: A Beginning*. New York: Macmillan, 1935; rpt. 1937; Baltimore: Penguin Books, 1944; London: Penguin Books, 1955; Harmondsworth: Penguin Books, 1957.

——. *Poets and Puritans*. London: Methuen, 1915; 2nd rev. ed. 1916; 3rd ed. 1923.

Godshalk, William L. "Prior's Copy of Spenser's 'Works' (1679)." *PBSA*, 61 (1967), 52–55.

Gohn, Ernest S. "A Note on Spenser's Use of Trope." *MLN*, 64 (1949), 53–55.

Golder, Harold. "Bunyan and Spenser." *PMLA*, 45 (1930), 216–37.

Goldsmith, Robert N. "The Wild Man on the English Stage." *MLR*, 53 (1958), 481–91.

Goodman, R. A. "A Reconsideration of the Poetry of Edmund Spenser, with Special Reference to the Mutability Theme." Diss. University of Nottingham, 1953.

Gordon, George. *The Discipline of Letters*. Oxford: Clarendon Press, 1923; rpt. 1946.

——. "The Trojans in Britain." *Essays and Studies by Members of the English Association*, 9 (1924), 9–30.

——. "Virgil in English Poetry." *Proceedings of the British Academy*, 17 (1931), 39–53; rpt. London: Haskell House, 1964.

Gordon, R. K. "Notes on Keats's 'Eve of St. Agnes.'" *MLR*, 41 (1946), 413–19.

Gottfried, Rudolf B. "Our New Poet: Archetypal Criticism and *The Faerie Queene*." *PMLA*, 83 (1968), 1362–77.

——. "The Pictorial Element in Spenser's Poetry." *ELH*, 19 (1952), 203–13.

——. "Spenser and *The Historie of Cambria*." *MLN*, 72 (1957), 9–13.

——. "Spenser and the Italian Myth of Locality." *SP*, 34 (1937), 107–25.

——. "Spenser Expands his Text." *RN*, 16 (1963), 9–10.

Gough, A. B. "Who Was Spenser's Bon Font?" *MLR*, 12 (1917), 140–45.

Gransden, K. W. "Allegory and Personality in Spenser's Heroes." *EK*, 20 (1970), 298–310.

———. *A Critical Commentary on Spenser's "The Faerie Queene."* London: Macmillan, 1969.

Gray, Jack Cooper. "Major Patterns of Imagery in *The Faerie Queene.*" Diss. Syracuse University, 1964.

Gray, M. M. "The Influence of Spenser's Irish Experiences on *The Faerie Queene.*" *RES*, 6 (1930), 413–28.

Graziani, Rene. "Elizabeth at Isis Church." *PMLA*, 79 (1964), 376–89.

———. "Philip II's *Impresa* and Spenser's Souldan." *JWCI*, 27 (1964), 322–24.

Greaves, Margaret. *The Blazon of Honor: A Study in Renaissance Magnanimity.* London: Barnes and Noble, 1964.

Greco, Francis G. "Torquato Tasso's Theory of the Epic and Its Influence on Edmund Spenser's *The Faerie Queene.*" Diss. Duquesne University, 1970.

Green, A. Wigfall. "Platonism in the Works of Edmund Spenser." *UMSE*, 6 (1965), 23–38.

Green, Charles H. "Sir John Salisbury as Spenser's Timias." *TxSE*, 31 (1952), 27–34.

Green, Zaidee E. "Observations on the Epic Similes in *The Faerie Queene.*" *PQ*, 14 (1935), 217–28.

———. "Swooning in *The Faerie Queene.*" *SP*, 34 (1937), 126–33.

Greene, Thomas. *The Descent from Heaven.* New Haven: Yale University Press, 1963.

Greenlaw, Edwin A. "Britomart at the House of Busirane." *SP*, 26 (1929), 117–30.

———. "The Captivity Episode in Sidney's *Arcadia.*" In *Manly Anniversary Studies.* Chicago: University of Chicago Press, 1923, pp. 54–63.

———. "*The Faerie Queene.*" In *Encyclopedia Americana.* New York: Americana Corp., 1918, pp. 708–10.

———. "The Influence of Machiavelli on Spenser." *MP*, 7 (1909), 187–202.

———. "Proceedings of Dr. Greenlaw's Seminary C, 1926–1931." Johns Hopkins University Library, Baltimore.

———. "Review of Herbert Ellsworth Cory's *Edmund Spenser: A Critical Study.*" *MLN*, 35 (1920), 165–77.

———. "Shakespeare's Pastorals." *SP*, 13 (1916), 122–54.

———. "Sidney's *Arcadia* as an Example of Elizabethan Allegory." In *Kittredge Anniversary Papers.* Boston: Ginn and Co., 1913, pp. 327–37.

———. "Some Old Religious Cults in Spenser." *SP*, 20 (1923), 216–43.

———. "Spenser and British Imperialism." *MP*, 9 (1912), 347–70.

———. "Spenser and Lucretius." *SP*, 17 (1920), 439–64.

———. "Spenser and the Earl of Leicester." *PMLA*, 25 (1910), 535–61.

Greenlaw, Edwin A. "Spenser's Fairy Mythology." *SP*, 15 (1918), 105–22.

———. "Spenser's Influence on *Paradise Lost.*" *SP*, 17 (1920), 320–59.

———. "Spenser's 'Mutabilitie.'" *PMLA*, 45 (1930), 684–703.

———. *Studies in Spenser's Historical Allegory.* Baltimore: The Johns Hopkins Press, 1932; rpt. New York: Octagon Books, 1967.

———. "Two Notes on Spenser's Classical Sources." *MLN*, 41 (1926), 323–26.

Greenough, Chester Noyes. *A Bibliography of the Theophrastan Character in English with Several Portrait Characters.* Cambridge, Mass.: Harvard University Press, 1947.

Grellner, Mary Adelaide, S.C.L. "Britomart's Quest for Maturity." *SEL*, 8 (1968), 35–43.

Grierson, H. J. C. *Cross Currents in English Literature of the Seventeenth Century.* London: Chatto and Windus, 1929; rpt. 1948; new ed. 1958.

Groom, Bernard. *The Diction of Poetry from Spenser to Bridges.* Toronto: University of Toronto Press, 1955.

———. *The Formation and Use of Compound Epithets in English Poetry from 1579.* Oxford: Clarendon Press, 1937.

Grubb, Marion. "A Brace of Villains." *MLN*, 50 (1935), 168–69.

Grundy, Joan. "Keats and the Elizabethans." In *John Keats: A Reassessment.* Ed. Kenneth Muir. Liverpool: University of Liverpool Press, 1958.

Gunn, Alan M. *The Mirror of Love: A Reinterpretation of "The Romance of the Rose."* Lubbock, Texas: Texas Tech Press, 1952.

Guth, Hans P. "Allegorical Implications of Artifice in Spenser's *Faerie Queene.*" *PMLA*, 76 (1961), 474–79.

———. "Unity and Multiplicity in Spenser's *Faerie Queene.*" *Anglia*, 74 (1956), 1–15.

Haase, Gladys. "Spenser's Orthography: An Examination of a Poet's Use of the Variant Pronunciations of Elizabethan English." Diss. Columbia University, 1952.

Hagstrum, Jean H. *The Sister Arts: The Tradition of Literary Pictorialism and English Poetry from Dryden to Gray.* Chicago: University of Chicago Press, 1958.

Hales, J. W. "Poet's Poet." In *Modern English Essays.* 3 vols. Ed. E. Rhys. New York: E. P. Dutton, 1922, II, pp. 241–46.

Hall, Edgar A. "Spenser and Two Old French Grail Romances." *PMLA*, 28 (1913), 539–54.

Hall, Vernon. *Renaissance Literary Criticism: A Study of Its Social Content.* New York: Columbia University Press, 1946; rpt. Gloucester, Mass.: Peter Smith, 1959.

Haller, William. *The Rise of Puritanism . . . from Thomas Cartwright to John Lilburne and John Milton, 1570–1643.* New York: Columbia University Press, 1938; rpt. New York: Harper, 1957.

Hamann, Albert. *An Essay on Spenser's "Faerie Queene."* Berlin: Gaertner, 1888.

Hamer, Douglas. "Some Spenser Problems." *N&Q*, 180 (1941), 165–67, 183–84, 206–9, 220–24, 238–41.

Hamilton, A. C. *"The Faerie Queene."* In *Critical Approaches to Six Major Works: "Beowulf" through "Paradise Lost."* Ed. Robert Lumiansky and Herschel Baker. Philadelphia: University of Pennsylvania Press, 1968, pp. 132–66.

———. "'Like Race to Runne': The Parallel Structure of *The Faerie Queene*, Books I and II." *PMLA*, 73 (1958), 327–34.

———. "Spenser and Langland." *SP*, 55 (1958), 533–48.

———. "Spenser's Letter to Ralegh." *MLN*, 73 (1958), 481–85.

———. "Spenser's Treatment of Myth." *ELH*, 26 (1959), 335–54.

———. *The Structure of Allegory in "The Faerie Queene."* Oxford: Clarendon Press, 1961.

———. "A Study of the Allegory of Spenser's *Faerie Queene*." Diss. Cambridge University, 1953.

———. "A Theological Reading of *The Faerie Queene*, Book II." *ELH*, 25 (1958), 155–62.

———. "The Visions of *Piers Plowman* and *The Faerie Queene*." In *Form and Convention in the Poetry of Edmund Spenser*. Ed. William Nelson. New York: Columbia University Press, 1961, pp. 1–34.

Hamilton, G. Rostrevor. *The Tell-Tale Article: A Critical Approach to Modern Poetry*. London: Heinemann, 1949.

Hammerle, Karl. "Das Laubenmotif bei Shakespeare und Spenser und die Frage: wer waren Bottom und die Little Western Flower?" *Anglia*, 71 (1953), 310–30.

———. "Ein Muttermal des deutschen Pyramus und die Spenserechos in *A Midsummer Night's Dream*." *WBEP*, 66 (1958), 52–66.

Hankins, John E. "The Sources of Spenser's Britomartis." *MLN*, 58 (1943), 607–10.

———. "Spenser and the Revelation of St. John." *PMLA*, 60 (1945), 364–81.

———. "Spenser's Lucifera and Philotime." *MLN*, 59 (1944), 413–15.

Haraszti, Zoltan. "The Poetry of Pure Fancy." *More Books*, 8 (1933), 213–22.

Hard, Frederick. "Princelie Pallaces: Spenser and Elizabethan Architecture." *SP*, 31 (1934), 293–310.

———. "Spenser's 'Clothes of Arras and of Taure.'" *SP*, 27 (1930), 162–85.

———. "Studies in the Aesthetic Influences on Edmund Spenser." Diss. Johns Hopkins University, 1928.

———. "Two Spenserian Imitations, by 'T. W.'" *ELH*, 5 (1938), 113–26.

Hardison, O. B., Jr. *The Enduring Moment: A Study of the Idea of Praise in Renaissance Literary Theory and Practice*. Chapel Hill, N. C.: University of North Carolina Press, 1962.

Harman, Edward G. *Edmund Spenser and the Impersonations of Francis Bacon*. London: Constable and Co., 1914.

———. *The "Impersonality" of Shakespeare*. London: C. Palmer, 1925.

Harmon, Alice Irene. "*Loci Communes* on Death and Suicide in the Literature of the English Renaissance." Diss. University of Minnesota, 1939.

Harper, Carrie A. *The Sources of British Chronicle History in Spenser's "Faerie Queene."* Philadelphia: John C. Winston Co., 1910; rpt. New York: Haskell House, 1964.

Harris, Victor. *All Coherence Gone.* Chicago: University of Chicago Press, 1949.

Harrison, Charles T. "The Ancient Atomists and English Humanism of the Seventeenth Century." Diss. Harvard University, 1932.

Harrison, John S. *Platonism in English Poetry of the Sixteenth and Seventeenth Centuries.* New York: Macmillan, 1903; rpt. 1919; New York: Russell and Russell, 1965.

————. *Types of English Poetry: A Study of Literary Organisms.* Indianapolis: Butler University Press, 1941.

Harrison, Thomas P., Jr. "Aspects of Primitivism in Shakespeare and Spenser." *TxSE*, 20 (1940), 39–71.

————. "Divinity in Spenser's Garden of Adonis." *TxSE*, 19 (1939), 48–73.

————. "*The Faerie Queene* and the *Diana*." *PQ*, 9 (1930), 51–56.

————. "Jonson's *The Sad Shepherd* and Spenser's." *MLN*, 58 (1943), 257–62.

————. "The Relations of Spenser and Sidney." *PMLA*, 45 (1930), 712–31.

————. "Spenser and Boccaccio's *Olympia*." *TxSE*, 14 (1934), 5–30.

————. *They Tell of Birds: Chaucer, Spenser, Milton, Drayton.* Austin, Texas: University of Texas Press, 1956; rpt. Westport, Conn.: Greenwood Press, 1969.

————. "The Whistler, Bird of Omen." *MLN*, 65 (1950), 539–41.

Hartley, Jesse Dyson, Jr. "A Study of the Imagery in Edmund Spenser's *The Faerie Queene*." Diss. University of Minnesota, 1963.

————. "Two Areas of Imagery Revealing Spenser, the Man and the Poet." *SCB*, 28 (1968), 138–41.

Hartman, Maurice M. "Spenser's Conceits." Diss. University of Virginia, 1937.

Hasker, Richard. "Spenser's 'Vaine Delight.'" *MLN*, 62 (1947), 334–35.

Hawkins, Sherman. "Mutabilitie and the Cycle of the Months." In *Form and Convention in the Poetry of Edmund Spenser.* Ed. William Nelson. New York: Columbia University Press, 1961, pp. 76–102.

Haydn, Hiram. *The Counter-Renaissance.* New York: Scribners, 1950; rpt. Gloucester, Mass.: Peter Smith, 1966; New York: Harcourt, Brace and World, 1967.

Heffner, Ray. "Edmund Spenser's Family." *HLQ*, 2 (1938), 79–84.

————. "Essex and Book V of *The Faerie Queene*." *ELH*, 3 (1936), 67–82.

————. "Essex, the Ideal Courtier." *ELH*, 1 (1934), 7–36.

————. "The Printing of John Hughes' Edition of Spenser, 1715." *MLN*, 50 (1935), 151–53.

————. "Spenser and the British Sea-Power." Diss. University of North Carolina, 1925.

————. "Spenser's Allegory in Book I of *The Faerie Queene*." *SP*, 27 (1930), 142–61.

Heinemann, Elfriede. *Das Bild der Dame in der Erzählendes Dichtung Englands von Malory bis Spenser*. Quakenbrück: Werkdruckerei von R. Kleinert, 1928.

Heise, Wilhelm. *Die Gleichnisse in Edmund Spensers "Faerie Queene" und ihre Vorbilder*. Konigsee: S. von Ende, 1902.

Heltzel, Virgil B. "Haly Heron: Elizabethan Essayist and Euphuist." *HLQ*, 16 (1952), 1–21.

Heninger, S. K., Jr. *A Handbook of Renaissance Meteorology, with Particular Reference to Elizabethan and Jacobean Literature*. Durham, N. C.: Duke University Press, 1960.

————. "The Orgoglio Episode in *The Faerie Queene*." *ELH*, 26 (1959), 171–87.

Henley, Pauline. *Spenser in Ireland*. Dublin: Cork University Press, 1928; rpt. New York: Russell and Russell, 1969.

————. "Spenser's 'Stony Aubrian.'" *TLS*, 35 (1936), 996.

Herford, C. H. "The Elizabethan Age in Recent Literary History." *QR*, 216 (1912), 353–73.

Herron, Dale S. "The 'Trial of True Curtesie': Book VII of *The Faerie Queene*." Diss. Northwestern University, 1970.

Heydorn, Marianne. "Spenser und der Calvinismus." Diss. University of Hamburg, 1939.

Hickey, E. "Catholicity in Spenser." *American Catholic Quarterly Review*, 32 (1907), 490–502.

————. "Sir Calidore: A Paper for Girls." *CW*, 93 (1911), 632–45.

Hieatt, A. Kent. "Milton's Comus and Spenser's False Genius." *UTQ*, 38 (1969), 313–18.

————. "Scudamour's Practice of *Maistrye* upon Amoret." *PMLA*, 77 (1962), 509–10.

————. *Short Time's Endless Monument: The Symbolism of Numbers in Edmund Spenser's "Epithalamion."* New York: Columbia University Press, 1960.

————. "Spenser's Atin from 'Atine'?" *MLN*, 72 (1957), 249–51.

Higgins, Dennis V. "Intellect-Will in Poetry of the English Renaissance." Diss. Claremont Graduate School, 1968.

Highet, Gilbert. *The Classical Tradition: Greek and Roman Influences on Western Literature*. New York: Oxford University Press, 1949; rpt. 1957, 1967.

Hill, John M. "Braggadochio and Spenser's Golden World Concept: The Function of Unregenerative Comedy." *ELH*, 37 (1970), 315–24.

Hill, R. F. "Colin Clout's Courtesy." *MLR*, 57 (1962), 492–503.

————. "Spenser's Allegorical 'Houses.'" *MLR*, 65 (1970), 721–33.

Hinckley, Henry B. "Theories of Vision in English Poetry." *MLN*, 24 (1909), 125.

Hintz, Howard W. "The Elizabethan Entertainment and *The Faerie Queene*." *PQ*, 14 (1935), 83–90.

Hogan, Patrick Galvin, Jr. "Sir Philip Sidney's *Arcadia* and Edmund Spenser's *Faerie Queene*: An Analysis of the Personal, Philosophic, and Iconographic Relationships." Diss. Vanderbilt University, 1965.

Holland, Joanne Field. "The Cantos of Mutabilitie and the Form of *The Faerie Queene*." *ELH*, 35 (1968), 21–31.

Holleran, James V. "The Minor Characters in Spenser's *Faerie Queene*." Diss. Louisiana State University, 1961.

————. "Spenser's Braggadochio." In *Studies in English Renaissance Literature*. Ed. Waldo F. McNeir. Baton Rouge: Louisiana State University Press, 1962, pp. 20–39.

————. "Spenser's Irony in Book II of *The Faerie Queene*." *McNeese Review*, 15 (1964), 11–17.

Holloway, J. "The Seven Deadly Sins in *The Faerie Queene*, Book II." *RES*, n.s. 3 (1952), 13–18.

Holme, James W. "Italian Courtesy-Books of the Sixteenth Century." *MLR*, 5 (1910), 145–66.

Honig, Edwin. *Dark Conceit: The Making of Allegory*. Evanston, Ill.: Northwestern University Press, 1959; rpt. Cambridge, Mass.: Walker de Barry, 1960; London: Faber and Faber, 1960; New York: Oxford University Press, 1966.

————. "Hobgoblin or Apollo." *KR*, 10 (1948), 664–81.

————. "Recreating Authority in Allegory." *JAAC*, 16 (1957), 180–93.

Hook, Julius Nicholas. "Eighteenth-Century Imitations of Spenser." Diss. University of Illinois, 1941.

Hoopes, Robert. " 'God Guide Thee, Guyon': Nature and Grace Reconciled in *The Faerie Queene*, Book II." *RES*, n.s. 5 (1954), 14–24.

Hope, Constance. "Alma. A Study from Spenser." *Month*, 96 (1900), 384–91.

Hopper, Vincent F. "Spenser's 'House of Temperance.' " *PMLA*, 55 (1940), 958–67.

Hotson, Leslie. "The Blatant Beast." In *Studies in Honor of T. W. Baldwin*. Urbana, Ill.: University of Illinois Press, 1958, pp. 34–37.

Hough, Graham. "First Commentary on *The Faerie Queene*." *TLS*, 63 (1964), 294.

————. *The First Commentary on "The Faerie Queene:" Being an Analysis of the Annotations in Lord Bessborough's Copy of the First Edition of "The Faerie Queene."* Privately published, 1964.

————. *A Preface to "The Faerie Queene."* London: Duckworth, 1962; New York: W. W. Norton, 1963.

Hough, Graham and Alastair Fowler. "Spenser and Renaissance Iconography." *EC*, 11 (1961), 233–38.

Houtchens, Lawrence H. and Carolyn Houtchens, eds. *Leigh Hunt's Literary Criticism*. New York: Columbia University Press, 1956.

Howarth, Enid. "Venus Looking Glas: A Study of Books III and IV of *The Faerie Queene*." Diss. University of New Mexico, 1968.

Howell, Wilbur Samuel. *Logic and Rhetoric in England, 1500–1700*. Princeton, N. J.: Princeton University Press, 1956; rpt. New York: Russell and Russell, 1961.

Huckabay, Calvin. "The Structure of Book IV of *The Faerie Queene*." *SN*, 27 (1955), 53–64.

Hudson, Hoyt H. *The Epigram in the English Renaissance*. Princeton, N. J.: Princeton University Press, 1947; rpt. New York: Octagon Books, 1966.

———. "The Transition in Poetry." *HLQ*, 5 (1942), 188–90.

Hughes, Merritt Y. "The Arthurs of *The Faerie Queene*." *EA*, 6 (1953), 193–213.

———. "A Boethian Parallel to *F.Q.* I, ii, 2–4." *MLN*, 63 (1948), 543.

———. "Burton on Spenser." *PMLA*, 41 (1926), 545–67.

———. "The Christ of *Paradise Regained* and the Renaissance Heroic Tradition." *SP*, 35 (1938), 254–77.

———. "England's Eliza and Spenser's Medina." *JEGP*, 43 (1944), 1–15.

———. "Some Aspects of the Relation of Edmund Spenser's Poetry to Classical Literature." Diss. Harvard University, 1921.

———. "Spenser and Utopia." *SP*, 17 (1920), 132–46.

———. "Spenser, 1552–1952." *TWA*, 42 (1953), 5–24.

———. "Spenser's Acrasia and the Circe of the Renaissance." *JHI*, 4 (1943), 381–99.

———. "Spenser's 'Blatant Beast.'" *MLR*, 13 (1918), 267–75.

———. "Spenser's Debt to the Greek Romances." *MP*, 23 (1925), 67–76.

———. "Spenser's Palmer." *ELH*, 2 (1935), 151–64.

———. *Virgil and Spenser*. University of California Publications in English, Vol. 2, No. 3. Berkeley: University of California Press, 1929, pp. 263–418.

———. "Virgilian Allegory in *The Faerie Queene*." *PMLA*, 44 (1929), 696–705.

Hulbert, Viola B. "The Belge Episode in *The Faerie Queene*." *SP*, 36 (1939), 124–46.

———. "A Possible Christian Source for Spenser's Temperance." *SP*, 28 (1931), 184–210.

———. "Spenser's Talus Again." *PQ*, 15 (1936), 413.

———. "Spenser's Twelve Moral Virtues 'According to Aristotle' and the Rest." Diss. University of Chicago, 1928.

Hume, Martin. "Spanish Influence in Elizabethan Literature." *Transactions of the Royal Society of Literature*, 2nd ser. 29 (1909), 1–35.

Hume, Theodore W. "*The Faerie Queene*—A Religious Romance." *Homiletic Review*, 48 (1904), 98–102.

Huston, J. Dennis. "The Function of the Mock Hero in Spenser's *Faerie Queene*." *MP*, 66 (1969), 212–17.

Hutcheson, W. J. Fraser. *Shakespeare's Other Anne: A Short Account of the Life and Works of Anne Whately or Beck, a Sister of the Order of St. Clare, Who Nearly Married William Shakespeare in November 1582 A. D.* Glasgow: MacLellan, 1950.

Hutton, James. "Spenser and the 'Cinq Points en Amours.'" *MLN*, 57 (1942), 657–61.

———. "Spenser's 'Adamantine Chains': A Cosmological Metaphor." In *The Classical Tradition: Literary and Historical Studies in Honor of Harry Caplan.* Ed. Luitpold Walloch. Ithaca, N. Y.: Cornell University Press, 1966, pp. 572–94.

Innes, Arthur Donald. *England under the Tudors.* London: Methuen, 1905; rpt. 1908, 1913, 1918, 1920, 1923, 1924, 1926, 1929, 1931; rev. ed. J. M. Henderson. London: Methuen, 1932; rpt. 1937, 1950, 1951, 1953.

Iredale, Roger O. "Book Five of Spenser's *Faerie Queene*: Justice and Her Enemies and the Coherency of the Imagery." Diss. University of Reading, 1959.

———. "Giants and Tyrants in Book Five of *The Faerie Queene*." *RES*, 17 (1966), 373–81.

Irving, William H. "An Imitation of *The Faerie Queene*." *MLN*, 43 (1928), 80.

Irwin, Margaret. *That Great Lucifer: A Portrait of Sir Walter Ralegh.* New York: Harcourt Brace, 1960.

Jack, A. A. *Chaucer and Spenser.* Glasgow: Maclehose and Jackson, 1920.

Jayne, Sears. "Ficino and the Platonism of the English Renaissance." *CL*, 4 (1952), 214–38.

Jeffery, Violet M. *John Lyly and the Italian Renaissance.* Paris: H. Champion, 1928.

Jenkins, Raymond. "Spenser and Ireland." *ELH*, 19 (1952), 131–42.

———. "Spenser at Smerwick." *TLS*, 32 (1933), 331.

———. "Spenser with Lord Grey in Ireland." *PMLA*, 52 (1937), 338–53.

Jessee, Jack Willard. "Spenser and the Emblem Books." Diss. University of Kentucky, 1955.

Jobson, Sister Florence Marie, S.C.N. "Dialogue in the Major Poetry of Edmund Spenser." Diss. St. Louis University, 1968.

Johnson, C. F. *Forms of English Poetry.* New York: American Book Co., 1904.

Johnson, Francis R. *Astronomical Thought in Renaissance England.* Baltimore: The Johns Hopkins Press, 1937.

———. *A Critical Bibliography of the Works of Edmund Spenser Printed before 1700.* Baltimore: The Johns Hopkins Press, 1933.

———. "The Progress of the Copernican Astronomy among English Scientists and Its Reflection in Literature from Spenser to Milton." Diss. Johns Hopkins University, 1935.

Johnston, Mary. "Once More Spenser and Ovid." *CW*, 22 (1929), 208.

———. "Parasites in Plautus and Spenser." *CW*, 26 (1933), 104.

Jones, Buford. "Hawthorne's Coverdale and Spenser's Allegory of Mutability." *AL*, 39 (1967), 215–19.

Jones, Frederick L. "Shelley and Spenser." *SP*, 39 (1942), 662–69.

Jones, H. S. V. "*The Faerie Queene* and the Medieval Aristotelian Tradition." *JEGP*, 25 (1926), 283–98.

———. "Magnanimity in Spenser's Legend of Holiness." *SP*, 29 (1932), 200–206.

———. *A Spenser Handbook*. New York: F. S. Crofts, 1930; rpt. London: George Bell, 1947.

———. *Spenser's Defense of Lord Grey*. Urbana: University of Illinois Press, 1919.

Jorgensen, Paul A. "Elizabethan Literature Today: A Review of Recent Scholarship." *TSLL*, 1 (1960), 562–78.

Jortin, John. *Remarks on Spenser's Poems*. New York: Garland, 1970.

Judson, A. C. *The Life of Spenser*. Baltimore: The Johns Hopkins Press, 1945.

———. "Samuel Woodford and Edmund Spenser." *N&Q*, 189 (1945), 191–92.

———. "The Seventeenth-Century Lives of Edmund Spenser." *HLQ*, 10 (1946), 35–48.

———. "Spenser's Theory of Courtesy." *PMLA*, 47 (1932), 122–36.

Jump, John D. "Spenser and Marlowe." *N&Q*, 209 (1964), 261–62.

Jusserand, J. J. "Spenser's 'Twelve Private Morall Vertues as Aristotle hath devised.'" *MP*, 3 (1906), 373–83.

Kahin, Helen Andrews. "Controversial Literature about Women: A Survey of Literature of This Type with Special Reference to the Writings of the English Renaissance." Diss. University of Washington, 1934.

———. "Spenser and the School of Alanus." *ELH*, 8 (1941), 257–72.

Kane, Robert J. "Tobacco in English Literature to 1700, with Special Reference to the Authorship of the First Work Thereon." Diss. Harvard University, 1929.

Kapp, Rudolf. "Heilige und Heiligenlegenden in England." In *Studien z. 16 u. 17 Jahrhundert*. Halle: Niemeyer, 1934.

Kaska, Thomas N. "A Study of Book VI of *The Faerie Queene*." Diss. Duquesne University, 1971.

Kaske, Carol V. "The Dragon's Spark and Sting and the Structure of Red Cross's Dragon Fight: *The Faerie Queene*, I. xi–xii." *SP*, 66 (1969), 609–38.

Kauffman, Corinne E. "Spenser and Tennyson: A Comparative Study." Diss. University of Texas, 1963.

Kellogg, Robert L. and Oliver L. Steele. "On the Punctuation of Two Lines in *The Faerie Queene*." *MLN*, 78 (1963), 147–48.

Kelso, Ruth. *The Doctrine of the English Gentleman in the Sixteenth Century*. University of Illinois Studies in Language and Literature, 14 (1929), 1–288.

Kendall, Lyle H., Jr. "Melt with Ruth." *N&Q*, 198 (1953), 145.

Kendrick, T. D. *British Antiquity*. London: Methuen, 1950.

———. "The Elfin Chronicle." *TLS*, 47 (1948), 79.

———. "The Elfin Chronicle." *TLS*, 47 (1948), 275.

Kennedy, William J. "Modes of Allegory in Ariosto, Tasso and Spenser." Diss. Yale University, 1970.

Kermode, Frank. "The Cave of Mammon." In *Elizabethan Poetry*. Ed. John Russell Brown and Bernard Harris. London: Edward Arnold, 1960, pp. 151–73.

———. "The Faerie Queene, I and V." *BJRL*, 47 (1964), 123–50.

———. "A Spenser Crux: *The Faerie Queene*, II, v, 12, 7–9." *N&Q*, 197 (1952), 161.

Kermode, J. F. "Spenser and the Allegorists." *PBA*, 48 (1962; pub. 1963), 261–79.

Kincaid, James R. "Tennyson's Mariners and Spenser's Despair: The Argument of 'The Lotus-Eaters.'" *PLL*, 5 (1969), 273–81.

King, Emma C. "Rhetorical Elements in the Poetry of Spenser." Diss. University of Chicago, 1912.

Kirk, Ruby. "An Inquiry into Elements of Time and Space in Spenser's *The Faerie Queene*." *ESRS*, 17, No. 3 (1968), 5–13.

Knight, G. Wilson. *The Burning Oracle: Studies in the Poetry of Action*. Oxford: Oxford University Press, 1939; rpt. Folcroft, Pa.: Folcroft Press, 1969.

———. *Poets of Action: Incorporating Essays from "The Burning Oracle."* London: Methuen, 1967.

Knight, W. Nicholas. "The Narrative Unity of Book V of *The Faerie Queene*: 'That Part of Justice Which Is Equity.'" *RES*, 21 (1970), 267–94.

Knowles, A. Sidney, Jr. "Spenser's Natural Man." In *RenP 1958, 1959, 1960*. Ed. George Walton Williams and Peter G. Phialas. Southern Renaissance Conference, 1961.

Knowlton, E. C. "The Genii of Spenser." *SP*, 25 (1925), 439–56.

———. "Genius as an Allegorical Figure." *MLN*, 39 (1924), 89–95.

———. "Spenser and Nature." *JEGP*, 34 (1935), 366–76.

Kocher, Paul H. *Science and Religion in Elizabethan England*. San Marino, Calif.: Huntington Library, 1953; rpt. New York: Octagon Books, 1969.

Koeppel, E. "Spenser's Florimel und die Britomartis Sage des Antoninus Liberalis." *Herrig's Archiv*, 107 (1901), 394–96.

Koller, Katherine. "Art, Rhetoric, and Holy Dying in *The Faerie Queene* with Special Reference to the Despair Canto." *SP*, 61 (1964), 128–39.

———. "Spenser and Raleigh." *ELH*, 1 (1934), 37–60.

———. "*The Travayled Pylgrime* by Stephen Batman and Book II of *The Faerie Queene*." *MLQ*, 3 (1942), 535–41.

———. "Two Elizabethan Expressions of the Idea of Mutability." *SP*, 35 (1938), 228–37.

Kostić, Veselin. "Ariosto and Spenser." *EM*, 17 (1966), 69–174.

———. "Spenser and the Bembian Linguistic Theory." *EM*, 10 (1959), 43–60.

———. "Spenser's Sources in Italian Poetry: A Study in Comparative Literature." Diss. University of Nottingham, 1958; Beograd: Filološki Fakultet Beogradskog Univerziteta, 1969.

Kuhl, E. P. "Hercules in Spenser and Shakespeare." *TLS*, 53 (1954), 860.

Kuhn, Bertha Mehitable. "Spenser's *Faerie Queene* and *Fowre Hymnes* in the Light of Some Medieval and Renaissance Evaluations of Plato's Doctrine of Ideas." Diss. University of Washington, 1941.

L., G. G. "Queries from Spenser." *N&Q*, 176 (1939), 190.

———. "Queries from Spenser." *N&Q*, 178 (1940), 445–46.

Lacey, William R., III. "Right Reason in Edmund Spenser's *Faerie Queene*." Diss. Louisiana State University, 1967.

La Guardia, Eric. *Nature Redeemed: The Imitation of Order in Three Renaissance Poems*. The Hague: Mouton, 1966.

Landrum, Grace W. "Imagery in *The Faerie Queene* Based on Domestic and Occupational Life." *SAB*, 17 (1942), 190–99.

———. "Imagery in *The Faerie Queene* Drawn from Flora and Fauna." *SAB*, 16 (1941), 89–101.

———. "Imagery of Fire in *The Faerie Queene*." *SAB*, 18 (1943), 22–29.

———. "Imagery of Water in *The Faerie Queene*." *ELH*, 8 (1941), 198–213.

———. "St. George Redivivus." *PQ*, 29 (1950), 381–88.

———. "Spenser's 'Clouded Heaven.'" *SAB*, 11 (1936), 142–48.

———. "Spenser's Use of the Bible and His Alleged Puritanism." *PMLA*, 41 (1926), 517–44.

Langdale, Abram Barnett. *Phineas Fletcher: Man of Letters, Science and Divinity*. New York: Columbia University Press, 1937; rpt. New York: Octagon Books, 1968.

Langdon, Ida. *Materials for a Study of Spenser's Theory of Fine Art*. Ithaca, N. Y.: Privately published, 1911.

———. "Spenser and Dante." *N&Q*, 125 (1912), 33.

Langendorf, Sister M. Loretta. "The Attitude toward History in English Renaissance Courtesy Literature." Diss. St. Louis University, 1948.

Langenfelt, Gosta. "'The Noble Savage' until Shakespeare." *ES*, 36 (1955), 222–27.

Lanham, Richard A. "The Literal Britomart." *MLQ*, 28 (1967), 426–45.

———. "Opaque Style in Elizabethan Fiction." *PCP*, 1 (1966), 25–31.

Larsen, Joan Elizabeth. "The Use of Natural Imagery and the Concept of Nature in Spenser's *Faerie Queene*." Diss. Radcliffe College, 1958.

Larson, Edwin. "Spenser and the Tradition of Italian Style." Diss. Vanderbilt University, 1951.

Latham, Minor White. *The Elizabethan Fairies: The Fairies of Folklore and the Fairies of Shakespeare*. New York: Columbia University Press, 1930.

Lavender, Andrew. "An Edition of Ralph Knevett's *Supplement of the Faery Queene* (1635)." Diss. New York University, 1955.

Law, Robert A. "Holinshed as Source of *Henry V* and *King Lear*." *TxSE*, 14 (1934), 38–44.

Law, Robert A. "Tripartite Gaul in the Story of King Leir." *TxSE*, 4 (1924), 39–48.

Lawrence, C. E. "English Humour." *QR*, 270 (1938), 132–45.

———. "The Poet's Poet." *Bookman*, 72 (1927), 261–62.

Lea, Kathleen M. "Conceits." *MLR*, 20 (1925), 389–406.

Le Comte, Edward S. "Milton: Two Verbal Parallels." *N&Q*, 184 (1943), 17–18.

Lee, Renselaer W. "Platonism in Spenser." Diss. Princeton University, 1926.

Legouis, Émile. *Edmund Spenser*. New York: E. P. Dutton, 1926; rev. ed. by Pierre Legouis. Paris: Didier, 1956.

Leibowitz, Herbert A. "Hawthorne and Spenser: Two Sources." *AL*, 30 (1959), 459–66.

Lemmi, Charles W. "Britomart: The Embodiment of True Love." *SP*, 31 (1934), 133–39.

———. "The Episode of Mordant and Amavia in *The Faerie Queene*, II, i." *PQ*, 13 (1934), 292–95.

———. "The Influence of Trissino on *The Faerie Queene*." *PQ*, 7 (1928), 220–23.

———. "Monster-Spawning Nile-Mud in Spenser." *MLN*, 41 (1926), 234–38.

———. "The Serpent and the Eagle in Spenser and Shelley." *MLN*, 50 (1935), 165–68.

———. "Symbolism in *The Faerie Queene*, II, xii." *MLN*, 50 (1935), 161–65.

———. "The Symbolism of the Classical Episodes in *The Faerie Queene*." *PQ*, 8 (1929), 270–87.

Lerch, Christie Ann. "Spenser's Ideal of Civil Life: Justice and Charity in Books V and VI of *The Faerie Queene*." Diss. Bryn Mawr College, 1968.

Le Sage, Deborah Dillon. "The Renaissance Heritage of Apocalyptic Tradition and Its Bearing upon Edmund Spenser's *Faerie Queene*." Diss. Pennsylvania State University, 1961.

Levinson, Ronald B. "Spenser and Bruno." *PMLA*, 43 (1928), 675–81.

Lewis, C. S. *The Allegory of Love: A Study in Medieval Tradition*. Oxford: Clarendon Press, 1936; rpt. London: Oxford University Press, 1946, 1959; New York: Oxford University Press, 1958.

———. *English Literature in the Sixteenth Century Excluding Drama*. Oxford History of English Literature. Ed. F. P. Wilson and Bonamee Dobrée. Oxford: Clarendon Press, 1954.

———. "Genius and Genius." *RES*, 12 (1936), 189–94.

———. *Spenser's Images of Life*. Ed. Alastair Fowler. Cambridge: Cambridge University Press, 1967.

———. "Spenser's Irish Experiences and *The Faerie Queene*." *RES*, 7 (1931), 83–85.

———. *Studies in Medieval and Renaissance Literature*. Cambridge: Cambridge University Press, 1966.

Lichtenegger, Wilhelm. "Antike Mythologie in Spensers *Faerie Queene.*" Diss. University of Graz, 1941.

Lievsay, John L. "An Immediate Source for *The Faerie Queene*, Book V, Proem." *MLN*, 59 (1944), 469–72.

———. "Braggadochio: Spenser's Legacy to the Character-Writers." *MLQ*, 2 (1941), 475–85.

———. "'D. T., Gent.,' Spenser, and the Defense of Women." *JEGP*, 47 (1948), 382–86.

———. "Spenser and Guazzo: A Comparative Study of Renaissance Attitudes." Diss. University of Washington, 1936.

———. "Spenser in Low Company." *SAB*, 19 (1944), 186–89.

———. *Stefano Guazzo and the English Renaissance, 1575–1675.* Chapel Hill, N. C.: University of North Carolina Press, 1960.

———. "Trends in Tudor and Stuart Courtesy Literature." *HLQ*, 5 (1942), 184–88.

Litchfield, Florence LeDuc. "The Treatment of the Theme of Mutability in the Literature of the English Renaissance: A Study of the Problem of Change between 1558–1660." Diss. University of Minnesota, 1935.

Lodge, Robert Aloysius. "The Elements of the Baroque in *The Faerie Queene* of Edmund Spenser." Diss. St. Louis University, 1955.

Long, P. W. "Review of Dodge's Edition of Spenser." *MLR*, 4 (1909), 529–31.

———. "Spenser and Lady Carey." *MLR*, 3 (1908), 257–67.

———. "Spenser's Sir Calidore." *Englische Studien*, 42 (1910), 53–60.

Lopach, John A. "Educative Allegory: Poet and Reader in *The Faerie Queene*, V." Diss. University of Notre Dame, 1970.

Lotspeich, Henry G. *Classical Mythology in the Poetry of Edmund Spenser.* Princeton, N. J.: Princeton University Press, 1932; rpt. New York: Octagon Books, 1965.

Louthan, Vincent A. "Spenser's Double: The Dark Conceit of Reality in *The Faerie Queene.*" Diss. University of Connecticut, 1969.

Low, Anthony. "The Image of the Tower in *Paradise Lost.*" *SEL*, 10 (1970), 171–81.

Lowes, J. L. "Spenser and Gower." *PMLA*, 29 (1914), 388–452.

Maar, Harko Gerit de. *Elizabethan Romance in the Eighteenth Century.* Zalt-Bommel: N. V. Van de Garde and Co., 1924.

MacArthur, J. R. "The Influence of Huon of Burdeux upon *The Faerie Queene.*" *JEGP*, 4 (1902), 215–38.

McAuley, James. *Edmund Spenser and George Eliot: A Critical Excursion.* Hobart: University of Tasmania Press, 1963.

McElderry, Bruce R., Jr. "Archaism and Innovation in Spenser's Poetic Diction." Diss. University of Iowa, 1925.

———. "Archaism and Innovation in Spenser's Poetic Diction." *PMLA*, 47 (1932), 144–70.

McGilley, Sister Mary Janet. "A Study of Illusion in *The Faerie Queene.*" Diss. Fordham University, 1957.

MacInnes, Margaret J. "Color Imagery in the Landscapes of *The Faerie Queene*: An Aspect of the Renaissance Visual Imagination." Diss. University of Minnesota, 1964.

MacIntire, Elizabeth. "French Influence on the Beginnings of English Classicism." *PMLA*, 26 (1911), 496–527.

MacIntyre, Jean. "Artegall's Sword and the *Mutabilitie Cantos*." *ELH*, 33 (1966), 405–14.

———. "*The Faerie Queene*, Book I: Toward Making It More Teachable." *CE*, 31 (1970), 473–82.

———. "Imagery, Mythology, and Romance, The Significance of the Marinell-Florimell Story in Spenser's *Faerie Queene*." Diss. Yale University, 1963.

———. "Spenser's *The Faerie Queene*, III, xi, 47–48." *Expl.*, 26 (1966), Item 69.

———. "Spenser's Herculean Heroes." *HAB*, 17 (1966), 5–12.

McIntyre, J. Lewis. *Giordano Bruno*. London: Macmillan, 1903.

Mackail, J. W. *The Springs of Helicon: A Study in the Progress of English Poetry from Chaucer to Milton*. London: Longmans Green and Co., 1909; rpt. Lincoln: University of Nebraska Press, 1962.

McKenzie, James J. "Two Possible Housman Sources." *N&Q*, 199 (1954), 539.

McKillop, Alan D. "The Poet as Patriot—Shakespeare to Wordsworth." *RIP*, 29 (1942), 309–35.

McLane, Paul E. "Was Spenser in Ireland in Early November, 1579?" *N&Q*, 204 (1959), 99–101.

McLennen, Joshua. "Allegory and *The Faerie Queene*." Diss. Harvard University, 1940.

———. *On the Meaning and Function of Allegory in the English Renaissance*. Ann Arbor: University of Michigan Press, 1947.

MacLure, Millar. "Edmund Spenser: An Introductory Essay." *QQ*, 73 (1967), 550–58.

———. "Nature and Art in *The Faerie Queene*." *ELH*, 28 (1961), 1–20.

McManaway, James G. "'Occasion' (*The Faerie Queene*, II, iv, 4–5)." *MLN*, 49 (1934), 391–93.

McMurphy, Susannah J. *Spenser's Use of Ariosto for Allegory*. Seattle: University of Washington Press, 1924.

McMurty, Josephine S. "Spenser's Narrative Imagery: The Visual Structure of *The Faerie Queene*." Diss. Rice University, 1969.

McNamee, Maurice B. *Honor and the Epic Hero: A Study of the Shifting Concept of Magnanimity in Philosophy and Epic Poetry*. New York: Holt, Rinehart and Winston, 1960.

MacNeice, Louise. *Varieties of Parables*. Cambridge: Cambridge University Press, 1965.

McNeir, Waldo F. "Ariosto's Sospetto, Gascoigne's Suspicion, and Spenser's Malbecco." In *Festschrift für Walther Fischer*. Heidelberg: Carl Winter, 1959, pp. 34–48.

———. "Barnfield's Borrowings from Spenser." *N&Q*, 200 (1955), 510–11.

————. "The Behavior of Brigadore: *The Faerie Queene*, V, iii, 33–34." *N&Q*, 199 (1954), 103–104.

————. "Canto Unity in *The Faerie Queene*." *PQ*, 19 (1940), 79–87.

————. "The Sacrifice of Serena: *The Faerie Queene*, VI, viii, 31–51." In *Festschrift für Edgar Mertner*. Munich: Fink, 1968.

McNeir, Waldo F. and George Foster Provost. *Annotated Bibliography of Edmund Spenser, 1937–1960*. Pittsburgh: Duquesne University Press, 1962.

McPeek, James A. S. "The Genesis of Caliban." *PQ*, 25 (1946), 378–81.

————. "The Influence of Catullus on English Literature to 1700." Diss. Harvard University, 1932.

MacQueen, John. *Allegory*. London: Methuen, 1970.

McShane, Mother Edith E. "Tudor Opinions of the Chivalric Romance: An Essay in the History of Criticism." Diss. Catholic University of America, 1950.

Magill, Andrew James. "Spenser and Ireland: A Synthesis and Revaluation of Twentieth-Century Scholarship." Diss. University of Texas, 1967.

————. "Spenser's Guyon and the Mediocrity of the Elizabethan Settlement." *SP*, 67 (1970), 167–72.

Magoun, F. P., Jr. "The Chaucer of Spenser and Milton." *MP*, 25 (1927), 129–36.

Maiberger, M. *Studien über den Einflüss Frankreichs auf die Elizabethanische Literatur*. Frankfurt: Knauer, 1903.

Maier, John Raymond. "Religious Melancholy and the Imagination in Book I of *The Faerie Queene*." Diss. Duquesne University, 1970.

Major, John M. "Paradise Regained and Spenser's Legend of Holiness." *RenQ*, 20 (1967), 465–70.

Major, John W., Jr. "The Education of a Young Knight." *UKCR*, 29 (1963), 269–74.

Manzalaoui, M. A. "The Struggle for the House of the Soul: Augustine and Spenser." *N&Q*, 206 (1961), 420–22.

Marinelli, Peter Vincent. "The Dynastic Romance: A Study in the Evolution of the Romantic Epics of Boiardo, Ariosto, and Spenser." Diss. Princeton University, 1964.

Marks, Emerson R. *Relativist and Absolute: The Early Neo-Classical Debate in England*. New Brunswick, N. J.: Rutgers University Press, 1955.

Marotti, Arthur F. "Animal Symbolism in *The Faerie Queene*: Tradition and the Poetic Context." *SEL*, 5 (1965), 69–86.

Marshall, William H. "Calvin, Spenser, and the Major Sacraments." *MLN*, 74 (1959), 97–101.

————. "Spenser and General Election." *N&Q*, 203 (1958), 95.

Masch, Werner. "Studien zum italienischen Einflüss in Spensers *Faery Queene*." Diss. University of Hamburg, 1922.

Matthes, Paula. "Das umschreibende 'do' in Spensers *Faerie Queene*." Diss. University of Tübingen, 1921.

Maxwell, Annie A. "A Glossary of the Non-Classical Proper Names of Spenser." Diss. Cornell University, 1904.

Maxwell, J. C. "Guyon, Phaedria, and the Palmer." *RES*, n.s. 5 (1954), 388–90.

———. "The Truancy of Calidore." *ELH*, 19 (1952), 143–49.

———. "A Virgilian Echo in Spenser," *N&Q*, 212 (1967), 458.

Maxwell, William C. "Word-Compounding in Spenser." Diss. University of Washington, 1925.

Mayhall, Jane. "Shakespeare and Spenser: A Commentary on Differences." *MLQ*, 10 (1949), 356–63.

Maynadier, Gustavus Howard. *The Arthur of the English Poets*. Boston: Houghton Mifflin, 1907; rpt. New York: Haskell House, 1966; New York: Johnson Reprint Company, 1969.

Maynard, Theodore. *The Connection between the Ballade, Chaucer's Modification of It, Rime Royal, and the Spenserian Stanza*. Washington, D. C.: Catholic University of America Press, 1934.

Meissner, Paul. *England im Zeitalter von Humanismus, Renaissance und Reformation*. Heidelberg: F. H. Kerle, 1952.

———. "England und die Europäischer Renaissance." In *Grundformen der Englischen Geistesgeschichte*. Ed. Paul Meissner. Stuttgart: W. Kohlhammer, 1941, pp. 191–273.

Mennine, Suzanne Ailman. "The Theory of World Harmony in Spenser's *The Faerie Queene*." Diss. University of California, Los Angeles, 1964.

Meres, Francis. *Palladis Tamia*. Ed. Don Cameron Allen. New York: Scholars' Facsimiles and Reprints, 1938.

Meynell, Alice. "Where *The Faerie Queene* Was Written." *Atlantic Monthly*, 103 (1909), 250–54.

Michie, Sara. "Celtic Myth and Spenserian Romance." Diss. University of Virginia, 1935.

———. "*The Faerie Queene* and *Arthur of Little Britain*." *SP*, 36 (1939), 105–23.

Miles, Josephine. *Eras and Modes in English Poetry*. Berkeley, Calif.: University of California Press, 1957.

———. *Major Adjectives in English Poetry from Wyatt to Auden*. Berkeley, Calif.: University of California Press, 1946.

———. *The Primary Language of Poetry in the 1640's*. Berkeley, Calif.: University of California Press, 1948.

———. *Renaissance, Eighteenth Century, and Modern Language in English Poetry: A Tabular View*. Berkeley, Calif.: University of California Press, 1960.

Milgate, W. "A Difficult Allusion in Donne and Spenser." *N&Q*, 211 (1966), 12–14.

Miller, Edwin Haviland. *The Professional Writer in Elizabethan England*. Cambridge, Mass.: Harvard University Press, 1959.

Miller, Frances S. "The Historic Sense of Thomas Warton, Jr." *ELH*, 5 (1938), 71–92.

Miller, Lewis H., Jr. "Arthur, Maleger, and History in the Allegorical Context." *UTQ*, 35 (1966), 176–87.

———. "Phaedria, Mammon, and Sir Guyon's Education by Error." *JEGP*, 63 (1964), 33–44.

———. "A Secular Reading of *The Faerie Queene*, Book II." Diss. Cornell University, 1964.

———. "A Secular Reading of *The Faerie Queene*, Book II." *ELH*, 33 (1966), 154–69.

Miller, Milton. "Nature in *The Faerie Queene*." *ELH*, 18 (1951), 191–200.

Millican, C. Bowie. "Note on Mulcaster and Spenser." *ELH*, 6 (1939), 211–16.

———. "Ralph Knevett, Author of the Supplement to Spenser's *Faerie Queene*." *RES*, 14 (1938), 44–52.

———. "Spenser and the Arthurian Legend." *RES*, 6 (1930), 167–74.

———. "Spenser and Drant's Poetical Names for Elizabeth: Tanaquil, Gloriana, and Una." *HLQ*, 2 (1939), 251–63.

———. *Spenser and the Table Round: A Study in Contemporaneous Background for Spenser's Use of the Arthurian Legend.* Cambridge, Mass.: Harvard University Press, 1932; rpt. New York: Octagon Books, 1967.

Milligan, Burton. "Spenser's Malengin and the Roguebook Hooker." *PQ*, 19 (1940), 147–48.

Mills, Jerry Leath. "A Source for Spenser's Anamnestes." *PQ*, 47 (1968), 137–39.

———. "Spenser's Castle of Alma and the Number 22: A Note on Symbolic Stanza Placement." *N&Q*, 212 (1967), 456–57.

Mills, Laurens J. *One Soul in Bodies Twain: Friendship in Tudor and Stuart Drama.* Bloomington, Ind.: Principia Press, 1937.

———. "The Renascence Development in England of Classical Ideas about Friendship." Diss. University of Chicago, 1926.

Mims, Edwin. *The Christ of the Poets.* Nashville: Abingdon-Cokesbury Press, 1948; rpt. New York: Greenwood Press, 1969.

Minto, William and Frederick John Snell. "Edmund Spenser." *Encyclopedia Britannica*, 25 (1911), 639–43.

Mizener, Arthur. "Some Notes on the Nature of English Poetry." *SR*, 51 (1943), 27–51.

Mock, H. B. "Influence of Ovid on Spenser." Diss. University of North Carolina, 1924.

Mohl, Ruth. *Studies in Spenser, Milton, and the Theory of Monarchy.* New York: King's Crown Press, 1949; rpt. New York: Ungar, 1962.

Moloney, Michael F. "St. Thomas and Spenser's Virtue of Magnificence." *JEGP*, 52 (1953), 58–62.

Moore, Courtenay. "The Bregoge," *J. Cork Hist. and Arch. Soc.*, 2nd ser. 19 (1913), 40–42.

———. "Spenser's Knowledge of the Neighborhood of Mitchelstown." *J. Cork Hist. and Arch. Soc.*, 2nd ser. 10 (1904), 31–33.

Moore, G. S. "The Influence of Dante on Spenser." *The Moraga Quarterly*, 3 (1932), 60–68.

Moorman, Charles. "The Allegorical Knights of *The Faerie Queene*." *SoQ*, 3 (1965), 131–50.

Moorman, F. W. *The Interpretation of Nature in English Poetry from Beowulf to Shakespeare*. Strassburg: K. J. Trübner, 1905.

Morgan, Kenneth Scott. "Formal Style in *The Faerie Queene*." Diss. Princeton University, 1966.

Morgan, Michael N. "Paradise and Lover in the Poetry of Spenser." Diss. University of Florida, 1969.

Morris, Christopher. *The Tudors*. New York: Macmillan, 1957.

Morris, Harry. "Some Uses of Angel Iconography in English Literature." *CL*, 10 (1958), 36–44.

Morris, Helen. *Elizabethan Literature*. London: Oxford University Press, 1958.

Morse, H. K. *Elizabethan Pageantry: A Pictorial Survey of Costume and Its Commentators from c. 1560–1620*. London: The Studio Ltd., 1934. rpt. New York: Benjamin Blom, 1969.

Mortenson, Peter. "Structure in Spenser's *Faerie Queene*, Book VI: Primitivism, Chivalry, and Greek Romance." Diss. University of Oregon, 1966.

Morton, E. P. "The Spenserian Stanza before 1700." *MP*, 4 (1907), 639–54.

———. "The Spenserian Stanza in the Eighteenth Century." *MP*, 10 (1913), 365–91.

Moulton, Charles Wells, ed. *The Library of Literary Criticism of English and American Authors*. Buffalo: Moulton Publishing Company, 1901–5; rpt. Gloucester, Mass.: Peter Smith, 1959.

Mounts, Charles E. "Coleridge's Self-Identification with Spenserian Characters." *SP*, 47 (1950), 522–33.

———. "The Evolution of Spenser's Attitude toward Cupid and Venus." *High Point College Studies*, 4 (1964), 1–9.

———. "The Influence of Spenser on Wordsworth and Coleridge." Diss. Duke University, 1941.

———. "The Place of Chaucer and Spenser in the Genesis of *Peter Bell*." *PQ*, 23 (1944), 108–15.

———. "Spenser and the Earl of Essex." In *RenP 1958–1960*, pp. 12–19. Southeastern Renaissance Conference, 1961.

———. "Spenser's Seven Bead-Men and the Corporal Works of Mercy." *PMLA*, 54 (1939), 974–80.

———. "Virtuous Duplicity in *The Faerie Queene*." *MLQ*, 7 (1946), 43–52.

"MS Notes to Spenser's *Faerie Queene*." *N&Q*, 202 (1957), 509–15.

Mueller, William R. *Spenser's Critics: Changing Currents in Literary Taste*. Syracuse: Syracuse University Press, 1959.

Mueller, William R. and Don Cameron Allen, eds. *That Soueraine Light: Essays in Honor of Edmund Spenser, 1552–1952*. Baltimore: The Johns Hopkins Press, 1952; rpt. New York: Russell and Russell, 1967.

Muir, Kenneth, ed. *John Keats: A Reassessment*. Liverpool: Liverpool University Press, 1958.

Munro, John. "Spenser Allusions." *N&Q*, 118 (1908), 121.

Murphy, Mallie John. "Hamlet's 'Sledded Polack.'" *N&Q*, 201 (1956), 509.

Murrin, Michael. *The Veil of Allegory*. Chicago: University of Chicago Press, 1969.

Murry, John Middleton. *Countries of the Mind: Essays in Literary Criticism*, 2nd ser. Oxford: W. Collins and Sons, 1931; rpt. Freeport, N. Y.: Books for Libraries Press, 1968.

Mustard, W. P. "Notes on Spenser, *The Faerie Queene*, V, v, 24." *MLN*, 20 (1905), 127.

Nagle, John D. "From Personification to Personality: Characterization in *The Faerie Queene*." Diss. Fordham University, 1969.

Naylor, Edward W. *The Poets and Music*. New York: E. P. Dutton, 1928.

Neale, J. E. "Elizabeth and the Netherlands. 1586–1587." *EHR*, 45 (1930), 373–96.

———. *Essays in Elizabethan History*. London: J. Cape, 1958.

Nearing, Homer. "Caesar's Sword (*Faerie Queene*, II, x, 49; *Love's Labour's Lost*, V, ii, 615)." *MLN*, 63 (1948), 403–5.

Neff, Merlin L. "Spenser's Allegory of the Toll Bridge." *PQ*, 13 (1934), 159–67.

Neill, J. Kerby. "The Degradation of the Red Cross Knight." *ELH*, 19 (1952), 173–90.

———. "*The Faerie Queene* and the Mary Stuart Controversy." *ELH*, 2 (1935), 192–214; rpt., with additions, as "*The Faerie Queene*" and the Mary Stuart Controversy. Baltimore: The Johns Hopkins Press, 1935.

———. "Spenser and the Literature of the Elizabethan Succession, A Study in Historical Allegory." Diss. Johns Hopkins University, 1935.

———. "Spenser on the Regiment of Women: A Note on *The Faerie Queene*, V, v, 25." *SP*, 34 (1937), 134–37.

———. "Spenser's Acrasia and Mary Queen of Scots." *PMLA*, 60 (1945), 682–88.

———. "Spenser's 'Shamefastnesse,' *The Faerie Queene*, II, ix, 40–44." *MLN*, 49 (1934), 387–91.

Nelan, Thomas P. "Catholic Doctrines in Spenser's Poetry." Diss., New York University, 1943.

Nellish, B. "The Allegory of Guyon's Voyage: An Interpretation." *ELH*, 30 (1963), 89–106.

Nelson, Herbert B. "Amidas v. Bracidas." *MLQ*, 1 (1940), 393–99.

Nelson, Louise A. "Muiopotmos." *Calcutta Review*, 3rd ser. 37 (1930), 339–41.

Nelson, William, ed. *Form and Convention in the Poetry of Edmund Spenser*. New York: Columbia University Press, 1961.

Nelson, William. *The Poetry of Edmund Spenser*. New York: Columbia University Press, 1963; rpt. 1965.

———. "Queen Elizabeth, Spenser's Mercilla and a Rusty Sword." *RN*, 18 (1965), 113–17.

Nelson, William. "A Source for Spenser's Malbecco." *MLN*, 68 (1953), 226–29.

Nesselhof, John Morrison. "Spenser's Book of Friendship: An Aspect of Charity." Diss. Princeton University, 1955.

Nestrick, William V. "The Virtuous Discipline of Gentlemen and Poets." *ELH*, 29 (1962), 357–71.

Neuse, Richard Thomas. "Book VI as Conclusion to *The Faerie Queene*." *ELH*, 35 (1968), 329–53.

————. "Diction in *The Faerie Queene*: Some of Its Principles and Patterns." Diss. Yale University, 1958.

Nevo, R. "Spenser's 'Bower of Bliss' and a Key Metaphor from Renaissance Poetic." In *Studies in Western Literature*. Ed. Daniel A. Fineman. Jerusalem: Magnes Press, 1962, pp. 20–31.

Newdigate, Bernard H. *Michael Drayton and His Circle*. Oxford: Basil Blackwell, 1941; corr. ed., 1961.

Nicholson, Margaret E. "Realistic Elements in Spenser's Style." *SP*, 21 (1924), 382–98.

Nitchie, Elizabeth. *Virgil and the English Poets*. New York: Columbia University Press, 1919; rpt. New York: AMS Press, 1966.

Northrop, Douglas A. "Spenser's Defense of Elizabeth." *UTQ*, 38 (1969), 277–94.

Notcutt, H. Clement. "*The Faerie Queene* and Its Critics." *Essays and Studies by Members of the English Association*, 12 (1926), 63–85.

Oakeshott, Walter. *The Queen and the Poet*. London: Faber and Faber, 1960.

Obrien, Kate, ed. *Romance of English Literature*. New York: Hastings House, 1944.

Oehninger, Ludwig. *Die Verbreitung der Königssagen der Historia Regum Brittaniae von Geoffrey of Monmouth in der Poetischen Elizabethanischen Literatur*. Munich: Meschett and Hissinger, 1903.

Okerlund, Arlene N. "Literature and Its Audience: The Reader in Action in Selected Works of Spenser, Dryden, Thackeray, and T. S. Eliot." Diss. University of California, San Diego, 1969.

Olson, Paul A. "*A Midsummer Night's Dream* and the Meaning of Court Marriage." *ELH*, 24 (1957), 95–119.

Ong, Walter J., S.J. "From Allegory to Diagram in the Renaissance Mind: A Study in the Significance of the Allegorical Tableau." *JAAC*, 17 (1959), 423–40.

Orange, Linwood E. "Sensual Beauty in Book I of *The Faerie Queene*." *JEGP*, 61 (1962), 555–56.

————. "Spenser's Old Dragon." *MLN*, 74 (1959), 679–81.

————. "Spenser's *The Faerie Queene*, Book Four, IX 3xxx, 5–9." *Expl.*, 17 (1959), Item 22.

————. "Spenser's Word-Play." *N&Q*, 203 (1958), 387–89.

————. "Wordplay in Spenser." Diss. Duke University, 1955.

Oras, Ants. "Intensified Rhyme Links in *The Faerie Queene*: An Aspect of Elizabethan Rhymecraft." *JEGP*, 54 (1955), 39–60.

————. "Spenser and Milton: Some Parallels and Contrasts in the Handling of Sound." In *Sound and Poetry*. New York: Columbia University Press, 1957, pp. 109–33.

Orsini, Napoleone. "'Policy' or the Language of Elizabethan Machiavellianism." *JWCI*, 9 (1946), 122–34.

Oruch, Jack B. "Spenser, Camden, and the Poetic Marriages of Rivers." *SP*, 64 (1967), 606–24.

Osenburg, Frederick Charles. "The Ideas of the Golden Age and the Decay of the World in the English Renaissance." Diss. University of Illinois, 1939.

Osgood, Charles G. "Comments on the Moral Allegory of *The Faerie Queene*." *MLN*, 46 (1931), 502–7.

————, ed. *A Concordance to the Poems of Edmund Spenser*. Washington, D. C.: Carnegie Institution of Washington, 1915; rpt. Gloucester, Mass.: Peter Smith, 1963.

————. *Creed of a Humanist*. Seattle: University of Washington Press, 1963.

————. *Murals Based upon Edmund Spenser's "Faerie Queene" by Lee Woodward Zeigler*. Baltimore: Enoch Pratt Free Library, 1945.

————. *Poetry as a Means of Grace*. London: Oxford University Press, 1941; rpt. New York: Gordian Press, 1965.

————. "Spenser and the Enchanted Glass." *Johns Hopkins Alumni Magazine*, 19 (1930), 8–31.

————. "Spenser, Edmund." *Collier's Encyclopedia*, 17 (1960), 591–92.

————. "Spenser's English Rivers." *Transactions of the Connecticut Academy*, 23 (1920), 65–108.

————. "Virgil and the English Mind." In *The Tradition of Virgil*. With Junius S. Morgan and Kenneth McKenzie. Princeton: Princeton University Press, 1930, pp. 23–40.

Osmond, Percy H. *The Mystical Poets of the English Church*. New York: Macmillan, 1919.

Owen, W. J. B. "'In these XII Books Severally Handled and Discoursed.'" *ELH*, 19 (1952), 165–72.

————. "Narrative Logic and Imitation in *The Faerie Queene*." *CL*, 7 (1955), 324–37.

————. "*Orlando Furioso* and Stanza-Connection in *The Faerie Queene*." *MLN*, 67 (1952), 5–8.

————. "Spenser and Ariosto." *N&Q*, 194 (1949), 316–18.

————. "A Spenser Note." *MLR*, 43 (1948), 239–41.

————. "Spenser's Letter to Raleigh." *MLR*, 45 (1950), 511–12.

————. "Spenser's Letter to Raleigh—A Reply." *MLN*, 75 (1960), 195–97.

————. "The Structure of *The Faerie Queene*." *PMLA*, 68 (1953), 1079–1100.

Owst, Gerald A. *Literature and Pulpit in Medieval England*. Cambridge: Cambridge University Press, 1933; 2nd rev. ed. New York: Barnes and Noble, 1961.

Padelford, F. M. "The Allegory of Chastity in *The Faerie Queene.*" *SP,* 21 (1924), 367–81.

———. "Anthony Copley's *A Fig for Fortune*: A Catholic Legend of Holiness." *MLQ,* 3 (1942), 525–33.

———. "Aspects of Spenser's Vocabulary." In *Renaissance Studies in Honor of Hardin Craig.* Ed. Baldwin Maxwell et al. Stanford, Calif.: Stanford University Press, 1941, pp. 87–91.

———. "*The Cantos of Mutabilitie*: Further Considerations Bearing on the Date." *PMLA,* 45 (1930), 704–11.

———. "E. W. 'His Thameseidos.'" *SAB,* 12 (1937), 69–76.

———. "The Muse of *The Faerie Queene.*" *SP,* 27 (1930), 111–24.

———. *The Political and Ecclesiastical Allegory of the First Book of "The Faerie Queene."* Boston: Ginn and Co., 1911.

———. "The Political, Economic, and Social Views of Spenser." *JEGP,* 14 (1915), 393–420.

———. "Spenser and the Arraignment of the Anabaptists." *JEGP,* 12 (1913), 434–48.

———. "Spenser and *The Pilgrimage of the Life of Man.*" *SP,* 28 (1931), 211–18.

———. "Spenser and the Puritan Propaganda." *MP,* 11 (1913), 85–106.

———. "Spenser and the Spirit of Puritanism." *MP,* 14 (1916), 31–44.

———. "Spenser's Use of 'Stour.'" *MLQ,* 2 (1941), 465–73.

———. "The Spiritual Allegory of *The Faerie Queene,* Book One." *JEGP,* 22 (1923), 1–17.

———. "Talus: The Law." *SP,* 15 (1918), 97–104.

———. "The Virtue of Temperance in *The Faerie Queene.*" *SP,* 18 (1921), 334–46.

———. "The Women in Spenser's Allegory of Love." *JEGP,* 16 (1917), 70–83.

Padelford, F. M. and W. C. Maxwell. "The Compound Words in Spenser's Poetry." *JEGP,* 23 (1926), 498–516.

Padelford, F. M. and Matthew O'Connor. "Spenser's Use of the St. George Legend." *SP,* 23 (1926), 142–56.

Page, F. "Keats and the Midnight Oil." *DubR,* 201 (1937), 87–97.

Palmer, George H. *Formative Types in English Poetry.* New York: Houghton Mifflin, 1918; rpt. Freeport, N. Y.: Books for Libraries Press, 1968.

Panofsky, Erwin. *Studies in Iconology: Humanistic Theories in the Art of the Renaissance.* New York: Oxford University Press, 1939; rpt. New York: Harper and Row, 1962, 1967.

Pansegrau, Günter. "'Leid' in der *Faerie Queene*: Studien zum literarischen und sprachlichen Charakter eines Wortfeldes bei Spenser." Diss. University of Mainz, 1955.

Paolina, M. "Spenser and Dante." *EM,* 14 (1963), 27–44.

Paolucci, Anne. "The Women in *The Divine Comedy* and *The Faerie Queene.*" Diss. Columbia University, 1966.

Parker, M. Pauline. *The Allegory of "The Faerie Queene."* Oxford: Clarendon Press, 1960.

————. "The Image of Direction in Dante, Spenser, and Milton." *EM*, 19 (1968), 9–23.

Parker, Roscoe E. "Let Gryll Be Gryll." *PQ*, 16 (1937), 218–19.

Parkes, H. B. "Nature's Diverse Laws: The Double Vision of the Elizabethans." *SR*, 58 (1950), 402–18.

Parks, George B. "Gloriana's Annual Feast." *TLS*, 32 (1933), 447.

Parrot, Alice. "A Critical Bibliography of Spenser from 1923–1928." *SP*, 25 (1928), 468–90.

Parsons, Coleman O. "Spenser's Braying Tiger." *N&Q*, 214 (1969), 21–24.

Parsons, Roger Loren. "Renaissance and Baroque: Multiple Unity and Unified Unity in the Treatment of Verse, Ornament, and Structure." Diss. University of Wisconsin, 1959.

Patch, H. R. "Notes on Spenser and Chaucer." *MLN*, 33 (1918), 177–80.

Paton, Lucy A. *Studies in the Fairy Mythology of Arthurian Romance.* Boston: Ginn and Co., 1903. Rev. ed. Roger Sherman Loomis. New York: Burt Franklin, 1960.

Patrick, John M. "Milton, Phineas Fletcher, Spenser, and Ovid—Sin at Hell's Gate." *N&Q*, 201 (1956), 384–86.

Pearce, Roy Harvey. "Primitivistic Ideas in *The Faerie Queene*." *JEGP*, 44 (1945), 139–51.

Pearson, L. E. *Elizabethan Love Conventions.* Berkeley: University of California Press, 1933; rpt. London: Allen and Unwin, 1966; New York: Barnes and Noble, 1967.

Pecheux, Mother M. Christopher. "Spenser's Red Cross and Milton's Adam." *ELN*, 6 (1969), 246–51.

Peck, H. W. "Spenser's *Faerie Queene* and the Student Today." *SR*, 24 (1916), 340–52.

Pellegrini, Angelo Mario. "Bruno and the Elizabethans." Diss. University of Washington, 1942.

————. "Bruno, Sidney, and Spenser." *SP*, 40 (1943), 128–44.

Perkinson, Richard H. "The Body as a Triangular Structure in Spenser and Chapman." *MLN*, 64 (1949), 520–22.

————. "The Plot of *The Faerie Queene*." *PMLA*, 48 (1933), 295–97, 299–301.

Petit, Herbert H. "The Fortuna-Vertu Conflict in Spenser's *Faerie Queene*." Diss. Western Reserve University, 1953.

Petriella, Teofilo. *La Novella di Britomarte nella Regina delle Fate di E. Spenser Riportata alle sue fonti italiane.* Salerno: Matteo Spudafore, 1913.

Pettet, E. C. *Shakespeare and the Romance Tradition.* London: Staples, 1949.

Phetzing, Amelia C. "The History of the Fair Unknown." Diss. University of Chicago, 1920.

Phillips, James E., Jr. "The Background of Spenser's Attitude toward Women Rulers." *HLQ*, 5 (1941), 5–32.

————. "Renaissance Concepts of Justice and the Structure of *The Faerie Queene*, Book V." *HLQ*, 34 (1970), 103–20.

Phillips, James E., Jr. "Spenser's Syncretistic Religious Imagery." *ELH*, 36 (1969), 110–30.

———. "The Women Rulers in Spenser's *Faerie Queene*." *HLQ*, 6 (1942), 211–34.

Pienaar, W. J. B. "Arthur's Shield in *The Faerie Queene*." *MP*, 26 (1928), 63–68.

———. *English Influences in Dutch Literature and Justus van Effen as Intermediary*. Cambridge: Cambridge University Press, 1929.

Pinto, V. De Sola. *The English Renaissance: 1510–1688*. New York: Robert M. McBride, 1938; 3rd rev. ed. London: Cresset Press, 1966.

Pons, M. "Apprecier l'art de Spenser d'apres le second livre de la *Reine des Fees*." *Rev. de l'Enseign. des Lang. Viv.*, 50 (1933), 150–55.

Pope, Emma Field. "A Comment on Criticism in the Cinquecento: A Reply." *PMLA*, 46 (1931), 276–87.

———. "The Critical Background of the Spenserian Stanza." *MP*, 24 (1926), 31–53.

———. "The Reflection of Renaissance Criticism in Edmund Spenser's *Faerie Queene*." Diss. University of Chicago, 1923.

———. "Renaissance Criticism and the Diction of *The Faerie Queene*." *PMLA*, 41 (1926), 575–619.

Porter, Mary Louise. "The Holy Wars in Medieval and Modern English Literature." Diss. Cornell University, 1921.

Pott, Constance M. "Francis St. Alban's 'Fair Lady.'" *Baconiana*, 3rd ser. 5 (1907), 190 ff.

Potts, Abbie Findlay. "Hamlet and Gloriana's Knights." *SQ*, 6 (1955), 31–43.

———. *Shakespeare and "The Faerie Queene"*. Ithaca, N. Y.: Cornell University Press, 1958; rpt. New York: Greenwood Press, 1969.

———. "Spenserian 'Courtesy' and 'Temperance' in *Much Ado About Nothing*." *SAB*, 17 (1942), 103–11, 126–33.

Powell, Chilton R. "The Castle of the Body." *SP*, 16 (1919), 197–205.

———. *English Domestic Relations, 1487–1653*. New York: Columbia University Press, 1917.

Praz, Mario. *The Flaming Heart: Essays on Crashaw, Machiavelli, and Other Studies in the Relations between Italian and English Literature from Chaucer to T. S. Eliot*. Garden City, New York: Doubleday, 1958; rpt. Gloucester, Mass.: Peter Smith, 1966.

Preston, Michael J. "The Folk Play: An Influence on *The Faerie Queene*." *AN&Q*, 8 (1969), 38–39.

Priest, Harold M. "Tasso in English Literature, 1575–1675." Diss. Northwestern University, 1933.

Purcell, J. M. "The Date of Spenser's *Mutabilitie Cantos*." *PMLA*, 50 (1935), 914–17.

Purpus, Jean R. "The Moral Philosophy of Book II of Spenser's *Faerie Queene*." Diss. University of California, Los Angeles, 1947.

Pyles, Thomas. "Dan Chaucer." *MLN*, 57 (1942), 437–39.

Quiller-Couch, Sir Arthur. *The Poet as Citizen and Other Papers.* New York: Macmillan, 1935.

Quitsland, Jon A. "Spenser's Image of Sapience." *SRen,* 16 (1969), 181–213.

———. "Studies in Spenser and the Platonic Tradition." Diss. Princeton University, 1967.

Rahilly, T. A. "Identification of Hitherto Unknown River 'Aubrian' of Spenser Fame." *Journal of Cork Hist. and Arch. Soc.,* 2nd ser., 22 (1916), 49–56.

Rajan, B. "Comus: The Inglorious Likeness." *UTQ,* 37 (1968), 113–35.

Ramsay, Judith C. "The Garden of Adonis and the Garden of Forms." *UTQ,* 35 (1966), 188–206.

Rashbrook, R. F. "*The Eve of St. Agnes* and Spenser." *N&Q,* 193 (1948), 29–31.

Rathborne, Isabel E. "The Elfin Chronicle." *TLS,* 47 (1948), 233.

———. *The Meaning of Spenser's Fairyland.* New York: Columbia University Press, 1937; rpt. New York: Russell and Russell, 1965.

———. "A New Source for Spenser's *Faerie Queene,* Book I." *SP,* 33 (1936), 166–81.

———. "The Political Allegory of the Florimell-Marinell Story." *ELH,* 12 (1945), 279–89.

Reaney, James. "The Influence of Spenser on Yeats." Diss. University of Toronto, 1958.

Rebora, Pietro. "Aspetti dell' Umanismo in Inghilterra." *LRin,* 2 (1939), 366–414.

———. "Spenser, Edmund." *Enciclopedia Italiana,* vol. 32. Rome: Instituto della Enciclopedia Italiana, 1936–40.

Reeve, Frederic Eugene, Jr. "The Stanza of *The Faerie Queene.*" Diss. Princeton University, 1942.

Reid, Margaret J. C. "The Arthurian Legend: Comparison of Treatment in Modern and Medieval Literature." Diss. University of Aberdeen, 1937.

Renwick, W. L. "The Critical Origins of Spenser's Diction." *MLR,* 17 (1922), 1–16.

———. "Edmund Spenser." In *The Great Tudors.* Ed. Katharine Garvin. London: E. P. Dutton, 1935, pp. 521–36; 2nd ed. London: Eyre and Spottiswoode, 1956.

———. *Edmund Spenser: An Essay On Renaissance Poetry.* London: Edward Arnold, 1925; rpt. 1961; London: Methuen, 1964.

———, ed. *Edmund Spenser: Selections with Essays by Hazlitt, Coleridge, and Leigh Hunt.* Oxford: Clarendon Press, 1923.

———. *Edmund Spenser: The R. A. Neil Lecture.* London: Cambridge University Press, 1952; rpt. Folcroft, Pa.: Folcroft Press, 1969.

———. "The Faerie Queene." *PBA,* 33 (1947), 149–61; rpt. London: Haskell House, 1964.

———. "Spenser, Edmund." *Chambers's Encyclopedia,* 13 (1955), 87–88.

Reschke, Hedwig. *Der Spenserstanze im neunzehten Jahrhundert*. Heidelberg: C. Winter, 1918.

Reuning, K. *Das Alterümliche im Wortschatz der Spenser-Nachahmungen das 18 Jahrhunderts*. Strassburg: K. Trübner, 1912.

Reyher, Paul. *Les Masques Anglais: Etude sur les Ballets et la Vie de cour en Angleterre (1512–1640)*. Paris: Hachette and Co., 1909; rpt. New York: Benjamin Blom, 1964.

Ribner, Irving. "Una's Lion: A Folklore Analogue." *N&Q*, 196 (1951), 114–15.

Richmond, Velma E. Bourgeois. "The Development of the Rhetorical Death Lament from the Late Middle Ages to Marlowe." Diss. University of North Carolina, 1959.

Richter, Margaret R. "Spenser's Use of Arthurian Romance." Diss. Stanford University, 1928.

Ricks, Beatrice. "Catholic Sacramentals and Symbolism in Spenser's *Faerie Queene*." *JEGP*, 52 (1953), 322–31.

Ringler, Richard N. "The Faunus Episode." *MP*, 63 (1965), 12–19.

———. "Spenser and the 'Archilleid.' " *SP*, 60 (1963), 174–82.

Ringler, William. "Spenser and Thomas Watson." *MLN*, 69 (1954), 484–87.

Rix, Herbert D. *Rhetoric in Spenser's Poetry*. University Park, Pa.: State College Press, 1940.

Robb, Nesca A. *Neoplatonism of the Italian Renaissance*. London: Allen and Unwin, 1935; rpt. New York: Octagon Books, 1968.

Robin, P. A. "Spenser's House of Alma." *MLR*, 6 (1911), 169–73.

Roche, Thomas P., Jr. "The Challenge to Chastity: Britomart at the House of Busyrane." *PMLA*, 76 (1961), 340–44.

———. *The Kindly Flame: A Study of the Third and Fourth Books of Spenser's "Faerie Queene."* Princeton, N. J.: Princeton University Press, 1964.

Rodgers, Catherine. "Time in the Narrative of *The Faerie Queene*." Diss. Brown University, 1963.

Roelofs, Gerrit. "The Law of Nature, the Tradition, and *The Faerie Queene*." Diss. Johns Hopkins University, 1954.

Rose, Mark. *Heroic Love: Studies in Sidney and Spenser*. Cambridge, Mass.: Harvard University Press, 1968.

Rosenbach, A. S. W. *Books and Bidders*. Boston: Little Brown and Co., 1927.

Rosenberg, Eleanor. *Leicester: Patron of Letters*. New York: Columbia University Press, 1955.

Rosenthal, Bruno. "Spensers Verhältnis zu Chaucer." Diss. University of Kiel, 1911.

Rosinger, Lawrence. "Spenser's Una and Queen Elizabeth." *ELN*, 6 (1968), 12–17.

Ross, Malcolm M. "History and Poetry." *Thought*, 26 (1951), 426–42.

Rossky, William. "Imagination in the English Renaissance: Psychology and Poetic." *SRen*, 5 (1958), 49–73.

Röstvig, Maren-Sofie. "Renaissance Numerology: Acrostics or Criticism?" *EIC*, 16 (1966), 6–21.

Rowe, Kenneth. "Sir Calidore: Essex or Sidney?" *SP*, 27 (1930), 125–41.

Rowse, A. L. *The England of Elizabeth: The Structure of Society*. London: Macmillan, 1950; rpt. 1951, 1961, 1964.

Rubel, Veré L. *Poetic Diction in the Renaissance from Skelton through Spenser*. New York: Modern Language Association of America, 1941.

Rusche, Harry. "Pride, Humility and Grace in Book I of *The Faerie Queene*." *SEL*, 7 (1967), 29–39.

Russell, R. W. "Spenser's Use of the Bible in Books I and II of *The Faerie Queene*. Diss. University of Oklahoma, 1938.

St. Clair, Foster Y. "The Myth of the Golden Age from Spenser to Milton." Diss. Harvard University, 1931.

Saintsbury, George. "Chaucer and Spenser." *Athenaeum*, 1 (1920), 698–99.

———. *A Last Vintage: Essays and Papers*. Ed. John W. Oliver, Arthur Melville Clark, and Augustus Muir. London: Methuen, 1950.

Sale, Roger. *Reading Spenser: An Introduction to "The Faerie Queene."* New York: Random House, 1968.

Salmon, Phillips C. "Spenser's Representations of Queen Elizabeth I." Diss. Columbia University, 1969.

Sandison, Helen E. "Spenser's 'Lost' Works and Their Probable Relation to *The Faerie Queene*." *PMLA*, 25 (1910), 134–51.

Satterthwaite, Alfred W. *Spenser, Ronsard, and Du Bellay: A Renaissance Comparison*. Princeton, N. J.: Princeton University Press, 1960.

Saunders, J. W. "The Façade of Morality." *ELH*, 19 (1952), 81–114.

Saurat, Denis. *Gods of the People*. London: John Westhouse, 1947.

———. *Literature and the Occult Tradition: Studies in Philosophical Poetry*. Trans. Dorothy Bolton. New York: Dial Press, 1930; rpt. Port Washington, N. Y.: Kennikat Press, 1966; New York: Haskell House, 1966.

———. "Spiritual Attitudes in Spenser, Milton, Blake, and Hugo." *CLS*, 13 (1944), 8–12; 14 and 15 (1944), 23–27.

Sawtelle, Alice Elizabeth. *The Sources of Spenser's Classical Mythology*. Boston: Silver, Burdette and Co., 1896; rpt. Ann Arbor, Mich.: University Microfilms, 1963; New York: AMS Press, 1970.

Schauer, Ruth Abbott. "Pastoral Satire in the Poetry of Edmund Spenser." Diss. University of Wisconsin, 1964.

Schirmer, Walter F. *Geschichte der englischen Literatur von den Anfängen bis zur Gegenwart*. Halle: Niemeyer, 1937.

———. *Geschichte der englischen und amerikanischen Literatur*. 2 vols. Tübingen: Niemeyer, 1954.

Schmidt, Karlernst. *Vorstudien zu einer Geschichte des komischen Epos*. Halle: Niemeyer, 1953.

Schoeck, R. J. "Alliteration as a Means of Stanza Connection in *The Faerie Queene*." *MLN*, 64 (1949), 90–93.

Schofield, W. H. *Chivalry in English Literature: Chaucer, Malory, Spenser, and Shakespeare.* Cambridge, Mass.: Harvard University Press, 1912; rpt. Port Washington, N. Y.: Kennikat Press, 1964; New York: AMS Press, 1970.

Schrinner, Walter. *Castiglione und die englische Renaissance.* Berlin: Junker and Dünnhaupt, 1939.

Schröer, A. "Zu Spenser im Wandel der Zeiten," *Die Neueren Sprachen,* 13 (1905), 449–60.

Schulze, Ivan L. "Elizabethan Chivalry and the Faerie Queene's Annual Feast," *MLN,* 50 (1935), 158–61.

———. "Elizabethan Chivalry, Pageantry, and Masque in Spenser." Diss. Johns Hopkins University, 1930.

———. "The Maiden and Her Lamb, *Faerie Queene,* Book I." *MLN,* 46 (1931), 379–81.

———. "Notes on Elizabethan Chivalry and *The Faerie Queene.*" *SP,* 30 (1933), 148–59.

———. "Reflections of Elizabethan Tournaments in *The Faerie Queene,* IV, iv and V, iii." *ELH,* 5 (1938), 278–84.

———. "Spenser's Belge Episode and the Pageants for Leicester in the Low Countries, 1585–1586." *SP,* 28 (1931), 235–40.

Scott, William O. "Proteus in Spenser and Shakespeare: The Lover's Identity." *ShS,* 1 (1965) 283–93.

———. "Structure and Repetition in Elizabethan Verse." Diss. Princeton University, 1959.

Scribner, Dora A. "The History of Spenser's Literary Reputation." Diss. University of Chicago, 1906.

Sedgwick, W. B. "Spencer [*sic*] and Ovid Again." *CW,* 22 (1929), 184.

Segura, Andrew R., F.S.C. "Primitivism in *The Faerie Queene.*" Diss. University of New Mexico, 1961.

Sehrt, Ernst. "Der Wald des Irrtums: zur allegorischen Funktion von Spenser's *Faerie Queene,* I, vii–ix." *Anglia,* 86 (1968), 463–91.

Sells, A. Lytton. *Animal Poetry in French and English Literature and the Greek Tradition.* Bloomington, Ind.: Indiana University Press, 1955.

———. *The Italian Influence in English Poetry.* Bloomington, Ind.: Indiana University Press, 1955.

Selwyn, E. G. "Some Philosophies in English Poetry." *QR,* 264 (1935), 224–37.

Sensabaugh, G. F. "A Spenser Allusion." *TLS,* 37 (1938), 694.

Seznec, Jean. *The Survival of the Pagan Gods: The Mythological Tradition and Its Place in Renaissance Humanism and Art.* Trans. Barbara F. Sessions. 1st English ed. New York: Pantheon Books, 1953; rpt. New York: Harper & Row, 1961.

Shaheen, Naseeb. "Spenser's Use of Scripture in *The Faerie Queene.*" Diss. University of California, Los Angeles, 1969.

Shanely, James Lyndon. "Spenser's Temperance and Aristotle." *MP,* 43 (1946), 170–74.

———. *A Study of Spenser's Gentleman.* Menasha, Wisc.: George Banta, 1940.

Sharp, Robert L. "The Revolt against Metaphysical Poetry: A Study in the Development of Neo-Classicism in England." Diss. Harvard University, 1932.

Shepard, Odell. *The Lore of the Unicorn*. Boston: Houghton Mifflin, 1930.

Shepperson, Archibald B. "Earth's Only Paradise. *VQR*, 33 (1957), 595–603.

Sheridan, Edward P. "Modes of Allegory in *The Faerie Queene*." Diss. Yale University, 1949.

Shih, Chung Wen. "The Criticism of *The Faerie Queene*." Diss. Duke University, 1955.

Shorey, Paul. *Platonism Ancient and Modern*. Berkeley: University of California Press, 1938.

Shroeder, John W. "Hawthorne's 'Egotism; or, The Bosom Serpent' and Its Source." *AL*, 31 (1959), 150–62.

————. "Hawthorne's 'The Man of Adamant': A Spenserian Source-Study." *PQ*, 41 (1962), 744–56.

————. "Miles Coverdale as Actaeon, as Faunus, and as October: With Some Consequences." *PLL*, 2 (1956), 126–39.

————. "Spenser's Erotic Drama: The Orgoglio Episode." *ELH*, 29 (1962), 140–59.

Siegel, Paul N. "Spenser and the Calvinist View of Life." *SP*, 41 (1944), 201–22.

Sills, Kenneth C. M. "Virgil in the Age of Elizabeth." *CJ*, 6 (1910), 123–31.

Simonini, R. C., Jr. *Italian Scholarship in Renaissance England*. Chapel Hill, N. C.: University of North Carolina Press, 1952.

Sirluck, Ernest. "*The Faerie Queene*, Book II, and the *Nichomachean Ethics*." *MP*, 49 (1951), 73–100.

————. "'God Guide Thee, Guyon,' etc. Letter." *RES*, 6 (1955), 401–2.

————. "Milton Revises *The Faerie Queene*." *MP*, 48 (1950), 90–96.

————. "A Note on the Rhetoric of Spenser's 'Despair.'" *MP*, 47 (1949), 8–11.

Smith, Charles G. "The Ethical Allegory of the Two Florimells." *SP*, 31 (1934), 140–51.

————. "Sententious Theory in Spenser's Legend of Friendship." *ELH*, 2 (1935), 165–91.

————. *Spenser's Proverb Lore*. Cambridge, Mass.: Harvard University Press, 1970.

————. "Spenser's Theory of Friendship." *PMLA*, 49 (1934), 490–500.

————. *Spenser's Theory of Friendship*. Baltimore: The Johns Hopkins Press, 1935; rpt. Folcroft, Pa.: Folcroft Press, 1969.

————. "Spenser's Theory of Friendship: An Elizabethan Commonplace." *SP*, 32 (1935), 158–69.

————. "Studies in the Fourth Book of *The Faerie Queene*." Diss. Johns Hopkins University, 1930.

Smith, G. C. Moore. "Printed Books with Gabriel Harvey's Autograph or MS Notes." *MLR*, 29 (1934), 68–70.

Smith, Hallett. *Elizabethan Poetry: A Study in Conventions, Meaning, and Expression.* Cambridge, Mass.: Harvard University Press, 1952; rpt. 1964; Ann Arbor, Mich.: University of Michigan Press, 1968.

Smith, J. C. "Edmund Spenser." *Encyclopedia Britannica,* 21 (1929), 204–8.

Smith, Paul Royce. "Studies in Spenser's Rimes." Diss. University of Florida, 1955.

Smith, Roland M. "A Further Note on Una and Duessa." *PMLA,* 61 (1946), 592–96.

———. "Irish Names in *The Faerie Queene*." *MLN,* 61 (1946), 27–38.

———. "Origines Arthurianae: The Two Crosses of Red Cross Knight." *JEGP,* 54 (1955), 670–83.

———. "Spenser's Irish River Stories." *PMLA,* 50 (1935), 1047–56.

———. "Spenser's 'Stony Aubrian.'" *MLN,* 59 (1944), 1–5.

———. "Spenser's Tale of the Two Sons of Milesio." *MLQ,* 3 (1942), 547–57.

———. "Una and Duessa." *PMLA,* 50 (1935), 917–19.

Snyder, Susan. "Guyon the Wrestler." *RN,* 14 (1961), 249–52.

———. "The Paradox of Despair: Studies of the Despair Theme in Medieval and Renaissance Literature." Diss. Columbia University, 1963.

Sonn, Carl R. "Sir Guyon in the Cave of Mammon." *SEL,* 1 (1961), 17–30.

———. "Spenser's Imagery." *ELH,* 26 (1959), 156–70.

South, Malcolm H. "A Note on Spenser and Sir Thomas Browne." *MLR,* 62 (1967), 14–16.

Spencer, Theodore. "The Poetry of Sir Philip Sidney." *ELH,* 12 (1945), 251–78.

Spens, Janet. "*The Faerie Queene*: A Reply." *MLR,* 44 (1949), 87–88.

———. *Spenser's "Faerie Queene": An Interpretation.* London: Edward Arnold, 1934; rpt. New York: Russell and Russell, 1967.

Spenser, Edmund. *The Faerie Queene.* 6 vols. Ed. Kate M. Warren. London: Constable and Co., 1897–1900.

———. *The Faerie Queene, Cantos I.—II. and The Prothalamion.* New York: Maynard, Merrill and Co., 1901.

———. *Faery Queen, Book I.* Ed. G. W. Kitchin. Oxford: Clarendon Press, 1901. New ed. 1929 (originally published 1867).

———. *Faerie Queene, Book I.* Ed. W. Keith Leask. London: Blackie, 1902.

———. *The Faerie Queene, Book I.* Ed. H. M. Percival. London: Macmillan, 1902; rpt. New York: St. Martin's Press, 1957.

———. *The Story of the Faerie Queene.* By Dr. Edward Brooks. Philadelphia: Penn Publishing Co., 1902.

———. *Tales from "The Faerie Queene."* By Clara L. Thomson. Shaldon: E. E. Speight, 1902.

———. *The Faerie Queene.* New York: T. Y. Crowell, 1903.

———. *Spenser. Book II of the "Faerie Queene."* Ed. G. W. Kitchin. 9th ed. Oxford: Clarendon Press, 1903 (originally published 1868).

————. *Spenser's The Faerie Queene, Book I.* Ed. George Armstrong Wauchope. New York: Macmillan, 1903; rpt. 1907, 1909.

————. *The Faerie Queene. Book I.* Ed. W. H. Hudson; London: J. M. Dent, 1904.

————. *Day-Book of Passages from "The Faerie Queene."* Edinburgh and London: William Blackwood and Sons, 1905.

————. *The Faerie Queene, Book One.* Ed. Martha Hale Shackford. Boston: Houghton Mifflin, 1905.

————. *The Faerie Queene. Book I.* Ed. C. L. Thomson. London: Carmelite Classic, 1905.

————. *Selections from Spenser's "The Faerie Queene."* Ed. John Erskine. New York: Longmans Green, 1905.

————. *Stories from "The Faerie Queene."* By Mary Macleod. New York: Frederick A. Stokes, 1905.

————. *Tales and Stories from Spenser's "Faery Queene."* By N. G. Royde Smith. London: Macmillan, 1905.

————. *Tales from Spenser Chosen from the "Faerie Queene."* By Sophia H. Maclehose. London: Macmillan, 1905.

————. *Una and the Red Cross Knight, and Other Tales from Spenser's "Faerie Queene."* By N. G. Royde-Smith. London: J. M. Dent, 1905; rpt. 1927.

————. *Britomart, Selections from Spenser's "Faerie Queene," Books III, IV, and V.* Ed. Mary E. Litchfield. Boston: Ginn and Co., 1906.

————. *The Faerie Queene.* 2 vols. London: George Newnes, 1906.

————. *"The Faerie Queene," First Book, Rewritten in Simple Language by Calvin Dill Wilson.* Chicago: A. C. McClurg, 1906.

————. *"The Faerie Queene," Told to the Children by Jeanie Lang.* New York: McLoughlin Brothers, 1906.

————. *Poems.* Edinburgh: T. C. and E. C. Jack, 1906; rpt. London: Caxton, 1960.

————. *Complete Poetical Works.* Ed. R. E. Neil Dodge. Boston: Houghton Mifflin, 1908; rpt. 1947.

————. *The Red Cross Knight and Sir Guyon.* By Mary Macleod. London: Wells, Gardner and Co., 1908.

————. *The Faerie Queene.* 2 vols. Cambridge: Cambridge University Press, 1909.

————. *The Faerie Queene and Her Knights, Stories Retold from Edmund Spenser, by the Rev. Alfred Church.* London: Seeley and Co., 1909.

————. *The Faerie Queene, Book I.* Oxford: Clarendon Press, 1909.

————. *The Faerie Queene, disposed into twelve books fashioning twelve moral vertues.* 2 vols. Ed. J. W. Hales. London: J. M. Dent, 1909; rpt. 1933, 1957, 1962.

————. *Spenser's "Faerie Queene."* Ed. J. C. Smith. Oxford: Clarendon Press, 1909; rpt. 1961.

————. *Stories from "The Faerie Queene," Retold from Spenser by Lawrence H. Dawson.* London: George G. Harrap, 1909.

Spenser, Edmund. *Tales from Spenser*. By R. W. Grace. London: T. Fisher Unwin, 1909.

———. *The Poetical Works of Edmund Spenser*. 3 vols. Ed. J. C. Smith and Ernest DeSelincourt. Oxford: Clarendon Press, 1910; rpt. 1964.

———. *The Gateway to Spenser. Tales Retold by Emily Underdown from "The Faerie Queene" of Edmund Spenser*. London: Thomas Nelson and Sons, 1911.

———. *The Quest of the Red Cross Knight. A Story from Spenser's "Faerie Queene."* By Mrs. F. S. Boas. London: Blackie, 1911.

———. *The Poetical Works of Edmund Spenser*. Ed. J. C. Smith and Ernest DeSelincourt. London: Oxford University Press, 1912; rpt. 1924, 1935, 1952, 1957, 1961.

———. *Stories from Spenser Retold from "The Faerie Queene."* London: Thomas Nelson and Sons, 1912.

———. *The Red Cross Knight. Scenes from Spenser's "Faerie Queene."* By William Scott Durrant. London: Year Book Press, 1913.

———. *Selections from "The Faerie Queene."* London: J. M. Dent, 1913.

———. *Spenser's "Faerie Queene." Book I*. Ed. S. E. Winbolt. London: Bell's English Texts, 1913.

———. *The Faerie Queene. Book II*. Ed. Lilian Winstanley. Cambridge: Cambridge University Press, 1914; rpt. 1928.

———. *"The Faery Queene." Book V*. Ed. E. H. Blakeney. London: Blackie, 1914.

———. *"The Faerie Queene." Book V*. Oxford: Clarendon Press, 1915.

———. *"The Faerie Queene." Book I*. Ed. Lilian Winstanley. Cambridge: Cambridge University Press, 1915; rpt. 1958.

———. *Spenser's "Faerie Queene," Book I*. Ed. S. E. Winbolt. London: Bell's Annotated English Classics, 1915.

———. *Spenser's "Faerie Queene." Book V*. Ed. S. E. Winbolt. London: Bell's English Texts, 1916.

———. *"The Faerie Queene." Book V*. Ed. Alfred Gough. Oxford: Clarendon Press, 1918.

———. *Stories from Spenser*. By Minna Steele Smith. Cambridge: Cambridge University Press, 1919.

———. *The Faerie Queene disposed into twelve bookes fashioning xii. morall vertues*. Chelsea: Ashendene Press, 1923.

———. *The Knights of "The Faerie Queene." Tales Retold from Spenser*. By M. Sturt and E. C. Oakden. London: Kings' Treasuries of Literature, 1924.

———. *The Approach to Spenser. Prose Tales by E. Underdown with Extracts from "The Faerie Queene."* London: T. Nelson and Sons, 1925.

———. *The Complete Works*. Ed. W. L. Renwick. London: Scholartis Press, 1928.

———. *Una and the Red Cross Knight, and Other Legends. Re-told from Spenser's "Faerie Queene."* London: James Brodie, 1928.

———. *"The Faerie Queene." The Second Booke, Contayning The Legend of Sir Guyon; or of Temperaunce.* Ed. George R. Potter and James Cline. New York: Harper, 1929.

———. *Stories from "The Faery Queen."* London: Epworth Press, 1929.

———. *Spenser's "Faery Queene." Book I.* Ed. Guy N. Pocock. London: J. M. Dent, 1930.

———. *The Works of Edmund Spenser.* 8 vols. Ed. W. L. Renwick. Oxford: Shakespeare Head Press, 1930–32.

———. *Legends and Pageants from "The Faerie Queene."* Ed. J. C. Smith. London: W. and R. Chambers, 1932.

———. *The Works of Edmund Spenser: A Variorum Edition.* 10 vols. Ed. Edwin Greenlaw et al. Baltimore: The Johns Hopkins Press, 1932–49; rpt. 1958, 1966.

———. *Edmund Spenser.* traduction par Paul de Reul. Paris: La Renaissance du Livre, 1933.

———. *The Faerie Queene.* Ed. R. Morris. London: J. M. Dent, 1933.

———. *"The Faerie Queene." Book I.* Ed. A. S. Collins. London: University Tutorial Press, 1937.

———. *"The Faerie Queene," Book I.* Ed. G. S. Dickson. London: Thomas Nelson and Sons, 1937.

———. *"The Faerie Queene." Book II.* Ed. A. J. F. Collins. London: University Tutorial Press, 1942.

———. *The Adventures of the Redcrosse Knight.* By Sister Mary Charitina. London: Sheed and Ward, 1945.

———. *La Reine des Fees.* Paris: Edition Montaigne, 1950.

———. *The Faerie Queene.* Coronation Edition. 2 vols. New York: Heritage Press, 1953.

———. *The Faerie Queene, disposed into twelve bookes fashioning xii morall vertues.* Oxford: Printed for the members of the Limited Editions Club at the University Press, 1953.

———. *La Regina delle Fate.* Ed. Carlo Izzo. Firenze: Biblioteca Sansoniana Straniera, 1954.

———. *Selected Poetry.* Ed. Leo Kirschbaum. New York: Rinehart, 1956; rev. ed., 1961.

———. *"The Faerie Queene." Book VI.* Ed. Tatiana A. Wolff. London: Macmillan, 1959.

———. *The First Book of "The Faerie Queene."* Ed. Robert L. Kellogg and Oliver L. Steele. Charlottesville, Va.: University of Virginia, 1961.

———. *"The Faerie Queene," Book First.* Ed. J. B. Singh. Agra: Nav Jeevan Prakashan, 1962.

———. *Saint George and the Dragon, Being the Legend of the Red Cross Knight from "The Faerie Queene."* By Sandol Stoddard Warburg. Boston: Houghton Mifflin, 1963.

———. *Selected Poetry.* Ed. William Nelson. New York: Modern Library, 1964.

———. *Books I and II of "The Faerie Queene," the Mutability Cantos, and Selections from the Minor Poetry.* Ed. Robert Kellogg and Oliver Steele. New York: Odyssey Press, 1965.

Spenser, Edmund. *"The Faerie Queene," Book II.* Ed. P. C. Bayley. London: Oxford University Press, 1965.

——. *From "The Faerie Queene"; Selections.* Ed. C. J. Dixon. London: Heinemann Educational Books, 1965.

——. *Selections.* London: Oxford University Press, 1965.

——. *Selections from the Minor Poems and "The Faerie Queene."* Ed. Frank Kermode. London: Oxford University Press, 1965.

——. *Antologia Spenseriana.* Verona: F. Ghidini, 1966.

——. *The Faerie Queene.* Ed. P. C. Bayley. London: Oxford University Press, 1966.

——. *Selected Poetry.* Ed. A. C. Hamilton. New York: New American Library, 1966.

——. *Edmund Spenser: A Selection of His Works.* Ed. Ian C. Sowton. New York: St. Martin's Press, 1968.

——. *The Mutabilitie Cantos.* Ed. S. P. Zitner. London: Thomas Nelson and Sons, 1968.

——. *Poetry: Authoritative Texts and Criticism.* Ed. Hugh Maclean. New York: Norton, 1968.

——. *Spenser.* Ed. Edwin Honig. New York: Dell, 1968.

——. *Edmund Spenser: "The Faerie Queene."* Ed. Catherine Myers. New York: Barnes and Noble, 1969.

——. *Edmund Spenser: A Critical Anthology.* Ed. Paul J. Alpers. Harmondsworth: Penguin, 1970.

——. *Edmund Spenser: A Selection of His Works.* Ed. Ian C. Sowton. New York: Odyssey, 1970.

——. *Selected Poetry.* Ed. A. Kent Hieatt and Constance Hieatt. New York: Appleton, 1970.

——. *Selections from the Poetical Works of Edmund Spenser.* Ed. S. K. Heninger, Jr. Boston: Houghton Mifflin, 1970.

Sprague, A. C. "Gloriana's Annual Feast." *TLS*, 32 (1933), 295.

Spurgeon, Caroline F. *Mysticism in English Literature.* Cambridge: Cambridge University Press, 1913.

Spurgeon, Patrick O. "The Poet Historical: Edmund Spenser—A Study of Renaissance Methods and Uses of History." Diss. University of Tennessee, 1963.

——. "Spenser's Muses." In *RenP 1969*, pp. 15–23.

Stack, Richard C. "From Sweetness to Strength: A Study of the Development of Metrical Style in the English Renaissance." Diss. Stanford University, 1968.

Stampfer, Judah L. "*The Cantos of Mutabilitie*: Spenser's Last Testament of Faith." *UTQ*, 21 (1952), 140–56.

Starnes, D. T. "The Figure Genius in the Renaissance." *SRen*, 11 (1964), 234–44.

——. "Spenser and the Graces." *PQ*, 21 (1942), 268–82.

——. "Spenser and the Muses." *TxSE*, 22 (1942), 31–58.

Starnes, Dewitt T. and Ernest W. Talbert. *Classical Myth and Legend in Renaissance Dictionaries.* Chapel Hill, N. C.: University of North Carolina Press, 1955.

Staton, Walter F., Jr. "Italian Pastorals and the Conclusion of the Serena Story." *SEL*, 6 (1966), 35–42.

———. "Ralegh and the Amyas-Aemylia Episode." *SEL*, 5 (1965), 105–14.

Stauffer, Donald A. *The Nature of Poetry*. New York: Norton, 1946.

Steadman, John M. "Acrasia in The Tablet of Cebes." *N&Q*, 205 (1960), 48.

———. "Errour and Herpetology." *N&Q*, 202 (1957), 333–34.

———. "Felicity and End in Renaissance Epic and Ethics." *JHI*, 23 (1962), 117–32.

———. "The 'Inharmonious Blacksmith': Spenser and the Pythagoras Legend." *PMLA*, 79 (1964), 664–65.

———. "Sin, Echidna and the Viper Brood." *MLR*, 66 (1961), 62–66.

———. "Spenser and Martianus Capella." *MLR*, 53 (1958), 545–46.

———. "Spenser and the *Virgilius* Legend: Another Talus Parallel." *MLN*, 73 (1958), 412–13.

———. "Spenser's 'Errour' and the Renaissance Allegorical Tradition." *NM*, 62 (1961), 22–38.

———. "Spenser's House of Care: A Reinterpretation." *SRen*, 7 (1960), 207–24.

———. "Stanzaic Patterns in the English Wagner Book." *N&Q*, 202 (1957), 376–77.

———. "Una and the Clergy: The Ass Symbol in *The Faerie Queene*." *JWCI*, 21 (1958), 134–37.

Stebbing, William. *Five Centuries of English Verse*. 2 vols. London: Henry Froude, 1913.

———. *The Poets, Chaucer to Tennyson: Impressions*. London: Henry Froude, 1907.

Steel, James H. "Style in Spenser." *Proceedings Royal Philosophical Society, Glasgow*, 46 (1914–15), 146–205.

Steele, Oliver Lee, Jr. "The Rhetorical Functions of the Narrator in *The Faerie Queene*. Diss. University of Virginia, 1966.

Stein, Arnold. "Stanza Continuity in *The Faerie Queene*." *MLN*, 59 (1944), 114–18.

Stewart, Bain T. "A Note on Spenser and Phineas Fletcher." *PQ*, 26 (1947), 86–87.

———. "The Psychology of Spenser's Anamnestes." *MLQ*, 1 (1940), 193–94.

Stewart, James Tate. "Elizabethan Psychology and the Poetry of Edmund Spenser." Diss. Vanderbilt University, 1954.

Stewart, Randall. "Hawthorne and *The Faerie Queene*." *PQ*, 12 (1933), 196–206.

Sterling, Brents. "The Concluding Stanzas of *Mutabilitie*." *SP*, 30 (1933), 193–204.

———. "The Philosophy of Spenser's Garden of Adonis." *PMLA*, 49 (1934), 501–38.

———. "Spenser's Garden of Adonis and *Cantos of Mutabilitie*: A Reinterpretation." Diss. University of Washington, 1934.

Sterling, Brents. "Spenser's Platonic Garden." *JEGP*, 41 (1942), 482–86.

———. "Two Notes on the Philosophy of *Mutabilitie*." *MLN*, 50 (1935), 154–55.

Stock, A. G. "Yeats on Spenser." In *In Excited Reverie: A Centenary Tribute to William Butler Yeats, 1865–1939.* Ed. A. Norman Jeffares and K. G. W. Cross. New York: Macmillan, 1965, pp. 93–101.

Stockton, Richard Engle. "The Christian Content of Edmund Spenser's *Mutabilitie Cantos*." Diss. Princeton University, 1954.

Stoger, H. "Ovid's Einfluss auf die poetischen Werke Spensers." Diss. University of Vienna, 1938.

Stoll, E. E. "Criticisms Criticized: Spenser and Milton." *JEGP*, 41 (1942), 451–77.

———. *Poets and Playwrights: Shakespeare, Jonson, Spenser, Milton.* Minneapolis: University of Minnesota Press, 1930; rpt. New York: Russell and Russell, 1965.

———. "The Validity of the Poetic Vision: Keats and Spenser." *MLR*, 40 (1945), 1–7.

Stovall, Floyd. "Feminine Rimes in *The Faerie Queene*." *JEGP*, 26 (1927), 91–95.

Strathmann, Ernest A. "A Scotch Spenserian: Patrick Gordon." *HLQ*, 1 (1938), 427–37.

———. "William Austin's 'Notes' on *The Faerie Queene*." *HLB*, 11 (1937), 155–60.

Strong, Sir Archibald. *Four Studies.* Adelaide: F. W. Preece, 1932.

Stroup, Thomas B. "Lycidas and the Marinell Story." In *SAMLA Studies in Milton.* Gainesville, Fla.: University of Florida Press, 1953.

Sugden, Herbert W. *The Grammar of Spenser's "Faerie Queene."* Philadelphia: Linguistic Society of America, 1936; rpt. New York: Kraus Reprint Co., 1966.

Super, R. H. "Spenser's *Faerie Queene*, II, i, 490–492," *Expl.*, 11 (1953), Item 30.

Swallow, Alan. "Allegory as Literary Method." *NMQ*, 10 (1940), 147–57.

Syford, Constance M. "The Direct Source of the Pamela-Cecropia Episode in the *Arcadia*." *PMLA*, 49 (1934), 472–89.

Sypher, Wylie. *Four Stages of Renaissance Style: Transformations in Art and Literature, 1400–1700.* Garden City, N. Y.: Doubleday, 1955; rpt. 1966.

Szoverffy, Joseph. "The Master of Wolves and Dragon-Killer (Some Aspects of the Popular St. George Traditions)." *SFQ*, 19 (1955), 211–29.

Tayler, Edward W. *Nature and Art in Renaissance Literature.* New York: Columbia University Press, 1964.

Taylor, A. E. "Spenser's Knowledge of Plato." *MLR*, 19 (1924), 208–10.

Taylor, H. O. *Thought and Expression in the Sixteenth Century.* New York: Macmillan, 1920; 2nd rev. ed. New York: Ungar, 1959; rpt. New York: Collier, 1962.

Thaler, Alwin. "Mercutio and Spenser's Phantastes." *PQ*, 16 (1937), 405–7.

———. "Spenser and *Much Ado About Nothing*." *SP*, 37 (1940), 225–35.

Thomas, Henry. "The Romance of Amadis of Gaul." *Transactions of the Bibliographical Society*, 11 (1911), 251–97.

Thomas, Sidney. "'Hobgoblin Runne Away with the Garland of Apollo.'" *MLN*, 55 (1940), 418–22.

Thompson, Edward. *Sir Walter Raleigh, Last of the Elizabethans*. New Haven: Yale University Press, 1936.

Thompson, Francis. *Collected Works*. 3 vols. Ed. Wilfrid Meynell. New York: Burnsand Oaks, 1913; rpt. Westminster, Md.: Newman Press, 1947.

Thompson, Phyllis J. "Archetypal Elements in *The Faerie Queene* with Special Reference to Book Six." Diss. University of North Carolina, 1965.

Thomson, Patricia. "The Literature of Patronage, 1580–1630." *EIC*, 2 (1952), 267–84.

———. "The Patronage of Letters under Elizabeth and James I." *English*, 7 (1949), 278–82.

———. "Phantastes and His Horoscope." *N&Q*, 211 (1966), 372–75.

Thornton, Frances Clabaugh. *The French Element in Spenser's Poetical Works*. Toulousse: Lion et Fils, 1938.

Tilley, M. P. "The Comedy *Lingua* and *The Faerie Queene*." *MLN*, 42 (1927), 150–57.

Tillotson, Geoffrey. *Essays in Criticism and Research*. Cambridge: Cambridge University Press, 1942; rpt. Hamden, Conn.: Archon Books, 1967.

Tillyard, E. M. W. "The Action of Comus." In *Essays and Studies by Members of the English Association*, 28 (1942), 22–37. Rpt. in *Studies in Milton*. London: Chatto and Windus, 1951, pp. 82–99; rpt. 1960.

———. *The Elizabethan World Picture*. London: Chatto and Windus, 1943; rpt. 1944, 1956; New York: Random House, 1959; Harmondsworth: Penguin, 1966; London: Chatto and Windus, 1967.

———. *The English Epic and Its Background*. New York: Oxford University Press, 1954; rpt. 1966.

———. *The English Renaissance: Fact or Fiction?*" Baltimore: The Johns Hopkins Press, 1952; rpt. London: Hogarth, 1960; New York: Greenwood Press, 1968.

———. "Milton and the English Epic Tradition." In *Seventeenth-Century Studies Presented to Sir Herbert Grierson*. Ed. J. Dover Wilson. Oxford: Clarendon Press, 1938, pp. 211–34.

———. *The Miltonic Setting: Past and Present*. London: Chatto and Windus, 1938; rpt. New York: Macmillan, 1949; London: Chatto and Windus, 1957; New York: Barnes and Noble, 1966.

———. *Poetry Direct and Oblique*. London: Chatto and Windus, 1934; rev. ed. 1945, 1948, 1959.

Tillyard, E. M. W. *Shakespeare's History Plays*. London: Chatto and Windus, 1944; rpt. New York: Macmillan, 1946; London: Chatto and Windus, 1956, 1966; Harmondsworth: Penguin, 1962; New York: Barnes and Noble, 1964.

Torczon, Vernon James. "The Pilgrimage of Red Cross Knight." Diss. University of Nebraska, 1960.

————. "Spenser's Orgoglio and Despair." *TSLL*, 3 (1961), 123–28.

Tosello, Rev. Matthew. "The Relationship between Dante Alighieri (1265–1321) and Edmund Spenser (1552–1599)." Diss. Duquesne University, 1970.

Traversi, D. A. "Revaluations (X): The Vision of Piers Plowman." *Scrutiny*, 5 (1936), 276–91.

————. "Spenser's *Faerie Queene*." In *The Age of Chaucer*. Ed. Boris Ford. London: Penguin Books, 1954.

Treneer, Anne. *The Sea in English Literature from Beowulf to Donne*. Liverpool: University of Liverpool Press, 1926.

Trienens, Roger J. "The Green-Eyed Monster: A Study of Sexual Jealousy in the Literature of the English Renaissance." Diss. Northwestern University, 1951.

Truesdale, Calvin William. "English Pastoral Verse from Spenser to Marvell: A Critical Revaluation." Diss. University of Washington, 1956.

Tuckwell, William. *Spenser*. London: G. Bell and Sons, 1906.

Tuell, Anne K. "The Original End of *The Faerie Queene*, Book III." *MLN*, 36 (1921), 309–11.

Turnage, Maxine. "Samuel Johnson's Criticism of the Works of Edmund Spenser." *SEL*, 10 (1970), 557–67.

Turner, W. J. *Romance of English Literature*. New York: Hastings House, 1944.

Tuve, Rosemond. *Allegorical Imagery: Some Medieval Books and Their Posterity*. Princeton, N. J.: Princeton University Press, 1966.

————. *Elizabethan and Metaphysical Imagery*. Chicago: University of Chicago Press, 1947; rpt. Chicago: University of Chicago Press, 1961.

————. *Essays by Rosemond Tuve*. Ed. Thomas P. Roche, Jr. Princeton, N. J.: Princeton University Press, 1970.

————. "A Medieval Commonplace in Spenser's Cosmology." *SP*, 30 (1933), 133–47.

————. "Notes on the Virtues and Vices: Part I; Two Fifteenth-Century Lines of Dependence on the Thirteenth and Twelfth Centuries." *JWCI*, 26 (1963), 264–303.

————. "The Red Cross Knight and the Medieval Demon Stories." *MLN*, 44 (1929), 706–14.

————. "Spenser and Medieval Mazars: with a Note on Jason in Ivory." *SP*, 34 (1937), 138–47.

————. "Spenser and Some Pictorial Conventions with Particular Reference to Illuminated Manuscripts." *SP*, 37 (1940), 149–76.

————. "Spenser and the *Zodiake of Life*." *JEGP*, 34 (1935), 1–19.

——. "Spenser's Reading: the *De Claris Mulieribus.*" *SP*, 33 (1936), 147–65.

Uhlig, Claus. "Ouroboros-Symbolik bei Spenser." *GRM*, 19 (1969), 1–23.
Upcott, L. E. "The Poet's Poet." *TLS*, 29 (1930), 190.
Ure, Peter. "The Poetry of Sir Walter Raleigh." *REL*, 1 (1960), 19–29.

Vallese, Tarquinio. *Spenser: Studio Critico della poesia di E. Spenser seguito dalla versione a fronte del I Canto del I Libro della "Faerie Queene."* Naples: Raffaele Pironti, 1946.
Vance, Eugene A. "Warfare as Metaphor in Spenser's *Faerie Queene.*" Diss. Cornell University, 1964.
Van Doren, Mark. *The Noble Voice: A Study of Ten Great Poems.* New York: Henry Holt and Co., 1946.
Van Heyningen, Christina. "Poet's Poet." *Theoria, A Journal of the Arts Faculty,* University of Natal (1950), 93–100.
Van Kranendonk, A. G. *Shakespeare en Zijn Tijd [Shakespeare and His Time].* Amsterdam: Querido's Uitgeversmij N.V., 1947.
——. "Spenserian Echoes in *A Midsummer Night's Dream.*" *ES*, 14 (1932), 209–17.
Ven-Ten Bensel, E. *The Character of King Arthur in English Literature.* Amsterdam: H. J. Paris, 1925; rpt. New York: Haskell House, 1966.
Vesci, Ornella. "Immagini della regina." *AION-SG*, 11 (1968), 145–70.
Viglione, Francesco. *L'Italia nel Pensiero degli Scrittori Inglese.* Milan: Fratelli Bocca, 1947.
Viswanathan, S. "Spenser's *The Faerie Queene,* Book I, i, v, 7." *Expl.,* 27 (1969), Item 44.
Vondersmith, Bernard J. "A History of the Criticism of *The Faerie Queene,* 1910–1947." Diss. Duquesne University, 1971.

Wade, Clyde Gregory. "The Comedy of *The Faerie Queene.*" Diss. University of Missouri, 1967.
Wagner, Geoffrey. "Talus." *ELH*, 17 (1950), 79–86.
Walker, Ralph S. "Literary Criticism in Jonson's Conversations with Drummond." *English*, 8 (1951), 222–27.
Wall, L. N. "Some Notes on Marvell's Sources." *N&Q*, 202 (1957), 170–73.
Walter, J. H. "*The Faerie Queene*: Alterations and Structure." *MLR*, 36 (1941), 37–58.
——. "Further Notes on the Alterations to *The Faerie Queene.*" *MLR*, 38 (1943), 1–10.
Walton, Charles E. " 'To Maske in Myrthe': Spenser's Theatrical Practices in *The Faerie Queene.*" *Emporia Research Studies,* 9 (1960), 7–45.
Wann, Louis. "The Role of the Confidant(e) in the Renaissance Epic." *Anglia,* 51 (1927), 63–74.
Wasserman, Earl R. "Elizabethan Poetry in the Eighteenth Century." *ISLL,* 32, Nos. 2–3 (1947), 1–291.

Wasserman, Earl R. "The Scholarly Origin of the Elizabethan Revival." *ELH*, 4 (1937), 213–43.

Waters, D. Douglas. "Duessa and Orgoglio: Red Cross's Spiritual Fornication." *RenQ*, 20 (1967), 211–20.

———. "Edmund Spenser's Theology." Diss. Vanderbilt University, 1960.

———. "Errour's Den and Archimago's Hermitage: Symbolic Lust and Symbolic Witchcraft." *ELH*, 33 (1966), 279–98.

———. "'Mistress Missa,' Duessa, and the Analogical Allegory of *The Faerie Queene*, Book I." *PLL*, 4 (1968), 258–75.

———. "Prince Arthur as Christian Magnanimity in Book One of *The Faerie Queene*." *SEL*, 9 (1969), 53–62.

———. "Spenser's 'Well of Life' and 'Tree of Life' Once More." *MP*, 67 (1969), 67–68.

Watkins, W. B. C. *Johnson and English Poetry before 1660*. Princeton, N. J.: Princeton University Press, 1936; rpt. New York: Gordian Press, 1965.

———. "The Kingdom of Our Language." *HudR*, 2 (1949), 343–76.

———. "The Plagiarist: Spenser or Marlowe?" *ELH*, 11 (1944), 249–65.

———. *Shakespeare and Spenser*. Princeton, N. J.: Princeton University Press, 1950; rpt. Cambridge, Mass.: Walker-de Berry, 1961; Princeton, N. J.: Princeton University Press, 1966.

Webb, William Stanford. "Spenser and Virgil." Diss. Johns Hopkins University, 1928.

———. "Virgil in Spenser's Epic Theory." *ELH*, 4 (1937), 62–84.

Weld, J. S. "The Complaint of Britomart: Wordplay and Symbolism." *PMLA*, 66 (1951), 548–51.

Wellek, Rene. "The Concept of Baroque in Literary Scholarship." *JAAC*, 5 (1946), 77–109.

———. *The Rise of English Literary History*. Chapel Hill, N. C.: University of North Carolina Press, 1941; rpt. New York: McGraw-Hill, 1966.

Wells, Minnie E. "'The Eve of St. Agnes' and 'The Legend of Britomartis.'" *MLN*, 57 (1942), 463–65.

Wells, Whitney. "Spenser's Dragon." *MLN*, 41 (1926), 143–57.

Welply, W. H. "Some Spenser Problems." *N&Q*, 180 (1941), 56–59, 74–76, 92–95, 151, 224, 248, 436–39, 454–59.

Wheeler, Harold P. "Studies in Sixteenth-Century English Literature of Rustic Life." Diss. University of Illinois, 1939.

Whitaker, Virgil K. *The Religious Basis of Spenser's Thought*. Stanford, Calif.: Stanford University Press, 1950; rpt. New York: Gordian Press, 1966.

———. "The Theological Structure of *The Faerie Queene*, Book I." *ELH*, 19 (1952), 151–64.

White, Harold O. *Plagiarism and Imitation during the English Renaissance*. Cambridge, Mass.: Harvard University Press, 1935; rpt. New York: Octagon Books, 1965.

Whitlock, Baird W. "The Counter-Renaissance." *BHR*, 20 (1958), 434–39.

Whitman, Charles Huntington. *A Subject Index to the Poems of Edmund Spenser*. New Haven, Conn.: Yale University Press, 1918; rpt. New York: Russell and Russell, 1966.

Whitney, J. E. "The Continued Allegory in the First Book of *The Faerie Queene*." *Transactions of the American Philological Association*, 19 (1888), 40–69.

Whitney, Lois. "Spenser's Use of the Literature of Travel in *The Faerie Queene*." *MP*, 19 (1921), 143–62.

Williams, Arnold. *The Common Expositor: An Account of the Commentaries on Genesis, 1527–1633*. Chapel Hill, N. C.: University of North Carolina Press, 1948.

———. *Flower on a Lowly Stalk: The Sixth Book of "The Faerie Queene."* East Lansing, Mich.: Michigan State University Press, 1967.

Williams, Charles. *Reason and Beauty in the Poetic Mind*. Oxford: Clarendon Press, 1933.

Williams, J. M. "A Possible Source for Spenser's Labryde." *MLN*, 76 (1961), 481–84.

Williams, Kathleen. "Courtesy and Pastoral in *The Faerie Queene*, Book VI." *RES*, 13 (1962), 337–46.

———. " 'Eterne in Mutabilitie': The Unified World of *The Faerie Queene*." *ELH*, 19 (1952), 115–30.

———. "The Present State of Spenser Studies." *TSLL*, 7 (1965), 225–38.

———. "Romance Tradition in *The Faerie Queene*." *RS*, 32 (1964), 147–60.

———. *Spenser's World of Glass: A Reading of "The Faerie Queene."* Berkeley, Calif.: University of California Press, 1966.

———. "Venus and Diana: Some Uses of Myth in *The Faerie Queene*." *ELH*, 28 (1961), 101–20.

———. "Vision and Rhetoric: The Poet's Voice in *The Faerie Queene*." *ELH*, 36 (1969), 131–44.

Williamson, George. "Mutability, Decay, and Seventeenth-Century Melancholy." *ELH*, 2 (1935), 121–50.

Wilson, Elkin Calhoun. *England's Eliza*. Cambridge, Mass.: Harvard University Press, 1939; rpt. New York: Octagon Books, 1966.

———. "The Idealization of Queen Elizabeth in the Poetry of Her Age." Diss. Harvard University, 1934.

Wilson, F. P. *Elizabethan and Jacobean*. Oxford: Clarendon Press, 1945; rpt. 1960.

Wilson, J. "Spenser and His Critics." In *Critical Essays of the Early Nineteenth Century*. Ed. R. M. Alden. New York: Scribner's, 1921.

Wilson, J. D. "A Note on Elisions in *The Faerie Queene*." *MLR*, 15 (1920), 409–14.

Wimsatt, W. K., Jr. *The Verbal Icon*. Lexington, Ky.: University of Kentucky Press, 1954; rpt. New York: Noonday Press, 1958; Lexington: University of Kentucky Press, 1967.

Winbolt, S. E. *Spenser and His Poetry*. London: C. G. Harrap, 1912. rpt. Folcroft, Pa.: Folcroft Press, 1969.

Wind, Edgar. *Pagan Mysteries in the Renaissance.* London: Faber and Faber, 1958; rev. ed. Harmondsworth: Penguin Books, 1967; rpt. London: Faber and Faber, 1968; New York: Barnes and Noble, 1968; New York: W. W. Norton, 1969.

Wingfield-Stratford, Esme C. *The History of English Patriotism.* 2 vols. New York: John Lane, 1913.

Winkelman, Sister Mary Anne, S.S.N.D. "Spenser's Modifications of the Renaissance Idea of Glory as the Motivation of *The Faerie Queene.*" Diss. St. Louis University, 1961.

Winslow, Anne. "Rhythmic Variations in Spenser's *Faerie Queene.*" *Vassar Journal of Undergraduate Studies,* 5 (1931), 179–93.

Winstanley, Lilian. "Spenser and Puritanism." *MLQ,* 3 (1900), 6–16, 103–10.

Winters, Yvor. "Problems for the Modern Critic of Literature." *HudR,* 9 (1956), 325–86.

Wion, Philip Kennedy. "The Poetic Styles of Edmund Spenser." Diss. Yale University, 1968.

Wolff, Emil. "England und die Antike." In *Grundformen der Englischen Geistesgeschichte.* Ed. Paul Meissner. Stuttgart: W. Kohlhammer, 1941, pp. 1–94.

Wolk, Anthony William. "Hercules and *The Faerie Queene.*" Diss. University of Nebraska, 1965.

Woodhouse, A. S. P. "The Argument of Milton's *Comus.*" *UTQ,* 11 (1941), 46–71.

———. "*Comus* Once More." *UTQ,* 19 (1950), 218–23.

———. "Nature and Grace in Spenser: A Rejoinder." *RES,* n.s. 6 (1955), 284–88.

———. "Nature and Grace in *The Faerie Queene.*" *ELH,* 16 (1949), 194–228.

———. *The Poet and His Faith: Religion and Poetry in England from Spenser to Eliot and Auden.* Chicago: University of Chicago Press, 1965.

———. "Spenser, Nature, and Grace: Mr. Gang's Mode of Argument Reviewed." *ELH,* 27 (1960), 1–15.

Woodruff, Bertram L. "Keats's Wailful Choir of Small Gnats." *MLN,* 68 (1953), 217–20.

Woodward, Frank L. "Bacon as Spenser and Shakespeare." *Baconiana,* 28, No. 110 (1944), 36–38.

Woodward, Parker. "Edmund Spenser's Poems." *Baconiana,* n.s. 9 (1901), 117–28, 177–85.

Woodworth, Mary K. "The Mutabilitie Cantos and the Succession." *PMLA,* 59 (1944), 985–1002.

Woolf, Virginia. *The Moment and Other Essays.* New York: Harcourt Brace, 1948; rpt. London: Hogarth Press, 1964.

Wordsworth, William. *The White Doe of Rylstone.* Ed. Alice Comparetti. Ithaca, N. Y.: Cornell University Press, 1940.

Wright, Carol von Pressentin. "The Lunatic, the Lover, and the Poet:

Themes of Love and Illusion in Three Renaissance Epics." Diss. University of Michigan, 1970.

Wright, Celeste Turner. "The Amazons in Elizabethan Literature." *SP*, 37 (1940), 433–56.

Wright, John. "Keats's Endymion as Spenserian Allegory." *AULLA Proceedings*, 1 (1965), 63–64.

Wright, Nathalia. "A Note on Melville's Use of Spenser: Hautia and the Bower of Bliss." *AL*, 24 (1952), 83–85.

Wurnig, Gertraud. "Arthur und sein Kreis in der englischen Literatur von Spenser bis Masefield." Diss., University of Innsbruck, 1951.

Wurtsbaugh, Jewel. "The 1758 Editions of *The Faerie Queene*." *MLN*, 48 (1933), 228–29.

———. "Thomas Edwards and the Editorship of *The Faerie Queene*." *MLN*, 50 (1935), 146–51.

———. *Two Centuries of Spenserian Scholarship (1609–1805)*. Baltimore: The Johns Hopkins Press, 1936; rpt. New York: AMS Press, 1970.

Yates, Frances A. "The Elfin Chronicle." *TLS*, 47 (1948), 373.

———. "Elizabethan Chivalry: The Romance of the Accession Day Tilts." *JWCI*, 20 (1957), 4–25.

———. "Elizabeth as Astraea." *JWCI*, 10 (1947), 27–82.

Young, John J. "Artegall and Equity: *The Faerie Queene*, Books III–V." Diss. Case-Western Reserve University, 1969.

Zacha, Richard Bane. "Ariosto and Spenser: A Further Study in the Relationship between *Orlando Furioso* and *The Faerie Queene*." Diss. Catholic University of America, 1962.

Zanco, Aurelio. *Storia della Letteratura Inglese: dalle Origini alla Restaurazione, 650–1660*. 2nd ed. Turin: Loescher, 1958.

Zander, Friedrich. "Stephen Hawes *Passetyme of Pleasure* verglichen mit Edmund Spensers *Faerie Queene*, unter Berücksichtigung der allegorischen Dichtung in England. Ein Beitrag zur Quellenfrage der *Faerie Queene*." Rostock: H. Warkentien, 1905.

Zimmerman, Dorothy Wynne. "Romantic Criticism of Edmund Spenser." Diss. University of Illinois, 1957.

Zitner, S. P. "Spenser's Diction and Classical Precedent." *PQ*, 45 (1966), 360–71.

Zocca, Louis. *Elizabethan Narrative Poetry*. New Brunswick, N. J.: Rutgers University Press, 1950; rpt. New York: Octagon Books, 1970.

NOTES   INDEX

Notes

INTRODUCTION

1. The five volumes of "The Proceedings" survive in the Milton Eisenhower Memorial Library of The Johns Hopkins University but no longer circulate because of their delicate condition.

2. In their general preface to the *Variorum* Charles Grosvenor Osgood and Frederick Morgan Padelford acknowledge the importance of Greenlaw to this work: "It will be the aim of the other editors to make the edition a worthy memorial to this distinguished scholar, though we know that it will suffer for want of his ripe scholarship, his sound judgment, and his literary acumen" (*The Works of Edmund Spenser: A Variorum Edition* [Baltimore: The Johns Hopkins Press, 1932] I, v).

3. *JEGP*, 25 (1926), 283–98.

4. *The Political and Ecclesiastical Allegory of the First Book of "The Faerie Queene"* (Boston: Ginn and Co., 1911); *The Faerie Queene, Book I* (Cambridge: Cambridge University Press, 1915).

5. We thank the Indiana State University Research Committee for two grants for this book.

1. TREATMENTS OF THEME AND ALLEGORY

1. *Edmund Spenser: A Critical Study* (Berkeley, Calif.: University of California Press, 1917; rpt. New York: Russell and Russell, 1965), p. 48.

2. Hopefully, the history of the criticism of *The Faerie Queene* which Dr. Carolyn Burgholzer, Dr. Bernard Vondersmith, and I are writing will make full amends for these omissions.

3. *The Complete Works in Verse and Prose of Edmund Spenser*, ed. Alexander B. Grosart (London: Privately printed, 1882–84), I, 304–39; rpt. in *Spenser's Critics: Changing Currents in Literary Taste*, ed. William R. Mueller (Syracuse, N. Y.: Syracuse University Press, 1959), pp. 108–27.

4. *Edmund Spenser: An Essay on Renaissance Poetry* (London: Edward Arnold).

5. *The Johns Hopkins Alumni Magazine*, 19 (Nov. 1930), 8–31; rpt. in *Spenser's Critics*, ed. Mueller, pp. 166–86.

6. (London: Edward Arnold.)

7. (London: Oxford University Press.)

8. (New York: Columbia University Press, 1937; rpt. New York: Russell and Russell, 1965.)

9. (London: Allen and Unwin.)

10. This assertion is made of the minor poems, but in the next sentence Arthos adds that "in so many ways this will be the principle to guide the knights of *The Faerie Queene*" (p. 41).

11. (New York and London: Columbia University Press.)

12. *SP*, 15, 105–22.

13. (Philadelphia: Winston.)

14. (Cambridge, Mass.: Harvard University Press.)

15. *Sources of British Chronicle History.*

16. Greenlaw had provided his own documentation in his more general lecture "The Battle of the Books" read at Johns Hopkins and at the MLA meeting in 1927, posthumously published as the first essay in Greenlaw's *Studies in Spenser's Historical Allegory* (Baltimore: The Johns Hopkins Press, 1932; rpt. London: Cass, 1967), pp. 1–58.

17. *The Allegorical Temper: Vision and Reality in Book II of Spenser's "Faerie Queene"* (New Haven: Yale University Press).

18. (Oxford: Clarendon Press.)

19. (London: Duckworth, 1962; rpt. New York: Norton, 1963.)

20. *Neoplatonism in the Poetry of Spenser* (Geneva: Droz, 1960).

21. *Allegorical Imagery: Some Medieval Books and Their Posterity* (Princeton: Princeton University Press).

22. " 'Eterne in Mutabilitie': The Unified World of *The Faerie Queene*," *ELH*, 19 (1952), 115–30.

23. *Spenser's World of Glass: A Reading of "The Faerie Queene"* (Berkeley and Los Angeles: University of California Press).

24. See especially "A Secret Discipline: *The Faerie Queene*, Book VI," in *Form and Convention in the Poetry of Edmund Spenser*, ed. William Nelson (New York and London: Columbia University Press, 1961), pp. 35–75; and "The Prospect of Imagination: Spenser and the Limits of Poetry," *SEL*, 1 (1961), 93–120.

25. *ELH*, 16, 194–228.

26. (New Haven and London: Yale University Press.)

27. (Princeton: Princeton University Press.)

28. (Princeton: Princeton University Press.)

29. (New York and London: Columbia University Press.)

30. (Lansing, Mich.: Michigan State University Press.)

31. (Oxford: Clarendon Press.)

32. *Spenser* (New York: Harper, 1879; rpt. New York and London: Harper, 1902), p. 124.

33. *PMLA*, 12, 151–204.

34. Quoted in the *Variorum Edition* of Spenser, I, 315.

35. "Nature and Grace in *The Faerie Queene*."

36. " 'Like Race to Runne': The Parallel Structure of *The Faerie Queene*, Books I and II," *PMLA*, 73 (1958), 327–34.

37. *"The Faerie Queene* and its Critics," *Essays and Studies by Members of the English Association*, 12 (1926), 66–70.

38. *Allegorical Imagery*, pp. 359–63.
39. "The Narrative-Technique of *The Faerie Queene*," *PMLA*, 39, 310–24.
40. *Spenser's "Faerie Queene": An Interpretation.*
41. "*The Faerie Queene*: Alterations and Structure," *MLR*, 36, 37–58.
42. *The Evolution of "The Faerie Queene"* (Chicago: University of Chicago Press; rpt. New York: Burt Franklin, 1960).
43. This sparseness might have been due to World War II, but other English studies were not so severely devastated by the war.
44. *MLN*, 35, 165–77.
45. (1917.)
46. (Cambridge: Cambridge University Press.)
47. *The Allegory of Love*, pp. 333–34.
48. *English Literature in the Sixteenth Century Excluding Drama* (Oxford: Clarendon Press, 1954), pp. 380–81.
49. *The Structure of Allegory in "The Faerie Queene"* (Oxford: Clarendon Press), pp. 128–29.
50. *The Kindly Flame*, pp. 200–201.
51. Berger's argument is reviewed below in the discussion of *The Allegorical Temper.*
52. Hamilton suggests this in *Structure of Allegory*, pp. 29–43, without using the word "cosmic," which is Angus Fletcher's (*Allegory*, pp. 70–146).
53. This assumption is implicit throughout M. Pauline Parker's *The Allegory of the "Faerie Queene"*; her view of the poem as a super-psychomachia, all taking place within Arthur's soul, is expressed on p. 169.
54. We note five studies of allegory as a genre: (1) Edward A. Bloom, "The Allegorical Principle," *ELH*, 18 (1951), 163–90; (2) Edwin Honig, *Dark Conceit: The Making of Allegory* (Evanston, Ill.: Northwestern University Press, 1959); (3) Angus Fletcher, *Allegory: The Theory of a Symbolic Mode* (Ithaca, N. Y.: Cornell University Press, 1964); (4) Michael Murrin, *The Veil of Allegory* (Chicago: University of Chicago Press, 1969); and (5) John MacQueen, *Allegory* (London: Methuen, 1970). Bloom's article defines allegory and discusses critical attitudes toward it as a literary mode in classical, medieval, and modern times; Honig's and Fletcher's books are largely inductive attempts to characterize the genre on the basis of the authors' wide reading in allegories; Murrin's and MacQueen's essays try to infer the poetic bases of the genre from historical surveys of the theory as well as the practice of allegory in ancient, medieval, and modern times. It is beyond the scope of my essay to review these works, but we must note that Honig's, Fletcher's, Murrin's, and Mac-Queen's books are all four radically different works. Honig is concerned primarily with the "external cultural determinants" of allegory, in Fletcher's phrase (*Allegory*, p. 12); Fletcher's work is descriptive, attempting to identify the form which literary allegories have in common; Murrin is primarily concerned with the rhetorical technique of deliberate obscurity; and MacQueen describes a wide range of clas-

sical, medieval, and Renaissance allegorical practices on the basis of contemporary theory. Two other works deserve mention. The first, A. D. Nuttall's *Two Concepts of Allegory* (London: Routledge and Kegan Paul, 1967), which attacks C. S. Lewis's distinction between symbolism and allegory, came to my attention too late for inclusion. The other, Humphrey Tonkin's "Some Notes on Myth and Allegory in *The Faerie Queene*," MP, 70 (1973), 291–301, appeared after the present chapter had been submitted.

55. There is a tendency in modern Spenserian criticism to embrace psychological significations, even though not specifically directed to right and wrong conduct, under the label "moral allegory" (sometimes "ethical allegory"); thus the presumed status of the various Houses in *The Faerie Queene* as symbols of so many states of mind might be referred to as a feature of the "moral allegory" or "ethical allegory," even though a more rigorous categorization would distinguish between a state of mind and the conduct which it gives rise to. If the House of Malecasta, for instance, is a symbol for erotic infatuation, we might validly distinguish between the infatuation symbolized by the house and the erotic conduct which takes place in the house, the second being an act and the first only an occasion.

56. It is the use of this popular device which perhaps more than anything else (except the blonde beauty) invites the application of Jungian dream-theory and symbol-theory to Spenser's poem, for locales, and especially houses, are very significant in Jung as symbols of the personality and of states of mind.

57. In this connection see A. Bartlett Giamatti, *The Earthly Paradise and the Renaissance Epic* (Princeton: Princeton University Press, 1966), pp. 33–47. Giamatti expands upon E. R. Curtius's treatment of the *locus amoenus* in *European Literature and the Latin Middle Ages*, trans. W. R. Trask (New York: Pantheon Books, 1953), p. 192; see also the whole chapter "The Ideal Landscape," pp. 183–202. In Giamatti see especially p. 34 and the statement, pp. 43–44, that for Ovid, as for Horace, "a landscape reflects one's interior state of soul."

58. My debt to Graham Hough's summary of the matter, *Preface*, pp. 123–25, will be apparent.

59. (Princeton: Princeton University Press; rpt. Cambridge, Mass.: Walker-de Berry, 1961.)

60. Watkins's argument, pp. 114–21, is too extensive to be paraphrased here.

61. (Princeton: Princeton University Press.)

62. (Princeton: Princeton University Press.)

63. By Edgar Wind (London: Faber and Faber, 1958).

64. *Paradoxia Epidemica: The Renaissance Tradition of Paradox*, by Rosalie L. Colie (Princeton: Princeton University Press, 1966).

65. *Mysteriously Meant: The Rediscovery of Pagan Symbolism and Allegorical Interpretation in the Renaissance*, by Don Cameron Allen (Baltimore: The Johns Hopkins Press, 1970).

66. (New York: Odyssey, 1965.)
67. (Cambridge: Cambridge University Press.)
68. (Oxford: Clarendon Press.)
69. (Boston: Silver, Burdette and Co.)
70. (Princeton: Princeton University Press.)
71. (Cambridge: Cambridge University Press.)
72. *Iconographie Chrétienne* (Paris: Imprimerie royale, 1843); *Christian Iconography*, trans. E. J. Millington (1st ed. 1851; rpt. New York: Ungar, 1965).
73. For example, *L'art Religieux du XIII*^e *Siecle en France*, 3rd ed. (Paris, 1910), translated as *The Gothic Image*, trans. Dora Nussey (New York: Dutton, 1913; rpt. New York: Harper Torchbooks, 1958).
74. *SP*, 37, 149–76.
75. *The Virtues Reconciled: An Iconographic Study* (Toronto: University of Toronto Press).
76. *Studies in Art and Literature for Belle da Costa Greene*, ed. D. E. Miner (Princeton: Princeton University Press).
77. (New Haven: Yale University Press.)
78. (New York: Oxford University Press.)
79. Trans. Barbara F. Sessions (New York: Pantheon Books).
80. (London: Chatto and Windus.)
81. *EIC*, 10, 334–41.
82. (London: Routledge and Kegan Paul.)
83. *SP*, 53, 114–40.
84. *The Prophetic Moment: An Essay on Spenser* (Chicago and London: University of Chicago Press).
85. *Major British Writers*, ed. G. B. Harrison (New York: Harcourt, Brace), I, 91–103.
86. *ELH*, 36, 470–92.
87. Diss. Duquesne University.
88. Frank Kermode, "The Cave of Mammon," *Elizabethan Poetry*, ed. John Russell Brown and Bernard Harris (New York: St. Martin's, 1960), pp. 151–73; M. Pauline Parker, *The Allegory of the "Faerie Queene,"* pp. 128–36; A. C. Hamilton, *Structure of Allegory*, pp. 97–112; Maurice Evans, "The Fall of Guyon," *ELH*, 28 (1961), 215–24; Priscilla Barnum, "Elizabethan 'Psychology' and Books I and II of Spenser's *Faerie Queene*," *Thoth*, 3 (1962), 55–68; Lewis Miller, "A Secular Reading of *The Faerie Queene*, Book II," *ELH*, 33 (1966), 154–69; Kathleen Williams, *Spenser's World of Glass*, pp. 54–64; Paul J. Alpers, *The Poetry of "The Faerie Queene,"* pp. 235–75; Humphrey Tonkin, "Discussing Spenser's Cave of Mammon," *SEL*, 13 (1973), 1–13.
89. These observations are of course relevant to the discussion in the text above of the locale as symbol for a state of mind.
90. *Spenser's Image of Nature*, pp. 49–54.
91. *Spenser's World of Glass*, pp. 15–19.
92. *MLQ*, 25 (1964), 106.

93. (Cambridge: Cambridge University Press.)
94. *Short Time's Endless Monument: The Symbolism of the Numbers in Edmund Spenser's "Epithalamion"* (New York: Columbia University Press).

2. ON ANNOTATING SPENSER'S *Faerie Queene*

All quotations from Spenser are taken from the two-volume Oxford edition of *Spenser's "Faerie Queene,"* ed. J. C. Smith (Oxford: Clarendon Press, 1909; rpt. 1961).

1. Donald Cheney, *Spenser's Image of Nature* (New Haven, Conn.: Yale University Press, 1966), p. 7. Paul J. Alpers, *The Poetry of "The Faerie Queene"* (Princeton, N. J.: Princeton University Press, 1967).
2. *Fables of Identity* (New York: Harcourt, Brace and World, 1963), 69–87. The essay first appeared in *UTQ*, 30 (1961), 109–27, and is reprinted in *Essential Articles for the Study of Edmund Spenser*, ed. A. C. Hamilton (Hamden, Conn.: Archon Books, 1972), pp. 153–70.
3. *The Prophetic Moment* (Chicago: University of Chicago Press, 1971).
4. *Source and Meaning in Spenser's Allegory* (Oxford: Clarendon Press, 1971).
5. *The First Commentary on "The Faerie Queene": Being an Analysis of the Annotations in Lord Bessborough's Copy of the First Edition of "The Faerie Queene,"* ed. Graham Hough (Privately published, 1964).
6. *Spenser's "Faerie Queene,"* ed. John Upton (London, 1758), II, p. 338.
7. Upton notes the source of the "vine-prop Elme." Later editions of the poem add little new annotation until the school editions of Kitchin and Percival. The quotation from Lyly is from *Euphues*, in *Complete Works of John Lyly*, ed. R. W. Bond (Oxford: Clarendon Press, 1902), I, p. 242.
8. A change in approach is found in recent critics, e.g., Cheney, who notes that the knight and Una are "content to identify the trees and append the appropriate moral or emblematic tags to each" and their identification of the maple exposes "the presumption of the human compilers of such a catalogue" (p. 25).
9. *Preface to Shakespeare* (1765), in *Johnson on Shakespeare*, ed. W. Raleigh (London: Oxford University Press, 1908), p. 61.
10. *The Faerie Queene, Book V*, ed. A. B. Gough (Oxford: Clarendon Press, 1921), p. 158.
11. *The Faerie Queene, Book I*, ed. G. W. Kitchin (Oxford: Clarendon Press, 1905), p. 184.
12. (London: Allen Lane, 1969), pp. 132–33.
13. *The Faerie Queene, Book I*, ed. H. M. Percival (London: Macmillan, 1964), p. 282. 1st ed. 1893. *Books I and II of "The Faerie Queene,"* ed. Robert Kellogg and Oliver Steele (New York: Odyssey Press, 1965), pp. 179–80.
14. All quotations from Scripture are from the facsimile of the 1560 edition of *The Geneva Bible* (Madison: University of Wisconsin Press, 1969).
15. I analyze Spenser's use of words in "Our new poet: Spenser, 'well of

English undefyld,'" in *A Theatre for Spenserians*, ed. J. M. Kennedy and J. A. Reither (Toronto: University of Toronto Press, 1973), pp. 101–23; rpt. in *Essential Articles*, pp. 488–506.

16. *The Faery Queene, Book II* (Oxford: Clarendon Press, 1872), p. 205.

17. H. Bayley, *The Lost Language of Symbolism* (London: Williams and Norgate, 1912), II, p. 277.

18. *The Study of Literature*, p. 135.

19. *Spenser's "Faerie Queene": The World of Glass* (Berkeley: University of California Press, 1966), p. 22.

20. In contrast to the Johns Hopkins Spenser *Variorum* which supplies "the fruits of all the significant scholarship and literary criticism" (I, v), the new Milton edition provides a variorum commentary.

21. "Concerning Spenser that I wrote at Mr May's Desire" (1638), rpt. in *Edmund Spenser: A Critical Anthology*, ed. Paul J. Alpers (Harmondsworth: Penguin Books, 1969), p. 60.

22. "Observations on the 22nd stanza of the 9th canto of Book II of The Faerie Queene" (1644), rpt. in *Edmund Spenser*, p. 61.

23. *Spenser's Images of Life*, ed. Alastair Fowler (Cambridge: Cambridge University Press, 1967), p. 1.

24. Ibid., p. 61.

25. This exuberant phrase is Sir John Harington's, which he makes in his commentary on Ariosto, *Orlando Furioso* (London, 1591).

26. *Preface to Shakespeare*, pp. 61–62.

27. S. J. Rosenberg, "On the Meaning of a Bosch Drawing," in *Essays in Honor of Erwin Panofsky*, ed. Millard Meiss (New York: New York University Press, 1961), p. 424.

28. "Nature and Grace in *The Faerie Queene*," *ELH*, 16 (1949), 221; rpt. in *Essential Articles*, p. 78.

29. "Comus Once More," *UTQ*, 19 (1950), 222.

30. *Spenser and the Numbers of Time* (London: Barnes and Noble, 1964), pp. 148–55.

31. Cf. Alastair Fowler, *Triumphal Forms* (Cambridge: Cambridge University Press, 1970), pp. 48–49, and C. S. Lewis, in *Spenser's Images of Life*, p. 27.

32. C. S. Lewis, in *Spenser's Images of Life*, pp. 27–28.

3. SPENSER RECOVERED

1. "Spenser," *North American Review*, 120 (1875), 334–94; quotation on p. 354. Parenthetical page references are made to this text hereafter. The revised version published in *The Collected Writings of James Russell Lowell* (Boston: Houghton, Mifflin, 1890–1901), IV, 265–353, includes minor changes in the earlier text, a few additions to the footnotes, and four new paragraphs toward the end of the essay.

2. *Edmund Spenser: A Critical Anthology*, ed. Paul J. Alpers (Harmondsworth: Penguin Books, 1969), pp. 69–72.

3. See W. I. Zeitler, "The Date of Spenser's Death," *MLN*, 43 (1928), 322–24.

4. Lowell should have known better by the time he revised and republished his essay in 1890: see A. B. Grosart in his editions of Spenser's *Complete Works* (1882–84), I, 190 ff., and of *The Lismore Papers* (1886–88), First Series, I, 189, 275; II, 94, 402–3; V, 254.

5. In the 1890 text, while retaining this passage, Lowell inconsistently adds a tribute to the "not only subtle but profound thinking" revealed by Artegall's debate with the giant in *F.Q.* V.ii.29–54 (*Collected Writings*, IV, 350).

6. *Collected Writings*, IV, 348.

7. *Spenser: A Collection of Critical Essays*, ed. Harry Berger, Jr. (Englewood Cliffs, N. J.: Prentice-Hall, 1968), p. 2. The same point of view has been obliquely expressed by Berger in an earlier review (*MLQ*, 25 [1964], 103).

8. *Icons of Justice* (New York: Columbia University Press, 1969), p. 1.

9. *Edmund Spenser*, pp. 181, 186.

10. See Waldo F. McNeir and Foster Provost, *Annotated Bibliography of Edmund Spenser, 1937–1960* (Pittsburgh: Duquesne University Press, 1962), pp. vii–viii.

11. *Edmund Spenser: The R. A. Neil Lecture* (London: Cambridge University Press, 1952), pp. 1–3.

12. *The Allegory of Love* (Oxford: Clarendon Press, 1936; rpt. 1967), pp. 324–26, 330–33.

13. *The Allegorical Temper* (New Haven, Conn.: Yale University Press, 1957), pp. 219, 226; in what follows, parenthetical references are made to the same text.

14. Berger, to be sure, supports the biblical interpretation with a few other references to Spenser's text.

15. Merrit Y. Hughes, *JEGP*, 58 (1959), 524–26.

16. In the most enthusiastic of these reviews Harold Bloom praises Fletcher for his "daemonic" kinship to Spenser and to the High Romantic tradition in Spenserian criticism (*VQR*, 47 [1971], 477–80).

17. *The Prophetic Moment* (Chicago: University of Chicago Press, 1971), pp. 39, 59; the parenthetical references which follow are made to this text.

18. Moreover, these long, unwieldy footnotes are not always, in themselves, models of the historical scholarship for which they speak. One of them, probably the outstanding example of its kind, has a representative importance which will justify examining it more closely. In this case, following the lead of William Empson, who uses the frequent occurrences of the word "all" in *Paradise Lost*, particularly in elegiac passages, as evidence that Milton is "an all-or-none man," Fletcher draws his own conclusion from the occurrences of "all" in *The Faerie Queene*:

Spenser's usage is in its way much more remarkable, and I believe it implies a marked change in his view of imperial expansion (with its poetical cognates of visionary possessiveness). In Book I: approximately 360 (about once in every fifteen lines, and more evenly distributed throughout the Book than throughout *Paradise Lost*); in Book II, 154 times. . . . Such "omnifics" express the fullness of the cosmos and the *pleroma* of Christian time. But note that there is a sudden disappearance of "all" after Book II. The mere count is extraordinary: Book III *three* uses (two of which occur in the Proem); Book IV *two*; Book V *six*; Book VI *zero*; and in the Mutabilitie Cantos *zero*. It may not be possible to explain these statistics, but I would argue that the avoidance of "all" marks a conscious resistance to elegiac introversion. Only by conscious attention could Spenser have so completely done away with a word that is almost synonymous with the elegiac mode. (pp. 298–99)

The footnote proceeds on its deliberate course, citing the elegiac use of "all" in Donne's sermons and in miscellaneous poems, but Fletcher's statistics on *The Faerie Queene* linger disconcertingly in a fellow Spenserian's mind: *zero* occurrences of "all" in the *Mutabilitie Cantos*? One seems to remember that word in the famous last stanza; in fact, it is used there three times, and a hasty check reveals some 134 occurrences of "all" in the 116 stanzas of the *Mutabilitie Cantos*, as compared with 68 in the first 116 stanzas of Book I. A little further investigation shows that Fletcher's counts for Books III, IV, V, and VI must be equally inaccurate. If Spenser, as we are told, is consciously resisting elegiac introversion in the later books of *The Faerie Queene*, he is not very attentive; he has everywhere allowed the fullness of the cosmos and the *pleroma* of Christian time to seep into his poem unobserved.

But Fletcher's hypothesis is perhaps less significant than the erroneous statistics on which it rests. Their source is clearly not the text itself, and one turns instinctively to Charles G. Osgood's *Concordance to the Poems of Edmund Spenser* (Washington, D. C.: Carnegie Institution of Washington, 1915), not mentioned by name in Fletcher's book though he seems to allude to it at one point (p. 100). The extraordinary statistics do indeed correspond to the number of entries in the *Concordance* under "all"; but the statistician has failed to note that at two places (pp. xi and 18) Osgood carefully explains that he has given only a partial listing of the occurrences of this very common word. If historical scholarship is still with us, it is still, as always, subject to egregious error: something which our time has tended to forget.

19. The Hermetic tradition, for example, seems to have suggested the identification of the round-dance on Mount Acidale as a temple (p. 127).

4. THE AESTHETIC EXPERIENCE OF READING SPENSER

1. Quoted in *Spenser: The Critical Heritage*, ed. R. M. Cummings (London: Routledge and Kegan Paul, 1971), p. 206.

2. *Spenser: The Critical Heritage*, p. 222.

3. "A Discourse on the Original and Progress of Satire" in *Prose Works of John Dryden,* ed. Edmond Malone (London: T. Cadell, 1800), III, 91.
4. *Spenser: The Critical Heritage,* p. 226.
5. *The defence of poesie* (London: William Ponsonby, 1595), C1ᵛ.
6. C. S. Lewis has some spirited comments about the difference between reading a novel and a romance in *Spenser's Images of Life,* ed. Alastair Fowler (Cambridge: Cambridge University Press, 1967), pp. 113–19.
7. See *Elizabethan Critical Essays,* ed. G. Gregory Smith (London: Oxford University Press, 1904), p. 232.
8. Cl.
9. For example, the apex of Peter Heylyn's extended praise of *The Faerie Queene* is this approbative statement: "There never was a *Poem* more *Artificial*" (*Cosmographie* [London, 1652], p. 196, quoted in *Spenser: The Critical Heritage,* p. 162).
10. Note that in this definition a poem does not require verse or rhyme. For Sidney his *Arcadia* was a poem, and it was so called by Milton (*Eikonoklastes* in *The Works of John Milton,* ed. Frank A. Patterson, et al. [New York: Columbia University Press, 1931–38], V, 86). Poetry and prose are not mutually exclusive categories.
11. "A letter of the authors" (appended to *The Faerie Queene*), line 14.
12. In 1628 Sir Kenelm Digby, the first serious and sustained critic of Spenser, advised: "You shall finde him a constant disciple of *Platoes* School" (quoted in *Spenser: The Critical Heritage,* p. 157). In an earlier essay, Digby commented on what later became a critical cliché, Spenser's learning:

His knowledge was not as many POETS are contented withall; which is but a meere sprinkling of severall superficiall notions to beautify their POEMS with; But he had a solide and deepe insight in THEOLOGIE, PHILOSOPHY (especially the PLATONIKE) and the MATHEMATICALL sciences, and in what others depend of these three, (as indeed all others doe). He was a Master of every one of them (quoted in *Spenser: The Critical Heritage,* p. 150).

13. The analogy between the divine maker and the poet was still expressed in these terms as late as 1675. Peter Sterry, for example, a fellow of Emmanuel College, Cambridge, made the following statement with reference to "*Homer, Virgil, Tasso,* our English *Spencer,* with some few others like to these":

The *Works* of these persons are called *Poems.* So is the Work of God in Creation, and contrivance from the beginning to the end, [*poiēma tō theō*], God's Poem (quoted in *Spenser: The Critical Heritage,* p. 207).

14. G1ᵛ.
15. This process by which a lover goes from earthly to celestial love is most straightforwardly delineated by Spenser in "An Hymne in Honour of Love," lines 176–217.

16. "To fashion" or "to make" is the usual Elizabethan translation of *poiein* and *fingere*.
17. "Letter of the authors," lines 49–55.
18. Ernst H. Kantorowicz, *The King's Two Bodies: A Study in Mediaeval Political Theology* (Princeton, N. J.: Princeton University Press, 1957).
19. I use the word "unfolding" (and later "infolding") in a special sense defined by Edgar Wind, *Pagan Mysteries in the Renaissance* (London: Faber and Faber, 1958), pp. 158 ff.; and brought into our critical vocabulary by Gerald Snare, "Spenser's Fourth Grace," *Journal of the Warburg and Courtauld Institutes*, 34 (1971), 353–55.
20. "Letter of the authors," lines 57–62.
21. While I am explaining terms, perhaps I may point out that "virtue" has L. *vir*, "man," as a root, and by its etymology it means "manliness" or "power."
22. *Prose Works of John Dryden*, III, 91. Thomas Warton took interesting issue with Dryden on this point and provided the most severely neo-classical criticism of *The Faerie Queene*. His verdict: "Spenser perhaps would have embarrassed himself and the reader less, had he made every book one entire detached poem of twelve cantos, without any reference to the rest" (*Observations on the Fairy Queen of Spenser*, 2nd ed. [London: R. and J. Dodsley, 1807], I, 10, 14).
23. "Letter of the authors," lines 27–29.
24. "Letter of the authors," lines 122–25.
25. II.i.32.6–7.
26. "Letter of the authors," lines 69–74.
27. At the risk of over-glossing this passage, I shall point out that "all" in Greek is *pan*, with its secondary meaning of "universe" (cf. *Timaeus*, 28C). "All" in Elizabethan usage also often has just such a secondary meaning; see *OED*, B.3, and cf. *Faerie Queene*, VII.vii.56.9.
28. "Letter of the authors," lines 76–79.
29. Coleridge makes the point in his inimitable way:

    You will take especial note of the marvellous independence and true imaginative absence of all particular space or time in the Faery Queene. It is in the domains neither of history or geography; it is ignorant of all artificial boundary, all material obstacles; it is truly in land of Faery, that is, of mental space (*Coleridge's Miscellaneous Criticism*, ed. T. M. Raysor [London: Constable and Co., 1936], p. 36).

30. This is essentially the reading arrived at by Richard Hurd, *Letters on Chivalry and Romance* [1762], ed. Hoyt Trowbridge (Augustan Reprints 101–2, Los Angeles: William Andrews Clark Memorial Library, 1963), pp. 62–75. Hurd is following the lead of John Hughes in comparing *The Faerie Queene* to a Gothic cathedral rather than a Roman temple (cf. Edmund Spenser, *Works*, ed. John Hughes [London: J. Tonson, 1715], I, lx).
31. See my article, "The Implications of Form for *The Shepheardes Calender*," *SR*, 9 (1962), 309–21.

32. *Observations, Anecdotes, and Characters of Books and Men,* ed. James M. Osborn (Oxford: Clarendon Press, 1966), I, 182. To visualize *The Faerie Queene* is, of course, to lead it into the realm of physical data and away from its conceptual home at Gloriana's court, thereby seducing the reader into the ephemeral world of sense experience and deflecting him from the intellectual experience which is the poem's aim. As Ralph Knevett opined about 1633: "The end of writeing Bookes, should be rather to informe the understanding, then please the fancy" (quoted in *Spenser: The Critical Heritage,* p. 170). The word "fancy" for Knevett meant the mental faculty which we, with a pretense of being precise, call "the mind's eye." By 1681, illustrating neatly the shift in aesthetics during the seventeenth century, Thomas D'Urfey was exclaiming: "Fancy! the brightest Jewel of Poetry, of which the Famous *English Spencer* was the great and only Master, as we may see in all his Descriptions" (quoted in *Spenser: The Critical Heritage,* p. 211). This trend toward a pictorial reading of *The Faerie Queene* reached a high-point with Leigh Hunt, who called Spenser "the painter of the poets . . . writing as with a brush instead of a pen" ("A New Gallery of Pictures," in *Leigh Hunt's Literary Criticism,* ed. Lawrence H. Houtchens and Carolyn W. Houtchens [New York: Columbia University Press, 1956], p. 421).

There is a lesson here for iconographical critics, but this is neither the time nor place to point it out. At present the best remedy I know to cure the infirmity of mistaking verbal imagery for visual imagery (an infirmity, incidentally, that killed off the New Critics and presently runs epidemic among the iconographers) is an article by Rudolph Gottfried, "The Pictorial Element in Spenser's Poetry," *ELH,* 19 (1952), 203–13.

33. It may be worthwhile to record here my own critical bias at the time of this writing. I contend that a poem exists as an object, a printed text, to which the individual reader comes as a unique percipient. The art-work itself occurs as a dynamic event, a happening which takes place in the intermundum between the objective text and the subjective response of the reader. Any reading of the poem must take into account the large subjective factor of individual response, or else the poem remains static at a literal level. Conversely, however, the individual's response must be confined within the poet's intention (yes, the intentional fallacy, but used as a limit rather than a genesis), or else critical anarchy ensues, with no one's reading having significance for anyone else. In any case, a critic may offer only *a* reading of the poem (*his* reading); there is no such thing as *the* reading.

5. A SPENSER TO STRUCTURE OUR MYTHS

1. Quotations of Spenser follow the *Variorum Edition,* with modernization of i, j, u, and v.

2. Cf. Botticelli's "Mars and Venus" (National Gallery, London), reproduced in Edgar Wind, *Pagan Mysteries in the Renaissance*, 2nd ed. (London: Faber and Faber, 1968), Plate 74.

3. A. Kent Hieatt, "Spenser's Atin from Atine?" *MLN*, 62 (1957), 249–51. The word is used in many Old French texts, including *Le Roman de la rose*.

4. More fully than elsewhere, the *Grand dictionnaire universel du XIXe siècle* (Paris, 1865), under "fleur-de-lis," assembles the curious traditional explanations of the origin of the fleur-de-lis in the French royal arms. The lily itself is said to be irrelevant.

5. See *OED*, "fleur-de-lis," 1, where sixteenth-century instances and a dictionary-entry of 1731–37 appear. See also Johnson's *Dictionary*, 1755, "Flour de Luce," where the flower is said to be a bulbous iris, and where Peacham is quoted: "The iris is the flower de luce." See also *Dictionary of American English*, under "Flower-de-luce." The title of Longfellow's poem "The Flower-de-Luce" signifies the iris.

6. See Du Cange, *Glossarium*, under *Flos deliciarum*, as well as etymology provided by *OED* and by Hans Kurath and Sherman M. Kuhn, *Middle English Dictionary*, under "flour-de-lice." Du Cange quotes two fifteenth-century examples. R. E. Latham, *Revised Medieval Latin Word List from British and Irish Sources* (London: Oxford University Press, 1965), shows a fourteenth- and a fifteenth-century example under *flos deliciarum*.

7. II.1: "Passer, deliciae meae puellae."

8. My only authority for this etymology is the *MED* as above, under "flour-de-lice."

9. "No drume nor trumpet peaceful sleepes should move, / Unles alar'me came from the campe of love" (9–10). The corresponding passage of Propertius is in II.xv, a poem in which he celebrates his and Cynthia's love-making. L1.41,43: "Qualem si cuncti cuperent decurrere vitam . . . non ferrum crudele neque esset bellica navis." See note in *The Works of Thomas Campion*, ed. Walter R. Davis (London: Faber and Faber, 1964), p. 18. Presumably Spenser as well is following Propertius.

10. Contrary to the false Genius of the Bower, II.xii.46–48. See A. Kent Hieatt, "Milton's Comus and Spenser's False Genius," *UTQ*, 38 (1969), 313–18. This appears as Chapter 11 in amplified form in my forthcoming "Chaucer, Spenser, Milton: Mythopoeic Continuities and Transformations," in which there are also further demonstrations of points below concerning the equation of Sun and Moon with Osiris and Isis, the coordination of the Isle of Venus with incidents in the rest of Book IV, and the relation of Medina's and Phaedria's mediations to the theme of Book II.

11. See Michael Baybak, Paul Delany, A. Kent Hieatt, "Placement 'In the Middest' in *The Faerie Queene*," *PLL*, 5 (1969), 227–34; rpt. in *Silent Poetry*, ed. Alastair Fowler (London: Routledge and Kegan Paul, 1970), pp. 141–52.

12. For mythic purposes Spenser occasionally blurs and equivocates the distinction between the natural as the just and right, and the natural as the vitally desirous and competitively acquisitive.

13. See Donald Cheney, "Spenser's Hermaphrodite and the 1590 *Faerie Queene*," *PMLA*, 87 (1972), 192–200.

14. See "Placement 'in the Middest' in *The Faerie Queene*."

15. The other passage is Luke 16.9–13.

16. See A. Kent Hieatt, "A Numerical Key for Spenser's *Amoretti* and Guyon in the House of Mammon," *YES*, 3 (1973), 14–27.

17. See A. Kent Hieatt, "Three Fearful Symmetries," in *A Theatre for Spenserians: Papers of the International Spenser Colloquium*, ed. Judith Kennedy and James Reither (Toronto: University of Toronto Press, 1973), pp. 19–52. Other supporting literature is cited there. See also the more completely developed interpretation in "Chaucer, Spenser, Milton."

6. SPENSER'S PLURALISTIC UNIVERSE

All citations from Spenser will be from *The Works of Edmund Spenser: A Variorum Edition*, ed. Edwin Greenlaw et al. (Baltimore: The Johns Hopkins Press, 1932–58).

1. My picture, based on Kathleen Williams's notion of widening circles in "Eterne in Mutabilitie: The Unified World of *The Faerie Queene*," *ELH*, 19 (1952), has always been of the successive books as successive growth-rings on a tree, with the rays representing the parallels and other cross-references between books. An entire volume of essays has recently been devoted to the problem, *Eterne in Mutabilitie*, ed. Kenneth John Atchity (Hamden, Conn.: Archon Books, 1972). Although the present essay talks more about meaning than about form, it draws on and contributes to this subject.

2. In a sermon translated by Arthur Golding (from which I shall quote at length here since it is relatively inaccessible but important to my argument) Calvin differentiates the pagan view of man, the *via media* of Christian humanism, which he identifies with the Papists, and his own Pauline views in terms of a progressively lower estimate of free will. The pagan, natural ethics ascribes all to man and his will as does our quotation from VI; the *via media* takes the Christian-humanist view of man expressed by our quotation from II, often in the same imagery: "True it is that the Papists will grant more than the heathen folk, namely, that we be corrupted by original sin, howbeit their meaning is, that notwithstanding the infirmity which is in man, yet there abideth some remnant of goodness in him: insomuch that we have half an understanding still, and also a will that is able to train us unto good, though it be weak of itself. To be short, such as will needs judge according to their natural understanding say, that men are as sound and incorrupted as angels. The papists, being convinced by so many records of the Scripture, will grant well enough, that we be fallen from

our original, and that there are many vices in us, but . . . they make such a partnership between God and man, that . . . it is right hard for us to submit ourselves to God, but yet that we . . . are able to do it, so that God aid us and reach us his hand. This is the concurrence (as they term it) (that is to say, the matching or marrowing together) of God's grace and of the goodness that remaineth in man, though we be corrupted." Calvin's own Pauline Christianity agrees with our quotation from Book I that will is useless and grace all-sufficient: "All they which follow common reason, and the things that man hath of himself, are blind wretches . . . God must be so fain to reform us, not by half, but all whole throughout." *Sermons . . . upon the Epistle to the Ephesians* (London: Nicolas Harison and George Bishop, 1527), Sermon xxviii on Eph. 4:17–19, fols. 199ᵛ–200ʳ⁻ᵛ; spelling has been modernized; henceforth designated simply as "Calvin." For the original French, see *Opera*, LI, ed. W. Baum, et al., Corpus Reformatorum (Brunswick: Schwetschke & Sons, 1895), cols. 597–98.

3. Robert Hoopes, " 'God Guide Thee, *Guyon*': Nature and Grace Reconciled in *The Faerie Queene*, Book II," *RES*, N.S., 5 (1954), 14–24.

4. VII.viii.2.6, cf. VII.vii.55.8, noted by S. P. Zitner in his edition of *The Mutabilitie Cantos* (London: Thomas Nelson and Sons, 1968).

5. A. S. P. Woodhouse, "Nature and Grace in *The Faerie Queene*," *ELH*, 16 (1949), 224–25. Judah L. Stampfer, "*The Cantos of Mutabilitie*: Spenser's Last Testament of Faith," *UTQ*, 21 (1951–52), 148–56.

6. I.iv; in *Erasmi Opera Omnia*, ed. J. Leclerc (Leiden: von der Aa, 1702–6), hereafter abbreviated LB, V, col. 13, my translation.

7. Besides passage in n. 2, (fol. 200ʳ⁻ᵛ; original, col. 597), see also 202ʳ; original, col. 601.

8. *Spenser's Image of Nature* (New Haven: Yale University Press, 1966), p. 141.

9. Paul J. Alpers, *The Poetry of "The Faerie Queene"* (Princeton, N. J.: Princeton University Press, 1967), pp. 114–15, hereafter cited by page numbers; he also neglects our first pluralistic passage, the double answer to Mutabilitie. Harry Berger, Jr., *The Allegorical Temper* (New Haven: Yale University Press, 1957), "The Chronicles," especially pp. 107–14; Thomas P. Roche, *The Kindly Flame* (Princeton, N. J.: Princeton University Press, 1964), pp. 32–50; Northrop Frye, *Fables of Identity* (New York: Harcourt, Brace & World, 1963), p. 585.

10. J. E. Hankins, "Spenser and the Revelation of St. John," *PMLA*, 60 (1945), 374–76; *Books I and II of "The Faerie Queene," the Mutability Cantos, and Selections from the Minor Poetry*, ed. Robert Kellogg and Oliver Steele (New York: Odyssey Press, 1965), p. 45; Carol V. Kaske, "The Dragon's Spark and Sting and the Structure of Red Cross's Dragon-Fight," *SP*, 66 (1969), 631.

11. In this I differ with Judith Anderson, "Perspectivism in Spenser: the July Eclogue and the House of Holinesse," *SEL*, 10 (1970), 29 ff., who sees Una's symbolism as present and as an integrating element here.

12. Maurice B. McNamee, S.J., *Honor and the Epic Hero* (New York: Holt, Rinehart, and Winston, 1960), pp. 137, 156; Ricardo Quinones, *The Renaissance Discovery of Time* (Cambridge, Mass.: Harvard University Press, 1972), pp. 245-46 (I do not proceed with him [pp. 243, 246] to see a synthesis here); Isabel Rathborne, *The Meaning of Spenser's Faeryland* (New York: Columbia University Press, 1937), pp. 4-5, 59, quotation from pp. 57-58. Succeeding references to these authors will be by page numbers. The essay of Edwin B. Benjamin, "Fame, Poetry, and the Order of History in the Literature of the English Renaissance," *SRen*, 6 (1959), 64-84, would seem to deny Spenser's uniqueness; but he proves only that fame became an important theme in the Renaissance, not that it was ever ranked as in Spenser among Christian values. In Benjamin's loose reading, Hawes seems to Christianize fame whereas, in fact, Hawes explicitly rejects it through his personification Eternity; see next note.

13. Petrarch, *The Triumph of Time*. Hawes, *The Passetyme of Pleasure* (1555) Percy Society (London: T. Richards for the Society, 1845), chapter 44, hereafter cited by chapter.

14. The pioneering work of Isabel Rathborne on the intermediate city has been learnedly continued by Thomas Roche, *The Kindly Flame*, pp. 39-43. I cannot agree with him, however, that there is also an ethical resolution in service to the state as the ideal represented by Cleopolis; the keynote of Cleopolis is personal fame.

15. Nicholas Love, *The Mirror of the Blessed Life of Christ*, rpt. in *Later Medieval English Prose*, ed. William Matthews (New York: Appleton-Century-Crofts, 1963), pp. 145-46.

16. Devoted as he is to the Active Life, Luther stresses that in themselves all good deeds are equal (*Werke* [Weimar: Hermann Böhlaus Nachfolger, 1883-], "Concerning Good Works," VI, 206-7), regarding fame as merely a temptation (Ibid., pp. 220-21), and attributing to what Erasmus called the noble deeds of philosophers and conquerors no more merit than to the meanest household task ("Lecture on Gen. 29:1-3," XLIII, 614 f.). Rita Belladonna, "Sperone Speroni and Alessandro Piccolomini on Justification," *RQ*, 25, 2 (1972), 162-63, 167, 171-72. Even Erasmus similarly extols a Christian Active Life but derogates fame. Charles Trinkaus, "The Problem of Free Will in the Renaissance and the Reformation," *JHI*, 10 (1949), 58.

17. J. S. Harrison, *Platonism in English Poetry of the Sixteenth and Seventeenth Centuries*, rpt. in Spenser, *Variorum Edition*, I, 503-5.

18. See for example his *Cántico espiritual*, second redaction, Commentary on Stanza 22.

19. For examples, see Joseph B. Collins, *Christian Mysticism in the Elizabethan Age* (Baltimore, Md.: The Johns Hopkins Press, 1940), pp. 90-91, and n. 23.

20. This twofold introduction of Arthur confirms from the text what several critics have surmised: that the label "magnificence" which Spenser assigns to Arthur in the *Letter* really includes magnanimity

too—perhaps by way of the Aquinian link suggested by Michael F. Moloney, "St. Thomas and Spenser's Virtue of Magnificence," *JEGP*, 52 (1953), 58–62.

21. "The Arthurs of *The Faerie Queene*," *EA*, 6 (1953), 193 ff.
22. Judith Anderson, "The Knight and the Palmer," *MLQ*, 31 (1970), 160–78; and " 'Nor Man It Is': The Knight of Justice in Book V of Spenser's *Faerie Queene*," *PMLA*, 85 (1970), 65–77.
23. John Edwin Sandys, "Education," in *Shakespeare's England*, ed. Walter Raleigh, Sidney Lee, and C. T. Onion (Oxford: Clarendon Press, 1916), I, 224. See also Lowell C. Green, "The Bible in Sixteenth-Century Humanist Education," *SRen*, 19 (1972), 112–34.
24. *Enarrationes Aliquot Librorum Ethicorum Aristotelis*, ed. H. E. Bindseil, Corpus Reformatorum, XVI (Halle: Schwetschke and Sons, 1850), 340.
25. "Spenser's Syncretistic Religious Imagery," *ELH*, 36 (1969), 110–30. Two Christian images surprising in their humanistic contexts are V.vi.27.2 and VII.vii.7.8.
26. Cambina's cup has been shown to be Christian by John Morrison Nesselhof, *Spenser's Book of Friendship: an Aspect of Charity*, Diss. Princeton, 1955. For the contrast between Isis and Mercilla, I am indebted to Mr. Donald Stump of Cornell University.
27. My position falls, therefore, halfway between that of Alpers as proponent of disunity and that of Kathleen Williams as the greatest of recent synthesizers. I side with Berger, Roche, and Frye insofar as they endorse the dualism of Briton and Faery, and I agree with Hoopes as to the syncretism of Book II, though not as to the central importance of this syncretism in the poem as a whole.

Index